KU-050-572

CORPORATE INSOLVENCY: LAW AND PRACTICE

AUSTRALIA
LBC Information Services—Sydney

CANADA AND USA
Carswell—Toronto

NEW ZEALAND
Brooker's—Auckland

SINGAPORE AND MALAYSIA
Sweet & Maxwell Asia
Singapore and Kuala Lumpur

CORPORATE INSOLVENCY: LAW AND PRACTICE

By

David Milman, LL.B., PH.D., F.R.S.A.
Herbert Smith Professor of Corporate and Commercial Law,
Centre for Law and Business, University of Manchester

Chris Durrant, B.A. Oxon., M.PHIL.
Solicitor
Partner at Lawrence Jones, London
Honorary Associate of the Centre for Law and Business at
the University of Manchester

THIRD EDITION

LONDON
SWEET & MAXWELL
1999

First Edition 1987
Second Edition 1994
Third Edition 1999

Published in 1999 by
Sweet and Maxwell Limited of
100 Avenue Road, London NW3 3PF
Typeset by Servis Filmsetting Ltd, Manchester
Printed and bound in Great Britain by
MPG Books Ltd, Bodmin, Cornwall

No natural forests were destroyed to make this product: only farmed timber was used and re-planted.

ISBN 0–421 65640–9

A CIP record for this book is available from the British Library

Preface to First Edition

From the viewpoint of the present authors, corporate insolvency law has one great attraction: it is an area where collaboration between the academic and the practitioner can be particularly fruitful. It is impossible for the practitioner to be effective in this field without the necessary conceptual grounding, and the "ivory tower" academic is unlikely to be able to acquire the necessary sense of proportion unless he takes steps to find out what is happening on the ground. Like it or not, such concepts as "the floating charge", "the fixed charge on future assets", and "title retention" involve abstract legal ideas of some subtlety, but they are of crucial practical importance. It is fair to say that, in purely monetary terms, millions of pounds each year turn upon the application of these concepts to practical situations. There can be few areas of law which are at once so conceptually satisfying and of such vital day-to-day importance to practitioners and their clients.

There are other reasons why at present a partnership of talents is particularly helpful in this field. One is that corporate insolvency principles have been evolving over the past couple of years at a rate so giddying that the busy practitioner cannot hope to keep fully abreast both of developments and his current workload without assistance from the academic. On the other hand, the practitioner will frequently encounter real situations to which new or undecided law must be applied long before anything like them has come before any court. As he is often concerned to make sure that, in his client's case at least, the matter never does come before a court, it may be many months or years before his academic colleague becomes aware of common problems which are of considerable importance but to which there are no clear or certain answers. The reader will find a number of "practice scenarios" in the following chapters illustrating problems of this type. The authors have enjoyed pooling their skills in suggesting solutions to these problems and hope the reader will consider the results worthwhile.

One thing which has recently united lawyers, whether academics or practitioners, and accountants working in the field of corporate insolvency, is their common feeling of righteous indignation at the extent to which their existence has been poisoned by the legislature lately. After years of delay Parliament at last produced the Companies Act 1985, the long awaited consolidating statute incorporating virtually the whole of company law into a single Act. The Department of Trade mounted a special campaign to acquaint practitioners with the contents of the new legislation, and even gave them additional time to familiarise themselves with its layout. Yet at the same time, in a belated and inadequate response to the 1982 Cork Report, the Bill which was to become the Insolvency 1985, was piloting its perilous course through the Houses of Parliament, attracting 1,200 amendments in the process. This Bill contained sections amending or replacing the consolidating Companies Act 1985!

Not content with this piece of lunatic legislative mismanagement, the Government chose to force the Bill through its last stages in the Lords in a manner little short of a national disgrace. The Upper House, in which this nonpolitical Bill had started its Parliamentary Odyssey, was threatened with the removal of its right to introduce major legislation into Parliament.

The brave new world under which company law was to be found in a single statute did not last long, therefore. It was hardly surprising that many lawyers pointed out the obvious, namely that the Government had put the cart before the horse in passing the Insolvency Act 1985 after a consolidating statute on company law. The Government responded by announcing on December 17, 1985 that it had decided to reconsolidate corporate insolvency law into a single statute, presumably by way of making a right out of two wrongs. In fact we have ended up with two statutes, the Insolvency Act 1986 and the Company Directors Disqualification Act 1986, and an unfortunate and artificial separation between the law on corporate insolvency and the general company law with which it is inextricably connected.

It is to be hoped that Parliament will now allow the dust to settle for a while on corporate insolvency law. Litigation in the courts observes no such moratorium, however, and there have been a number of important decisions over the past nine months, during the writing of this book. We have accommodated as many as possible.

Having outlined our aspirations, and recounted our troubles, in producing this monograph we must leave it to the reader to judge our efforts. We recognise that where we have ventured into uncharted waters, the map making may prove less than perfect but we hope at least to have saved those who follow a good deal of preliminary labour.

We would like to thank our respective wives, Catherine and Pam, and Chris's partners, for their help and encouragement, and also Alan Sugar without whose business acumen the writers of legal textbooks would be an even more diffident and under-rewarded race than they now are.

We have attempted to state the law as at March 1, 1987.

DAVID MILMAN,
CHRIS DURRANT
1987

Preface to Second Edition

It is now over seven years since we began work on the first edition of this book. We wrote the text in the immediate aftermath of the major insolvency reforms of 1985–6 and there was bound to be a certain amount of speculation in our comments. Some of the uncertainties inherent in new legislation have been clarified but others remain outstanding. Further problems have been exposed by judicial decisions.

Looking at the intervening years, two areas stand out for their productivity as far as contentious litigation is concerned. The administration order procedure (in spite of its statistical rarity) has taken up much judicial time, though this is hardly surprising in view of its innovatory character; there is no doubt that it was the most radical of the changes effected in the wake of the Cork Report. On the whole, the approach of the courts in interpreting Part II of the Insolvency Act 1986 has been constructive. Chapter 3 is devoted largely to administration, but also contains a brief treatment of the company voluntary arrangement (CVA), currently the subject of a government review, theoretically an alternative corporate rescue procedure but in practice closely linked with administration.

One of the less obvious, though most important, changes brought in by the 1985–6 reforms was the revitalisation of the disqualification of unfit directors regime by requiring insolvency practitioners to blow the whistle upon them. More cases are coming to the attention of the authorities, producing a corresponding increase in applications to the courts for disqualification. Attempts have been made to lay down flexible guidelines but inevitably, given the wide discretion enjoyed by the court and the infinite variety of circumstances in which corporate insolvency occurs, each case must in the end turn on its own facts.

The status of retention of title clauses, the uncertainties inherent in the nature of the floating charge, and the somewhat hazy boundaries of the fixed charge over future assets have continued to be productive of new case law. These areas are of considerable importance in practice, and we have dealt with them in as much detail as we practicably can in a general work of this kind.

The position with regard to legislation has been more stable.* The 1986 statutes have, thankfully, remained largely unscathed by Parliament, though there have been changes in the secondary legislation, most notably through the making of the Insolvency (Amendment) Rules 1987 (SI 1987/1919). Additionally, the Companies Act 1989 contained some highly technical provisions reforming the operation of insolvency laws in the financial markets. We have decided to give these a wide berth, putting our faith in the old maxim that discretion is the better part of valour.

More importantly, Part IV of the 1989 Act remodels the rules on charge registration. The circumstances under which this Part of the Companies Act 1989 came to appear on the statute book illustrate that the government has not learned the lessons of earlier incompetent law reform exercises. Consultation was inadequate, and the draft provisions were substantially amended late in the day and then subjected to the guillotine. The reasoning behind some of the new provisions on charge registration is unfathomable and we have no *travaux preparatoires* to light our way. This is doubly serious as the provisions in Part IV are so heavily dependent upon secondary legislation to give them any real meaning in practice. In spite of numerous rumours that Part IV is about to be put in force, nothing has happened and the government has now indicated in its DTI Annual Report for 1992–3 that the whole question of charge registration has become entwined in the "Hamilton Review" of Company Law in general. As authors our position is difficult, and we have decided to invest most of our effort in the well established charge registration rules as found in the 1985 consolidation. The implementation of Part IV of the 1989 Act (if it ever occurs) can then be used by us as ammunition to persuade our publishers to go for a third edition! The current review of a number of aspects of U.K. Company Law will strengthen our hand in this regard.

Our potential readership should have expanded over the last few years as Northern Ireland has now (with full effect from October 1991) introduced insolvency reforms along the same lines as those adopted in Britain. The provisions in the relevant Companies and Insolvency Orders of 1989 (S. Is., 1989 No. 2404, N.I. 18 and 1989 No. 2405, N.I. 19) and the Insolvency Rules (Northern Ireland) 1991 (SR No. 364) mirror their British counterparts in substance; the differences are largely cosmetic.

One other event deserves special mention. Sir Kenneth Cork died in 1991, having made a tremendous contribution to the law of insolvency in this jurisdiction. His legacy was not restricted to chairing the Committee that reported in 1982, but extended to his efforts over the next couple of years in keeping the pressure up on the government of the day to see that his committee's recommendations were not quietly shelved in the same way that the work of many of his illustrious predecessors was. All insolvency lawyers owe a great debt to him.

Chris would like to thank his partners in the Insolvency Department of Davies Wallis Foyster, Michael Jennings and Andrew Gregory, for their assistance with his contribution to this work (arising particularly, in Michael's case, from his uncanny knowledge of seemingly obscure yet practically important antipodean developments). Thanks are also due to various insolvency practitioners, mostly in Manchester and Liverpool, for their permission to print examples based on cases on which both Chris and they have been involved. This is not intended to be a purely academic work, and many difficult matters arise in practice which are rarely illuminated by decided cases. Alan Griffiths and Malcolm Shierson of Grant Thornton deserved a particular mention for their generosity in this regard. We are indebted also to Phillip Sykes of BDO Binder Hamlyn for permission to print the administration case study in Chapter 3 and to Phillip Ramsbottom of KPMG Peat Marwick for his permission to refer to the administration of Edington plc.

We have tried to state the law as it stands on November 30, 1993.

David Milman
Christopher Durrant
1993

*In making this comment we were foolishly tempting providence, for emergency amending legislation in the form of the Insolvency Act 1994 has had to be introduced to counteract an inconvenient judicial ruling that threatened the corporate rescue strategy. We have been able to accommodate this late development in Appendix I. Note—this Appendix has been deleted and its contents incorporated into the text for the Third Edition.

Preface to Third Edition

We were pleased to be able to revisit this text after an interval of some five years. The subject of corporate insolvency has become more high profile during that period and, if economic commentators are to be believed, its practitioners will be in great demand over the next five years.

Now that the great reforms in 1985–86 have bedded down the question must be asked as to whether there is scope for further significant change in the law? In the opinion of the present commentators that question must be answered in the affirmative. This view is shared by others. The issue of reform was addressed by JUSTICE in its 1994 paper *Insolvency Law: An Agenda for Reform*. This document places its main emphasis on the need for progress in the area of bankruptcy law, but it is clear that it identifies the issue of corporate rescue and on promoting the rights of unsecured creditors as areas for improvement. Crown preference is also questioned.

In spite of this influential report there has been little parliamentary intervention in the period under review. Promises of legislative action to promote corporate rescue have been frequent, but unfulfilled. To some extent, as with Company Law in general, an uneasy calm prevails, though a review of corporate rescue (yet again) and preferential status is currently underway. Major reforms of "core" Company Law are expected to be unveiled within the next year or so and, although corporate insolvency does not feature in that review as such, changes are bound to have a profound impact upon our subject. As it is we have been left to comment upon the Insolvency Act (No. 2) 1994, a niche statute if there ever was one, and the Social Security Act 1998, which revives a draconian financial penalty for errant company directors who permit their business to trade on Crown debts.

The primary focus of this revised text will therefore be upon the evolving jurisprudence of corporate insolvency law in the courts. Particular features will be the coming of age of the law on "corporate recovery", a politically correct phrase that threatens to supplant the more utilitarian "corporate insolvency" and thereby to disguise the fundamental rationale of the subject as a whole. The disqualification of directors regime, perhaps the most significant aspect of the 1985–86 reforms, does unquestionably dominate the scene. So much so indeed that political pressure to increase the number of disqualifications has lead to the courts being swamped with cases resulting in techniques having to be devised to save on public expenditure. Our response to the development of this area has been to allocate a discrete chapter to its study (see Chapter 13).

One of the central tenets of the Cork Committee was to tighten the law with regard to directors whose conduct with respect to an insolvent company has been found wanting. The disqualification mechanism has certainly helped to raise awareness and improve standards. Its partner in this new tougher policy, the wrongful trading sanction, had not had the same impact, mainly because there is no public subsidy for the litigation necessary to activate it.

The insolvency profession has become more high profile in the past five years. Leading practitioners are known nationally and are in demand internationally. The powers of insolvency practitioners were extended by the reforms in 1985–86; these office holders are the lynchpin of the system of corporate insolvency law as it operates in this country. It is pleasing to see office holders taking full advantage of their powers of investigation and transactional avoidance. However, the success of the profession and the high salaries on offer, has provoked a backlash. In the wake of criticism from Ferris J. in *Mirror Group Newspapers v. Maxwell* [1998] B.C.C. 324* (and from Mr Justice Lightman in well publicised comments) a Working Party headed by the same Mr Justice Ferris was established to review remuneration practices. Although the policy of the Working Party, which produced a report in July 1998, will manifest itself largely through self regulation, life will never be the same again for insolvency practitioners, and challenges from creditors directed towards ascertaining whether "value for money" has been secured will become more commonplace.

A pervasive conundrum centres upon the funding of insolvency litigation. To some extent this is merely a reflection of wider concerns about access to civil justice, issues that were addressed by the Woolf Report. Changes in insolvency litigation will necessarily result from the advent of the reforms contained in the Civil Procedure Rules 1998 (S.I. 1998/3132) (effective from April 6, 1999). Even though the rules as such do not apply to insolvency proceedings their influence is apparent from the new Insolvency (Amendment) (No. 2) Rules 1999 (S.I. 1999/1022). Matters relating to costs are, of course, more acute in insolvency cases where money is bound to be in short supply. The legal system must address the issue as to whether it is acceptable to permit statutory provisions to lie fallow for want of funding or should private enterprise be allowed to fill the vacuum by opening up the litigation market to external risk takers.

Although the question of cross border insolvency has grown in importance we have resisted the temptation to create a distinct niche for it in this edition. This is such a technical matter, of particular concern in major multinational corporate collapses, that in order to do it full justice would require a substantial expansion of the present text and this would upset the balance in what is meant to be a general commentary. We do refer to certain developments relating to cross border insolvency in passing, but reference to specialist monographs is recommended in order to grasp the full flavour of the subject.

The fundamental priority regime has remained stable. Our hunch that the provisions on charge registration found in Part IV of the Companies Act 1989 would not be implemented has proved to be right. The vexed issue of the boundary between fixed and floating charges has triggered litigation on a regular basis. Apart from raising intriguing theoretical issues, there are real practical consequences here in that the categorisation of a charge as "fixed" or "floating" will affect entitlements of preferential creditors. In a report in 1996 the National Audit Office commented upon the fact that some insolvency practitioners (presumably in deference to the influence of banks) have been too keen to label charges as fixed rather than floating and equally adept at attributing realisation costs exclusively to the floating charge portion of the security, thereby denying the public exchequer its legitimate entitlement on corporate

* It should be noted that the fees and disbursements claim, so heavily criticised in this case, was largely approved on taxation—see [1999] B.C.C. 684.

insolvency. A new Statement of Insolvency Practice has been devised to combat this abuse (see SIP 14).

Corporate insolvency law remains capable of springing the odd surprise. The *Paramount* litigation fulfilled this role in the previous edition (for an indication of this see pp 60–1 and Appendix I in the Second Edition). The ruling of Park J. in *Demite Ltd* v. *Protec Health Ltd* [1998] B.C.C. 638 is less high profile, but it has certainly given practitioners pause for thought when undertaking disposals. There is no prospect of this decision provoking front page headlines or emergency retrospective legislation, but the case has revealed a possible *lacuna* in the law that is likely to be addressed by the Law Commission as part of its review of Part VI of the Companies Act 1985.

David Milman
Christopher Durrant
May 31, 1999

Guide to Law Reports and Journals

A.C.	Appeal Cases (1891–)
A.C.L.R.	Australian Company Law Reports
A.C.S.R.	Australian Corporate and Securities Reports
App Cas	Appeal Cases (1875–90)
A.L.J.R.	Australian Law Journal Reports
A.L.R.	Australian Law Reports
All E.R.	All England Law Reports
B.C.C.	British Company Cases
B.C.L.C	Butterworths Company Law Cases
B.P.I.R	Bankruptcy and Personal Insolvency Reports
B.L.R.	Building Law Reports
C.B.N.S.	Common Bench New Series (English Reports)
C.F.I.L.R.	Company Financial and Insolvency Law Review
Ch.	Chancery Division (1891–)
Ch. App.	Chancery Appeals (1865–75)
Ch. D.	Chancery Division (1875–90)
C.L.C.	Current Law Consolidated
C.L.D.	Company Law Digest
C.L.R.	Commonwealth Law Reports (Australia)
C.L.Y.B.	The Current Law Yearbook
Co. Law	The Company Lawyer
Com.L.R.	Commercial Law Reports
Cony.	The Conveyancer and Property Lawyer
Crim.L.R.	Criminal Law Review
De G.J. & S.	De Gex, Jones & Smith
D.L.R.	Dominion Law Reports (Canada)
E. & B.	Ellis & Blackburn (English Reports)
E.B. & E.	Ellis, Blackburn & Ellis (English Reports)
E.C.R.	European Court Reports
E.G.	Estates Gazette
F.T.C.L.R.	Financial Times Commercial Law Reports
F.T.L.R.	Financial Times Law Reports
G.W.D.	Green's Weekly Digest
I.C.R.	Industrial Cases Reports
I.L. & P.	Insolvency Law and Practice
I.L.R.M.	Irish Law Reports Monthly
Ir.L.T.	Irish Law Times
Ins. Int.	Insolvency Intelligence

Ins. Law.	Insolvency Lawyer
I.R.	Irish Reports
I.R.L.R.	Industrial Relations Law Reports
J.B.L.	Journal of Business Law
J.P.	Justice of the Peace
KB	Kings Bench
L.J.	Law Journal
L.J. Ch.	Law Journal (Chancery)
Lloyd's Rep.	Lloyd's Law Reports
L.R. Eq.	Law Reports Equity (1896–75)
L.T.	Law Times
L.T. J.	Law Times Journal
M.L.R.	Modern Law Review
M. &. W.	Meeson & Welsby (English Reports)
N.I.	Northen Irish Reports
N.I.J.B.	Norhern Irish Judicial Bulletin
N.I.L.Q.	Northern Ireland Legal Quarterly
N.L.J.	New Law Journal
N.S.W.L.R.	New South Wales Law Reports
N.S.W.R.	New South Wales Reports
N.Z.C.L.C.	New Zealand Company Law Cases
N.Z.L.R.	New Zealand Law Reports
P.C.C.	Palmer's Company Cases
P. & C.R.	Property and Compensation Reports
Q.B.	Queens Bench
R.A.L.Q.	Receivers, Administrators and Liquidators Quarterly
R.T.R.	Road Traffic Reports
S.A.	South African Reports
S.C.	Session Cases
S.J.	Solicitors Journal
S.L.T.	Scots Law Times
S.T.C.	Simons Tax Cases
Times	The Times
T.L.R.	Times Law Reports
Tr. L.R.	Trading Law Reports
V.R.	Victoria Reports
W.L.R.	Weekly Law Reports
W.N.	Weekly Notes

Table of Contents

Chapter 6
Compulsory Liquidation

Table of Cases

NORTHERN IRELAND

SCOTLAND

Table of Non-U.K. Cases

AUSTRALIA

CANADA

EUROPE

IRELAND

KENYA

NEW ZEALAND

SOUTH AFRICA

Table of Statutes

Table of Statutory Instruments

CHAPTER 1

Corporate Insolvency Regimes

1-01 The object of this short Chapter is to set the scene, so to speak, by dealing with the aims of corporate insolvency law and the scope of the authors' treatment of the subject, and by giving a brief preliminary outline of the main types of insolvency regime within that scope. A brief account will also be given of the rules relating to insolvency litigation, and in particular the critical aspect of funding legal proceedings.

AIMS OF CORPORATE INSOLVENCY LAW

Basic aims

1-02 Throughout this monograph reference will be made to certain basic aims of the corporate insolvency law in this country, an appreciation of which is necessary to make the subject intelligible. They are:

(1) To protect creditors—*e.g.*, by providing facilities and procedures designed to allow them to enforce their claims against the company.

(2) To balance the interests of competing groups on corporate insolvency. Chapters 7–11 of this book will be devoted to the manner in which the law seeks to achieve this balance.

(3) To control or punish directors responsible for the financial collapse of the company. Directors will be dealt with in some detail in Chapters 12 and 13.

(4) To promote rescues. This is an aim that is becoming increasingly valued in this area of the law, as society recognises the need to minimise unemployment resulting from corporate insolvency. The Cork Committee in its Herculean report on the subject in 1982, laid great emphasis on the need to promote rescues and suggested changes in the law in order to achieve this purpose. The administration order procedure was introduced with this aim in mind. This procedure, together with the companies' voluntary arrangement mechanism will be discussed in Chapter 3.

1-03 During the course of this work, these aims will be frequently highlighted by the authors and they should be borne in mind by the reader as he or she approaches the subject.

CORPORATE AND PERSONAL INSOLVENCY

Bankruptcy and insolvency

1-04 This book is concerned only with corporate insolvency regimes for registered companies.[1] No consideration will be given to the question of bankruptcy—*i.e.* individual or personal insolvency which applies to sole traders and partnerships.[2] One often hears of companies becoming bankrupt, but, in legal terms, this is as misleading as the signpost saying "Trespassers will be prosecuted." However, despite the distinction in English law between corporate and personal insolvency, there are a large number of broad similarities between these two regimes. The Insolvency Act 1986, which supersedes its 1985 namesake, has (at a superficial level) continued the recent trend towards harmonising the personal and corporate insolvency law systems. Thus winding up and bankruptcy procedures have been greatly assimilated and the doctrine of reputed ownership, which only applied in personal, as opposed to corporate insolvency, has at last been abolished.[3] Equally, the enhanced risks of personal liability faced daily by company directors mean that in practice there can be a tragic link between corporate and personal insolvency. On the other hand, the direct link between the two systems (Companies Act 1985, s.612) has now been abandoned and in its place the Insolvency Rules 1986 make special provision for matters formerly dealt with by bankruptcy law—*e.g.* the rules on set off.

INSOLVENCY DEFINED

1-05 Before embarking upon our analysis of the law of corporate insolvency, it is appropriate to explain what the concepts of solvency and insolvency mean to lawyers.

1-06 The traditional view prior to 1985 was that the crucial method for determining solvency was the "cash flow test".[4] Thus, a company that could pay its debts as they fell due was deemed solvent, no matter what the state of its balance sheet was. The source of the funding used to settle debts was largely irrelevant.

1-07 After 1985, this test was supplemented by the "balance sheet test".[5] A company that could manage to pay its debts as they fell due was nevertheless deemed insolvent if, according to its balance sheet, liabilities exceeded assets. Contingent liabilities were brought into the equation for these purposes. As a result of these

---

[1] We are not concerned with the insolvency of specialised companies such as insurance companies—see here *Re Continental Assurance Co of London*, *The Times*, January 14, 1999 for the distinct law here. Separate insolvency regimes also operate for banking companies, railway companies, building societies, friendly societies, etc.

[2] For the winding up of insolvent partnerships see Insolvency Act 1986, s.420 and the Insolvent Partnerships Order 1994 (S.I. 1994 No. 2421) (as amended by S.I. 1996 No. 1308). The effect of the 1994 Order (which replaced S.I. 1986 No. 2142) was to open up the possibility of administration orders and voluntary arrangements in respect of financially distressed firms. For relevant case law see *Re Kyrris (No. 1)* [1998] B.P.I.R. 103, *Re Kyrris (No. 2)* [1998] B.P.I.R. 111, *Re Greek Taverna* [1999] B.C.C. 153 and *Re HS Smith & Sons*, *The Times*, January 6, 1999.

[3] This is the effect of the repeal of the Bankruptcy Act 1914, s.38 and its replacement by Insolvency Act 1986, s.283. Reputed ownership in a rather different sense survives in the law of distress—see Law of Distress Amendment Act 1908, s.4.

[4] *Re Patrick & Lyon Ltd* [1933] Ch. 786.

[5] See now Insolvency Act 1986, s.123.

changes many more companies came within the purview of the corporate insolvency laws.

1-08 Thus, there are now two alternative tests to determine whether a company is or is not insolvent. It is clear that a company with a healthy balance sheet can still be the subject of a winding-up petition if it is unable to pay its debts within the extended meaning given to it in the statutory provisions, including failure of execution for recovery of a judgment debt and failure to pay an undisputed debt worth more than £750.[6] However, these two tests do not always operate in tandem. For example, the only criterion in determining whether a company is insolvent in the context of imposing liability for wrongful trading, is the balance sheet test.[7]

1-09 Why is it important to determine whether a company is or is not insolvent? Insolvency in one form or another is a prerequisite to the initiation of formal insolvency proceedings. Whether a company is solvent or not will determine whether a voluntary liquidation is controlled by creditors or members. Once a company becomes insolvent, members lose their right to petition for a winding-up because they will cease to have a tangible interest in its assets.[8] Late registration of a company charge is unlikely to be granted if the borrowing company is insolvent, even if it is not undergoing formal insolvency procedures.[9] If a company is insolvent when it enters into a property transaction and it then undergoes formal insolvency proceedings within a specified time, that transaction may be open to challenge. More interestingly, it now seems that the latent duty owed by directors to protect the interests of creditors will be triggered once the company falls into a state of insolvency.[10]

Court appointed receivers and Scottish receivers

Court-initiated receivership

1-10 Having excluded bankruptcy from our survey, there are also other species of corporate insolvency regime which we have decided not to cover. One of these is the court-initiated receivership, which, as far as corporate insolvency law is concerned, is virtually obsolete in English law.[11] This is partly because modern commercial lending documentation normally makes it unnecessary, and partly because it is expensive and cumbersome both to initiate and operate.

Scottish receivers

1-11 Moreover, no attempt will be made to consider the Scottish law of receivership, which is now to be found in sections 50–71 of the Insolvency Act 1986 as

---

[6] See *Cornhill Insurance v. Improvement Services Ltd* [1986] B.C.L.C. 26 and *Taylor's Industrial Flooring v. M. &. H. Plant Hire* [1990] B.C.L.C. 216.

[7] Insolvency Act 1986, 2.214(6).

[8] *Re Rica Gold Washing Co.* (1879) 11 Ch.D 36 and *Re Expanded Plugs Ltd* [1966] 1 W.L.R. 514. But see *Re Wessex Computer Stationers Ltd* [1992] B.C.L.C. 366.

[9] *Re Ashpurton Estates Ltd* [1983] Ch. 110.

[10] *West Mercia Safetywear v. Dodd* [1988] B.C.L.C. 250.

[11] Strangely, such receiverships are more frequent in Commonwealth jurisdictions. It is possible that they may enjoy a renaissance in this country as receiverships instituted out of court are more likely to be challenged these days. In the event of an out of court appointment being ruled unlawful substantial damages for trespass might be awarded against the debenture holder. Receivers are sometimes appointed by the court to act as caretakers pending the resolution of a dispute within a solvent company. See *BCCI v. BRS Kumar Bros* [1994] B.C.L.C. 211.

supplemented by the Receivers (Scotland) Regulations 1986 (S.I. 1986 No. 1917 (s.141)), and does differ from English law in a number of key respects. Turnings to more positive matters, which species of corporate insolvency regime can the reader expect to encounter in the following pages?

ADMINISTRATORS AND CVA SUPERVISORS

1-12 These are two new forms of corporate insolvency regime which were introduced as a result of the reforms in 1985–6. Both are considered fully in Chapter 3 but a few general comments are appropriate here. First in spite of initial optimism that they would be attractive possibilities for a company in financial difficulties, they have in fact been rarely used. If one examines the statistics it quickly becomes apparent that, even taken together, they comprise about four per cent of all corporate insolvencies. The reasons for this will be considered in Chapter 3. Of the two regimes, the administration order has the higher profile, partly because some of the companies involved have been very substantial and partly because it has generated considerable litigation, particularly with regard to the effect of the moratorium.[12] The court plays a key role in the administration procedure, whereas the CVA is necessarily much more dependent on co-operation between all concerned, as it lacks any mechanism for the freezing of creditors enforcement procedures. Both the administration order facility and the CVA are available to solvent as well as insolvent companies. However, in the case of administrations, the procedure is only available to those solvent companies which are likely to become unable to pay their debts.[13] A company voluntary arrangement appears to be available to solvent companies[14] that are encountering financial problems, though it has to be said that in practice, such a company would be unlikely to use the CVA procedure because of the adverse publicity entailed.

RECEIVERS APPOINTED OUT OF COURT

Administrative receivers

1-13 We shall then be dealing (in Chapter 4) with the company receiver. In the vast majority of cases this means a receiver appointed out of court by a debenture holder, normally a bank, in pursuance of an express power to do so contained in his debenture. As a result of the Insolvency Act 1986 such receivers can now be subdivided into administrative receivers, and, for want of a better word, ordinary receivers. The confusing term "administrative receiver" (introduced into English law by the now defunct Insolvency Act 1985), is defined as follows by section 29(2) of the 1986 Act:

"(a) a receiver or manager of the whole (or substantially the whole) of a company's property appointed by or on behalf of the holders of any debentures of the company, secured by a charge, which, as created, was a floating charge, or by such a charge and one or more other securities, or

[12] See Insolvency Act 1986, ss.9 and 10.
[13] Or companies likely to become insolvent in some other sense—*ibid.*, s.8(1)(*a*).
[14] This would seem to follow by default from a perusal of Part I of the Insolvency Act 1986.

(b) a person who would be such a receiver or manager but for the appointment of some other person as the receiver of part of the company's property."[15]

1-14 In practice, therefore, most receivers appointed under a debenture containing a general floating charge will fall into this category. Other types of receiver, appointed over a specific part of the company's assets (*e.g.* under section 109 of the Law of Property Act 1925), are less common in the context of corporate insolvency. What is the practical significance of a receiver being categorised as an administrative receiver?

(1) He must be qualified as an insolvency practitioner.[16]

(2) He is an "office holder" within the meaning of sections 230–237 of the Insolvency Act 1986.

(3) He has broader statutory powers than an ordinary receiver.[17]

(4) He enjoys the protection of the Insolvency Act 1994.

LIQUIDATORS

1-15 The third species of insolvency practitioner we will encounter is the liquidator. How does he differ from a receiver? The main practical point of distinction is that a liquidator acts primarily in the interests of unsecured creditors and members, whereas a receiver is essentially concerned with the welfare of the secured creditors who appointed him. This distinction was graphically illustrated by the decision of Hoffmann J. in *Re Potters Oils Ltd (No. 2)*,[18] where a liquidator tried to exercise his power under what is now section 36 of the Insolvency Act 1986 to question the fees and disbursements claimed by the receiver. This challenge failed—these items had been properly incurred by the receiver in the course of his duty to protect the interests of the debenture holders.

1-16 Historically speaking, the two regimes have different roots. Liquidators are creatures of and governed by statute law, whereas receivers are a creation of equity. The law of receivership therefore contains a stronger case law element, although the statutory element continues to gain ground. Receivers are normally appointed by secured creditors as a contractual remedy requiring no recourse to the court, whereas liquidators are appointed by the company itself or by the court usually on an unsecured creditor's petition, in either case pursuant to a statutory right. Notwithstanding these points of distinction, the two regimes are not completely divorced from each other. Thus, for example, both liquidators and administrative receivers must be qualified insolvency practitioners and the orders of repayment of debts is similar. Indeed,

---

[15] It is important to note that where the security contains a combination of fixed and floating charges, the appointment of the administrative receiver is effected under the floating charge—*Meadrealm Ltd v. Transcontinental Golf Construction Ltd* (Vinelott J., 1991, unreported). For general discussion of the concept of the administrative receiver see *Re International Bulk Commodities Ltd* [1993] Ch. 77. For an interesting discussion as to whether it is possible to have a court appointed administrative receiver see *Schummacher* (1993) 9 *Insolvency Law & Practice* 43. The courts have clarified this matter by indicating that they have no power to appoint administrative receivers—*Re A & C Supplies* [1998] B.P.I.R. 303.

[16] See Insolvency Act 1986, s.388(1)(*a*).

[17] *ibid.*, ss.42 and 43 plus Sched. 1.

[18] [1986] 1 W.L.R. 201.

the two regimes can operate concurrently with regard to the same company,[19] but in such a case, the receiver will take precedence.[20]

Voluntary liquidation

1-17 Liquidations of insolvent companies are of two types. First, there is the voluntary liquidation. If members of the company realise that the company is insolvent, they can resolve to place it in liquidation. If the directors cannot or do not make a declaration to the effect that the company is solvent, the liquidation is a creditors' voluntary liquidation and the creditors have the major say in the running of the liquidation. If, in fact, the company turns out to be solvent, the creditors are not involved. Unfortunately, there have in the past been abuses of the procedure for initiating a voluntary liquidation where the company is insolvent, and creditors have been deprived of their statutory rights by underhand tactics. Measures were introduced in the Insolvency Act 1986 to combat this problem (see chapter 5).

Liquidation by the court

1-18 As an alternative to voluntary liquidation, if the company refuses to do the honourable thing, it is possible for creditors owed in excess of £750 to petition the court for the liquidation of the company. If, in the opinion of the court, the company is unable to pay its debts, the court may order the winding up of the company. A provisional liquidator may be appointed by the court[21] immediately after the presentation of the petition, if the company's assets are believed to be at risk. The word "provisional" here relates to the temporary nature of such a liquidator's appointment.[22] The provisional liquidator will often be the Official Receiver (unfortunately there is room for terminological confusion here). These matters are considered fully in Chapter 6.

Liquidation under court supervision abolished

1-19 Formerly, there was a third type of liquidation available in the event of corporate insolvency—*i.e.* a winding-up under the supervision of the court. This involved the court supervising a company, which was in the process of being wound up voluntarily during the period of the winding-up. This facility was rarely used and in fact was abolished (some 20 years after a recommendation to that effect from the Jenkins Committee) by section 88 of the Insolvency Act 1985. It should be noted that the safety valve of a compulsory liquidation is always available if the court is unhappy with the conduct of a voluntary winding-up.[23] Section 116 of the Insolvency Act 1986 expressly preserves the rights of creditors and members to apply to the court for the exercise of this discretion.

---

[19] *Foxhall & Gyle (Nurseries) Ltd, Petitioners* 1978 S.L.T. (Notes) 29.

[20] *Re Joshua Stubbs Ltd* [1891] 1 Ch. 475, *Manley, Petitioner* 1985 S.L.T. 42.

[21] Under Insolvency Act 1986, s.135. For a novel use of the procedure see *Integro v. Demite Ltd* [1998] 11 Insolvency Intelligence 69.

[22] *Re A.B.C. Coupler and Engineering Co. Ltd (No. 3)* [1970] 1 W.L.R. 702 at 715 *per* Plowman J.

[23] For cases where a voluntary liquidation was superseded by a compulsory liquidation see *Re Millward & Co. Ltd* [1940] Ch. 333, *Re B. Karsberg Ltd* [1956] 1 W.L.R. 57, *Re J. D. Swain Ltd* [1965] 1 W.L.R. 909, *Re Surplus Properties (Huddersfield) Ltd* [1984] B.C.L.C. 89, *Re Lowestoft Traffic Services Ltd* [1986] B.C.L.C. 81, *Re Palmer Marine Surveys Ltd* [1986] 1 W.L.R. 573, *Re Falcon R. J. Developments Ltd* (1987) 3 B.C.C. 147 and *Re M.C.H. Services Ltd* (1987) B.C.L.C. 535. [1986] 1 W.L.R. 573. Compare *Re Russell Electronics Ltd* [1968] 2 All E.R. 559, *Re Rhine Film Corp. Ltd* (1986) 2 B.C.C. 98, 949 and *Re Fitness Centre (South East) Ltd* [1986] B.C.L.C. 518. See also Chaps 5 and 6.

INSOLVENCY COURTS AND PROCEDURE

1-20 The courts responsible for administering corporate insolvency law in England and Wales are the High Court (Chancery Division) and the county courts. Section 117 of the Insolvency Act 1986 confers unlimited winding-up jurisdiction on the High Court in England and Wales, whereas the county courts are given such jurisdiction in the case of companies with a paid up share capital of less than £120,000 and having a registered office within the relevant district (unless the Lord Chancellor excludes a particular county court from that jurisdiction). Notwithstanding these provisions insolvency proceeding are not, according to section 118, to be invalidated by reason of having been started in the wrong court.

Insolvency procedures

1-21 The rules governing corporate insolvency procedures are to be found in the Insolvency Rules 1986 (S.I. 1986 No. 1925) (as amended). The introduction of the new civil procedure rules on April 26, 1999 has necessitated some further modification and these amendments are set forth in the Insolvency (Amendment) (No. 2) Rules 1999 (S.I. 1999 No. 1022). The purpose of these modifications is to ensure consistency between the new civil procedure regime and the discrete procedures to be followed in insolvency cases. The general rule is expressed in rule 7.51, namely that general rules of civil procedure apply to insolvency cases before the High Court or county court unless inconsistent with the Insolvency Rules. A new version of rule 7.49 clarifies the matter of insolvency appeals.

1-22 These procedural rules are detailed in the extreme and, for the most part, are mandatory. The courts frown upon departures from specified procedures and are reluctant to add a gloss upon them. Having said that, the court does enjoy some discretion under rule 7.55 to forgive procedural lapses. Whether they will exercise this power of judicial pardon is unpredictable; the critical question is whether the procedure was introduced to protect creditors, and, if so, whether permitting deviation would undermine that legislative policy.[24] Another significant component of the Insolvency Rules 1986 is rule 7.47 which permits any court enjoying winding up jurisdiction to review, rescind or vary any of its orders.[25]

Foreign courts

1-23 Sometimes the courts of the United Kingdom may be asked by foreign counterparts to invoke their jurisdiction in the case of an overseas company. Section 426 of the Insolvency Act 1986 is the key provision in such a context. This section makes possible the enforcement of insolvency court orders throughout the United Kingdom. Furthermore, section 426(4) and (5) state that on receiving a request for assistance from a court of another part of the United Kingdom or of a relevant territory[26] may invoke their insolvency jurisdiction. This provision was first utilised in *Re*

---

[24] See here *Re Continental Assurance Co of London (No. 2)* [1998] 1 B.C.L.C. 583.

[25] For a full consideration of the jurisdiction and the multiplicity of authorities here see Sealy and Milman, *An Annotated Guide to the 1986 Insolvency Legislation* (5th ed., 1995) 924. Note also *Re Piccadilly Property Management Ltd*, *The Independent*, November 30, 1998.

[26] The jurisdictions whose courts may request such assistance are specified in s.426(11) and (12) and in the Cooperation of Insolvency Courts (Designation of Relevant Countries and Territories) Order 1986 (S.I. 1986 No. 2123) as extended by (S.I. 1989 No. 2409, S.I. 1996 No. 253 and S.I. 1998 No. 2766).

Dallhold Estates (U.K.) Pty Ltd, Re[27] where the courts of Western Australia asked the English courts to appoint an administrator of a company incorporated in Western Australia which had assets located in the United Kingdom. Notwithstanding the fact that in general, an administrator could not be appointed in respect of such a company (because it was not a "company" for the purposes of the Companies and Insolvency Acts) Chadwick J. held that section 426 gave him power to respond positively to the request from his Western Australian brethren. More recently in *Re Bank of Credit and Commerce International SA*[28] a question arose as to whether section 426 only entitled the English courts to invoke procedural rules of United Kingdom insolvency law (such as by appointing an administrator) or whether it permitted the application of substantive rules of insolvency law to foreign companies where such application had been requested by the appropriate foreign court. Rattee J. decided that substantive provisions such as those relating to wrongful and fraudulent trading, misfeasance or the avoidance of transactions may all be invoked if the foreign court seeks assistance.

1-24 Another example of the courts offering assistance to foreign courts is found in the case of *Re Business City Express*.[29] Here the section 426 facility was invoked to modify the rights of creditors to persuade them to support a court examiner's rescue scheme in Ireland.

1-25 Although it is clear from the above examples that the English courts are keen to support the concept of judicial comity that support is not unqualified. For example in *Re Focus Insurance Co Ltd*[30] it was stressed by Scott VC that assistance would not be forthcoming if the result would be to undermine insolvency procedures taking place in this country. Equally differences in substantive law may militate against offering assistance. Thus in *England v. Purves*[31] a request by administrators to interrogate company officers was rejected because legal proceedings were already afoot against such officers and it was clear that such an application if made by an English office holder would not find favour with the UK courts.

1-26 The leading case on the section 426 jurisdiction is *Hughes v. Hannover re (Re EMLICO)*.[32] This case involved a company that had been redomesticated from the US to Bermuda and which had then gone into liquidation in that new jurisdiction. A request for assistance from the Bermudan liquidators which took the form of a request to debar a German claimant from suing the company in the UK or in any other jurisdiction was rejected by the English courts. In giving judgment the Court of Appeal laid down the following guidelines:

(1) The phrase "insolvency law" as used in section 426(10) was exhaustive. However this comprised both substantive law of England and Wales together with such foreign law as was consistent with the former. The inherent and general jurisdiction of the court was also covered.

---

[27] [1992] B.C.C. 394.
[28] *The Times*, August 11, 1993.
[29] [1997] 2 B.C.L.C. 510.
[30] [1996] B.C.C. 659.
[31] Reported *sub nom Re JN Taylor Pty Ltd* [1998] B.P.I.R. 347. A similar conclusion was arrived at in *Re Southern Equities Corporation* [1999] B.P.I.R. 589 where the possibility of an examination being carried out in this country by an Australian judge under the Corporations Law, an idea accepted in principle but rejected on the facts.
[32] [1997] 1 B.C.L.C. 497. For comment on this case and the general issues raised by section 426, see Smart (1996) 112 L.Q.R. 397, (1998) 114 L.Q.R. 46, Fletcher [1997] J.B.L. 470 and Dawson (1998) 22 *Insolvency Lawyer* 14.

(2) The court did retain discretion as to whether it was proper to offer assistance. In so doing it could look at matters of public policy and other considerations.

Official Receiver

1-27 The office of the Official Receiver plays an important role in corporate insolvency law.[33] The Official Receiver will act as liquidator of many companies, particularly those whose assets are insufficient even to fund the expenses of a private liquidator. The appointment of a provisional liquidator will often involve the Official Receiver.

1-28 As liquidator a full range of duties is imposed on the Official Receiver. However some immunity from liability may be afforded as a result of the controversial decision in *Mond v. Hyde*.[34] This case involved the responsibilities of a trustee in bankruptcy under the pre 1985 law and the Court of Appeal ruled that the Official Receiver could not be held liable in tort for carrying out his public functions under the law. The full implications of this policy decision are unclear.

Insolvency records

1-29 Information about debtors is an important commercial commodity. Court records are an excellent source of such information. To what extent should the law permit free access to such records (and copying thereof) for an overtly commercial purpose? The Insolvency Rules 1986, r.7.28 deal with this matter. The issue was addressed recently in *Re Austintel Ltd*[35] where the Court of Appeal held that the wholesale copying of court records by a company specialising in business/credit information was not to be authorised. In so deciding the court emphasised its unwillingness to depart from the exercise of discretion by the judge at first instance. Having reached this conclusion with reluctance the Court of Appeal invited the Insolvency Rules Committee to review the matter.

Insolvency litigation

1-30 Now is an opportune moment to say a few words about insolvency litigation in general. Litigation initiated by insolvent companies poses particular problems.[36] There is inevitably a shortage of funds and the law should be alert to the danger of a successful defendant being unable to recover his costs. Equally, it should be careful not to deny insolvent companies a right of access to the courts.

1-31 All companies are as a general rule debarred from seeking support from the Legal Aid Fund.[37] One way around this difficulty is for a liquidator to assign the company's cause of action to a private individual (often a director or leading shareholder) who then may pursue the claim with the support of legal aid. After some uncertainty[38] the House of Lords has ruled in *Norglen Ltd v. Reeds Rains Prudential*

[33] See Insolvency Act 1986, ss.399–401.
[34] [1998] B.C.C. 44.
[35] [1997] B.C.C. 362.
[36] For discussion of some of the issues raised below see Ife [1996–97] 3 R.A.L.Q. 53, Walters (1996) 17 Co Law 165, Fennell (1997) 13 I.L. & P. 106 and Parry [1998] 2 C.F.I.L.R. 121.
[37] Legal Aid Act 1988, s.2(10). For recent confirmation see *R v. Chester and North Wales Legal Aid Area Office, ex parte Floods of Queensferry Ltd* [1998] B.C.C. 685.
[38] *Advanced Technology Structures v. Cray Valley Products* [1993] B.C.L.C. 723.

Ltd[39] that here is nothing intrinsically unlawful about such a stratagem. Policy issues as to whether this was an abuse of public funds were best left to the legal aid authorities, and indeed Parliament has offered guidance on the relevance of such factors.[40]

1-32 Liquidators who have sufficient funds at their disposal to institute proceedings may nevertheless lack a sufficiently deep pocket to meet the risk of adverse costs should the action fail. A defendant in such a case would be well advised to seek an early security for costs order pursuant to section 726 of the Companies Act 1985.[41] Failure to take this precautionary step could be damaging because the courts are reluctant to make a personal order for costs against a liquidator in the event of the action failing. Provided the liquidator is acting in good faith the court will not seek to deter him from exercising his legitimate power to realise assets. This point was stressed in *Mettaloy Supplies Ltd v. MA (UK) Ltd.*[42]

1-33 It is apparent from the above commentary that liquidators have the power to assign causes of action. This power is recognised in cases such as *Ramsay v. Hartley*[43] as an exception to the rules on champerty. However the assignment must be absolute. An attempt to share the fruits of the action in return for litigation finance, where the financier was to have conduct of the action, was frowned upon by Lightman J in *Grovewood Holdings Ltd v. James Capel & Co.*[44] This censorious approach has attracted criticism and has not been followed in Australia.[45] Moreover it is clear that certain causes of action are vested exclusively in liquidators and are therefore incapable of assignment. The best example of this genre would be a wrongful trading action pursued under section 214 of the Insolvency Act 1986. This limitation on a liquidator's power to realise assets was confirmed by the Court of Appeal in *Re Oasis Merchandising Services Ltd.*[46]

1-34 There is no objection to a liquidator seeking outside finance for the pursuit of a claim. Offering a share of the proceeds is acceptable[47] as the Court of Appeal acknowledged in *Katz v. McNally*,[48] but the liquidator must retain control of the proceedings. The court is not happy when one of its officers acts under the directions of a third party as this may compromise his independence and duty to act in the interests of all parties. Where a creditor offers finance to a liquidator in return for a share of the proceeds this transaction is not without risk because if the action fails the funding creditor may[49] be exposed to liability (although not a party to the proceedings) by virtue of the operation of section 51 of the Supreme Court Act 1981.

1-35 Another option, which is likely to become more commonplace is the use of

---

[39] [1997] 3 W.L.R. 1177.

[40] Legal Aid (General) (Amendment) (No. 2) Regulations 1996 (S.I. 1996 No. 1257).

[41] For a review of the security for costs jurisdiction in company law see Milman, "Security for Costs; Principles and Pragmatism in Corporate Litigation", in *The Realm of Company Law: Essays in Honour of Len Sealy*, (Rider, 1998) pp. 167–181.

[42] [1997] B.C.C. 165.

[43] [1977] 1 W.L.R. 686. However, this power may be reviewed by the courts—see *Re Edennote Ltd* [1996] 2 B.C.L.C. 389.

[44] [1995] Ch. 80.

[45] *Re Movitor Pty Ltd* (1996) 19 A.C.S.R. 440.

[46] [1997] 2 W.L.R. 764. A similar conclusion (with regard to s.127) was arrived at in *Re Ayala Holdings (No. 2)* [1996] 1 B.C.L.C. 467.

[47] In Australia there is a formal mechanism to enable liquidators to reward funding creditors—see *Re Clenisia Investments Pty Ltd* (1996) 19 A.C.S.R. 84. Note generally *Re Wm Fetton Co Pty Ltd* (1998) 28 A.C.S.R. 228.

[48] [1997] B.C.C. 784.

[49] *Eastglen v. Grafton Ltd* [1996] 2 B.C.L.C. 279. It is clear from the judgment of Lindsay J. in this case that the courts will be reluctant to impose such liability upon a funding creditor.

a conditional fee agreement to fund insolvency litigation.[50] Under such an agreement some of the risk of litigation is transferred from the client to the lawyer who agrees to accept a commission on this basis.[51] However this is not a panacea and in particular does not deal with the risk of adverse costs should the action fail.

[50] See Conditional Fee Agreements Order (S.I. 1995 No. 1647)—made under s.58 of the Courts and Legal Services Act 1990.
[51] The Insolvency Lawyers' Association has produced a model contract—see (1996) 17 *Insolvency Lawyer* 24.

CHAPTER 2

Insolvency Practitioners

2-01 This Chapter will deal with certain general features of the law applicable to the various types of insolvency practitioner already identified in Chapter 1. Matters of qualification, status, remuneration and control raise common issues and are most conveniently discussed comparatively, though certain of these topics have aspects which will require more detailed treatment subsequently.

2-02 A key feature of U.K. corporate insolvency law is the degree to which the operation of the system depends upon self-regulation within private practice. In more recent times the method of regulation has been characterised as "government monitored self regulation" to indicate that there is a considerable degree of state supervision.[1] This system is unlikely to change in the near future.[2]

2-03 All insolvency practitioners must be licensed (or "authorised", to use the statutory language). However while most insolvency practitioners are accountants or (to a much lesser extent) solicitors, the profession of insolvency practitioner as such is a relatively new one and is still working out the manner of its self-regulation. The Society of Practitioners of Insolvency plays a key role in promoting high standards. Worthy of particular mention are its Statements of Insolvency Practice. These deal with everyday matters of insolvency administration ranging from the mundane to the ultra technical. Although these statements do not have the force of law there is little doubt that failure to comply with established practice might place an insolvency practitioners in jeopardy in the event of a challenge to his conduct in litigation. Having a reputation for good practice is not merely a matter of professional pride. In some areas the reputation of an insolvency practitioner for probity is critical to the fate of a company. No creditor is going to vote for a voluntary arrangement if the company's nominee has a reputation as a soft touch who fails to deliver on the company's promises.

QUALIFICATION OF INSOLVENCY PRACTITIONERS

Limited companies bar

2-04 Prior to the Insolvency Act 1985 the law on qualification lacked cohesion. Certainly there were common strands. Thus, there was the prohibition on the appointment of limited companies as receivers or liquidators.[3] Indeed, it was held by

---

[1] For discussion see Finch [1998] J.B.L. 334.

[2] This conclusion was drawn in the Garwood Report, "A Review of Insolvency Practitioner Regulation" (February 1999).

[3] See Companies Act 1985, ss.489 and 634. See now Insolvency Act 1986, ss.30 and 390. The *Chancery Lane Registrars Case* which came before Harman J. (unreported, 1985, but noted in (1985) 1 Ins L. & P. 54) revealed a situation where there had been a breach of this statutory prohibition. The company concerned was wound up on a petition by the Secretary of State for Trade on the grounds of public interest.

Wynn-Parry J. in *Portman Building Society v. Gallwey*[4] that the appointment of a corporation as a receiver would be regarded as a total nullity, and would not have the desired effect of crystallising a floating charge.

Other restrictions

2-05 There was a more justifiable restriction placed on the appointment of an undischarged bankrupt to such a position.[5] Moreover, where the court was involved in any appointment, it applied a rule of practice to the effect that a minimum of five years relevant experience was an essential qualification.[6] A director who had been disqualified from managing companies would also be precluded from acting as a receiver or liquidator.[7] Finally, it was unlawful to procure an appointment as a liquidator by corrupt inducements.[8]

2-06 Apart from these isolated forms of negative regulation, there was no overall control matrix. There was nothing to stop a company officer being appointed as a liquidator or receiver. Furthermore, there was no requirement that insolvency practitioners be members of recognised professional bodies, with the result that their actions were not subject to control through the medium of rules of professional discipline. Thus, in one case, a former taxi driver set himself up as a voluntary liquidator in Sheffield and then fled to Spain with sums of money which had been paid over to him on the understanding that it would be forwarded to the employees of the liquidated companies. On the other hand, it must not be imagined that a requirement of professional qualification would constitute a panacea. The problem of "cowboy" insolvency practitioners was less acute in the case of receivers because banks as debenture holders tended only to appoint respected professionals whom they knew and trusted to protect their interests. The real difficulty arose in the case of voluntary liquidations, where directors of insolvent companies, looking for an easy ride, sometimes procured the appointment of non-qualified or even professionally qualified "cowboys" to the position of voluntary liquidator. This practice, coupled with the abuse of Centrebinding,[9] seriously prejudiced the rights of creditors.

Reform

2-07 The Cork Committee rightly viewed this situation as highly unsatisfactory.[10] It therefore proposed a system based essentially on a special professional qualification, and this is now to be found in Part XIII of the Insolvency Act 1986.

2-08 Thus, in the corporate context, it is now an offence under sections 388 and 389 of the Insolvency Act 1986 for a person to act as an insolvency practitioner (*i.e.* liquidator, provisional liquidator, administrator, administrative receiver[11] or

---

[4] [1955] 1 All E.R. 227 at 230.
[5] See Companies Act 1985, s.490. See now Insolvency Act 1986, ss.31 and 390(4).
[6] This rule was not inflexible. In *Re Icknield Developments Ltd* [1973] 1 W.L.R. 537, Plowman J. agreed to the appointment of the son of Sir Kenneth Cork as a liquidator to act in a compulsory winding-up even though he had only three years experience. This experience was sufficiently varied and extensive to qualify him for such a position.
[7] See Companies Act 1985, s.295. The relevant provision is now to be found in s.1 of the Company Directors Disqualification Act 1986 and Insolvency Act 1986, s.390(4).
[8] See Companies Act 1985, s.635. This provision is now to be found in Insolvency Act 1986, s.164.
[9] See Ch. 4.
[10] See Cmnd. 8558, para. 756.
[11] As defined by Insolvency Act 1986, s.29(2).

supervisor of a voluntary arrangement) without being properly qualified. Section 390 provides that in order to qualify, the insolvency practitioner must either be a member of a recognised professional body or obtain authorisation to act under section 393.

Disqualifications

2-09 Disqualifications are imposed on corporations, undischarged bankrupts, persons subject to disqualification orders under the Company Directors Disqualification Act 1986, and the mentally ill from acting as insolvency practitioners.[12] It is also a condition of qualification that the insolvency practitioner provides the requisite security under section 390(3) and rule 12.8 of the Insolvency Rules 1986. Further details on the question of security are provided by part III of the Insolvency Practitioners Regulations 1986 (S.I. 1986 No. 1995) as amended by (S.I. 1993 No. 221).

2-10 The Secretary of State is empowered to draw up a list of recognised professional bodies under section 391; such bodies must satisfy certain criteria as to function, training and professional discipline. Reference should be made here to the Insolvency Practitioners (Recognised Professional Bodies) Order 1986 (S.I. 1986 No. 1764). The Secretary of State can remove a body from this list if it fails to fulfil the requirements of the law.

"Competent authorities"

2-11 An alternative route to obtaining qualification as an insolvency practitioner for those persons who are not members of recognised professional bodies is to apply for authorisation to a "competent authority" under section 392. The Secretary of State can identify such authorities and, if he does not do so, he is the competent authority himself. Under section 393, the competent authority has some discretion when dealing with an application for authorisation, though it must grant the application if it is satisfied that the applicant is a fit and proper person and meets the prescribed requirements as to education and training. These matters are now dealt with by Part III of the Insolvency Practitioners Regulations 1986 (S.I. 1986 No. 1995). Authorisation can be revoked if the competent authority is satisfied that the applicant no longer fulfils the required criteria.[13]

2-12 Section 394 deals with notification of the decision of the competent authority. If authorisation is granted, the applicant should receive a certificate bearing the date from which the authorisation is to take effect. Refusal or revocation of authorisation should take the form of a reasoned written notice, which should refer the disappointed party to his rights under sections 395 and 396. These include the right to make written representations to the competent authority, challenging its decision. On receipt of such representations, the competent authority is obliged to reconsider the matter. Moreover, within 28 days of receiving notice from the competent authority of either its initial decision, or its final ruling the aggrieved party can require the competent authority to refer the matter to the Insolvency Practitioners' Tribunal, estab-

[12] There are prohibitions placed on corporations and undischarged bankrupts acting as any type of receiver imposed by Insolvency Act 1986, ss.30 and 31.

[13] Loss of qualification means that the insolvency practitioner should vacate office *Re Adams (Builders) Ltd* [1991] B.C.C. 62.

lished under Schedule 7 of the Act. On receipt of such a requirement, the competent authority has a final opportunity to reconsider the application but, if it remains unmoved, it must refer the matter to the Tribunal. The 28 day time limit must be strictly observed.[14]

Tribunal

2-13 The Tribunal is appointed by the Secretary of State from lawyers and experienced insolvency practitioners. Schedule 7 governs the remuneration of panel members and the number of sittings, and sets down ground rules for the procedure to be followed. Basically, the procedure must be designed to afford a reasonable opportunity for representations to be made on behalf of the aggrieved party. The Tribunal has powers to compel the attendance of witnesses. Further details on the procedure are provided by the Insolvency Practitioners Tribunal (Conduct of Investigations) Rules 1986 (S.I. 1986 No. 952).

2-14 Where a reference is made to the Tribunal, section 397 requires the tribunal to investigate the matter and report back to the competent authority on what it believes should be the appropriate decision in the particular case. The competent authority must abide by the Tribunal's ruling. The competent authority can publish the decision of the Tribunal if it thinks fit.

Incomptence and dishonesty

2-15 No doubt the compulsory qualification of insolvency practitioners will greatly reduce the number of incompetent and dishonest operators in the field of voluntary liquidations.[15] However some of the pre-1986 cases suggest that qualification is unlikely to cure all problems of this type. Thus, in the *Chancery Lane Registrars* affair in 1985, Harman J. was faced with gross misconduct on the part of voluntary liquidators, who were qualified accountants. He disqualified them for 12 years from acting as receivers or liquidators. In another case (which again was never properly reported), a professionally qualified liquidator was sent to prison for six years for misappropriating funds belonging to the companies which were under his control as liquidator. Malpractices of this kind can only be controlled by the regulatory procedures discussed later in this Chapter.

THE STATUS OF INSOLVENCY PRACTITIONERS

2-16 The legal status of insolvency practitioners was always somewhat vague, and unfortunately has been further complicated by the Insolvency Act 1986.

Receivers

2-17 In the case of receivers, there is a basic distinction between receivers appointed out of court and those appointed by the court on the petition of debenture holders. There is a standard contractual provision in most debentures providing that

---

[14] Note under s.398 the courses of action to be followed by the competent authority where the 28 days elapse without objections being raised.

[15] The courts are more willing to place trust in qualified insolvency practitioners—see for example *Capital Cameras v. Harold Lines Ltd* [1991] B.C.L.C. 884.

a receiver appointed out of court is deemed to be the agent of the company over whose assets he has control.[16] In the absence of such a provision, he will naturally be regarded as the agent of the debenture holders who appointed him, and on whose behalf he is really working.[17] An express agency provision is not necessary in the case of a receiver appointed by a mortgagee under section 109 of the Law of Property Act 1925, nor, now, in the case of an administrative receiver, because in both instances, Parliament has established a statutory agency relationship with the company.[18] Receivers appointed by the court are neither agents of the company nor of the debenture holders who procured their appointment.[19] Instead, they enjoy the special status of being officers of the court, which carries with it both advantages and disadvantages.

Liquidators, administrators, etc.

2-18 A liquidator appointed by the court is also viewed as one of its officers,[20] as are provisional liquidators and special managers. An official receiver is accorded similar status by section 400(2) of the Insolvency Act 1986. Administrators are officers of the court and so it appears are CVA supervisors[21] However, it is less clear whether a voluntary liquidator would be so regarded. In *Re John Bateson & Co. Ltd*,[22] a case which dealt with the question of whether a voluntary liquidator could exploit the non-registration of a company charge to the benefit of the unsecured creditors, Harman J. held that a voluntary liquidator was an officer of the court. The Court of Appeal took the opposite view in *Re T. H. Knitwear (Wholesale) Ltd.*[23]

Officers of the court

2-19 What is the significance of an insolvency practitioner falling into the category of an officer of the court? It is sometimes argued that the appointment of such a person is more likely to have a deleterious effect on company contracts, but, on closer analysis, this is not necessarily so.[24] Furthermore, it is unclear whether an officer of the court as such incurs personal liability on contracts entered into by him; the position appears to differ for receivers appointed by the court[25] as compared to court-appointed liquidators.[26] In any event an administrator escapes personal liability by virtue of his statutory status as agent for the company under section 14(5).

---

[16] See *Milman* (1981) 44 M.L.R. 658.

[17] *Re Vimbos Ltd* [1900] 1 Ch. 470.

[18] See Law of Property Act 1925, s.109(2) and Insolvency Act 1986, s.44(1)(*a*). This relationship can be rebutted.

[19] *Corporation of Bacup v. Smith* (1890) 44 Ch.D. 395 at 398, *per* Chitty J. See also *Maritime Life Assurance Co. v. Chateau Gardens* [1984] 2 D.L.R. (4th) 553 at 556, *per* Van Camp J.

[20] *Re Icknield Development Ltd* [1973] 1 W.L.R. 537 at 539 *per* Plowman J.

[21] By analogy with *King v. Anthony* [1998] 2 B.C.L.C. 517.

[22] [1985] B.C.L.C. 259 at 264. See also *Re Anglo-Moravian Junction Railway Co. ex p. Watkin* (1875) 1 Ch.D. 130 at 133 *per* James L.J., *Knowles v. Scott* [1891] 1 Ch. 717 at 723 *per* Romer J.

[23] [1988] B.C.L.C. 195—overruling *Re Temple Fire and Accident Assurance Co. Ltd* (1910) 129 L.T. Jo. 115.

[24] See *Parsons v. Sovereign Bank of Canada* [1913] A.C. 160. In *Reid v. Explosives Co.* (1887) 19 Q.B.D. 264 it was held that the appointment of a receiver by the court would automatically terminate contracts of employment. This case has attracted much criticism and was not followed in *International Harvester Export Co. v. International Harvester (Australia) Ltd* (1983) 7 A.C.L.R. 391.

[25] *Burt, Boulton & Hayward v. Bull* [1895] 1 Q.B. 276.

[26] *Re Anglo-Moravian Junction Railway Co. ex p. Watkin* (1875) 1 Ch.D. 130; *Stead Hazel & Co. v. Cooper* [1933] 1 K.B. 840.

What is clear, however, is that officers of the court are protected by the law of contempt against undue interference from outside parties.[27] Most importantly of all, it would appear that officers of the court are subject to a duty to act honourably, because the bankruptcy rule in *Ex parte James*[28] will apply to them. It is not easy to define with precision the nature of the duty imposed by this rule, though it has been variously described as an obligation not to use dirty tricks, nor to behave in a shabby manner, nor to act contrary to natural justice.[29] Thus, in *Re Regent Finance and Guarantee Corp. Ltd*,[30] Maugham J. held that a liquidator appointed by the court ought to repay a sum of money which had been paid to the company at the time of liquidation, because it would in the circumstances of that particular case have been unfair for the liquidator to retain it.

Office holders

2-20 In terms of status, an additional label was introduced into the law of insolvency practitioners by sections 230–246 of the Insolvency Act 1986—namely, that of an office holder. Unfortunately an analysis of the sections shows that the "office holder" is not in fact a definite class of insolvency practitioner, but a somewhat clumsy drafting expedient. The expression is differently defined for the purposes of different sections, and simply means the class of insolvency practitioner to which the particular section or group of sections is intended to apply.

2-21 Section 230 is headed "Office Holders." It contains no definition but provides that administrators, administrative receivers, liquidators and provisional liquidators must be qualified insolvency practitioners. Section 231 provides that those persons can be appointed jointly but the instrument of appointment must say whether they can act separately or must act together. By section 232 their acts remain valid notwithstanding defects in their appointment, nomination or qualification.

Public utility services

2-22 An important right vested in every office holder (except a non administrative receiver) is the right under section 233 to receive a continued supply of essential public utility services without first settling arrears incurred by the company before his appointment. Formerly, receivers and liquidators could be compelled to settle arrears by the threat of withdrawal of supply. This right to receive a supply now extends to administrators, administrative receivers, supervisors of voluntary arrangements, liquidators and provisional liquidators. It does not extend to non-administrative receivers.

---

[27] See *Helmore v. Smith (No. 2)* (1886) 35 Ch.D. 449, *Re Wm Thomas Shipping Co. Ltd* [1930] 2 Ch. 368 and *Re Exchange Travel Holdings Ltd* [1991] B.C.L.C. 728. In *Re Maidstone Palace of Varieties Ltd* [1909] 2 Ch. 283 it was held that to institute proceedings against a court appointed receiver without the leave of the court might constitute contempt. This decision is inconsistent with the subsequent case of *Cleary v. Brazil Railway Co.* (1915) 113 L.T. 96 and was criticised in Canada in *Badior v. North American Wood Preserving Ltd* (1981) 124 D.L.R. (3d) 571.

[28] (1874) L.R. 9 Ch. App. 609.

[29] For a recent discussion of the rule see *Re Byfield* [1982] Ch. 271, *Re John Bateson & Co. Ltd* [1985] B.C.L.C. 259 and *Re T. H. Knitwear (Wholesale) Ltd* (1988) 4 BCC 102.

[30] [1930] W.N. 84. See also *Downs Distribution Co. v. Associated Blue Star Stores* (1948) 76 C.L.R. 463, *Re Associated Dominions Assurers Society* (1962) 109 C.L.R. 516 and *Re Paddington Town Hall Centre Ltd* (1979) 4 A.C.L.R. 673.

Right of seizure

2-23 The definition of office holder is further narrowed for the purposes of sections 234–7, in that supervisors of voluntary arrangements are excluded from the benefit of these provisions. Section 234 confers rights of seizure of company documents on office holders. Moreover, in the event of a wrongful seizure of property, an office holder who had reasonable grounds for believing that he was entitled to effect a seizure, and who had not acted negligently, is given immunity from suit. Office holders can demand cooperation from company officers, past and present, to assist them in the performance of their duties.

Investigations

2-24 Office holders have considerable powers under subsections 235 and 236 of the Insolvency Act 1986 to investigate the company's affairs, to interrogate officers and to seek information from third parties.[31]

2-25 In this connection two issues have repeatedly come before the courts in the last few years. The first question is the extent to which an officer can refuse to answer questions put to him by an office holder on the grounds that the answer might incriminate him and lead to a criminal prosecution. Of course, at common law there is a general presumption in favour of maintaining the right of silence where the accused runs the risk of self-incrimination by responding to the interrogator's questions. The status of this presumption in the context of the powers of office holders under insolvency legislation was considered by the Court of Appeal in *Maxwell v. Bishopsgate Investment Trusts*.[32] In a judgment that confirmed a number of first instance authorities[33] decided under the Insolvency Act 1986, the Court of Appeal ruled that the privilege against self-incrimination had been expressly excluded by Parliament in cases where an office holder was making section 236 inquiries—the legislature had decided as a matter of policy to confer the widest investigatory powers upon insolvency practitioners.

2-26 However, this clear statement of English law must now be open to doubt. The decision of the European Court of Human Rights in *Saunders v. U.K.*[34] does pose difficulties for the authorities with regard to follow up action in the wake of an investigation of managerial misconduct. Here the European Court ruled that it was an infringement of Article 6 of the European Convention on Human Rights for a citizen having being compelled to give evidence without the benefit of the right of silence then to be prosecuted for criminal offences on the basis of that evidence. Although this case was concerned with evidence obtained via a DTI inspection process the principle laid down by the case is surely relevant to section 236 inquiries. In *R v. Secretary of State v. McCormick*[35] the English Court of Appeal took an optimistic view of the principle by accepting an argument from the authorities that it was only relevant to compelled evidence in criminal cases and not apposite to follow up civil proceedings (e.g. director disqualification proceedings). We doubt that such a limitation applies and the matter will surely be revisited, perhaps when the Human Rights Act 1998 becomes fully operational.

[31] Individual creditors cannot invoke these procedures—*Re James McHale Automobiles Ltd* [1997] B.C.C. 202.

[32] [1992] 2 W.L.R. 991.

[33] *Re Jeffrey S. Levitt Ltd* [1992] B.C.C. 137, *Re Arrows Ltd (No. 1)* [1992] B.C.C. 121.

[34] [1997] B.C.C. 872.

[35] [1998] B.C.C. 379.

2-27 The second issue concerns the position of third parties when an office holder is exercising his or her wide powers of investigation. To what extent can the office holder gain access to or possession of information which the company itself might not be entitled to? In *Cloverbay v. Bank of Credit and Commerce International*[36] the Court of Appeal, in a majority ruling, held that an office holder could not pursue inquiries against a third party where it would be oppressive, and indicated that the section 236 power should only be used to glean information which the company itself would have been entitled to acquire. More recent consideration of these issues has been provided by the judgment of the House of Lords in *Re British and Commonwealth Holdings plc (Nos. 1 and 2)*.[37] This case concerned the wish of the administrators of British and Commonwealth to gain access to documents in the possession of accountants who had audited a company (A plc) which had been taken over by British and Commonwealth, and then became insolvent and went into administration. Among these documents was a working capital analysis of the financial prospects of A plc and other material prepared in connection with the audits of the company. The request for access was based upon section 236(2) and (3) of the Insolvency Act 1986, but access was refused by the accountants, who argued that to require them to produce the large amount of documentation required would be oppressive. The accountants further argued, relying upon dicta of Browne-Wilkinson V.-C. in *Cloverbay Ltd v. Bank of Credit and Commerce International*[38] that the information could only be extracted from them if it could be said to be essential to reconstitute the state of the company's (*i.e.* B & C's) knowledge.

2-28 Hoffmann J. after carefully weighing the merits of the respective cases, was of the opinion that the burden placed on the accountants was not oppressive, in the circumstances, but he concluded that the limitation upon the use of section 236 as suggested by the accountants was indeed supported by *Cloverbay*.[39] The Court of Appeal differed on this latter point, denying that *Cloverbay*[40] had sought to lay down a rigid rule restricting applications by office holders under section 236.

2-29 The House of Lords unanimously upheld the ruling of the Court of Appeal, with Lord Slynn summarising his reason for dismissing the accountants' appeal as follows:[41]

> "I am therefore of the opinion that the power of the court to make an order under section 236 is not limited to documents which can be said to be needed 'to reconstitute the state of the company's knowledge' even if that may be one of the purposes most clearly justifying the making of an order".

2-30 In making this statement Lord Slynn went to some lengths to point out that no such restrictive condition upon the operation of section 236 had been imposed by the legislature in the provision itself, nor by Browne-Wilkinson V.-C. in *Cloverbay*.[42]

2-31 The ruling in favour of the administrators was, however, not an unqualified

---

36 [1991 Ch. 90.

37 [1992] 3 W.L.R. 853. Section 236 can be used in the context of a foreign company—*Re Mid East Trading Ltd* [1998] B.C.C. 726.

38 [1991] Ch. 90.

39 *Supra*.

40 *Supra*.

41 [1992] 3 W.L.R. 853 at 862.

42 [1991] Ch. 90.

victory. In the first place, Lord Slynn was quick to acknowledge that this was an exceptional decision promoted by the need to investigate all aspects of the financial collapse of British and Commonwealth. Ordinarily, the courts would only be willing to order the delivery of such documents where the effect would be to reconstitute the state of knowledge of the insolvent company, but this was not an ordinary case.

2-32 In examining the exercise of discretion on the part of Hoffmann J., their Lordships could find no fault with the way in which he had conducted the requisite balancing operation, and agreed that it would not be unduly burdensome to ask the accountants to produce the relevant documents. The effort and inconvenience involved was outweighed by the administrators' need for full disclosure.

2-33 Similar issues arose in *Re Brook Martin & Co. (Nominees) Ltd*[43] where Vinelott J. had to consider the position of solicitors who had acted for and had also been directors of the failed company. It was held that the defence of professional privilege could not be used in the face of section 236 inquiries carried out by an office holder seeking reasons for the collapse of the client company. Furthermore, the fact that any documents handed over might be used against the respondents was not a valid reason to resist delivery up, nor was delay by the office holder in exercising section 236 powers.

2-34 The power conferred by section 236 must not be abused, however, as shown by the case of *Re Sasea Finance Ltd.*[44] Here the liquidators of a company wished to use section 236 to issue interrogatories with respect to documents (which the liquidators held) relating to the company's audits. The auditors resisted this request and Scott VC upheld their objections. Here the liquidators already held the relevant documentation and the purpose of the interrogatories was not to obtain information but to elicit damaging admissions from the auditors who were being sued by the liquidators for alleged negligence. Scott V.C. also criticised the practice adopted by some office holders of issuing protective negligence writs against auditors and then seeking to exploit section 236 to secure admissions from the intended defendants—this might be viewed as an abuse of process.

Criminal Investigations

2-35 Office holders are of course not the only persons who may wish to investigate the causes of a corporate collapse. The DTI may wish to appoint inspectors to examine certain matters, and where criminality is suspected, the Serious Fraud Office may wish to exercise its powers of inquiry under the Criminal Justice Act 1987.[45] As far as a director is concerned, the fact that one investigatory authority is looking into the collapse of the company with a view to laying criminal charges does not relieve that director from his statutory duty to cooperate with the office holder, a point stressed by Ferris J. in *Re Wallace Smith Trust Co. Ltd.*[46] Problems have arisen in defining the precise relationship between office holders and the SFO.

2-36 In *Re Barlow Clowes Gilt Managers Ltd.*[47] Millett J. held that where infor-

---

[43] [1993] B.C.L.C. 328.

[44] [1998] 1 B.C.L.C. 559. On the relevance of costs of compliance see *Re B.C.C.I. SA* [1997] B.C.C. 561 (*sub nom Morris v. Bank of America*).

[45] For a discussion of the investigatory powers of the SFO see *R v. Director of the SFO, ex parte Smith* [1992] 3 W.L.R. 66.

[46] [1992] B.C.C. 707.

[47] [1991] B.C.C. 608.

mation had been provided to office holders who had given an undertaking of confidentiality, that undertaking should be respected by the office holders, who should not voluntarily disclose the information to the SFO (or to the accused?). The need to maintain the flow of information to office holders lay behind the decision of Millett J. However, in *Re Arrows Ltd (No. 4)*[48] the House of Lords (overturning a ruling by Vinelott J.) held that documents obtained by office holders exercising section 236 powers could be released to the SFO without placing restrictions on the use of those documents in the terms outlined by section 2(8) of the Criminal Justice Act 1987. The effect of this ruling may be to hamper investigations by office holders who will no longer be able to give binding undertakings as to the ultimate use of information uncovered under section 236.

2-37 The opposite scenario arose in *Morris v. SFO*,[49] namely under what circumstances could the SFO be compelled to hand over material seized during its inquiries to liquidators seeking access pursuant to the exercise of their section 236 powers? Nicholls V.-C. held that the SFO has no general power to make *voluntary* disclosure of such documents without the permission of the owners of these documents, but that the court might, in the exercise of its discretion under section 236 of the Insolvency Act 1986, *order* the SFO to deliver up this material, (although the rights of the owners of the material in question have to be weighed against the need of the office holder to obtain information). The owner of the documents should be informed of the application and given an opportunity to present an argument supporting his objection to production of the material.

2-38 The powers contained in sections 238–246 (relating to avoidance of transactions at an undervalue, preferences, certain floating charges and extortionate credit bargains) apply to an even narrower class of office holder, being an administrator or liquidator only. These provisions are fully discussed in Chapter 11. The definition then widens slightly in section 246 to include a provisional liquidator in a special class of office holder against whom a lien on the company's books and papers (not including documents of title held as such) is unenforceable.

REMUNERATION AND EXPENSES OF INSOLVENCY PRACTITIONERS

2-39 In view of the generous priority accorded to an insolvency practitioner's claim in respect of his remuneration and expenses (discussed in Chapter 10), it was essential that the law should establish a number of control mechanisms to prevent such claims getting out of hand.

Level of remuneration of s.109 receiver

2-40 Where a receiver is appointed under section 109 of the Law of Property Act 1925, that legislation regulates the question of his remuneration. Thus under section 109(6) the rate is to be fixed by agreement with the mortgagee, subject to an upper ceiling of 5 per cent. of gross realisations. In the absence of express agreement between the parties, the 5 per cent. rate is adopted, unless the court orders

---

48 [1994] 3 W.L.R. 646. See also *Ex parte Trachtenberg* [1993] B.C.C. 492. The accused does not enjoy such a favourable right of access to section 236 documents—*Re Headington Investments Ltd* [1993] B.C.C. 500.

49 [1993] 1 All E.R. 788.

otherwise. It should be noted that the global figure of 5 per cent. includes any claim by the receiver for his costs, charges and expenses. In *Marshall v. Cottingham*[50] Megarry V.-C. held that in the case of a receiver appointed under a debenture incorporating the provisions of the 1925 Act,[51] where no rate of remuneration was explicitly agreed, the receiver would be entitled to claim his 5 per cent. and it was not necessary to make an application to the court to confirm this level of remuneration. Moreover, on the facts of this particular case, it was held that the receiver's realisation costs did not have to come out of his 5 per cent. share because the debenture had made it clear that these were to be paid in addition to any remuneration.[52]

Remuneration of administrative receiver

2-41 In the more common case where an administrative receiver is appointed out of court to enforce a general security over the company's assets, his level of remuneration will be determined by the debenture and instrument of appointment. In the absence of an appropriate clause, recourse to an action based on a quantum meruit might prove necessary.[53] Normally remuneration is fixed as a percentage of total realisations.

2-42 The key mechanism designed to prevent receivers claiming excessive remuneration out of the company's assets is now to be found in section 36 of the Insolvency Act 1986:

> "(1) The court may, on application made by the liquidator of a company, by order fix the amount to be paid by way of remuneration to a person who, under powers contained in an instrument, has been appointed receiver or manager of the company's property.
>
> (2) The court's power under subsection (1), where no previous order has been made with respect thereto under the subsection—
> (a) extends to fixing the remuneration for any period before the making of the order or the application for it,
> (b) is exercisable notwithstanding that the receiver or manager has died or ceased to act before the making of the order or the application, and
> (c) where the receiver or manager has been paid or has retained for his remuneration for any period before the making of the order any amount in excess of that so fixed for that period, extends to requiring him or his personal representatives to account for the excess or such part of it as may be specified in the order.
>
> But the power conferred by paragraph (c) shall not be exercised as respects any period before the making of the application for the order under this

---

[50] [1980] 3 W.L.R. 235.

[51] In *Re Greycaine Ltd* [1946] Ch. 269, it was made clear that the debenture should clearly establish whether the provisions of s.109 of the 1925 Act are being incorporated in toto or merely in part.

[52] For recent authorities on a receiver's claim to remuneration see *Choudri v. Palta*, [1992] B.C.C. 787 (remuneration cannot be paid out of the charged assets until prior charges have been satisfied) and *Rottenberg v. Monjack*, [1992] B.C.C. 688 (receiver cannot realise further assets comprised in security if he already has sufficient funds in hand to repay mortgagee and meet his own claim to remuneration). See also *Phoenix Properties v. Wimpole Street Nominees* [1992] B.C.L.C. 737.

[53] *Prior v. Bagster* (1887) 57 L.T. 766.

> section, unless in the court's opinion there are special circumstances making it proper for the power to be exercised.
>
> (3) The court may from time to time on an application made either by the liquidator or by the receiver or manager, vary or amend an order made under subsection (1)."

2-43 There has been a dearth of litigation centred on this provision and its predecessors, if only because there are good reasons for insolvency practitioners being reluctant to take issue with one another over such matters. Insolvency practitioners form a close-knit professional community and depend to some degree on their relationship with each other for their effectiveness. Today's liquidator with misgivings about the receiver's remuneration may well find the roles reversed when he is appointed receiver of another company tomorrow. Apart from plain cases, therefore, there is much practical commonsense in a policy of live and let live. It remains to be seen whether the increased pressure on liquidators to maximise assets available for unsecured creditors will affect the matter.

2-44 The leading case on what is now section 36 is *Re Potters Oils Ltd (No. 2)*,[54] a decision of Mr Justice Hoffmann. Stripped of its complications, this case involved an application by a liquidator, who had been appointed by the court to wind up the company, challenging a claim for remuneration and disbursements submitted by a receiver who had subsequently been appointed over the company's assets to protect the interests of a chargee. The liquidator alleged that the appointment of the receiver was unnecessary and that his claim for remuneration and disbursements was excessive. Hoffmann J. held that the appointment of the receiver was not unjustified. On the question of the receiver's remuneration, Hoffmann J., whilst conceding that what is now section 36 is interventionist in nature, declared:[55]

> "interference should be confined to cases in which the remuneration can clearly be seen as excessive, rather than take the form of a routine taxation by the court of the receiver's remuneration."

Hoffmann J. had few guidelines to help him, and decided that the remuneration claimed in this particular case was not excessive.

2-45 Turning to the receiver's claim for disbursements, Hoffmann J. stated:[56]

> "the scope of . . . (section 36) . . . is, however, confined to the receiver's remuneration. It confers no jurisdiction to interfere with his right to indemnity for disbursements. This remains subject to the ordinary law of agency."

One of the items listed under the receiver's claim for disbursements was in respect of solicitors' costs and Hoffmann J. mooted the possibility of the liquidator asking for these costs to be taxed under section 71 of the Solicitors Act 1974.

2-46 Where the appointment is made by the court, the receiver's claim for remuneration and expenses is entirely a matter for the court itself.

---

[54] [1986] 1 W.L.R. 201. For an Irish review see *Re City Car Sales Ltd* [1995] 1 I.L.R.M. 221.
[55] *ibid.*, at 207.
[56] *ibid.*, at 207.

Remuneration of administrators and supervisors

2-47 An administrator is clearly going to expect that his or her claim to remuneration will be met out of the assets of the company whose custodianship has been entrusted to him. His remuneration is to be paid in priority to the claim of any floating charge holder,[57] a fact contributing to the reluctance of such chargees to allow an administration to proceed (as an alternative to administrative receivership) in certain cases. Specific provisions on the quantum of the remuneration are laid down in rule 2.47 of the Insolvency Rules 1986—the rate will be calculated by reference to the value of assets under the control of the administrator, or by reference to the time expended on the administration. Essentially, the appropriate rate is to be determined by the creditors' committee, though recourse to the creditors as a whole may be necessary. Both the administrator[58] and any disgruntled creditor[59] can appeal to the court for a review of the remuneration awarded. However, hostile review application by a creditor must be supported by 25 per cent. (in value) of the total debts held by the creditors.

2-48 The provisions on the remuneration payable to nominees (and then, supervisors) of voluntary arrangements are set forth in rule 1.28 of the Insolvency Rules 1986. Essentially, it is for the nominees to negotiate the issue of fees before the arrangement is approved with the company (or its liquidator or administrator), and also to make provision for fees as a supervisor in the terms of the arrangement to be approved by creditors.

Remuneration of liquidators

2-49 In the case of remuneration payable to liquidators there is less scope for a challenge and no statutory provision equivalent to section 36 of the Insolvency Act 1986. The matter is instead dealt with by the Insolvency Rules. Rule 4.127 provides that the liquidator's remuneration is to be based either on a percentage of realisations and distributions, or on time spent on the work,[60] but not, apparently, on both. The liquidation committee is to decide which, taking into account the complexity of the winding-up, any special responsibility the liquidator has had to assume, the value of the assets, and the liquidator's apparent effectiveness. The liquidator has a right of appeal to a meeting of creditors if he thinks the committee has been too mean, and a further right of appeal to the court under rules 4.129–4.130 (as amended). On the other hand, creditors can complain to the court under rule 4.131 (at their own expense unless the court orders otherwise) if they consider the remuneration allowed by the committee excessive.

2-50 If the liquidator's remuneration is not fixed by the liquidation committee, the liquidator is entitled to charge his fees on the Official Receiver's scale.[61] Details of this scale are now to be found in the Insolvency Regulations 1986 (S.I. 1986 No. 1994) (regs 19–22). If the liquidator realises charged property on behalf of a secured

[57] Insolvency Act 1986, s.19(4).
[58] R. 2. 49.
[59] R. 2. 50.
[60] The time basis for charging remuneration is now in disfavour as a result of the report of the Ferris Working Party, which was published in July 1998 (see para. 2.56 post). Where this method of quantification is used it is imperative that meticulous records are kept.
[61] This scale was the subject of some discussion in the Ferris Working Party on Remuneration—this report is cited below at para. 2.56.

creditor he has the right under rule 4.128 in any event to keep a fee calculated on this scale out of the proceeds of realisation.

2-51 Problems can arise where a voluntary liquidator is supplanted in the event of the company subsequently going into compulsory liquidation. Such a situation arose recently in *Re A. V. Sorge & Co. Ltd.*[62] A voluntary liquidator was appointed after a winding up petition had been presented to the court for the compulsory liquidation of the company. On the making of the winding-up order, the new liquidator objected to his predecessor's claim for remuneration and costs, on the ground that his intervention had been both unnecessary and counterproductive. The voluntary liquidator thereupon applied to the court to have his claim to remuneration and costs fixed. Hoffmann J. held that the power of the court, under the Winding Up Rules to have the remuneration of a voluntary liquidator fixed extended to the period before the presentation of the petition as well as before the making of the winding-up order. Costs incurred by a voluntary liquidator before the date of the resolution for winding up (*e.g.* the expense involved in preparing a statement of the company's assets to be laid before a creditors' meeting) could also be claimed by the voluntary liquidator. Finally, a voluntary liquidator who had been displaced on the appointment of a liquidator by the court could claim not only his costs of handing over the assets, but also costs incurred after that date where loose ends, such as replying to letters, had to be tied up.

Liquidators appointed by the court

2-52 In the case of liquidators appointed by the court, the level of remuneration is fixed by the court according to standard scale fees. An interesting example of judicial attitudes in this context is to be found in *Re U.S. Ltd.*[63] Here, the court had appointed a special manager under what is now section 177 of the Insolvency Act 1986 with a view to selling certain high fashion clothes. The company's ownership of these garments was contested by one of its suppliers, but, in view of the need to catch the current fashion wave, both parties agreed that the sale should proceed. After the sale it was then discovered that the garments did not belong to the company. Nevertheless Nourse J. held that as the special manager was merely carrying out the instructions given to him by the court, he was not to be deprived of his remuneration.

Claims against associated companies

2-53 The claim of a liquidator in respect of his remuneration and expenses can only be enforced against the assets of the insolvent company under his charge. He has no right to pursue such a claim against an associated company.[64] The moral of the tale is clear—an insolvency practitioner should not accept an appointment unless he is sure that the company's assets are sufficient to pay for his fees and expenses. It seems that there is no obstacle to the practitioner agreeing with members proposing to appoint him that they will make up any deficiency in this respect, so long as no

---

[62] (1986) 2 B.C.C. 99, 306. See also *Re Sandwell Copiers Ltd* (1988) 4 B.C.C. 227 and *Re Tony Rowse Ltd* [1996] B.C.C. 196. Slightly different issues arose in *Re Salters Hall School Ltd* [1998] 1 B.C.L.C. 401 where there was a succession of liquidators in a creditors' voluntary liquidation. As there were insufficient funds to satisfy both claims to remuneration it was determined that they should abate rateably.

[63] (1984) 1 B.C.C. 98, 985.

[64] *Taylor, Petitioner* 1976 S.L.T. (Sh. Ct.) 82.

agreement is made whereby the liquidator is to receive more than his entitlement under rules 4.127 and 4.128.

Remuneration of insolvency practitioners: a new regime

2-54 The principles set out above governing the remuneration of insolvency practitioners have been settled for many years. Although consisting of piecemeal decisions they have operated without serious criticism for generations. The position today is much less settled.

2-55 The House of Commons Select Committee[65] reviewing the fees and expenses of the office holders undertaking the realisation of the Maxwell empire was aghast at the amounts being charged for what appeared to be little in the way of return to ordinary creditors. The spotlight increased in intensity in the wake of the judgment of Ferris J. in *Mirror Group Newspapers v. Maxwell*[66] where the court appointed receivers who were winding up the private affairs of the late Robert Maxwell submitted a bill for the courts approval. Ferris J reviewed the current law and practice on the issue and made a number of criticisms of current practices. The views of Ferris J. were supported from other quarters.[67]

2-56 In response to these criticisms and general public disquiet a committee was set up headed by Mr Justice Ferris. The Ferris Working Party produced its first report[68] in July 1998 and called for a number of changes. These may be summarised as follows:

— a need for clarification of the relevant principles;

— the importance of the "value for money" criterion;

— regulatory changes must be proportionate, that is they must not unduly increase the costs of administering the estate for no appreciable benefit;

— formal remuneration scales for private insolvency practitioners are not favoured, but more information should be available on going rates;

— the procedures under which the court fixes remuneration should be updated;

— insolvency practitioners need to be more alert when checking bills submitted by lawyers for work completed for the estate;

— a standing consultative committee should be set up to keep this area (and others) under constant review.

2-57 Thus the new regime will be dominated by the need to show value for money and the ability of every office holder to produce detailed records as to how time was spent and costs incurred. It seems likely that many of these recommendations will be implemented through a new Statement of Insolvency Practice.[69]

---

[65] Third Report (1994).

[66] [1998] B.C.C. 324. Ironically the claims for fees and disbursements were largely upheld on closer scrutiny—see [1999] B.C.C. 684.

[67] Even more caustic criticism of the practices of office holders when submitting claims for remuneration and expenses was made by Le Pinchon J. in the Hong Kong case of *Re Peregrine Investments Holdings* (unreported June 25, 1998). Lightman J. has also criticised remuneration practices in a number of *ex cathedra* speeches—see [1996] J.B.L. 113.

[68] For comment see Theobald (1998) 14 I.L. & P. 300. Ferris J. outlines how he sees the way forward in his piece in [1999] *Insolvency Lawyer* 48.

[69] This will in effect be a revised SIP 9.

REGULATORY CONTROLS ON INSOLVENCY PRACTITIONERS

2-58 The rules on qualification and remuneration are two important examples of the way in which corporate insolvency law exercises a degree of control over insolvency practitioners. However, they are not the only forms of regulation to note.

Misfeasance proceedings

2-59 An important instrument of regulation is to be found in section 212 of the Insolvency Act 1986. This provides a summary procedure for instituting misfeasance proceedings against company officers, liquidators, administrative receivers[70] and administrators. The Official Receiver, the liquidator, or any creditor or contributory, can take advantage of the procedure where there is evidence of misfeasance, breach of fiduciary duty, or indeed any other duty owed to the company.[71] If the action is against a liquidator or administrator who had already been given his release, the leave of the court must be obtained before misfeasance proceeding can be instituted. On a successful misfeasance action the court can order that the miscreant officer or insolvency practitioner restore assets to the company, or compensate the company for any loss caused by the breach of duty in question.[72]

2-60 Let us examine a few illustrations of successful misfeasance actions against company liquidators. In *Re Home and Colonial Insurance Co. Ltd*,[73] Maugham J. held a liquidator, who admitted a proof of an invalid claim, to be liable on the grounds of misfeasance. The fact that he was not negligent did not preclude a misfeasance finding. It was held in *Argylls Ltd v. Coxeter*[74] that it could constitute misfeasance for a voluntary liquidator to distribute the company's assets whilst ignoring certain outstanding claims. A liquidator who made a secret profit from his position would surely be guilty of misfeasance.[75]

Application to the court

2-61 The court exercises an apparently benign control over liquidators by way of the liquidator's power to apply to the court for directions where a thorny issue of law has arisen[76]—*e.g.* the validity of a particular title retention clause, or the legality of a specific claim against the company's assets. All insolvency practitioners, whether appointed by the court or out of court, can and should take advantage of this facility. In *Re Windsor Steam & Coal Co.*,[77] Lawrence L.J. indicated that this right to apply for judicial guidance can be double edged:[78]

---

[70] In *Re B. Johnson and Co. (Builders) Ltd* [1955] Ch. 634, the Court of Appeal held that misfeasance proceedings could not be launched against receivers. Although this decision no longer retains its authority for administrative receivers, presumably it still applies to non-administrative receivers.

[71] It is interesting to note that the statutory provision was remodelled in 1985–6 to encompass breaches of any other duty, and this may well indicate the possibility of liability in negligence.

[72] As to the fate of the proceeds of a successful misfeasance claim, see *Re Anglo-Austrian Printing and Publishing Co. Ltd* [1895] Ch. 152.

[73] [1929] W.N. 223.

[74] (1913) 29 T.L.R. 355. See also *Re New Zealand Stock and General Corporation Ltd* (1907) 23 T.L.R. 238.

[75] *Cf. Silkstone & Haigh Moor Coal Co. v. Edey* [1900] 1 Ch. 167.

[76] See Insolvency Act 1986, ss.35 and 112 (receivers and voluntary liquidators). Court appointed insolvency practitioners have always had this right.

[77] [1929] 1 Ch. 151.

[78] *ibid.*, at 167.

"It is difficult to conceive a much stronger case of negligence than the omission to apply to the Court where a claim is put forward against the company which the liquidator realises may be wholly invalid, and which even if valid is difficult to assess; and the liquidator knows that the persons out of whose money he intends to pay it object to the payment."

Controls on financial dealing

2-62 There are various controls over the financial dealings of insolvency practitioners when handling the proceeds of their realisations. Firstly, the sums generated by realisations must be paid into the Insolvency Services Account at the Bank of England, and must never be mixed with the insolvency practitioner's private funds.[79] The relevant rules governing such matters are now to be found in the Insolvency Regulations 1986 (S.I. 1986 No. 1994). More importantly, insolvency practitioners are subject to a number of statutory obligations requiring them to file periodic returns at the Companies Registry.[80] Certain records must also be kept under the Insolvency Regulations 1986 (S.I. 1986 No. 1994) (as amended by S.I. 1994 No. 2507) and the Insolvency Practitioners Regulations 1986 (S.I. 1986 No. 1995) (as amended by S.I. 1990 No. 439 and S.I. 1993 No. 221).

Failure to submit returns

2-63 The courts are adopting an increasingly strict attitude towards insolvency practitioners who fail to fulfil their obligations in this area. For example, a voluntary liquidator who neglects to file accounts runs the risk of being supplanted by a liquidator appointed by the court.[81] In *Re Diane (Stockport) Ltd*[82] a seventy-five year old liquidator who had, on a number of occasions, not only failed to submit returns but who had also ignored orders of the court to do so, was fined £500 by Nourse J. and narrowly avoided being sent to prison for contempt of court. In *Re Grantham Wholesale Fruit, Vegetable and Potato Merchants Ltd.*,[83] Megarry J. was faced with a liquidator who had failed to submit returns to the Companies Registry and whose default had persisted for no less than three and a quarter years! He had also not bothered to reply to many letters from the Companies Registry and had failed to appear at earlier court proceedings relating to his default. Megarry J. described his behaviour as "wholly deplorable", and ordered him to pay the costs of the proceedings. The attention of his professional body was also drawn to his behaviour. Megarry J. indicated that he would have preferred to have fined him for contempt, but resisted the temptation because it was clear that the impression had grown up amongst insolvency practitioners that the authorities were soft on defaulters. However, he reminded liquidators that they were well rewarded and that one of their responsibilities was to file returns. Megarry J. stated:[84]

---

[79] One of the complaints levelled against the voluntary liquidators in the *Chancery Lane Registrars* case in 1985, noted in (1985) 1 Ins L. & P. 54, was failure to maintain the separation of funds. Harman J. disqualified the offending liquidators for 12 years. In another case a liquidator was jailed for six years for misappropriating funds from companies under his control as liquidator—see (1985) 1 Ins L. & P. 127.
[80] See Insolvency Act 1986, ss.38, 41, 46–48 and 130.
[81] See the decision of Buckley J. in *Re Ryder Installations Ltd* [1966] 1 W.L.R. 524.
[82] See *The Times*, July 15, 1982 and August 4, 1982. The liquidator was initially sentenced to eight months imprisonment for contempt but subsequently the judge relented and suspended this sentence.
[83] [1972] 1 W.L.R. 559.
[84] *ibid.*, at 567.

> "I must also say something about the Registrar of Companies. On his shoulders rest great responsibilities in the important field of the proper administration of companies. It is right that he should exercise a proper tolerance in the process of administration, and that he should not exercise his powers or perform his duties in such a way as to appear, for instance, to be unduly hounding a liquidator. A liquidation is often not a simple process, and there may be many reasons for delays. At the same time, it seems to me that there is an important distinction between a liquidator who, though in default, offers reasonable explanations and provides information, and on the other hand a liquidator who remains persistently inert."

Megarry J. concluded that liquidators falling in the latter category should be kept on a shorter rein.

Persistent default

2-64 The lessons of this case do not appear to have been learned and, in spite of changes of practice at the Companies Registry, persistent default by insolvency practitioners in the filing of returns continues. This state of affairs raised its ugly head again in *Re Arctic Engineering Ltd (No. 2)*,[85] where another insolvency practitioner came close to disqualification and thereby losing his career. In this case, a former President of the Insolvency Practitioners' Association admitted that over the previous five years he had failed to submit returns on 35 occasions. However, he had never been convicted for these defaults. This was an important test case dealing with the meaning of "persistent default." Three previous convictions are deemed to constitute conclusive proof of persistent default, but it was held by Hoffmann J. in this case that this is not the only way in which persistent default can be established. It was not necessary to show deliberate or culpable disregard of the obligation to file returns, though the culpability of the particular insolvency practitioner would be relevant when fixing the duration of the disqualification. The fact that many insolvency practitioners viewed the filing requirements as a tiresome formality was no defence. Hoffmann J. issued a stern warning to the profession as a whole that the courts would not in future cases treat lightly any failure to submit accounts:[86]

> "There has been widespread public concern in recent years over the activities of dishonest or incompetent liquidators or receivers. At present the only form of control over their activities which does not require an initiative to be taken by some individual creditor or contributory is the obligation to make regular returns to the registrar, which are then available for public inspection. It is therefore very important that these obligations should be adhered to and considerable public money is spent on maintaining the register and providing the enforcement mechanisms which I have described."

Removal

2-65 The ultimate method of control lies in the sanction of removal. The court has always had this power both in the case of insolvency practitioners appointed by

[85] [1986] 1 W.L.R. 686.

[86] *ibid.*, at 693. See also *Re S. & A. Conversions Ltd* (1988) 4 B.C.C. 384 and *Re Allan Ellis (Transport & Packing) Services Ltd* (1989) 5 B.C.C. 835.

it and also those appointed out of court.[87] The main change effected in this area by the Insolvency Act 1986 was to make the power of removal a matter exclusively for the courts in the case of administrative receivers.[88] Gone are the days when administrative receivers appointed out of court could be quietly removed for failure to carry out the instructions of their appointing creditors. Administrative receivers are now viewed as independent professionals and can only be removed by the court on good cause being shown.[89] For reasons best known to itself, Parliament has decided to retain the rule that liquidators can be removed, in some cases, without the court being involved.[90]

2-66 Although the court does enjoy a power of removal in the case of office holders, needless to say it will be most reluctant to exercise it. This is apparent from the Court of Appeal in *Re Edennote Ltd*[91] where an assignment of a cause of action had been set aside by Vinelott J, who had concluded that in undertaking this unwise assignment the liquidator had lost the confidence of certain creditors and should therefore leave office. On appeal, the Court of Appeal agreed with the trial judge that the assignment should be set aside but indicated that it would only remove a liquidator on the grounds of loss of confidence if that loss was reasonable, which was not the case here.

2-67 The issue of replacement of insolvency practitioners has become a common conundrum in recent years. The problem is compounded by the fact that in strict law insolvency practitioners hold appointments in a personal capacity, though in reality the appointment is made with respect to the firm of which they are member. Difficulties are multiplied by virtue of the fact that insolvency practitioners are not subject to any upper limit on the number of appointments they can hold. When an individual leaves a firm it is standard practice for another partner in the firm to be nominated as successor but effecting that transfer, even in a case where the parties are in agreement, can be difficult and expensive.

2-68 The mechanics of a transfer of office have troubled the courts. Uncertainties have arisen as to which court has the authority to approve the transfer[92] and as to whether full meetings of creditors should be required. A good illustration of some of the difficulties that can arise in this context is afforded by *Re A and C Supplies Ltd*.[93] Here an insolvency practitioner holding numerous appointments, both in sole name and jointly, left his firm as a result of a dispute. He was reluctant simply to resign his

---

[87] Formerly receivers appointed out of court could be removed by their appointors—*Re Chic Ltd* [1905] 2 Ch. 345. The court enjoyed residual power to remove such receivers—*Re Maskelyne British Typewriters Ltd* [1898] 1 Ch. 133, *Re Slogger Automatic Feeder Ltd* [1915] 1 Ch. 478.

[88] See Insolvency Act 1986, s.45(1). Receivers appointed under the Law of Property Act 1925 can still be removed by the mortgagees who appointed them.

[89] For illustrations of what might constitute "good cause" see *Re Sir John Moore Gold Mining Co* (1879) 12 Ch.D. 325, *Re Charterland Gold Fields Ltd* (1909) 26 T.L.R. 132 and *Re Rubber and Produce Inv. Trusts* [1915] 1 Ch. 382. These cases involved the removal of liquidators, but presumably the same principles will apply. See also *Wheeler* (1990) 6 I. L. & P. 5.

[90] See Insolvency Act 1986, ss.171 and 172.

[91] [1995] 2 B.C.L.C. 248 (Vinelott J.), [1996] 2 B.C.L.C. 389 (CA).

[92] The real problem has concerned IVAs where it has been unclear as to whether the removal/replacement of a supervisor could only be effected by the court which made the original interim order—see *Re Parkdown Ltd* (1993, unreported), *Re Bridgend Goldsmiths Ltd* [1995] B.C.C. 266, *Re Bullard and Taplin Ltd* [1996] B.C.C. 973. The better view now seems to be that this supposed difficulty can be overcome—see *Re A & C Supplies Ltd* [1998] 1 B.C.L.C. 603.

[93] [1998] 1 B.C.L.C. 603. For other instructive cases see *Re Abbot* [1997] B.C.C. 666, *Re Stella Metals Ltd* [1997] B.C.C. 626, *Re Bullard and Taplin Ltd* (*supra*), *R v. Stankey Furniture Ltd, ex parte Harding* [1995] 2 B.C.L.C. 594.

offices and his firm therefore applied to the court for his removal. Blackburne J laid down the following rules:

— an application for removal could be made by the firm in which the office holder had formerly been a partner.[94]

— the court has the power to remove any liquidator on cause shown (see ss.108, 171 and 172). This did not require fault to be shown on the part of the office holder.

— on removal the court could appoint a replacement liquidator.

— the court had the power to remove an administrative receiver but not to appoint a successor.

— if the need for a change of office holder can be traced back to a dispute within the firm it should bear the legal costs of effecting a replacement and these expenses should not be borne by the estate.

2-69 It has to be conceded that the rules governing replacement are inefficient. To a large extent it is a product of the legal fiction that appointments are held in the name of individuals rather than being vested in the firm. The Garwood Report[95] identified this as an area for reform and suggested that much of this procedure could be dealt with out of court thus saving considerable expense.

[94] In appropriate cases a recognised professional body might enjoy *locus standi*—*Re Stella Metals Ltd* (*supra*).

[95] See recommendation 8 of A Review of Insolvency Practitioner Regulation, (Insolvency Regulation Working Party) (February 1999).

CHAPTER 3

Administration Orders and Voluntary Arrangements

3-01 The Cork Report recommended[1] that English law should acknowledge the benefits that might flow from having corporate insolvency procedures designed specifically for corporate rescue rather than mere asset realisation. It was acknowledged that receivership could lead to rescue where a receiver and manager was able to sell the business as a going concern, but that was only an incidental result of the transaction, which was primarily designed to generate cash to repay the debenture holder. Furthermore, this sort of rescue was only possible where the company had created a general floating charge over its undertaking, thereby making it possible for a receiver and manager to be appointed. The only other option that might produce a corporate rescue was by exploiting the complex statutory procedure for an arrangement or reconstruction under sections 425–427A of the Companies Act 1985, but this had proved unpopular in practice. It was expensive to implement as class meetings of members and creditors and the sanction of the court were required and, crucially, there was no interim protection for the company's assets while details of the arrangement or reconstruction were being worked out and steps were being taken for securing the necessary approvals from creditors and the court. An obstructive creditor could therefore frustrate the whole process by petitioning for winding up. The corporate rescue mechanisms found in Parts I and II of the Insolvency Act 1986 (which operate alongside schemes of arrangement) owe much to the rescue philosophy embraced by Cork, though they differ from the proposals of the Cork Committee in a significant number of respects.

ADMINISTRATION ORDERS

> **3-02** "An administration order is an order directing that, during the period for which the order is in force, the affairs, business and property of the company shall be managed by a person (*the administrator*) appointed for the purpose by the court." (Insolvency Act 1986, s.8(2)).

Availability of administration

3-03 Even if the criteria for the grant of an administration order are satisfied, certain companies cannot take advantage of this procedure. The most important exception is where the company has already entered liquidation; in such a case, as section 8(4) makes clear, the administration option is lost forever. It is a pity that the law is so inflexible here, and there ought to be a safety valve to allow the conversion of a liquidation into an administration in exceptional cases, where the administra-

[1] Cmnd. 8558, Chap. 9.

tion option had not been properly considered. By way of contrast it should be noted that a supervisor of a company voluntary arrangement can present an administration petition (see Insolvency Rules 1986 r.2.1.(4) here).

3-04 It used to be the case that an administration order could not be granted in respect of a banking company, but that *lacuna* was plugged[2] in 1987. Since that time, a number of banks have gone into administration. The administration of *Edington plc* in 1989 provides an interesting example of an administration petition presented by the directors of a bank that was not insolvent—although it was prospectively insolvent, as the directors feared that insolvency would result from a likely run on the bank, as local authorities withdrew their deposits from secondary banks like Edington following the Chancery Bank affair. However, for reasons that are not immediately apparent to the present authors, insurance companies still fall outside the scope of the administration order jurisdiction.[3]

3-05 Companies incorporated in England, Wales and Scotland have been able to take advantage of the administration procedure since 1985 and this option was extended to Northern Irish companies in 1991.[4] One issue left unclear by the legislation that has tested the courts recently, is whether a foreign company could be placed into administration under English law. The statutory provision here uses the word "company" without expanding upon its meaning. We are then confronted with the general rule of interpretation[5] in English company law which excludes foreign companies from the catchment of the companies legislation. Thus, the view has been expressed that foreign companies trading in this country cannot be placed in administration.[6] This may be inconvenient and is certainly inconsistent with an analogous authority involving administrative receiverships.[7] Foreign companies may, however, enter administration by a circuitous route based upon section 426 of the Insolvency Act 1986 which, by allowing a principle of judicial comity, allows insolvency courts from specified overseas jurisdictions to request assistance from their English counterparts.[8] This jurisdiction was invoked most recently in *Re, Dallhold Estates (U.K.) Pty Ltd*[9] where a company which had been incorporated in Western Australia was placed in administration in this country, in an effort to protect assets located here from the demands of creditors.

1. Procedural aspects

Petitions for administration orders

3-06 Administration is a court activated form of insolvency regime and is initiated through a petition. In this sense, it has some similarities with compulsory

[2] See Banks (Administration Proceedings) Order 1989 (S.I. 1989/1276) which was made under s.422 of the Insolvency Act 1986.
[3] Insolvency Act 1986, s.8(4)(*a*). Though the Financial Services and Markets Bill when enacted may change this.
[4] Insolvency (Northern Ireland) Order 1991 (S.I. 1989/2405, N.I. 19) brought into effect on October 1, 1991 by S.R. 1991/411 (Commencement Order No. 4).
[5] See Companies Act 1985, s.735. Generally speaking, definitions applicable to the Companies Act 1985 will also apply to the Insolvency Act 1986—on the interplay between these two Acts see Sched. 13 Part II of the Insolvency Act 1986 (which inserts a s.735A into the Companies Act 1985).
[6] *Felixstowe Dock & Railway Co. v. United States Lines* [1989] Q.B. 360.
[7] *Re International Bulk Commodities Ltd* [1992] 3 W.L.R. 238.
[8] See Cooperation of Insolvency Courts (Designation of Relevant Countries and Territories) Order 1986 (S.I. 1986 No. 2123) as extended by (S.I. 1989 No. 2409) and (S.I. 1998 No. 2766).
[9] [1992] B.C.C. 394.

liquidation. On the other hand, it was originally intended to be a transient regime[10] that would last for much shorter periods than are normally encountered in liquidation cases. However, many complex administrations of multinational public companies currently in hand are likely to be long drawn out affairs.

3-07 By virtue of section 9(1), a petition can be presented by the company, its directors or creditors. In the most common scenario it is the directors who activate the procedure, but it should be noted that the petition can only be presented if all of the directors are petitioners or the petition is based upon a board resolution. This limitation was accepted by Millett, J. in *Re Equiticorp International plc*[11] in which the learned judge based his ruling on an analogous winding-up case.[12] The practical importance of this restriction on the availability of administration is that it makes it impossible for a dissenting director concerned about his position in the event of continued trading being later viewed as wrongful, to raise the administration possibility before the court. The Cork Committee favoured allowing individual directors to do this, but in the privacy of an *in camera* hearing.[13]

3-08 Creditor petitions for administration orders are extremely rare.[14] An unsecured creditor would normally favour a compulsory winding-up, or collective pressure from unsecured creditors would force the directors to initiate some form of insolvency. Where a creditor does present an administration petition that is opposed by the directors, a cross undertaking in damages may be required of him.[15]

3-09 There is no general requirement that the petition be advertised[16] but section 9(2) requires that any person having the right to appoint an administrative receiver must be notified, to allow him to exercise his *de facto* power of veto. This notification is effected by service under rule 2.6(2). Where there is an extant winding-up petition, the petitioner must also be served. If the petitioner is aware of the sheriff being about to levy execution or of any other person having levied distress against the company's assets, they must be notified under rule 2.6A.

3-10 The petition must state that the company is (or is likely to become) insolvent and that the order would be likely to promote one or more of the four purposes outlined in section 8(3). It is possible to hedge one's bets and refer to more than one purpose in the alternative. However, the petitioning directors (or creditors) must swear an affidavit under rules 2.1 and 2.3 in support of the petition, not only giving particulars of the company's financial and security position but also stating which of the statutory purposes the deponent expects to be achieved. Clearly, this limits the scope for merely regurgitating all four of the permissible purposes, which would in any case suggest that no clear strategy is being proposed. In *Re West Park Golf and Country Club*[17] the court stressed how important it was for the affidavits sworn in support of the petition to be both accurate and realistic.

---

[10] For a judicial indication to this effect see *Re Atlantic Computer Systems Ltd (No. 1), Re* [1992] 2 W.L.R. 367 at *381 per* Nicholls L.J.

[11] [1989] B.C.L.C. 597. This conclusion would also appear to be supported by the wording of rule 2.1(2) of the Insolvency Rules 1986. Normally directors will not be liable to costs if the petition fails—*Re Tajik Air Ltd* [1996], B.C.L.C. 317.

[12] *Re Instrumentation Electrical Services Ltd* [1988] B.C.L.C. 550 Cmnd. 8558 para. 500.

[13] Cmnd. 8558 para. 500.

[14] For rare examples see *Re Imperial Motors Ltd* (1988) 5 B.C.C. 214, *Re Gallidoro Trawlers Ltd* [1991] B.C.L.C. 856.

[15] *Re Gallidoro Trawlers Ltd* (*supra*).

[16] In contrast to the position in compulsory liquidation—see Insolvency Rules 1986 r.4.11.

[17] [1997] 1 B.C.L.C. 20.

3-11 By way of further support for the chances of achievement of the selected purpose or purposes, the petition (the form of which is governed by rule 2.4) should ideally contain a report from an independent expert commending the administration option to the court. Although this is not a mandatory requirement, it is clear that the courts place great reliance upon this form of expert opinion when deciding whether to grant an administration order or not.[18] This is the celebrated "rule 2.2 report" named after the relevant provision in the Insolvency Rules 1986. The real practical value of rule 2.2 reports has led to a situation where they are regarded as indispensable by certain practitioners. Indeed the weightier the report the more likely it is to impress the court. This has made the procedure for obtaining an administration order more complex and increasingly expensive. This in turn has induced the courts to remind practitioners of what Parliament intended the function of such reports to be. Accordingly the Vice Chancellor, Sir Donald Nicholls has issued a *Practice Note (Administration order applications: Independent reports)*[19] designed to cut the cost of, and therefore encourage the use of, administration orders. Rule 2.2 reports should not be unnecessarily detailed. There was no need to outline in advance details of how the administrator was planning to finance future trading by the company. Practitioners were reminded that these reports were not mandatory and may not be essential in straightforward cases.

2. Effect of the petition

3-12 A petition for an administration order can have important consequences for the company both internally and, more importantly on an external level.

3-13 As the petition will normally be presented by the directors and as the period between petition and hearing is so short (a minimum of 5 days according to rule 2.7), there is normally no danger of directors dissipating assets in the run up to the hearing. This may not be the case however, where a hostile petition is presented by a creditor. In *Re Gallidoro Trawlers Ltd*[20] the petitioning bank held security over the company's fishing vessels, but had reason to suppose that the directors intended to separately dispose of fishing licences, without which the market value of the vessels would have been much reduced. The court abridged the period for service of the petition (which had been neither presented nor served) and exercised its power under section 9(5) to restrict the activities of the directors, by granting an injunction preventing them from dealing with the assets otherwise than in the ordinary course of business, and for full value.

3-14 The court has wide power under section 9(4) to adjourn the hearing of the petition, or to make an interim order, or any other order it thinks fit. It has been held that despite the wide terms of section 9(4) the court has no power to appoint an interim administrator,[21] but can (and in a proper case will) appoint a person, such as the proposed administrator, to take control of the company and manage its affairs pending the hearing. It does not matter that there may be a secured creditor who is in a position to appoint an administrative receiver, unless such a receiver is appointed,

---

[18] *Re Primlaks (U.K.) Ltd* [1989] B.C.L.C. 734.
[19] [1994] B.C.L.C. 347.
[20] [1991] B.C.L.C. 411.
[21] *Re A Company (00175 of 1987)* 3 B.C.C. 124. For a discussion of s.9(4) see *Re W. F. Fearman Ltd* (1988) 4 B.C.C. 139.

in which case the interim manager will have to vacate office. An order of this kind has been made where the only active director felt unable (possibly through ill health) to take the responsibility of continuing to trade, thereby having to deal with employees and creditors.[22]

Partial Moratorium

3-15 Of much greater importance is the partial moratorium made possible by section 10, which protects the company's assets from external threats, and is activated by the mere presentation of a petition for an administration order. The purpose of this freeze is to allow a period of calm both prior to and after the making of the order, to ensure a climate to promote rescue or an orderly breakup of assets. Assets protected by this moratorium include property leased to the company[23] and property owned by the company, but in the possession of third parties (such as lessees).[24] The moratorium covers:

(a) the enforcement of security[25] (subject to the important limitation noted below). This is a wide concept, and is not restricted to the enforcement of security in the usual sense of that word. Thus, the legislation makes clear that the snatch back of goods held on hire purchase, lease and conditional sale agreements, or subject to title retention, is covered.[26] The courts have also endeavoured to maximise the scope of the concept. Thus, the exercise of a lien (whether contractual[27] or statutory[28] in nature) is covered. The most contentious issues with regard to the enforcement of security concerns the right of a landlord to reenter the premises and forfeit the lease. The legislation here is opaque and the judiciary have been left to ponder on this matter. Early case law suggested that the courts would treat this as akin to a form of security enforcement and therefore such action would require the leave of the court.[29] This view has been questioned within the profession and by other judges. In *Razzaq v. Pala*[30] Lightman J. took the opposite view to Harman J. and concluded that it was wrong to characterise a right of reentry as a form of security enforcement. This contrary view has most recently been supported in *obiter dicta* by Lord Millett in the House of Lords in *Re Park*

---

[22] See *Re A Company (00175 of 1987) (supra)*. For the effect of an interim order on the limitation period for instituting disqualification proceedings against directors see *Secretary of State v. Palmer* [1994] B.C.C. 990.

[23] *Bristol Airport v. Powdrill* [1990] 2 W.L.R. 1362.

[24] *Re Atlantic Computer Systems Ltd (No. 1), Re* [1992] 2 W.L.R. 367.

[25] Insolvency Act 1986, s.(10)(1)(*b*).

[26] Insolvency Act 1986, s.10(4). See *Re David Meek Access Ltd* [1993] B.C.C. 175.

[27] *Re Sabre International Products Ltd* [1991] B.C.L.C. 341.

[28] *Bristol Airport v. Powdrill* [1990] 2 W.L.R. 1362.

[29] *Exchange Travel Agency Ltd v. Triton Property Trust* [1991] B.C.C. 341 (Harman J.). This case represented an early authority on the moratorium arising on an administration and it is clear that Harman J. was keen to maximise the protective impact of this moratorium. For comment see Milman and Davey [1996] J.B.L. 541.

[30] [1997] 1 W.L.R. 1336, in so deciding Lightman J. recanted his earlier tentative and contrary opinion expressed in *Gunmark v. March Estates* [1996] B.P.I.R. 439 on the grounds that the issue had not been fully argued before him. See also the unreported High Court case of *Clarence Café v. Colchester Properties* (1998) (unreported), but noted in *The Lawyer*, March 8, 1999, where Judge Cooke concluded that exercising a right of reentry did not constitute the enforcement of security. For comment see Byrne and Doyle [1999] *Insolvency Lawyer* 167.

Air Services plc.[31] The end result of this difference of judicial opinion is that landlords are once again given special privileges on insolvency, an all too common scenario.

(b) instituting or continuing legal proceedings against the company;[32]

(c) levying distress or any other form of execution against the company's assets;[33]

3-16 In the administration of *Discounter Catalogue Showrooms*, the moratorium provided by administration protected the company from possible forfeitures and distraints by the landlords of its numerous shops. It also afforded protection against the repossession of stock allegedly subject to substantial retention of title claims, as well as the many fixtures and fittings which were subject to hire purchase or retention of title claims.

Veto by debenture holder

3-17 Useful though the moratorium may be, however, it provides only partial protection at this stage. It is still possible for a debenture holder entitled to appoint an administrative receiver, to intervene and make such an appointment. This statutory power of veto reasserts the traditionally strong position of secured creditors in all forms of corporate insolvency. Lending documentation has been modified to allow for the creation of lightweight floating charges which offer no real security in the proprietorial sense, but do take advantages of this statutory right of veto. The legitimacy of such artificial forms of security was reluctantly upheld by Vinelott J. in *Re Croftbell Ltd*.[34]

3-18 The mere presentation of an administration petition does not prevent the directors from summoning a meeting of members to consider voluntary liquidation (though no resolution can be passed) nor does it preclude another creditor from presenting a winding-up petition.[35] However, it has been held that the courts do have power to restrain advertisement of a winding-up petition in such circumstances, for fear of the damage it might cause to the commercial well-being of the company at such a sensitive time.[36] Winding-up procedures can thus continue to be initiated, though it is clear from section 10(1)(*a*) that entry into liquidation is not permitted until the administration petition has been heard.

3-19 In a rare case in which the court refused to support the strengthening of the moratorium, it was held that the actions of an administrative or regulatory body in

---

[31] [1999] 2 W.L.R. 396. Neuberger J. came to the same conclusion in *Re Lomax Leisure Ltd*, *The Times*, May 4, 1999.

[32] Insolvency Act 1986, s.10(1)(*c*). See *Scottish Exhibition Centre v. Mirestop* 1993 GWD 9–586. In *Exchange Travel Agency Ltd v. Triton Property* (*supra*) it was held that the exercise of a contractual power to forfeit a lease could be regarded as the commencement of a legal process against the company, but this view was doubted by Millett J. in *Re Olympia and York Canary Wharf Ltd* [1993] B.C.C. 154. An equally narrow view of what was a "legal process" for the purposes of the moratorium operating in the context of an IVA was taken in *McMullen & Sons Ltd v. Cerrone*, [1994] B.C.C. 25. Compare *Carr v. British International Helicopters* [1993] B.C.C. 855 (leave required to apply to industrial tribunal).

[33] Insolvency Act 1986, s.10(1)(*c*).

[34] [1990] B.C.C. 781. For discussion see *Oditah* [1991] J.B.L. 49.

[35] Insolvency Act 1986, s.10(2).

[36] See *Re A Company (001992 of 1988)* [1989] B.C.L.C. 9, *Re A Company (001448 of 1989)* [1989] B.C.L.C. 715.

revoking what may be an essential trading licence were not covered.[37] This could turn out to be an important and unfortunate Achilles heel for the moratorium. More recently it has been held[38] that the moratorium does not prevent a contracting party from relying on a contractual provision terminating his or her contract with the company in the event of its entering into administration. Undoubtedly, there are still a number of important long term contracts[39] drafted before 1986 which do not provide for termination on appointment of an administrator, but clearly, their days must be numbered.

Judicial attitudes

3-20 It should be remembered that even if a hostile activity falls within the scope of the moratorium, that does not mean that it will not be allowed to proceed. The administrator is empowered (in fact, sometimes even encouraged) to allow restricted hostile actions to proceed, provided they are not unduly detrimental. As a last resort an application can be made to the court under section 11 for leave to proceed. A brief review of selected section 11 cases is informative when trying to assess current judicial attitudes.

3-21 In *Bristol Airport v. Powdrill*[40] the Court of Appeal was faced with the question of whether an airport authority was entitled to maintain its statutory power of detention over aircraft which had been leased to a company in administration. After analysing the aim of the moratorium in the context of the administration process as a whole, it was determined that the rights of the airport should yield to the interests of all the creditors of the company. The aircraft were ordered to be released.

3-22 The issues raised in *Re Atlantic Computer Systems Ltd (No. 1), Re*[41] were slightly different. Here the company in administration had acquired computers under an equipment leasing arrangement and the ownership was retained by head lessor financiers (the funders). The company in turn let out those same computers to sub lessees. The funders wished to have the head lease rentals, which the administrators were not paying, treated as expenses of the administration (entitling the funders to be compensated in priority to the administrators remuneration and all other creditors) or alternatively, to recover the computers from sub-lessees. The Court of Appeal refused to extend the so-called "liquidation expenses" principle[42] to administration and the claim for head lease rentals failed. However, after considering the merits of the funders' claim, the court allowed them to terminate the head leases and repossess the computers from the hands of the sub-lessees.[43] The Court of Appeal reluctantly laid down general guidelines governing the exercise of their discretion under section 11, but on close scrutiny these rules amount to little more than an exhortation to con-

---

[37] *Air Ecosse v. Civil Aviation Authority* (1987) 3 B.C.C. 492—followed in *Bristol Airport v. Powdrill (supra)*.

[38] *Re Olympia and York Canary Wharf Ltd* [1993] B.C.C. 154.

[39] This was an important consideration in the appointment of administrators to *Eclipse Copper Ltd*, which had a number of contracts in the old JCT form. Head leases are another important example.

[40] [1990] 2 W.L.R. 1362.

[41] [1992] 2 W.L.R. 367.

[42] As typified by cases such as *Re Oak Pits Colliery Co. Ltd* (1882) 21 Ch.D. 322—see the discussion in Chap. 6.

[43] Compare *Re David Meek Access Ltd* [1993] B.C.C. 175 where the owners of goods let out on hire purchase were refused permission to repossess.

sider all the circumstances and to weigh up the balance of disadvantage judiciously. More interestingly the Court of Appeal, worried about being flooded with applications for leave, urged administrators to be reasonable when dealing with original requests and not to strike too hard a bargain.

3-23 Another case to consider is that of *Royal Bank v. Buchler*.[44] Here a company had borrowed money on security to buy a block of flats. The company went into administration and the lender sought to enforce its security over the office block. However, the administrator of the company aimed to maximise the value of the company's assets and attempted to find tenants for all of the office space before selling the property. Peter Gibson J. while recognising that the administrator should be given a chance to see his policy reap dividends, did, in effect, impose a three month deadline upon him by inviting the mortgagee to make another application for leave to enforce security once that period had elapsed.

3-24 One final caveat must be entered. The moratorium on administration is exactly that; it does not involve an expropriation of property rights once and for all, a point stressed in *Barclays Bank Mercantile Finance v. Sibec Developments*.[45]

Hearing the petition

3-25 The hearing of the petition should in theory not occur until 5 days have elapsed from the date of the petition.[46] In practice, in spite of judicial protestations[47] that this is undesirable, it is not uncommon to find petitions being heard on the same day as they were presented where there is need for urgency—this is often the case where wrongful trading liability may be a matter of concern for the directors.[48]

3-26 Assuming that the company is susceptible to the administration order jurisdiction and that the correct procedures have been undertaken, what conditions need to be fulfilled before an order will be granted? Firstly the company must, under section 8(1), either be insolvent or likely to be so in the near future. Either the cash flow test or the balance sheet approach can be used to establish insolvency. The position with regard to prospective insolvency is uncertain, although in all reported cases so far the Rubicon had been crossed long before the petition was presented.[49]

3-27 Provided insolvency (or prospective insolvency) can be established, it then must be shown that the grant of the order would be likely to promote any of four specified purposes mentioned in section 8(3). Before considering these, the criterion of likelihood must be commented upon. The initial view taken by the courts was that a test using the balance of probabilities had to be satisfied.[50] However, this somewhat restrictive view was decisively rejected by Hoffmann J. in *Re Harris Simons Construction Ltd*[51] in favour of simply requiring that there was a reasonable prospect

---

[44] [1989] B.C.L.C. 130. Also reported as *Re Meesan Investments Ltd* (1988) 4 B.C.C. 788. Leave was refused in *Re Polly Peck International (No. 4)*, *The Times*, May 18, 1998.
[45] [1992] 1 W.L.R. 1253.
[46] I.R. 1986 r.2.7.
[47] See for example, the comments of the court in *Re Cavco Floors Ltd* [1990] B.C.L.C. 940 and *Re Shearing and Loader Ltd* [1991] B.C.C. 232.
[48] This fear was apparently influential in *Re Chancery plc* [1991] B.C.C. 171.
[49] It is interesting to note that the Cork Committee (Cmnd. 8558) did not want to restrict the procedure to cases of insolvency—see para. 506. Edington plc went into administration on the grounds of prospective insolvency.
[50] *Re Consumer and Industrial Press* [1987] B.C.L.C. 177, *Re Manlon Trading Ltd* (1988) 4 B.C.C. 455.
[51] [1989] 1 W.L.R. 368.

(which might be less than a 50/50 possibility) that the desired consequences would ensue. This test is now universally applied, though not always satisfied in practice.[52]

3-28 What are these desired consequences? Essentially, they break down into two groups—those concerned with corporate rescue and those promoting an efficient break up of assets. Thus an administration order can be granted if it would be likely to promote a scheme of arrangement under section 425 of the Companies Act 1985 or a voluntary arrangement under Part I of the Insolvency Act 1986.[53] More crucially, an order is possible under section 8(3)(*a*) if it would promote "the survival of *the* company and *its* undertaking". Some explanation should be offered here. Clearly a total rescue of the company in its existing form is not a requirement, but there must be a survival of both the company and part of its undertaking.[54] The company and the undertaking cannot be completely divorced if reliance is placed on section 8(3)(*a*). This would appear to exclude a complete hive-down of the company's viable businesses, although any sort of hive-down would of course be possible as part of a voluntary arrangement or a realisation of the assets in administration.

3-29 It is sometimes easy to forget in all the ballyhoo about corporate rescue that the administration order procedure is essentially two dimensional; the possibility of using the procedure as a more effective means of liquidation is a real one and is often cited in petitions. This can occur, for example, where the company holds large stocks of goods subject to valid title retention clauses. An administrator using his power under section 15 of the Insolvency Act 1986 can exploit these stocks to the best commercial advantage of the company in a way that a liquidator cannot. On the other hand, there may be situations where the court, faced with a choice between administration or compulsory liquidation prefers the latter outcome.[55] This may be the favoured policy where the actions of the directors require full investigation, as was the case in *Re West Tech plc*.[56]

3-30 An administration order can be appealed against. In *Cornhill Insurance v. Cornhill Financial Services Ltd*[57] it was held by the Court of Appeal that the court can use its general jurisdiction under rule 7.47(1) to rescind an administration order that should not have been made.

Effect of entry into administration

3-31 Once the order is granted and the administrator (who must be a qualified insolvency practitioner) is appointed, control of the management of the company ceases to be vested in the directors,[58] though they are not automatically removed from office. The administrator can effect their removal if he wishes by using section 14(2).

---

[52] *Re Primlaks (U.K.) Ltd* [1989] B.C.L.C. 734, *Re SCL Building Services Ltd* (1989) 5 B.C.C. 746. *Re Chelmsford City F.C. (1980)* [1991] B.C.C. 133. For unsuccessful attempts see *Re Rowbotham Baxter Ltd* [1990] B.C.C. 113, *Re Land and Property Trust Co. Ltd (No. 1)* [1991] B.C.L.C. 845.

[53] Arrangements with creditors not falling under either statutory scheme are frowned upon—*Re Bradwin Ltd's; Petition* [1997] N.I. 394.

[54] This point was made by Harman J. in *Re Rowbotham Baxter Ltd. (supra)*.

[55] See *Re Arrows Ltd (No. 3)* [1992] B.C.C. 131. Compare *Re Maxwell Communications plc* [1992] B.C.C. 372 where administration was preferred to liquidation.

[56] [1989] B.C.L.C. 600.

[57] [1992] B.C.C. 818. See also *Re MTI Trading Systems Ltd* [1998] B.C.C. 400.

[58] This is in contrast with the "debtor in possession" policy pursued in the U.S.A. under Chap. 11 of the Bankruptcy Code.

3-32 The order must be properly notified to the outside world by the administrator, who must by virtue of rule 2.10(2) see that it is gazetted. The creditors must (by virtue of section 21) be told within 28 days and all business letters must disclose the fact of the appontment, as section 12 makes clear.

3-33 On the making of the order, the moratorium that was activated on the presentation of the petition becomes virtually impenetrable (see section 11). In addition to the restrictions that have been noted above, it is now impossible to initiate any winding-up or to place the company into administrative receivership.[59]

The administrator: role and powers

3-34 Essentially an administrator has three key functions. In chronological order they are, securing control of the assets, preparing proposals for the approval of creditors and, finally, carrying out those proposals. The jurisdiction of the administrator extends to the totality of the "affairs" of the company, a concept that is widely construed by the courts.[60]

3-35 An administrator has wide powers to secure the company's assets and to protect those assets once they are under his control. Indeed, he is under a statutory duty to ensure this (section 17(1)). One of his first tasks is to demand under section 22 a statement of affairs from the directors, who have 21 days in which to provide this. Rules 2.11 and 2.12 of the Insolvency Rules 1986 should be noted here. A copy of the statement of affairs should be filed in court by the administrator, but he can seek the permission of the court to keep sensitive information secret (see rule 2.13).

3-36 The administrator can decide whether to grant leave to persons wishing to enforce security, or levy execution, etc., against the company's assets, though if he refuses, an appeal can be made to the court. An administrator enjoys the status of being an officer of the court, and any attempt to obstruct him in this task might constitute contempt.[61] He can apply to the court for directions under section 14(3). Additionally, as all of the statutory definitions of "office holder" in sections 230–246 of the Insolvency Act 1986 include an administrator, he has all the additional powers flowing from that status.[62] These include the right to supplies of gas, water and telecommunications services under section 233, the powers of seizure of property, books, papers and records under section 234, the power to require co-operation and information, if necessary on oath, under sections 235 and 236. The administrator's powers as an office holder extend also to the power to attack certain pre-administration transactions, namely transactions at an undervalue, unfair preferences, certain floating charges, and extortionate credit bargains. These powers arise from sections 238 to 245 and are discussed in Chapter 11.

3-37 The timescale envisaged by section 23 of the Insolvency Act 1986 is that the administrator should have three months to prepare his or her plans to put to the creditors for their approval under section 24. Procedural aspects of creditors' meetings are dealt with by rules 2.18 *et seq.* but it should be noted that decisions are taken by majority vote (in value). The administrator's plans must be consistent with the

---

[59] Insolvency Act 1986, s.11(1).
[60] See *Denny v. Yeldon* [1995] 3 All E.R. 624 and *Polly Peck International v. Henry*, *The Times*, December 16, 1998.
[61] *Re Exchange Travel Holdings Ltd* [1991] B.C.L.C. 728.
[62] See the discussion in Ch. 2 here.

specified aims of the administration, and if they cannot be made to fit in with those aims the administrator must return to court to get the terms of his appointment modified. Provision is made for revision under section 25. The three month period can be extended by the court if the administrator can show good cause.[63]

3-38 An administrator is endowed by section 14(1) with a wide range of statutory powers as outlined in schedule 1 of the Act. In exercising these powers he acts as the company's agent (section 14(5)). As these powers are identical to those conferred on administrative receivers, little further comment is required. For a full analysis see Chapter 4. An administrator has the power to sell company property. However, Peter Gibson J. in *Re Consumer and Industrual Press (No. 2)*[64] indicated that the courts are cautious about allowing major disposals prior to the creditors having an opportunity to vote on the administrator's plans. In practice therefore, his or her powers may be more circumscribed during this initial three month period than is apparent at first sight.

3-39 However, there are other powers possessed by an administrator that are unique, most notably the power to override security and property rights under section 15 of the Act. This power extends to hire purchase, lease, conditional sale and retention of title assets, as well as property subject to a security interest. It enables the administrator to convert such assets into money, on the condition that he or she must account to the owner or security holder for the greater of the proceeds of sale or the market value. The exercise of this power can enable the administrator, in certain cases, to achieve a much better realisation of the undertaking and assets than would be possible in receivership or liquidation. This might be the case where the company's business depends on important capital equipment owned by a supplier or financier who is unwilling to leave its realisation to the receiver or liquidator.

3-40 The administrator must account for the market value of the asset, whatever may be apportioned to it in the sale agreement. However, in practice, this obligation leaves considerable scope for negotiation and presents no greater drawback than in other insolvency procedures in which the office holder is unable to dispose of assets without the owner's co-operation. In recent years, finance houses in particular have been less ready than they formerly were to accept outstanding lease rentals or hire purchase instalments in settlement of their interests in valuable assets. On the contrary, they have been inclined to look for "windfall" profits from high residual values where there is an opportunity to terminate finance agreements on the insolvency of the customer. Administrators are immune from this pressure.

3-41 The administrator can dispose of floating charge assets without leave, but must have leave of the court to dispose of assets owned by third parties or subject to a fixed charge. In dealing with the application for leave, the court will undertake the familiar exercise of weighing up competing claims, but will be greatly influenced by the desirability of promoting corporate rescue, a point recognised by Knox J. in *Re ARV Aviation Ltd.*[65]

3-42 Although it is not the primary function of the administrator to settle pre

---

[63] In *Re Newport County A.F.C.* [1987] B.C.L.C. 582 the court granted an extension to counteract problems caused by local government elections.

[64] (1988) 4 B.C.C. 72. Compare *Re NS Distribution Ltd* [1990] B.C.L.C. 169. In *Re P.D. Fuels Ltd* [1999] B.C.C. 450 Rimer J. authorised an immediate sale without creditor approval as it was an emergency situation.

[65] [1989] B.C.L.C. 664. Compare *Re Newman Shopfitters Ltd* [1991] B.C.L.C. 407.

administration debts the courts will confer a power on him or her to undertake this task if it is deemed necessary for the attainment of the purposes of the administration.[66]

Extensive as the administrator's power are, he or she lacks certain powers, or at least immunities, available to other "office holders". An administrator does not enjoy the *de facto* right which may (depending on one's view of the authorities) apparently be accorded to receivers[67] to disregard most current company contracts with impunity, a point made forcefully by Vinelott J. in *Astor Chemicals v. Synthetic Technology*.[68] Certainly the administrator lacks the statutory power possessed by liquidators to disclaim onerous contracts.[69]

Liability for contracts

3-43 An administrator is deemed by virtue of section 14(4) of the Insolvency Act 1986 to act as the agent of the company in exercising his powers. He is therefore not personally liable on contracts made by him in doing so, although he must pay any debts or liabilities incurred under contracts entered into, or contracts of employment adopted, during the administration out of floating charge assets, in priority to the chargee and to his own remuneration (section 19(5)). Contracts are not adopted by reason of anything done or omitted within 14 days after the administrators' appointment, but until recently it was not clear what did amount to adoption. In *Re Paramount Airways Ltd (No. 3)*[70] the House of Lords held that an administrator adopts contracts of employment if in substance he continues after the statutory 14 days to employ staff and pay them in accordance with their previous contracts, unless he takes the trouble to negotiate new contracts which are not a sham. The "ritual incantation" commonly used by administrative receivers in writing to employees whose services they wish to retain, to the effect that the writers do not intend to adopt their contracts, has no effect. This former practice was based on an unreported and indeed unwritten judgment of Harman J. in *Re Specialised Mouldings Limits* (1987). The administrators in *Re Paramount Airways Ltd (No. 3) (supra)* were held to have adopted the contracts of the company's staff despite such a statement, having in fact continued to employ them on the same terms as before, and, therefore, sums payable under those contracts were payable in priority to the administrators' claim for remuneration and expenses.

3-44 The significance of this case for contracts of employment adopted on or after March 15, 1994 has been lessened by the passing of the Insolvency Act 1994. Under that Act[71] the question of whether a contract had been adopted was left untouched; this was still to be governed by the common law principles outlined above. However the financial consequences of adoption were mitigated for administrators (s.1) and administrative receivers (s.2) by restricting the liability incurred on adoption to what were categorised as "qualifying liabilities". These were less extensive than those identified at common law and essentially related only

[66] *Re WBSL Realisations 1992 Ltd* [1995] B.C.C. 1118.
[67] The conventional wisdom as reflected by *Airlines Airspares Ltd v. Handley Page* [1970] Ch. 193 is increasingly being challenged—see Chap. 4.
[68] [1990] B.C.C. 97.
[69] Insolvency Act 1986, s.178 *et seq*. But see *Re P. & C. and R. & T. (Stockport) Ltd* [1991] B.C.C. 98.
[70] Reported *sub nom. Powdrill v. Watson* [1995] 2 W.L.R. 312.
[71] For general discussion see Mudd (1994) 10 I.L. & P 38, Fenn (1994) 10 I.L. & P 99.

to liabilities accruing under the contract of employment after the date of adoption (see ss.1(6) and 2(2)). Comparable provision is made for Scotland and Northern Ireland by sections 3 and 4. The 1994 Act does not apply to non administrative receivers and this may cause difficulties in certain cases, for example a receiver of a hotel business appointed under the Law of Property Act 1925. In spite of pleas from the insolvency profession the concessions granted in the 1994 Act were not extended to this latter group. The provisions of the 1994 Act have not attracted judicial comment in English law.[72]

Duties of administrators

3-45 Once the administrator's plan has been approved by the creditors with the requisite majority, it then falls to the administrator to carry out the scheme. In the event of unforeseen difficulties the administrator should return to the creditors to seek their approval for modifications, though in an urgent case he or she may be entitled to act on his or her own initiative.[73]

3-46 Like other insolvency practitioners, an administrator is not given powers without corresponding responsibilities. His or her basic duty is to manage the company's affairs in accordance with the terms of the appointing order and with the plan approved by creditors (section 17). Moreover, as an officer of the court the administrator is always subject to its overall control and, more specifically, is presumably bound to act honourably by application of the anomalous rule in *ex parte James*,[74] a subject of much legal debate.[75] In addition, an administrator may assume general responsibilities under law (*e.g.* to employees) by virtue of his position as operator of the business.[76]

3-47 An administrator is susceptible to being sued for misfeasance under section 212 of the Insolvency Act 1986. Where such an action is brought he or she may be entitled to seek refuge in the judicial pardon facility of section 727 of the Companies Act 1985. In *Re Home Treat Ltd*[77] an administrator was granted immunity from any liability that might result from carrying on the company's business in a potentially *ultra vires* manner.

3-48 Creditors can exercise control over administrators in a variety of ways. They can decide whether or not to approve his plans in the first place. Creditors whose debts exceed 10 per cent. of the company's total indebtedness can, under section 17(3), compel administrators to convene meetings at which their grievances may be aired. Section 26 permits them to establish a creditors' committee, which can summon the administrator to attend and furnish them with such information as they might reasonably require. The constitution and procedure of this committee is dealt with by rules 2.32–2.46A.

3-49 As a last resort, a disgruntled creditor might petition the court to invoke its jurisdiction under section 27 to remedy alleged unfair prejudice. It is clear from the

---

[72] But the Scottish courts did discuss them in passing in *Lindop v. Stuart Noble & Sons Ltd*, *The Times Scots Report*, June 25, 1998.
[73] *Re Smallman Construction Ltd* (1988) 4 B.C.C. 784.
[74] (1874) 9 Ch.App. 609.
[75] See Dawson [1996] J.B.L. 437.
[76] For example, the duty to consult when proposing redundancies—see *Re Hartlebury Printers Ltd* [1992] B.C.C. 428.
[77] [1991] B.C.C. 165.

comments of Millett J. in *Re Charnley Davies Ltd*[78] that this is very much a jurisdiction of last resort which should not be used where a more appropriate remedy (such as a simple misfeasance action) is available. It is also apparent from the judgment in that same case, that the courts are not keen to encourage this type of unfair prejudice action: they are acutely aware of the difficulties faced by administrators as they go about their tasks.

The conclusion of administration

3-50 The administration procedure may produce a successful outcome, either by effecting a corporate rescue or enabling the assets to be realised in a manner more efficiently than would be allowed on liquidation. On the other hand, it sometimes happens that the original aims of an administration prove impossible to achieve, as the case study below illustrates. In such circumstances, section 18 requires either that the administrator go back to the court for those aims to be modified or supplemented, or that the administration order be discharged. In any event, there is a strange *lacuna* in the administration procedure, the result of which is that an administrator apparently has no power to distribute the proceeds of realisation of the company's assets, even when the purpose of the administration is the more effective realisation of those assets. In such a case, the administrator must seek a winding-up before any distribution to creditors can be made.

3-51 The administrator can also be compelled to apply for the discharge or variation of the administration order by the company's creditors, at a meeting summoned for the purpose in accordance with the rules (see section 18(2)(b)).

3-52 Once the administrator's task is completed he or she should seek release under section 20 and vacate office. Release does not absolve an administrator from any liability for misfeasance under section 212 of the Insolvency Act 1986. The court has power to delay the release if there are outstanding complaints against the administrator requiring investigation.[79] Where the company subsequently goes into compulsory liquidation the court can invite the official receiver to examine the conduct of the administration by the administrator.[80]

3-53 The question of exit routes from administration had troubled the courts in recent times. The problem here is that because of a quirk in the legislation preferential creditors may enjoy better rights if the exit is via the compulsory (rather than voluntary) liquidation procedures. However, this method of liquidating a company is acknowledged as being less efficient and more expensive. A sensible way of dealing with this dilemma would be for the administrator to compensate preferential creditors for agreeing to this way of exiting administration. Unfortunately in *Re Powerstore Ltd*[81] Lightman J. felt constrained by the legislation to rule that there was no obvious way of permitting this sensible compromise. The administrators could not make payments to the preferential creditors nor could the hands of the incoming

---

[78] [1990] B.C.C. 605. A similar reluctance to interfere with the exercise of discretion and professional judgments of administrators is apparent from the ruling of Nicholls V.-C. in *Re Olympia and Canary Wharf Holdings Ltd* [1993] B.C.C. 866, which was not a s.27 case but rather an application to discharge the administration order once a C.V.A. had been approved. See also *MTI Trading Systems Ltd* [1998] B.C.C. 591.

[79] *Re Sheridan Securities Ltd* (1988) 4 B.C.C. 200.

[80] *Re Exchange Travel Holdings* [1992] B.C.C. 954.

[81] [1997] 1 W.L.R. 1280—discussed by Fennessy [1998] 22 *Insolvency Lawyer* 11.

liquidator be tied. Fortunately this conclusion has been found to be less compelling by other judges. It was sidestepped by Neuberger J. in *Re Philip Alexander Securities Ltd (No. 2)*[82] where a neat compromise was sponsored and then questioned by Jacob J. in *Re Mark One (Oxford Street) plc*[83] where the inherent power of the court to control its officers so as to achieve a sensible solution was stressed as an aid to interpreting the statutory framework applicable to administrators. In this later case Jacob J. held that the court could direct payments to be made by the administrators on trust so that the preferential creditors would not suffer financially from the court approving the voluntary liquidation exit mode.

3-54 An administrator is, under section 19(4), entitled to have his or her claim for remuneration and expenses settled in priority to the claims of any floating charge holder. Further discussion of this matter is to be found in Chapter 2.

A case study in administration

3-55 The stated purpose of the order in the *Sock Shop*[84] administration was the survival of the company and the whole or part of its undertaking as a going concern. When the order was made, it appeared that the company had a viable United Kingdom business which had been brought down by a disastrous expansion into the United States. There appeared to be a number of interested buyers, and a strong possibility of achieving a sale of the company after putting in place a suitable voluntary arrangement. A sale of the company itself (which could not have been achieved in a receivership) was particularly desirable, as the company was entitled to over £1 million worth of transitional relief for the uniform business rate on its 108 shops, which would not be available on a mere sale of the business and assets.

3-56 The administration procedure also offered a number of other substantial advantages, including the protection offered against a threatened distraint at various leasehold shops in respect of rent arrears approaching £1 million, and apparently extensive retention of title claims to the company's stocks. Furthermore, an administration was at that time perceived as less harmful to the standing and goodwill attached to a strong brand name than any other insolvency procedure.

3-57 The originally intended purpose of the administration could not be achieved, for two reasons. The first was the general decline of the retail sector after the appointment of the administrators in early 1990, which accounted for a waning of interest among likely buyers. Secondly, however, it became clear that an unknown number of parent company guarantees were outstanding in favour of United States creditors. The result of this was that as some guarantee creditors could not be traced, they could not be summoned to a creditors meeting, and thereby brought into and bound by the proposed voluntary arrangement (see below). The administrators therefore applied to the court for an order extending the purposes of the administration order to include that of achieving a more advantageous realisation of the company's assets than would be effected in a winding-up. The administrators thereby achieved a sale of the business and 85 of the 108 shops (having closed a number of outlets) less than six months after their appointment.

[82] [1999] 1 B.C.L.C. 124. Here the judge indicated that the unsecured creditors could agree to surrender certain rights on liquidation to ensure that the preferentials did not lose out.

[83] [1998] B.C.C. 984. For full discussion see Fennessy [1999] *Insolvency Lawyer* 169.

[84] The authors are indebted to Philip Sykes of BDO Binder Hamlyn, one of the former joint administrators of Sock Shop, for permission to print this case study.

VOLUNTARY ARRANGEMENTS FOR COMPANIES

3-58 This procedure (known by its acronym, the CVA) is to be found in Part I of the Insolvency Act 1986 and Part I of the Insolvency Rules 1986. The Act provides the following guidance:

> "A proposal under this Part is one which provides for some person (the nominee) to act in relation to the voluntary arrangement either as trustee or otherwise for the purpose of supervising its implementation . . ." (section 1(2)).

3-59 This guidance is amplified by section 1(2) which continues by explaining that a voluntary arrangement means a composition in satisfaction of the company's debts or a scheme of arrangement of its affairs.

Introduction

3-60 Prior to 1985 a company wishing to enter into an arrangement with its creditors would have had to use the cumbersome scheme of the arrangements procedure now contained in section 425 of the Companies Act 1985. The Deeds of Arrangement Act 1914 was not available to companies,[85] though, even if it had been, its practical utility would have been open to question. The need for a new informal yet binding procedure was therefore obvious.

3-61 The company voluntary arrangement (or CVA) procedure was at first the junior partner in the corporate rescue double act introduced in 1985–6. However despite its considerable limitations (discussed in some detail below) in 1997–98 approximately 490 supervisors of CVAs were appointed, compared to about 230 administrators. No doubt this reflects the relative ease and affordability of the procedure compared to administration. Nevertheless from a technical legal viewpoint, there is comparatively little case law to flesh out the skeletal statutory provisions.

Availability of the CVA procedure

3-62 The CVA procedure is more widely available than administration. It can be exploited by a solvent company in financial difficulties, a company in administration, and by a company already in the process of being wound up, as section 1(3) makes clear.

Initiation of a CVA: the proposal

3-63 The essence of the voluntary arrangement procedure for companies is that it is initiated by the directors making a written proposal to creditors (*e.g.* for a moratorium or exchange of debt for equity). It is an offence under rule 1.30 for directors to procure a CVA by false representations. If the company is already in administration or liquidation, then the proposal should emanate from the insolvency practitioner responsible for conducting the administration or winding-up; in such instances the procedure will vary slightly to reflect the different circumstances of the case.

---

[85] *Re Rileys Ltd* [1903] 2 Ch. 590. It used to be the case (see Companies Act 1948, s.320(2)) that any general assignment of assets to trustees for the benefit of creditors was void—this provision did not survive the insolvency reforms of 1985 and has no counterpart in the current legislation.

3-64 The proposal should identify an insolvency practitioner who has agreed to take responsibility for the voluntary arrangement. This person is known initially as the nominee. Once in receipt of the proposal, the nominee has 28 days to mull it over and to report to the court on its possible viability. A nominee is entitled to receive a statement of affairs from the directors within 7 days of receipt of the proposal (rule 1.4) and can require officers to furnish additional information (rule 1.6). In his report to the court, the nominee should be prepared to indicate whether meetings of the members and creditors of the company should be summoned. It is important to note that during this period of reflection, and indeed until the creditors have had their say, there is no protection for the company or its assets from actions by impatient creditors. In this sense there is a fundamental difference between the CVA and the Individual Voluntary Arrangement or (IVA) provided for by Part VII of the Act in the case of individual debtors. This possibly explains why the former regime has, statistically speaking, performed badly as compared to the latter.

Securing consent to the proposal

3-65 Once the proposal has been formulated it must then attract sufficient support amongst the company's members and creditors. If the company is insolvent (and this will often be the case) it is difficult to see why members should be involved, unless there is reason to suppose that they have a residual interest in the company's assets. The nominee is required by section 3 to summon meetings of the company and of all known creditors. Fourteen days notice is required by rule 1.9. A high threshold of support, namely 75 per cent. (in value) of the company's creditors (present and voting) have to support the scheme for a voluntary arrangement.[86] The chairman of the meeting must, in accordance with section 4(6) and rule 1.24, report its outcome to the court which will note its date of filing. The court does not, however, participate in the decision whether the voluntary arrangement should go ahead or not.

Voting rights

3-66 Determining voting rights of creditors on a voluntary arrangement has not been easy. In particular uncertainty has arisen as to the position of creditors with disputed, unliquidated or unascertained debts. In practice such creditors will have the value of their claims estimated by the chair of the creditors' meeting. This estimate may not always meet with their approval and they may wish to pursue their rights outside the arrangement by denying that they were creditors entitled to vote on (and therefore be bound by) the arrangement. After some initial uncertainty,[87] the Court of Appeal ruled in *Doorbar v. Alltime Securities Ltd*[88] that a unilateral decision by a chair to place a valuation on an unascertained debt was binding unless challenged under rule 1.17. It was not necessary for the particular creditor to agree to the valuation in order for him to be bound by it. Equally the courts were reluctant to double guess bona fide estimates of debt. The effect of this ruling was to reassure insolvency practitioners faced with the difficult task of

---

[86] Insolvency Rules r.1.19. A simple majority will suffice for the members meeting—r.1.20.
[87] *Re Cranley Mansions Ltd* [1994] B.C.C. 576.
[88] [1995] B.C.C. 1149.

valuing nebulous claims and thereby to give an important boost to the voluntary arrangement regime.

3-67 In *Re Millwall Football Club*[89] the court ruled that an individual may be estopped by his conduct from denying that he is a creditor bound by the arrangement.

Implementation of the proposal

3-68 Once the scheme has been approved it becomes the responsibility of the nominee (who is then transformed by section 7 into the supervisor) to see that the voluntary arrangement is put into effect. On the CVA receiving approval, either the directors (or the liquidator/administrator, if he is not the supervisor) must by virtue of rule 1.23 hand over the assets subject to the arrangement to the supervisor. These can be many or few; proposals for voluntary arrangements in which the directors merely propose to pay unsecured instalments of some kind to the supervisor over a limited period, leaving the directors to run the company free of debt to the participating creditors, are not uncommon. On the other hand, the arrangement may require a transfer of assets to the supervisor as trustee, for realisation on behalf of creditors, or the grant of security to him for due performance of the voluntary arrangement. The fact is that no assets vest in the supervisor at all unless the scheme provides otherwise, and the company makes the necessary transfers. In carrying out his role, the supervisor can apply to the court for directions, as section 7(4) makes clear.[90]

3-69 The supervisor can also petition for the winding-up or administration of the company (section 7(4)(b)), and the threat of doing this may well be his only means of enforcing the voluntary arrangement in many cases. If the company is already in liquidation or administration, the court can lend assistance by staying further proceedings in the wind-up or administration, so as to allow the voluntary arrangement to take effect (section 5(3)). The court can also appoint additional supervisors or substitute supervisors where that is required and there is no more convenient means of achieving it.

3-70 If the supervisor carries on the company's business, realises its assets or deals with its funds, proper accounts must be maintained (see rules 1.26 and 1.27). On completion of the CVA the supervisor must, as a result of rule 1.29, make a final report within 28 days to members and creditors. The supervisor's entitlement to remuneration and costs and expenses is governed by rule 1.28.

Effect of the proposal: creditor protection

3-71 One question that has repeatedly arisen has been the effect of a CVA on a range of parties connected with the company. The position can be summarised as follows:

— unsecured creditors who had notice of the relevant meeting and were entitled to vote are bound (section 5(2)), irrespective of whether they voted for or against the proposal.[91] However, such creditors are not bound with

[89] [1998] 2 B.C.L.C. 272.

[90] On an application for directions the court enjoys no power to vary the CVA terms—*Re Alpa Lighting Ltd* [1997] B.P.I.R. 341.

[91] See *Re A Company (No. 00392 of 1995)*, *The Times*, July 25, 1995.

regard to future debts becoming due from the company unless these have been brought within the terms of the arrangement.[92]

— secured creditors and preferential creditors are not according to section 4(3) and (4) to be prejudiced by an arrangement which is essentially a method of compounding unsecured debts. However, if a secured creditor allows a CVA to proceed without taking adequate precautions it may find itself in a position of disadvantage if it subsequently wishes to enforce its security because assets which would otherwise fall within the security may be impressed with a "trust" in favour of participating creditors.[93]

— third parties, by virtue of the doctrine of privity of contract, are not generally affected by a CVA.[94] Thus a creditor of a company can pursue a surety of the company in respect of a debt owed by that company, a debt now caught by the arrangement.[95]

3-72 Under section 6, members and creditors have 28 days to petition the court alleging either unfair prejudice or some material irregularity in the procedure. The court enjoys wide powers on such an application.[96] Furthermore, even after this period has elapsed, an application to the court under section 7(3) is possible to challenge the implementation of voluntary arrangement by the supervisor.

3-73 Where the proposal has been put forward on behalf of a company that is in administration or liquidation on approval of the CVA, the court can stay the winding-up proceedings or discharge the administration order (section 5(3)).

3-74 A company voluntary arrangement only binds those creditors who had notice of the scheme and were entitled to vote at the relevant meeting. It does not bind or other creditors, or indeed participating creditors with respect to new debts unless this has been specifically provided for. Moreover, if a company fails to honour its commitments under a CVA the supervisor can (and indeed should) petition for winding up. In the light of this evidence the fact that a company which is undergoing a CVA may also find itself placed in liquidation should come as no surprise. But what is the effect of that liquidation on the CVA, the supervisor and funds in his hands?

— If the liquidation has been initiated by a creditor outside the scheme the CVA survives and the supervisor will continue to implement it. Assets/funds caught by the arrangement are not available for general creditors in a liquidation.[97]

— It is possible for an arrangement to explicitly provide for a subsequent liquidation and to indicate that this will terminate the CVA.[98]

---

[92] Future debts can be included by specific reference—see *Re Cancol Ltd* [1995] B.C.C. 1133, *Burford Midland Properties v. Marley Extrusions* [1994] B.C.C. 604.

[93] *Re Leisure Study Group Ltd* [1994] 2 B.C.L.C. 65.

[94] *Mytre Investments v. Reynolds* [1995] 3 All E.R. 558, *March Estates v. Gunmark* [1996] 2 B.C.L.C.

[95] *Johnson v. Davies* [1998] 2 B.C.L.C. 252.

[96] There have been few cases brought under s.6. For a rare unsuccessful example see *Re Primlaks (U.K.) Ltd (No. 2)* [1990] B.C.L.C. 234. The 28 day period cannot be extended—*Re Bournemouth and Boscombe AFC* [1998] B.P.I.R. 183.

[97] *Re Halson Packaging Ltd* [1997] B.P.I.R. 194, *Re Arthur Rathbone Kitchens Ltd* [1998] B.P.I.R. 1 and *Re Excalibur Airways Ltd* [1998] 1 B.C.L.C. 436. The following cases involving IVAs are consistent with that approach—*Re McKeen* [1995] B.C.C. 412 and *Re Bradley-Hole* [1995] 1 W.L.R. 1097.

[98] *Re Excalibur Airways Ltd* (*supra*).

— If the liquidation has been brought about by the supervisor exercising his power of intervention under the Act[99] this will automatically terminate the CVA.[1]

OVERVIEW OF THE ADMINISTRATION AND CVA PROCEDURES

3-75 The two forms of corporate insolvency regime covered in this chapter are fascinating in many respects, but their significance must be placed in perspective. Even taken together they represent little more than 4 per cent. of the total corporate insolvencies each year but this figure is on the increase.[2] This relative rarity is disguised by the high profile of certain cases in which administration orders have been granted, which directly reflects the type of company for which administration is likely to be appropriate, and results from the fact that the relative novelty and nature of the administration procedure has led to considerable reported litigation.

3-76 It is not difficult to identify why administration has been under-utilised. Banks and other floating charge holders have an effective power of veto over the making of an administration order, and there are a number of good reasons in most cases for exercising it. Firstly, administration removes from the floating charge holders the control over the realisation of their security, both fixed and floating. Once the administrator is in place, even fixed security cannot be enforced without leave, and the benefit of income generated by such property goes to general creditors.[3] Secondly, unless the administrator has been able to trade at an overall profit, the floating charge assets will be depleted not only by the administrator's remuneration and expenses, but by all debts and liabilities (including certain taxes) incurred by the administrator in respect of contracts he has entered into (section 19). Third, as the administrator has no power to make distributions, the secured creditor may wait a long time for his money.

Cost

3-77 Even where the floating charge holders have no objection to administration, however, the nature of the procedure dictates that the overhead cost of obtaining an administration order is high. Figures as high as £20,000 have been cited as a minimum starting cost—this is prohibitively expensive for the small private company, especially as this money has to be provided "up front" to persuade the necessary practitioners to lend their support and services. The problem is worsened by the fact that unless the company survives the administration as a trading entity, inevitably another insolvency procedure has to be initiated and followed through.

---

[99] See s.7(4)(b). Supervisors who fail to exercise this default power run the risk of losing their professional credibility and even incurring the wrath of the regulatory authorities—see the note in [1999] Insolvency Intelligence 16.

[1] See *Re Arthur Rathbone Kitchens Ltd (supra)* and the analogous IVA case of *Davies v. Martin-Sklan* [1995] 2 B.C.L.C. 483.

[2] Latest figures contained in the D.T.I. Annual Report for 1997–98 show that in 1997–98 there were in Great Britain only 225 administration orders made and the total of C.V.A.s was 512. The total of corporate insolvencies was 15,000.

[3] As in *Re Atlantic Computer Systems Ltd (No. 1), Re* [1992] 2 W.L.R. 367, although, as that case shows this may be a ground for leave to enforce rights of repossession.

Flaws

3-78 The main weakness of the voluntary arrangement procedure is the lack of a moratorium, but this can be overcome by combining the CVA with administration, a combination that is anticipated by section 8(3). On the other hand, such a combination of corporate insolvency procedures as this will greatly increase the cost of the exercise and would seem to defeat the purpose in having a CVA alternative to administration. Some practitioners have sought to provide themselves with a *de facto* moratorium by applying to a county court for an administration order, persuading the court to adjourn the petition without consideration of the merits, and pursuing a CVA before the adjourned hearing takes place. This practice appears to be an abuse of the process of the court, and it is to be hoped that it will not spread.

3-79 The lack of a moratorium is not the only weakness of the CVA procedure, however. Reference was made above to the fact that it is only the creditors who received notice of the meeting who are bound by the arrangement. There is no procedure for advertising for, and binding, creditors of whom the company may not be aware. It used to be the case that the release of debts under the voluntary arrangement was treated as a receipt by the debtor company, giving rise to a charge to corporation tax. Clearly, this represented an unwelcome obstacle to corporate recovery, but fortunately it was removed by s.144 of the Finance Act 1994.

Reform

3-80 Taken together, these two procedures have at least raised the profile of corporate rescue as a legitimate aim of corporate insolvency law. The topic is now firmly on the political agenda, and further enhancement of the above procedures now seems likely. In October 1993 the D.T.I. Working Party which considered the issue of corporate rescue, proposed a number of changes both to the CVA procedure and the administration order concept. Amongst the many changes suggested would be the introduction of a 1 month moratorium in the case of certain company voluntary arrangements and the removal of the practical requirement of an independent expert's report (under rule 2.2) for certain cases of short term administrations involving only a 28 day moratorium.

3-81 These proposals were revisited in another Insolvency Service Consultative Document (*Revised Proposals for a New Company Voluntary Arrangement Procedure*) in April 1995. The proposed 28 day moratorium was now to be capable of being extended by application to the court. More significant was the proposal that floating charge holders give the company five days notice of intention to appoint a receiver, thereby enabling the company to take immediate steps to enter into an arrangement with creditors. Subsequently governments of all persuasions have repeatedly indicated their intention to legislate to introduce a moratorium for CVA cases (especially for small companies) but these promises as yet have failed to materialise. In July 1997 The British Bankers' Association, presumably in an effort to stave off legislation that might hinder the enforcement of security, introduced a code of practice designed to promote the rescue culture and the statistics do show receivership to be in decline, as compared to the growing number of administrations/arrangements. At present a government working group (set up in February 1999) is developing detailed proposals for a CVA moratorium and the only question now would appear to be one of timing.

CHAPTER 4

Receivers

INTRODUCTION

4-01 For present purposes a receiver is a person appointed to take possession of property which is the subject of a charge and to deal with it primarily for the benefit of the holder of the charge.

Jurisdiction of court to appoint

4-02 The court has an inherent jurisdiction to appoint a receiver in order to put property in safe hands until the rights of those interested in it can be determined.[1] Where the property includes a business, the court can also appoint a manager of that business.[2] From this ancient jurisdiction is derived the debenture holder's action, under which the court can appoint a receiver and manager of property subject to a debenture even if it contains no express power of appointment.[3] However such a case is rare today—if there is a charge at all it is overwhelmingly more common than not to find an express power, and all mortgages by deed contain an implied power by reason of section 101 of the Law of Property Act 1925.

Administrative Receivers

4-03 The Insolvency Act 1986 created the term "administrative receiver," which means a receiver or manager of the whole (or substantially the whole) of a company's property appointed by the holders of a debenture secured by a charge which when created was a floating charge.[4] Aspects of this term have been considered above in Chapter 1. Apparently it does not matter that there was also a fixed charge and that most of the assets are covered by the fixed and not the floating charge. The Act gives important powers to administrative receivers (including the power to carry on the company's business) which will be examined later in this Chapter. In the meantime, unless otherwise stated, in this Chapter the word "receiver" is used to mean an administrative receiver.

Typical circumstances of appointment

4-04 A receiver today is, in practice, appointed by a secured lender under the terms of his floating charge, invariably at a time of acute crisis for the company. If he

[1] Supreme Court Act 1981 s.37. For the best account of this type of receivership, see Picarda *Law relating to Receivers and Managers* (2nd ed., 1990) Butterworths.

[2] For the distinction, see *Taylor v. Neate* (1889) 39 Ch.D. 538; *Re Newdigate Colliery Ltd* [1912] 1 Ch. 468.

[3] The court can also appoint a receiver where the debenture does not contain an express power, or for example where the trustee has not used his power of appointment in the proper manner for the benefit of the debenture holders generally as his fiduciary duty requires—*Re Maskelyne British Typewriter Ltd* [1898] 1 Ch. 133.

[4] s.29(2). In the case of composite security the appointment must be made under the floating charge element—*Meadrealm Ltd v. Transcontinental Golf Construction* (1991, unreported).

is to be effective he must do what the directors have failed to do quickly, and under considerable pressure from creditors, guarantors, directors, the workforce, and often the lender himself. The receiver owes duties of one sort and another to all, and his task therefore calls for a high degree of professionalism and integrity.

4-05 Sometimes the directors ask the lender to appoint the receiver so that he can take steps to save the company which, for some reason, are not open to the directors. If the company is basically sound but has been thrown into cash flow difficulties by delay in completing a contract, a receiver may have a much better chance of persuading creditors to be patient than the directors who have been promising a cheque for months. Alternatively, the directors may know perfectly well that the company needs to reduce its overheads drastically, but feel they will have a better chance of working with a much reduced workforce if the bank and its receiver are perceived as being responsible for the inevitable hive-down of the profitable part of the business. Occasionally there may be good reasons for appointing an administrator in these circumstances, but receivership is generally more popular with the banks, quicker, less cumbersome and therefore less expensive.

4-06 Usually, however, the bank will be appointing the receiver against the wishes of the directors, and often without warning.[5] Often the bank will have been trying for some time without success to obtain promised management information, or been driven to the conclusion that the directors are hopelessly inadequate to their task, and the security may be in jeopardy. One way or another, the arrival of the receiver is likely to provoke considerable resentment.

4-07 The first problem of the receiver will be to satisfy himself that his appointment is valid, or that he has taken a suitable indemnity from his appointing creditor to cover him in the event that it is not. A receiver who takes possession of the assets under an invalid appointment will be a trespasser[6] and will not normally be short of enemies to take the point.

THE VALIDITY OF THE APPOINTMENT

Validity of the debenture

4-08 An administrative receiver must be a qualified insolvency practitioner within the meaning of Part XIII of the Insolvency Act 1986.[7] So long as he is qualified, the validity of the appointment will normally depend on the interpretation of the debenture in the events which have happened, but first the validity of the debenture itself will have to be considered carefully. The receiver will normally want his legal advisers to check whether the debenture is liable to be set aside for any of the reasons discussed in detail in Chaper 11. For example:

- the floating charge element may be found to be void, wholly or in part, if it was granted less than one year before the appointment, and the company goes into liquidation or an administrator is appointed before that period expires (Insolvency Act 1986, s.245)

---

[5] The bank may have engaged accountants to investigate the company's finances. For the responsibilities of such investigators see *Huxford v. Stoy Hayward & Co.* (1989) 5 B.C.C. 421.

[6] See *Re Goldburg (No. 2)* [1912] 1 K.B. 606 and *Ford & Carter Ltd v. Midland Bank* (1979) 129 N.L.J. 543.

[7] See Chap. 2.

— the charge may be liable to be set aside as a voidable preference or as a transaction at an undervalue (ss.238–241)

— if the debenture was granted as part of an extortionate credit transaction and the company goes into liquidation or administration within three years of the transaction, the receiver may have to account to the liquidator or administrator for some or all of the assets of which he has taken possession (s.244)

— the grant of the debenture may have been *ultra vires* the company[8] or have involved the provision of illegal financial assistance in connection with an acquisition of shares in a company or its holding company[9]

— the debenture may not have been duly registered under section 395 of the Companies Act 1985.

4-09 The formalities and procedure associated with the appointment of a receiver depend upon a mixture of contractual interpretation, common law and statutory regulation. The starting point must be the terms of the debenture under which the receiver was appointed. Normally the debenture requires the appointment to be made in writing[10] but any other formalities laid down must be observed.

Entitlement to appoint

Examples

4-10 Many debentures contain a list of events entitling the debenture holder to appoint a receiver. The following are typical:

(i) failure by the company to meet a demand to pay principal or interest. There has been considerable discussion in recent years as to how this should operate in practice. The demand must be in the form (if any) stipulated by the debenture.[11] Subject to that, however, it appears from the comments of Walton J. in *Bank of Baroda v. Panessar*[12] that the demand need not be for a specific sum—a demand for "all sums due" is sufficient.

There has also been doubt over the extent to which the company should be given time to meet the debenture holder's demand for repayment. It is axiomatic that the demand must have been justified in terms of the debenture, but beyond this the position is not entirely settled. Some English cases[13] have been interpreted to mean that the company is not entitled to any breathing space. However, on closer analysis, it seems that these authorities do not go as far as this, and rather hinge on their own individual facts. It is apparent that the "reasonable opportunity" test to meet repayment is widely

---

[8] The *ultra vires* rule is likely to be abolished in the future. In any case, its impact has been substantially weakened by the Companies Act 1989.

[9] See here Companies Act 1985, s.151 and *Re S.H. & Co. Realisations (1990) Ltd* [1993] B.C.C. 60.

[10] On this see *Windsor Refrigeration Co. v. Branch Nominees* [1961] Ch. 375.

[11] *Elwick Bay Shipping Co. v. Royal Bank of Scotland* 1982 S.L.T. 62. But see *Byblos Bank v. Al Khudhairy* F.T.C.L.R. 7/11/86.

[12] [1986] B.C.L.C. 497.

[13] See *Cripps v. Wickenden* [1973] 2 All E.R. 606 and *Williams and Glyns Bank v. Barnes* (1981) 2 Co. Law 80.

accepted.[14] The advantage of adopting such a criterion is obviously its inherent flexibility. On the other hand, the Scylla of flexibility must inevitably be coupled with the Charybdis of uncertainty, which may, by its very existence, provoke litigation.

An illuminating insight into current English judicial attitudes towards this question was provided by Walton J in *Bank of Baroda v. Panessar*,[15] where the "reasonable opportunity" test was rejected in favour of an equally vague formula. The essential requirement was held to be that the company must be given an "adequate time" to find the money, with the proviso that the adequacy of the time allowed will depend on the circumstances of each particular case. In *Sheppard and Cooper Ltd v. TSB Bank (No. 2)*[16] the issue of the propriety of a receiver's appointment was once again raised. Here the debenture was repayable on demand and having made a fruitless request for some £680,000 the bank appointed a receiver within the hour. Blackburne J. upheld the appointment on the grounds that all that was required of it was to give the company time to collect the money from a convenient source and that as it was clear that the money could not be made available an immediate appointment was appropriate. What is apparent from the case law on the subject is that the practice of handing the demand for repayment and the letter of appointment of the receiver over together, could well lead to the appointment being challenged even if that challenge fails.[17]

(ii) The presentation of a winding-up petition or the passing of a resolution to liquidate the company voluntarily. If the court has already appointed a liquidator its leave must first be obtained before a receiver can be appointed, though such leave will normally be granted.[18]

(iii) The presentation of a petition for administration or the initiation of a CVA.[19]

(iv) The levying of distress or execution against the company's assets.

(v) Failure by the company to perform any of its obligations or observe any of the restrictions placed upon it under the debenture. Such a breach could include the grant by the company of new security interests in contravention of the terms of the original debenture, or payment of the proceeds of book debts into some bank other than the debenture holder.

---

[14] See, for instance, *A.N.Z. Banking Group v. Gibson* [1981] 2 N.Z.L.R. 513, *Ronald Elwyn Lister Ltd v. Dunlop Canada Ltd* (1982) 135 D.L.R. (3d) 1, *Bunbury Foods v. National Bank of Australasia* (1984) 153 C.L.R. 491 and *NRG Vision v. Churchfield Leasing Ltd* [1988] B.C.L.C. 624.

[15] [1986] B.C.L.C. 497.

[16] [1996] B.C.C. 965. A similar approach was adopted by the Court of Appeal in *Lloyds Bank v. Lampert* [1999] B.C.C. 507. Although the Court of Appeal refused to be drawn on choosing between the stricter English approach and the more liberal Commonwealth authorities (because it would have made no difference on the facts of the case before it) it seems likely that the Court of Appeal would not have been prepared to extend the degree of latitude to debtors as is suggested by some of the Commonwealth authorities.

[17] This practice was an important factor behind the decision in *Ronald Elwyn Lister Ltd v. Dunlop Canada Ltd* (1982) 135 D.L.R. (3d) 1.

[18] *Henry Pound & Sons Ltd v. Hutchins* (1889) 42 Ch.D. 402, and see Insolvency Act 1986, s.130(2).

[19] For charges created before the Insolvency Act 1986 came into force this is unnecessary in view of Sched. 11, para, 1(1) of the Act. Under the Insolvency Act 1986, s.9(2)(*a*), a debenture holder entitled to appoint an administrative receiver must be notified of a petition for an administrator.

(vi) The company ceasing to trade. In view of the decision of Nourse J. in *Re Woodroffes (Musical Instruments) Ltd*,[20] such an eventuality may well cause the floating charge to crystallise automatically without requiring intervention by the debenture holder.

(vii) The assets being in jeopardy. Guidance on the meaning and scope of "jeopardy" is to be found in numerous cases dealing with the appointment of court appointed receivers on this ground.[21]

(viii) Inability of the company to pay its debts. Where such a clause is relied upon the court will not take into account fanciful possibilities that assets might accrue to the company in the future.[22]

Burden of proof

4-11 It is clear that the burden of proof is placed on the debenture holder to show that an event has occurred justifying the appointment of the receiver. This principle was confirmed in the case of *Kasofsky v. Kreegers*.[23] In practice therefore the receiver must satisfy himself that such an event has occurred.

Appointment of investigating accountant

4-12 A controversial issue concerns the appointment of a receiver by a bank on the recommendation of an investigating accountant nominated by the bank to undertake a review of a company's prospects. It is often the case that the receiver will be a partner in the firm that conducted the investigation. There would appear to be a potential conflict of interest here in that the investigating accountants may be tempted to recommend receivership with one eye on maximising future fee income. The counter argument is that it makes commercial sense to appoint a receiver from the firm that is already in possession of the relevant background financial information.

4-13 The insolvency profession does not consider appointment in these circumstances to be unacceptable. Although its statement of ethics disapproves of appointment where there is a material professional relationship with the company, holding a prior appointment as an investigator does not fall within this category.[24] The courts are also prepared to countenance the practice,[25] but public concern has surfaced with the presentation of a Private Members Bill in 1999 to outlaw it.[26]

4-14 Banks invariably insist that their faltering corporate customers engage (and pay) the investigating accountants themselves. This may give the subject company the opportunity to reduce the risk of a premature appointment of a receiver by including a term in the engagement letter to the effect that the accountant's firm will not

---

[20] [1985] 3 W.L.R. 543. See also Chap. 7.

[21] For guidance here see *McMahon v. North Kent Iron Works* [1891] 2 Ch. 148, *Re Victoria Steamboats Ltd* [1897] 1 Ch. 158, and *Re London Pressed Hinge Co.* [1905] 1 Ch. 576. The courts will not imply such a facility in a debenture—*Cryne v. Barclays Bank* [1987] B.C.L.C. 548.

[22] *Byblos Bank v. Al Khudhairy* F.T.C.L.R. 7/11/86.

[23] [1937] 4 All E.R. 374.

[24] See here ICAEW Guide to Professional Ethics section 1.201 and paras 8.4–8.5.

[25] See the discussion in *Huxford v. Stoy Hayward* (1989) 5 B.C.C. 421.

[26] The Bill was introduced by Richard Page M.P. on February 2, 1999. It was more of a gesture than a serious attempt at legislation but its appearance at this particular time in the debate is significant.

undertake any responsibility for the management of the company at any time. In *Sheppard and Cooper Ltd v. TSB Bank*[27] the Court of Appeal held that such a term could be enforced by an injunction. In this case the prohibition was enforced some three years after the investigation in circumstances where the appointment of the firm as receivers had nothing to do with that earlier review.

Duty of care in appointment?

4-15 In recent times the courts have also had to consider whether the debenture holder owes any sort of duty of care to the company when making the appointment. The position appears to be that provided the debenture holder allows the company an adequate opportunity to meet the demand, he has no additional obligation to be kind. The debenture holder is perfectly entitled to protect his own legitimate interests even though in so doing he may inevitably damage the position of the company. This is clear from the decision of Hoffmann J. in *Shamji v. Johnson Matthew Bankers Ltd*:[28]

> "The appointment of a receiver seems to me to involve an inherent conflict of interests. The purpose of the power is to enable the mortgagee to take the management of the company's property out of the hands of the directors and then trust it to a person of the mortgagee's choice . . . It seems to me that a decision by the mortgagee to exercise the power cannot be challenged except perhaps on grounds of bad faith."

The same judge reinforced this point in *Re Potters Oil Ltd (No. 2)*,[29] where the importance of the debenture holder's contractual right to appoint a receiver was stressed together with the fact that he could not be expected to subordinate his interests to those of the company. Thus the fact that there was already a liquidator in post who could adequately realise the security did not preclude the appointment of a receiver:[30]

> "The debenture holder is under no duty to refrain from exercising his rights merely because doing so may cause loss to the company or its unsecured creditors."

Acceptance of appointment

4-16 If, after making all the necessary enquiries, the receiver decides to accept the appointment, he must by virtue of section 33 of the Insolvency Act 1986 do so before the end of the next business day after receiving his letter of appointment. It follows, therefore, that his investigations must be conducted with considerable despatch. This acceptance does not need to be in writing but if it is not he must confirm his appointment in writing with his appointor within seven days. This confirmation must state both the time and date of his receiving his letter of appointment and of his acceptance.[31] The appointment takes effect, once accepted, from the time

---

[27] [1997] 2 B.C.L.C. 222.
[28] [1986] B.C.L.C. 278 at 284. Confirmed by the Court of Appeal—see [1991] B.C.L.C. 36.
[29] [1986] 1 W.L.R. 201.
[30] *ibid.*, at 206.
[31] Insolvency Rules 1986, r. 3.1 (as amended).

at which it was received, as section 33 of the Insolvency Act 1986 makes clear. If the appointment is joint, it does not take effect until all have accepted, but one may accept on behalf of the other if authorised.

Notification of others

4-17 On acceptance, the receiver and his appointor must take a number of steps to alert the outside world of the change in the stewardship of the company. For example, the appointor must notify the Companies Registry at Cardiff within seven days.[32] Failure to do this will expose the appointor to criminal penalties but will not prejudice the appointment. All invoices, business letters, etc., (whether from the receiver or the liquidator) must indicate the fact that a receiver has been appointed.[33] Section 46 of the Insolvency Act 1986 imposes a new requirement on an administrative receiver to notify the company and all known creditors of his appointment within 28 days. The contents of this notice are detailed in the Insolvency Rules 1986.[34] The notice should be advertised in the Gazette and in a local newspaper. Once again, the penalties for non-compliance are criminal in nature.

Unlawful appointment

4-18 If the appointment is prima facie unlawful the court may order the removal of the receiver on an interlocutory application, though it will not do so if the balance of convenience favours him remaining in office.[35] The wrongful appointment of a receiver with the resultant damage to the company's assets and financial standing constitutes a serious tort, entitling the company to a remedy in trespass. It is well established at common law that both the receiver, and the debenture holder who procured his appointment, risk incurring liability in tort in the event of a wrongful appointment.[36] The Insolvency Act 1986, acting on a recommendation of the Cork Committee (para. 830), made an interesting change in the law in section 34 by allowing the court a discretion to order that the appointor indemnify the receiver against any liability resulting from an unlawful appointment. It is too early to predict how this new discretionary power will be exercised, though the degree of culpability of the receiver will clearly be a relevant consideration.

Joint receivers

4-19 For practical reasons, insolvency practitioners commonly wish to take appointments jointly, often with another partner in the same firm. It is settled law that a joint appointment cannot be validly made without an express power in the debenture. Usually, the provisions of the Interpretation Act 1978 can be prayed in aid, under which, generally speaking, a power to appoint a receiver will be interpreted as a power to appoint one or more receivers. There is, however, one problem here that may appear trivial at first sight, but in fact crops up frequently in practice.

---

[32] Companies Act 1985, s.405(1).
[33] Insolvency Act 1986, s.39.
[34] Insolvency Rules 1986, r. 3.2 (as amended).
[35] *Byblos Bank v. Rushingdale* 1986 P.C.C. 249.
[36] See *Re Goldburg (No. 2)* [1912] 1 K.B. 606 and *Ford & Carter Ltd v. Midland Bank* (1979) 129 N.L.J. 543. The debenture holder will not be liable if the receiver is installed as the company's agent—*Re Simms* [1934] Ch. 1.

Where receivers have been appointed jointly, does that confer authority on them to act jointly and severally? The advantage in having joint and several powers is of course that either receiver can do or authorise an act or execute a document even if the other is absent or unavailable. Section 231(2) of the Insolvency Act 1986, which applies to office holders, may appear to permit joint appointees to act severally if their appointment specifically authorises them to do so, but it has to be said that the statute is less than clear on this point. If the debenture under which the appointment is made explicitly authorises joint and several appointments, and such an appointment is made, then the matter is cut and dried. However, it is common to find debentures authorising joint appointments without mentioning the possibility of the appointees acting severally. One analysis of such cases is that the receivers cannot act severally. This view would cause great difficulties in practice, and fortunately it has now been rejected by the New South Wales Court of Appeal in *NEC Information Systems Australia Pty. Ltd v. Lockhart*.[37] Here a debenture authorised joint receivers to be appointed to realise the security conferred by the debenture. The debenture holder later appointed receivers with power to act jointly and severally. Was this a valid appointment? At first instance Giles J. thought not, but on appeal it was held that, on a proper construction of the debenture charge, and having regard to the commercial contemplation of the parties, it was permissible to appoint joint receivers with joint and several powers. However, it was indicated that had the debenture not expressly contemplated a joint appointment, the conclusion of the court might have been different.[38] The advantage of inserting an express mention of a joint appointment in the debenture, rather than relying on the operation of the Interpretation Act 1978, is therefore apparent, and in the absence of recent English authority the better practice must be to provide specifically for joint and several powers.

THE IMPACT OF RECEIVERSHIP ON THE COMPANY

Legal implications

4-20 In a legal sense the appointment of a receiver will have a minimal impact on the company though the economic effect on goodwill can be severe. The receiver's appointment does not effect a cessation of trade, most of the company's contracts remain enforceable by and against it, its directors remain in office, and it retains the ownership of its assets.[39] Moreover, there is no change in the occupation of its premises for rating purposes.[40] For priority purposes, the appointment of the receiver operates as notice of the equitable assignment of the property subject to the deben-

---

[37] (1991) 101 A.L.R. 95, following the New Zealand Court of Appeal in *DFC Financial Services Ltd v. Samuel* (1990) 5 N.Z.C.L.C. 96, 403. *NEC Information Systems Australia Pty: Ltd v. Lockhart (supra)* went on to the High Court of Australia on constitutional and procedural grounds (see (1992) 108 A.L.R. 561). The ruling on the New South Wales Court of Appeal on the point discussed above in the text was not at issue in those later proceedings.

[38] See *Wrights Hardware Pty. Ltd v. Evans* (1988) 13 A.C.L.R. 631 *Kerry Lowe Management Pty. Ltd v. Isherwood & Sherlock* (1989) 15 A.C.L.R. 615 and *Melson v. Velcrete Pty Ltd* (1996) 20 A.C.S.R. 291. For discussion see Picarda 2 [1995–96] 2 R.A.L.Q. 261.

[39] Certain 19th century cases suggest that this is not so for some purposes of the law of distress, but see Chap. 10. For the ownership of company documents see *Gomba Holdings v. Minories Finance* [1989] B.C.L.C. 115.

[40] *Peat Marwick Ltd v. Consumers Gas Co.* (1981) 113 D.L.R. (3d) 754. Compare *Lord Advocate v. Aero Technologies* 1991 SLT 134. See also Chap. 9.

ture,[41] but otherwise the receiver stands in much the same position as the company itself.[42] There has been a crucial change in that *de jure* control has passed to the receiver.[43] Depending on the degree of supervision exercised by the receiver, the *de facto* management of the business and assets may appear unaltered. However, the result is that the receiver is legally entitled to give instructions to the directors as to the management of the business.[44] In *Gomba Holdings Ltd v. Homan*, Hoffmann J. declared:[45]

> "There are, I think, certain principles which can be deduced from what the parties may be supposed to have contemplated as the commercial purpose of the power to appoint a receiver and manager. The first is that the receiver and manager should have the power to carry on the day to day process of realisation and management of the company's property without interference from the board."

Thus the receiver is entitled to demand a statement of affairs from the company's directors. This is now supported by a statutory duty under section 47 of the Insolvency Act 1986 and rules 3.3–3.8 of the Insolvency Rules 1986 (as amended). This statement must be prepared in accordance with the statutory provisions, under which the administrative receiver can also release certain persons from their obligations in this respect.[46] The relationship between the receiver and the directors will be examined in more depth in Chapter 12.

Employees

4-21 So far as employees are concerned, the general rule, once again, is that their contracts of employment are not affected by the appointment of a receiver out of court[47] (the position may be different in the case of court appointed receivers).[48] This general rule preserving the status quo, is however, subject to a number of exceptions. Thus it has been said that contracts of employment will be terminated:

(i) where the receiver sells the business. This was the position at common law, but is no longer so in the case of a person who was employed in the business "immediately before" the sale. By reason of the Transfer of Undertakings (Protection of Employment) Regulations 1981 (as amended), the contract of employment of such a person is automatically transferred to the purchaser;[49]

---

[41] See *Tullow Engineering Ltd* [1990] I.R. 452. The appointment of the receiver will of course crystallise any floating charge.

[42] See *Rother Iron Works v. Canterbury Precision Engineers* [1974] Q.B. 960, *George Baker Transport Ltd v. Eynon* [1974] 1 All E.R. 960 and *Re Diesels Components Pty Ltd* (1985) 9 A.C.L.R. 825.

[43] A receiver enjoys the confidence of the court not to wrongfully dissipate assets—*Capital Cameras v. Harold Lines Ltd* [1991] 1 W.L.R. 54.

[44] *Meigh v. Wickenden* [1941] 2 K.B. 160 at 166 *per* Viscount Caldecote C.J. and *Macleod v. Alexander Sutherland* 1977 S.L.T. (Notes) 44. See also *Joshua Shaw & Sons Ltd* [1989] B.C.L.C. 362.

[45] [1986] 1 W.L.R. 1301 at 1306.

[46] Rule 3.6.

[47] *Re Foster Clark Ltd's Indenture Trust* [1966] 1 All E.R. 43, *Re Macks Trucks (Britain) Ltd* [1967] 1 W.L.R. 780, *Deaway Trading Ltd v. Calverley* [1973] 3 All E.R. 773 and *Griffiths v. Secretary of State for Social Services* [1973] 3 All E.R. 1184.

[48] Compare *Reid v. Explosives Co.* (1887) 19 Q.B.D. 264 with *International Harvester Export Co. v. International Harvester (Australia) Ltd* (1983) 7 A.C.L.R. 391.

[49] Regs. 4 and 5. For discussion see para. 4-32.

(ii) if the receiver arranges for new inconsistent contracts of employment, and

(iii) where the continued employment of a particular employee is incompatible with a receiver and manager taking over the running of the company.[50] It is thought that in these circumstances the contract of employment will in effect have been repudiated by the company on the appointment of the receiver as its agent. Presumably the question whether a particular employee's contract has been terminated will turn upon whether that repudiation has been accepted by the employee.[51]

Contracts

4-22 In the context of company contracts, the basic rule is that the appointment of a receiver is of no significance, unless the contract provides otherwise.[52] Existing contracts remain binding on the company (but not on the receiver). The receiver will incur personal liability for contracts of employment, if he adopts them,[53] though his actions during the first two weeks of the receivership are not to be taken into account when considering whether he has indeed adopted a particular contract. A receiver, unlike a liquidator, has no statutory power to disclaim onerous contracts.[54]

4-23 If the receiver decides not to honour such a contract, the disappointed party will obviously be entitled to sue the company for damages.[55] Normally there would be no point in this, as any judgment debt would rank as a mere unsecured claim against the insolvent company. It may nevertheless be worthwhile for set-off purposes if the insolvent company has some cross-claim.

4-24 It was widely assumed as a result of the decision of Graham J. in *Airlines Airspaces v. Handley Page*[56] that the equitable remedy of specific performance was not available to compel a receiver to honour existing company contracts. However, that case only decided that receivers could not be restrained from, or made liable for, a breach of contract for which the only remedy was damages. The case concerned a "hive down" of a profitable part of Handley Page's business and the subsequent sale of the subsidiary's shares, which would have put it out of the company's power to honour its obligations to pay commissions due to the plaintiff on sale of aircraft.

4-25 In *Freevale Ltd v. Metrostore Holdings Ltd*,[57] Rattee Q.C. (sitting as deputy judge of the High Court) distinguished *Airline Airspaces (supra)*, holding that it did not apply to specifically performable contracts, a feature of which was that the complaining party had acquired an equitable interest in the property which was the subject of the contract. A receiver who fails to honour current company contracts of this type may be liable in tort for interfering with the plaintiff's equitable rights, as

[50] On this see *Re Mack Trucks (Britain) Ltd* [1967] 1 W.L.R. 780 and *Griffiths v. Secretary of State for Social Services* [1973] 3 All E.R. 1184.
[51] If major dismissals are planned the unions must be consulted with—*GMB v. Rankin* [1992] I.R.L.R. 514. Compare *Warner v. Adnet Ltd*, *The Times*, March 12, 1998.
[52] See *Barclays Bank v. Simms (W.J.) and Son and Cooke (Southern) Ltd* [1980] 2 W.L.R. 218 at 221. Where, in a hire purchase contract, the entry of the hirer into receivership terminates the contract, the court may restrain an attempt by the owner to snatch back the goods on equitable grounds—*Transag Haulage v. Leyland DAF Finance* [1994] B.C.C. 356.
[53] For the position at common law see *Nicoll v. Cutts* (1985) 1 B.C.C. 99, 427.
[54] See Chap. 4 on this.
[55] *Telsen Electric Co Ltd v. Eastick & Sons* [1936] 3 All E.R. 266.
[56] [1970] Ch. 193.
[57] [1984] B.C.L.C. 72. See also *Schering Pty Ltd v. Forrest Pharmaceuticals* Co. [1982] N.S.W.L.R. 287 and *Re Diesels Components Pty Ltd* (1985) 9 A.C.L.R. 825.

was acknowledged by Peter Gibson J. in *Telemetrix plc v. Modern Engineers of Bristol (Holdings) plc.*[58] These decisions have recently been reinforced by the Court of Appeal in *Amec Properties v. Planning and Research Systems Ltd*,[59] in which the Court rejected the argument that it would be contrary to the principle of equality of treatment to allow specific performance to claimants who would otherwise have no more than an unsecured claim for damages. There would now seem to be no reason why specific performance should not be available against a receiver in appropriate circumstances, such as contracts for the sale or purchase of land.

4-26 The Privy Council revisited this issue in *Village Cay Marina Ltd v. Acland*[60] and clarified matters by indicating that an incoming receiver was unlikely to be rebuked by the court for honouring existing contracts, even if such contracts were disadvantageous to the company. In summary, therefore, the courts seem prepared to give considerable latitude to receivers when dealing with ordinary commercial contracts.

Powers of an administrative receiver

Implied powers

4-27 The receiver's powers are normally to be found in the debenture under which he was appointed, but unless the debenture provides otherwise certain powers are implied by statute. A list of implied powers is now set out in Schedule 1 of the Insolvency act 1986.[61] This format has been used in Scotland for a number of years[62] and the Cork Committee recommended[63] that it should be adopted by English law. The list is fairly comprehensive (though presented in a haphazard fashion).

4-28 An administrative receiver has power to take possession of and get in the company's assets.[64] In order to do so he can institute legal proceedings,[65] refer disputes to arbitration,[66] or compromise them[67] or prove for debts owed to the company by an insolvent debtor.[68]

4-29 An administrative receiver can carry on the company's business[69] and can borrow money using the company's assets as security.[70] He is entitled to make

---

[58] [1985] B.C.L.C. 213. However the opposite conclusion was arrived at by Sir Neil Lawson in *Lathia v. Dronsfield Bros. Ltd* [1987] B.C.L.C. 321. This was an interlocutory appeal and *Telemetrix (supra)* was not cited. The difference between these two cases may well lie in the different nature of the property which was the subject of the contract in the two cases. *Telemetrix (supra)* concerned land options, while *Lathia (supra)* was about the sale of goods. However, specific performance is available in sale of goods cases (see Sale of Goods Act 1979 s.52) and the cases are not easy to reconcile.

[59] [1992] 13 E.G. 109. See also *Ash & Newman Ltd v. Creative Devices Research Ltd* [1991] B.C.L.C. 403.

[60] [1998] B.C.C. 417.

[61] This is made applicable by s.42(1) of the Act. An administrator enjoys similar powers.

[62] See now Insolvency Act 1986, s.55 and Sched. 2.

[63] Cmnd. 8558 para. 820.

[64] Sched. 1 para. 1. He can act in Scotland by virtue of s.72 of the Act—*Norfolk House v. Repsol Petroleum* 1992 SLT 235.

[65] *ibid.*, para. 1. See also *Wheeler & Co. v. Warren* [1928] Ch. 840.

[66] *ibid.*, para. 6.

[67] *ibid.*, para. 18.

[68] *ibid.*, para. 20.

[69] *ibid.*, para. 14.

[70] *ibid.*, para. 3.

necessary payments[71] and to issue cheques in the company's name.[72] The employment of agents and other professionals to assist him is also envisaged by Schedule 1.[73]

4-30 Having collected the assets, the administrative receiver is empowered to sell them to generate funds to repay the debenture holder.[74] He can execute documents in the company's name and use the company's seal to this end,[75] whether or not the appointment was made by deed.[76] The grant of leases of company property is permitted.[77] The administrative receiver is entitled to establish subsidiary companies,[78] transfer viable portions of the company's business to them and ultimately to sell them.[79] In other words, Schedule 1 authorises an administrative receiver to engage in "hiving down" transactions, a favourite method of packaging receivership assets for sale.

Hiving down

4-31 A typical mechanism is as follows:

Step 1

(a) the company in receivership ("RCo") buys a newly formed company with a £2 issued share capital, ("SCo").

Step 2

(b) RCo sells a selection of its assets to SCo, for a price to be settled by valuation by the receiver, payable on demand. RCo's trade premises are often excluded at this stage, the hive down agreement giving SCo merely a non exclusive licence to occupy them. The receiver's personal liability is excluded. Usually RCo contracts to supply key employees to SCo on subcontract terms, and often to carry on SCo's business as its agent.

Step 3

(c) The receiver sells the shares of SCo to a third party, PCo, for a nominal consideration but PCo undertakes to cause SCo to pay the debt due to RCo and to inject the necessary funds into SCo. For the purposes of the original agreement between RCo and SCo, the receiver values the assets at the moment PCo has agreed to pay. An agreement is made, supplemental to the hive down agreement, dealing with the fixing of the price and if necessary varying the assets included in the original agreement to suit the purchaser's requirement. Arrangements are made to govern the transfer of key employees to PCo and to indemnify the receiver and RCo against claims by them.

4-32 The measures formerly taken to enhance the value of SCo by passing on

[71] *ibid.*, para. 13.
[72] *ibid.*, para . 10.
[73] *ibid.*, paras. 4 and 11.
[74] *ibid.*, para. 2.
[75] *ibid.*, para. 8. This was the result of a Cork Committee recommendation (Cmnd. 8558 para. 824).
[76] *Phoenix Properties Ltd v. Wimple Street Nominees* [1992] B.C.L.C. 737.
[77] Sched. 1, para. 17.
[78] *ibid.*, para. 15.
[79] *ibid.*, para. 16.

RCo's accrued tax losses[80] are no longer of any great practical importance if the parent company is insolvent (taking into account the proceeds of sale of the assets).[81]

4-33 Cash will always be excluded from the sale, and book debts will often be excluded, although arrangements may be made for SCo to collect them as agent for RCo.

4-34 In all hive down cases the receiver and PCo will have to take account of the possible impact of the Transfer of Undertakings (Protection of Employment) Regulations 1981,[82] which can operate to transfer to SCo the contracts of employment of all RCo's employees engaged in the hive-down business. These Regulations were passed in order to implement a European Community Directive (The Acquired Rights Directive, E.C. 77/187). Great care has to be taken to ensure that at most, only the employees that PCo actually wants are employed by RCo "immediately before" the sale of SCo. The significance of these Regulations to receivers was confirmed by the House of Lords ruling in *Lister v. Forth Dry Dock & Engineering Co. Ltd.*[83] Here the respondents had gone into receivership and the receivers had agreed to sell its business assets to another company. One hour before the transfer was due to take place the employees of the respondents were dismissed with immediate effect. The transferee of the business did recruit fresh labour from the respondents, including some of the former staff. The applicants who were not found jobs with the transferee claimed unfair dismissal. A key issue to be decided was whether the applicants were employed by the respondents "immediately before" transfer of the undertaking. If so, the solvent transferee would be responsible for compensating them for the dismissal that was clearly a result of the transfer. The House of Lords upheld the arguments of the applicants; the phrase "immediately before" in the 1981 Regulations had to be construed in a purposive light and in a manner that was consistent with the aims of the Directive.[84] Thus, it could be said that the applicants were employed immediately before the transfer and that their dismissal was effected as a result of that transfer. The purchaser of the business from the receiver was liable for their compensation.

4-35 The interrelationship between TUPE, the Acquired Rights Directive and the hiving down activities of insolvency practitioners continues to create uncertainty throughout Europe. Real concerns have been raised that the protective provisions in the ARD are hampering the activities of those professionals seeking to rescue business or at least to give them a decent burial. The European Court of Justice has responded to these concerns by indicating that certain transfers are exempt from the employee protective provisions of the ARD.[85] Nearer to home the English Court of Appeal in

---

[80] Under s.252 Income and Corporation Taxes Act 1970. It was important to complete the hive down and for the hive down company to trade before any binding arrangement was made with PCo.

[81] Finance Act 1986, s.42 and Sched. 10 applies to hive downs after March 18, 1986. See now ICTA 1988 s.343(9).

[82] S.I. 1981 No. 1794 as extended by the Transfer of Undertakings (Protection of Employment) (Amendment) Regulations 1987 (S.I. 1987 No. 442) and the Collective Redundancies and Transfer of Undertakings (Protection of Employment) (Amendment) Regulations S.I. 1995 No. 2587. For discussion see *De Groot* (1993) 30 C.M.L. Rev. 332.

[83] [1990] 1 A.C. 546. The Irish courts have also concluded that their equivalent regulations apply to disposals by receivers—see *Mythen v. Employment Appeals Tribunal* [1989] I.L.R.M. 844.

[84] This approach is consistent with that adopted by the European Court of Justice in *Bork International A/S v. Foreningen of Arbejdsledere i Danmark* [1989] I.R.L.R. 41.

[85] See *Abels (Case 135/83)* [1985] E.C.R. 469. This concession is not however extended to all insolvency proceedings; the aim of the proceedings must be considered—*Jules Dethier Equipement SA v. Dassy (Case 319.94)* [1998] I.R.L.R. 266.

Warner v. Adnet Ltd[86] has ruled that an administrative receiver will continue to enjoy considerable freedom of action in conducting hive downs because a pre transfer dismissal of employees can often be justified by reference to the "economic reason" loophole in Regulation 8(2) of TUPE. The position is likely to be further improved for insolvency practitioners when proposed amendments to the Acquired Rights Directive kick in because these will not only allow Members States some freedom to derogate from the ARD but will also offer concessions to insolvency practitioners.[87]

Other powers

4-36 The administrative receiver can effect two important legal changes as far as the company is concerned. He can relocate its registered office, (Schedule 1 para. 22) this was a reform engineered by the Cork Committee to enable an administrative receiver to move the company's registered office to an area of lower rents and rates (Cmnd 8558, para. 22). Moreover, he is entitled to petition for its winding up.[88] He may wish to opt for this latter course of action if a winding up could assist the successful completion of the receivership.

4-37 These specific powers of the receiver are supplemented by two generalised powers and a number of other statutory provisions. Thus, the administrative receiver can do all things as may be necessary for the realisation of the property of the company,[89] and also anything incidental to the exercise of his other powers.[90]

4-38 The powers contained in Schedule 1 must be read in the light of a number of other statutory provisions. For example, under section 35 of the Insolvency Act 1986, a receiver (or his appointor) can apply to the court for directions. In *Re Therm-a-Stor (Morris v. Lewis)*[91] the jurisdiction of the court with regard to the giving of directions under section 35 was reviewed. An extensive interpretation of this jurisdiction was adopted. This is in stark contrast to the approach of the Scottish courts in *Jamieson, Petitioners*[92] where the court was unable to make the necessary directions, which would have had the effect of binding a third party, because of the narrow language used in the Scottish counterpart (Insolvency Act 1986, s.63). Under section 43 he can seek the court's permission to sell company property which is within the debenture but subject to a prior specific mortgage.[93] Rule 3.31 of the Insolvency Rules 1986 states that the administrative receiver must give the chargee notice of the venue of the hearing and of any order made.

4-39 This valuable facility allows an administrative receiver to override the selfish objections of an obstructive first mortgagee. It is therefore a matter of regret that it was not extended to cover property held by the company subject to title retention, as the Cork Committee had recommended.[94] The law maintains a balance of interests by providing that the proceeds of sale must be paid over to the mortgagee

---

[86] *The Times*, March 12, 1998. This case also permits deviations from established consultation practices where the financial difficulties were such as to constitute an emergency. See Roberts (1998) 14 I.L. & P. 204 for comment on this case.

[87] For discussion of these changes, found largely in Art. 4a of the Amended Directive, see Sargeant [1998] J.B.L. 577 and (1999) 15 I.L. & P. 6.

[88] Sched. 1 para. 21. For example see *Re Television Parlour Ltd* (1988) 4 B.C.C. 95.

[89] *ibid.*, para. 12.

[90] *ibid.*, para. 23.

[91] [1996] 1 W.L.R. 1238.

[92] [1997] B.C.C. 682.

[93] See Cork Report Cmnd. 8558, para. 1512 for this recommended power.

[94] *ibid.*, para. 1650.

and, that, in the event of a sale at an undervalue, the court can order the receiver to pay compensation to the mortgagee.

1. Receiver's new contracts

Legal characteristics

4-40 In practice a receiver will exercise his powers mostly by making contracts on behalf of the company. What are the legal characteristics of such a contract? Although a receiver makes the contract as agent of the company he can nevertheless incur personal liability on it.[95] This is clear from the language of sections 37(1)(*a*) and 44(1)(*b*) of the Insolvency Act 1986. However this liability will be covered by his indemnity from the company so far as assets permit. The statutory provisions do allow the receiver to contract out of personal liability, and it is usual for him to do so.[96] It is true that so far as representations and warranties are concerned, the receiver is peculiarly dependent on what he is told, and this may explain the general willingness of purchasers from him to accept the exclusion of his liability, even though the purchaser is left with no practical right of redress against the insolvent company.

4-41 The receiver will not normally become personally liable on company contracts he adopts, unless they are contracts of employment. Like an administrator, a receiver (administrative or otherwise) is not to be taken to have adopted a contract of employment by reason of anything done or omitted within 14 days after his appointment (Insolvency Act 1986, s.44(2)). It is clear from *Re Paramount Airways Ltd (No. 3)*[97] that a receiver will be taken to have adopted a contract of employment if in substance he continues after the statutory 14 days to employ staff and pay them in accordance with their previous contracts, unless he takes the trouble to negotiate new contracts which are not a sham. A letter to the employees denying an intention to adopt the contracts will not protect the receiver from personal liability, but there is nothing in *Re Paramount Airways Ltd (No. 3) supra* to suggest that personal liability cannot be validly excluded where new contracts are negotiated. In any case, his personal liability will extend to contractual claims only and not to claims for unfair dismissal or other purely statutory remedies, as is clear from the first instance ruling of Evans-Lombe J. in this case.

2. The effect of liquidation on a receiver's powers

Powers of realisation

4-42 After some doubt, it now seems clear that although liquidation will strip a receiver of his right to act as the company's agent,[98] it does not impinge upon his

---

[95] The position is much the same for court appointed receivers—*Burt, Boulton and Hayward v. Bull* [1895] 1 Q.B. 276. for the enforceability of a receiver's contract, see *McCarter v. Roughan and McLaughlin* [1986] I.L.R.M. 447.

[96] For an unusual case where contracting out of liability might be appropriate see *Amec Properties v. Planning Research and Systems Ltd* [1992] 13 E.G. 109.

[97] Reported *sub nom. Powdrill v. Watson* [1995] 2 W.L.R. 312—the practical difficulties posed by this case for administrative receivers are largely neutralised by the Insolvency Act 1994.

[98] See Insolvency Act 1986, s.44(1)(*a*) for the position with regard to administrative receivers. The same rule applies to ordinary receivers—*Gosling v. Gaskell* [1897] A.C. 575, *Thomas v. Todd* [1926] 2 K.B. 511, *Re Northern Garage Ltd* [1946] Ch. 188, *Re Peek, Winch & Tod Ltd* (1979) 129 N.L.J. 494 and *Bacal Contracting Ltd v. Modern Engineering (Bristol) Ltd* [1980] 2 All E.R. 655 at 658. For an Australian perspective see O'Donovan [1994] 1 R.A.L.Q. 283.

powers of realisation.[99] In this connection, it is worth noting that a provision is often inserted in debentures *ex abundanti cautela* conferring on a receiver a power of attorney. In *Sowman v. David Samuel Trust Ltd*,[1] Goulding J. held that such a power of attorney remains unaffected by the subsequent liquidation of the company. Thus, the receiver can convey a good title to registered land and this should prove acceptable to the Land Registry. Goulding J. also held that what is now section 127 of the Insolvency Act 1986 (invalidation of dispositions of company property after the date of the winding-up petition) does not prejudice realisations of charged company property by a receiver appointed under the terms of the charge, because such realisations are not dispositions of company property within the meaning of the section. The "disposition" of which the realisations form part occurred with the original grant of security by the company.[2] This is a matter which we shall return to in Chapter 11.

3. Receiver exceeding his powers

Effect on outsiders

4-43 In spite of the breadth of the powers conferred on an administrative receiver, they can, of course, be exceeded. What effect would this have on an outsider dealing with the company? One way in which this problem might arise is where the initial appointment of the receiver turns out to be invalid. Section 232 of the Insolvency Act 1986 offers relief, by providing that the acts of an "office holder" (which includes an administrative receiver) shall be valid notwithstanding any defect in his appointment, nomination or qualifications. Where a properly appointed receiver simply exceeds his powers, the outsider has the protection of section 42(3) of the Insolvency Act 1986, which states that a person dealing with an administrative receiver in good faith and for value is entitled to assume that the receiver was acting within the ambit of his powers. Outsiders would probably also be protected by the established common law rules.[3]

DUTIES OF AN ADMINISTRATIVE RECEIVER

1. The common law

Complex position

4-44 An administrative receiver occupies a most complicated position in legal terms. He will be acting on behalf of his debenture holder yet technically will be installed as the agent of the company. While his prime concern must be to further the interests of his debenture holder, it now seems clear that he may owe certain responsibilities to the company as his principal. This conundrum was explained as follows by Hoffmann J. in *Gomba Holdings Ltd v. Homan*:[4]

---

[99] *Gough's Garages v. Pugsley* [1930] 1 K.B. 615.
[1] [1978] 1 W.L.R. 22. See also *Barrows v. Chief Land Registrar, The Times*, October 20, 1977.
[2] See also *Re Margart Pty Ltd* [1985] B.C.L.C. 314.
[3] See *Freeman & Lockyer v. Buckhurst Park Properties Ltd* [1964] 2 Q.B. 480.
[4] [1986] 1 W.L.R. 1301 at 1305.

> "A receiver is an agent of the company and an agent ordinarily has a duty to be ready with his accounts, and to provide his principal with information relating to the conduct of his agency. But these generalisations are of limited assistance because a receiver and manager is no ordinary agent. Although nominally the agent of the company, his primary duty is to realise the assets in the interests of the debenture holder, and his powers of management are really ancillary to that duty."

Bearing this comment in mind, how does the law cope with these tensions?

Agency relationship

4-45 It is standard practice for the debenture under which a receiver was appointed to provide that he will act as the company's agent.[5] This is no longer strictly necessary, as such an agency relationship is now implied by virtue of section 44(1)(*a*) of the Insolvency Act 1986. The statutory presumption of agency is rebuttable.[6] The agency is a legal fiction the purpose of which is to insulate the debenture holder from any contractual liabilities incurred[7] and the consequences of any wrongful acts committed by the receiver.[8] On the other hand, it does impose certain duties on the receiver, *vis-à-vis* the company. The full range of fiduciary duties normally expected to be fulfilled by an agent does not apply. Thus there is clearly no obligation to obey his principal,[9] the company, but he may be under a duty not to injure his principal's interests by failing to take reasonable care in the discharge of his functions.[10] This point was confirmed by the Court of Appeal in *Standard Chartered Bank Ltd v. Walker*,[11] where it was held in principle that if a receiver conducts a negligent sale of company property, he can be forced to compensate the company for any loss caused. Lord Denning M.R. declared:[12]

> "He owes a duty to use reasonable care to obtain the best possible price which the circumstances of the case permit."

This duty of care was subsequently extended by Mann J. in *American Express v. Hurley*[13] to cover guarantors of the company's debts. In *Knight v. Lawrence*,[14] a case involving a Law of Property Act receiver, Browne-Wilkinson V.-C. held that a receiver was in effect the custodian of the charged property, and must take reasonable care to ensure that its value is not diminished. Here, failure to serve rent review

---

[5] See *Milman* (1981) 44 M.L.R. 658.
[6] On this point, see *Inverness District Council v. Highland Universal Fabricators* 1986 S.L.T. 556.
[7] See *Cully v. Parsons* [1923] 2 Ch. 512.
[8] See *Re Simms* [1934] Ch. 1. In *Re John Willment (Ashford) Ltd* [1979] 2 All E.R. 615 it was stated that the company would be liable for breaches of VAT regulations committed by the receiver. See also *Jarvis v. Islington B.C.* (1909) 73 J.P. 323.
[9] See *Meigh v. Wickenden* [1942] 2 K.B. 160.
[10] This duty (in relation to sales) has been placed on a statutory basis in New Zealand by section 19 of the Receiverships Act 1993. See also s.316A of the Irish Companies Act 1963.
[11] [1982] 1 W.L.R. 1410.
[12] *ibid.*, at 1416. See also *Lambert Jones Estates Ltd* (1982) unreported but discussed by Tomkin in (1982–4) 3 C.L.D. 4.
[13] [1985] 3 All E.R. 564. See also *McGowan v. Gannon* [1983] I.L.R.M. 516 and Rule 3.32(4) of the Insolvency Rules 1986. The conflicting decision in *Latchford v. Beirne* [1981] 3 All E.R. 705 has now been overruled. See also *Routestone Ltd v. Minories Finance Ltd* [1997] B.C.C. 180.
[14] [1991] B.C.C. 41.

notices was held to be negligent because an opportunity had been missed to improve the income derived from the property.

Negligence liability: the renewed debate

4-46 Cases imposing liability on receivers for pure negligence took something of a blow in the Privy Council case of *Downsview Nominees Ltd v. First City Corporation Ltd.*[15] In that case it was held that a receiver owed no duty to a mortgagor or subsequent encumbrancer to use reasonable care in the exercise of his powers under a debenture. He had only the equitable duty to act in good faith, owed to those having an interest in the equity of redemption. This odd ruling seemed to owe more to general trends in the law of negligence, including the much criticised decision in *Caparo Industries v. Dickman*,[16] than to the requirements of modern receivership law. It was regrettable to say the least that the cases cited above were not fully considered by the Privy Council and hardly surprising that the case has been subject to fierce criticism not merely by academics but also by judges in *ex cathedra* pronouncements.

4-47 It is perhaps worth bearing in mind the actual result in *Downsview (supra)*, in which the receivers were held liable for breach of their duty of good faith in failing to accept an offer by second debenture holders to pay off the first debenture under which they were appointed. However, in any event in the case of *Douglas Medforth v. Peter Blake et alia*[17] the Court of Appeal seems to have made a large step towards realigning English law with the trend in other jurisdictions towards imposing duties of reasonable care on receivers. In that case the question arose whether receivers of a pig farm, when carrying on the business, should have heeded the farmer's warnings about the importance of securing discounts on pig feed. The court robustly denied that receivers had no duty other than a duty of good faith, and held that there was a duty of care. A flexible duty, including but not limited to the duty of good faith, was owed to anybody with an interest in the equity of redemption. The scope of that duty depended on the circumstances, but did not oblige the receiver to carry on the business.[18] If he did carry on the business, he had to take reasonable steps to do so profitably.

Duty to render accounts

4-48 Similar problems involving the balancing of a receiver's *de jure* and *de facto* responsibilities have arisen with regard to his duty to render accounts. In *Smiths Ltd v. Middleton*,[19] Blackett-Ord V.-C. held that the receiver was subject to the agent's

---

[15] [1993] 2 W.L.R. 86. For analysis see Berg [1993] J.B.L. 2 and Hogan (1996) 17 Co. Law 226. *Downsview* has many eminent detractors—Lightman (1996) 16 Insolvency Lawyer 2, Goode, *Modern Principles of Corporate Insolvency Law* (2nd ed., 1997) at 242 and Arden in Patfield (ed.) *Perspectives on Company Law I* (1995) at 159. For rare support see Rajak (1997) 21 *Insolvency Lawyer* 7.

[16] [1990] 2 AC 605—this much criticised ruling appears to exempt auditors from the full extent of liability to third parties in the event of a negligently conducted audit. Undoubtedly a policy decision, it has been the subject of much debate. A more relevant platform for the Privy Council ruling in *Downsview* was *Re B Johnson & Co (Builders) Ltd* [1955] Ch. 634, but that case was decided prior to developments in modern professional negligence law and for that reason its authority is open to question.

[17] [1999] B.C.C. 771.

[18] See here *Kernohan Estates v. Boyd* [1967] N.I. 27, *Re Northern Developments Holdings Ltd* (1978) 128 N.L.J. 86, *Consolidated Traders Ltd* v. Downes [1981] 2 N.Z.L.R. 247 and *AIB Finance v. Debtors* [1998] B.P.I.R. 533.

[19] [1979] 3 All E.R. 842.

duty to render true accounts to his principal despite the existence of the statutory regime relating to the provision of information about the conduct of the receivership. This was reinforced by Hoffmann J. in *Gomba Holdings Ltd v. Homan*:[20]

> "It has been suggested that these provisions are exhaustive of a receiver's obligations to provide accounts or other information but I do not think that this can be right. For one thing, there can be no doubt that a receiver under a fixed charge is under an equitable duty to account to the mortgagor. . . . If this is correct in the case of receivers under fixed charges, it is hard to see why Parliament should have taken a different view of receivers under floating charges."

4-49 However, Hoffmann J. qualified the duty by holding that a receiver does not have to disclose information that might harm the interests of the debenture holder on whose behalf he is acting:[21]

> "If the receiver considers that disclosure of information would be contrary to the interests of the debenture holder in realising the security, I think he must be entitled to withhold it and probably owes a duty to the debenture holder to do so. The company may be able to challenge the receiver's decision on the grounds of bad faith or possibly that it was a decision which no reasonable receiver could have made, but otherwise I think that the receiver is the best judge of the commercial consequences of disclosing information about his activities."

The key question is whether the company can establish a "need to know". This will obviously depend upon the precise circumstances of each individual case, though it might be present where the company is in a position to redeem the security.[22]

Not officer of court

4-50 One further complication in this arena of conflicting interests has fortunately been avoided. It now seems clear that the acts of an administrative receiver will only be judged by the standards of commercial, rather than any other, morality. A receiver appointed out of court is not regarded as an officer of the court and therefore will not be subject to the duty to act honourably, imposed by the rule in *Ex p. James*.[23]

2. Statutory duties

4-51 There are superimposed upon this matrix of common law duties owed by a receiver an increasingly large number of statutory obligations. For instance, it follows from section 40 of the Insolvency Act 1986, and authorities culminating in *I.R.C. v. Goldblatt*,[24] that a receiver, appointed to enforce a floating charge (but not

---

[20] [1986] 1 W.L.R. 1301 at 1305.

[21] [1986] 1 W.L.R. 1301 at 1307. See also *Irish Oil & Cake Mills v. Donnelly* (1984) unreported but discussed by Tomkin in (1982–4) 3 C.L.D. 4.

[22] See [1986] 1 W.L.R. 1301 at 1308 *per* Hoffmann J.

[23] (1874) L.R. 9 Ch. App. 609. A court appointed receiver will be regarded as an officer of the court—*Toronto-Dominion Bank v. Fortin (No. 2)* (1978) 88 D.L.R. (3d) 232.

[24] [1972] Ch. 498. See also *Woods v. Winskill* [1913] 2 Ch. 303 and *Westminster C.C. v. Haste* [1950] Ch. 442. A receiver of an industrial and provident society is under no such duty—*Re Devon and Somerset Farmers Ltd* [1993] B.C.C. 410.

a fixed security),[25] is under a positive obligation to ensure that the statutory preferential claims regime is correctly applied. Where receivership and liquidation coincide the receiver has the primary duty of settling preferential claims.[26] Indeed in *Re Pearl Maintenance Services Ltd*[27] the court emphasised that it was not permissible for a receiver to defer the payment of preferential claims and to leave this chore to a later liquidator. By way of contrast section 11(5) of the Insolvency Act 1986 stresses that where an administrative receiver has been replaced by an administrator he is excused the duty to settle preferential claims.

4-52 The practices adopted by receivers in dealing with preferential claims have attracted criticism from the National Audit Office. In a report[28] that was published in 1996 the National Audit Office noted that some receivers were adept at artificially stretching the scope of the fixed charge element in the security so as to frustrate preferential claims and to deprive the public exchequer of recoveries. Another common abuse was to treat realisation costs as being largely attributable to the floating charge element of the security, thereby reducing the amount of funds from which preferential claims could be discharged. In the light of these criticisms the Society of Practitioners of Insolvency has produced a new Statement of Insolvency Practice (SIP 14) to remind practitioners of their responsibilities.

A full consideration of the law on preferential claims will be undertaken in Chapter 8.

Duty to furnish information

4-53 The Insolvency Act 1986 and the Insolvency Rules 1986 have made a considerable number of modifications to the administrative receiver's duty to furnish information about the progress of the receivership. The administrative receiver's duty to furnish annual accounts to the Companies Registry, the company, his appointor, and the creditors' committee is now set forth in rule 3.32 of the Insolvency Rules 1986.[29]

Information prejudicial to the receivership

4-54 Section 48 requires the receiver to prepare a report within three months after he has received the statement of affairs submitted by company officers under section 47. By section 48 the report must deal with what he knows of the events leading up to his appointment, what he has done and intends to do about disposing of the company's property, and carrying on its business, the state of the account with the debenture holder, the amounts due to preferential creditors and the prospects for other creditors. It must contain a summary of the directors' statement of affairs, but the receiver is permitted by section 48(6) to exclude information the disclosure of which would seriously prejudice the conduct of the receivership. A copy of the receiver's report and the summary must be sent to the Companies Registry together with a copy of the directors' statement of affairs.[30] If the latter contains information

---

[25] *Re G.L. Saunders Ltd* [1986] 1 W.L.R. 215.
[26] *Manley, Petitioner* 1985 S.L.T. 42. See also *Re Eisc Teo Ltd* [1991] I.L.R.M. 760.
[27] [1995] 1 B.C.L.C. 449.
[28] HCP 1995–96 No. 695 (October 17, 1996). Note also House of Commons Public Accounts Committee (18th Report). See Keay and Walton [1999] *Insolvency Lawyer* 112.
[29] See also Form 3.6 here. For the position with regard to an ordinary receiver, see Insolvency Act 1986, s.38.
[30] r. 3.8(3).

prejudicial to the conduct of the receivership, a court order can be obtained under rule 3.5 to exclude that information from disclosure. Copies of the report (but not the statement of affairs) must also be sent to the debenture holders, the liquidator (if there is one) and all known unsecured creditors. As an alternative to sending the report to unsecured creditors, the receiver can advertise the place from which copies of it may be obtained free of charge.[31]

Unsecured creditors

4-55 Unless the court orders otherwise, the administrative receiver must also summon a meeting of unsecured creditors to consider his report.[32] The procedure is spelled out by the Insolvency Rules 1986.[33] Creditors' votes at the meeting are weighted according to the value of their debts. The unsecured creditors may decide at this meeting to establish a committee, in which case the administrative receiver must comply with reasonable requests for information from it. The committee[34] has a statutory duty to help the receiver and is to consist of between three and five creditors, with a quorum of two. The administrative receiver must file details of the committee and of any changes in it at the Companies Registry. The receiver determines when committee meetings are to be held, though the first must be summoned within three months of the establishment of the committee. Committee decisions are made by simple majority. The receiver can obtain decisions of the committee by post without calling a meeting, but in such a case a committee member may require a meeting to be called. An interesting provision in the rules dealing with the committee is rule 3.30, which provides as follows:

> "(1) Membership of the committee does not prevent a person from dealing with the company while the receiver is acting, provided that any transactions in the course of such dealings are entered into in good faith and for value.
>
> (2) The court may, on the application of any person interested set aside a transaction which appears to it to be contrary to the requirements of this Rule, and may give such consequential directions as it thinks fit for compensating the company for any loss which it may have incurred in consequence of the transation."

This rule contrasts sharply with the position of members of a liquidation committee, who are precluded from obtaining any benefit out of the assets unless the transaction is approved by the court or sanctioned by the committee.[35] This is understandable in that it is very much more common for a receiver than for a liquidator to carry on the company's business, and this often involves dealings with those who supplied the company before receivership.

---

[31] s.48(2)(*b*).
[32] s.48(2).
[33] rr. 3.9–3.15. Rule 3.13 has been deleted.
[34] r. 3.18. For the law on the creditors' committee generally, see Insolvency Rules 1986, rr 3.16–3.30 (as amended).
[35] r. 4.170.

Other legal responsibilities

4-56 Looking further afield, receivers are subject to wider statutory responsibilities. Thus, if they assume the running of the company's business, they may incur liability under the Factories Acts,[36] the Health and Safety at Work Act 1974, Environmental Protection Act 1990 and Employment Rights Act 1996.[37] They are also obliged to operate the system of VAT bad debt relief by issuing certificates of insolvency and notifying creditors.[38]

4-57 One further obligation imposed by the new insolvency regime deserves special mention. Under section 7(3) of the Company Directors Disqualification Act 1986, administrative receivers are obliged to report to the Secretary of State the names of directors of insolvent companies who appear unfit. This matter is considered fully in Chapter 13.

Enforcement

4-58 The receiver's duties can be enforced in a variety of ways. The statutory obligations are normally reinforced with criminal sanctions in the form of fines, and default fines. The common law duties can be enforced by the appropriate types of action in the ordinary courts, usually the Chancery Division of the High Court.

4-59 It was confirmed in 1985 by Peter Gibson J. in *Watts v. Midland Bank plc*[39] that the company can bring a direct action against the receiver. The learned judge reasoned:[40]

> "There is no doubt that a mortgagor can sue a mortgagee improperly exercising a power of sale. Why should not a mortgagor company in receivership sue the receiver appointed by the mortgagee to realise the security so as to repay the mortgagee if the receiver acts improperly and to the detriment of the company? Of course the court will not allow any interference by a company in receivership with the proper exercise by a receiver of a power of sale, but I can see no reason in principle why the court should not allow the company to sue the receiver in respect of an improper exercise of his powers."

Having said that, it must be stressed that the duties of a receiver are owed to the company over whose undertaking he has been appointed. It is the company that has the legal interest in the equity of redemption. Thus in *Burgess v. Auger*[41] Lightman J. was at pains to point out that it was not possible for a person claiming through a company (for example a director, shareholder, employee or guarantor) to bring a direct action against a receiver. In a sense this is merely a reflection of the principle of separate corporate personality.

4-60 Where the company has gone into liquidation it is now possible to exploit the summary misfeasance procedure prescribed by section 212 of the Insolvency Act

---

[36] *Meigh v. Wickenden* [1942] 2 K.B. 160.
[37] See *GMB v. Rankin* [1992] I.R.L.R. 514.
[38] See Insolvency Rules 1986, rr. 3.36–3.38. Note receivers are not liable for unpaid VAT—*Sargent v. Customs and Excise* [1995] 2 B.C.L.C. 34—however, if VAT is collected it must be forwarded to the Customs and Excise.
[39] [1986] B.C.L.C. 15.
[40] *ibid.*, at 22.
[41] [1998] 2 B.C.L.C. 478.

1986 against an administrative receiver.[42] It would appear to follow from the decision of the Divisional Court in *R. v. Board of Trade, ex p. St. Martin's Preserving Co. Ltd*[43] that a D.T.I. investigation of the conduct of the receiver is technically possible. Apart from these established legal procedures, a receiver may be subject to disciplinary proceedings by the appropriate professional body or the withdrawal of his qualification as an insolvency practitioner.

THE CONCLUSION OF THE RECEIVERSHIP

Normal method

4-61 The receivership can come to an end in a variety of ways. The normal scenario is where the receiver has realised all available assets covered by the debenture and has made all possible distributions to interested parties in the priority sequence determined by law. Immediate notification must be given to the company and the creditors' committee.[44] If the receiver has surplus funds in hand, he must return them to the company. In *Re G. L. Saunders Ltd*,[45] Nourse J. indicated that any surplus left in the hands of a receiver appointed under the Law of Property Act 1925 to realise a fixed charge must be handed back to the company or its liquidator and not distributed to the preferential creditors. They were only the concern of a receiver appointed to enforce a floating charge.

Resignation

4-62 However, the receiver can terminate the receivership in other ways. Firstly, he may decide to resign his office. Certain formalities are required here in the case of resignation by an administrative receiver. Notice must be given within two weeks to the Companies Registry.[46] The Insolvency Rules 1986 also require at least 7 days of notice of intention to resign to be given to the appointor, the company, any liquidator and creditors' committee, where appropriate.[47] An administrative receiver will also have to vacate office if he loses his qualification as an insolvency practitioner or where an administrator has been appointed by the court.[48] In the latter case, special provision is made by section 11(4) of the Insolvency Act 1986 to protect the administrative receiver's entitlement to remuneration and expenses.

Removal

4-63 Removal is obviously a more contentious matter. Prior to the Insolvency Act 1986 a debenture holder could remove his receiver without recourse to the court provided the debenture or the instrument of his appointment allowed this. As a last resort, recourse to the court was possible.[49] However, as a result of section 45(1) of

---

[42] Thus the decision in *Re B. Johnson & Co. (Builders) Ltd* [1955] Ch. 634 is not longer good law on this point.

[43] [1965] 1 Q.B. 603.

[44] Insolvency Rules 1986, r. 3.35 (as amended).

[45] [1986] 1 W.L.R. 215.

[46] Insolvency Act 1986, s.45(4).

[47] Insolvency Rules 1986, r. 3.33 (as amended).

[48] The relevant provisions here are ss.45(2) and 11(1)(*b*) of the Insolvency Act 1986 respectively.

[49] *Re Slogger Automatic Feeder Co. Ltd* [1915] 1 Ch. 478. See also *Re Maskelyne British Typewriter Ltd* [1898] 1 Ch. 133.

the Insolvency Act 1986, removal can now only be effected by successful application to the court. The aim of this reform is to make an administrative receiver independent, and less the creature of the debenture holder who appointed him. Clearly, the debenture holder will have to produce compelling reasons for the removal, and it may be that the authorities on removal of liquidators by the court will provide some guidance.[50] It should be noted that although the court can remove an administrative receiver it has no power of replacement.[51]

4-64 Where the company goes into liquidation the court might be faced with a request from the unsecured creditors that the receiver be displaced and that his task be carried out by the liquidator.[52] In the normal course of events, the court will not accede to such a request but will respect the debenture holder's contractual right to have the task of realisation carried out by his own appointee.[53]

4-65 Whenever and however a receivership has been terminated, the receiver must give notice to the Companies Registry within 14 days of his departure.[54]

---

[50] See Chap. 2 here.
[51] *Re A & C Suppliers Ltd* [1998] B.P.I.R. 303.
[52] See *Re Chic Ltd* [1905] 2 Ch. 345.
[53] *Re Joshua Stubbs Ltd* [1918] 1 Ch. 475.
[54] Insolvency Act 1986, s.45(4). See also Companies Act 1985, s.405(2).

CHAPTER 5

Voluntary Liquidations

TYPES OF VOLUNTARY LIQUIDATION

5-01 In the context of insolvency law, the term voluntary liquidation is misleading.[1] Generally, the voluntary liquidation of an insolvent company is about as much an act of free will as a resignation extracted from a person faced with dismissal.

5-02 Voluntary liquidations fall into two categories. If the company is solvent, there is a true voluntary liquidation, which is technically called a members' voluntary winding-up. If the company is insolvent, the liquidation is correctly called a creditors' voluntary winding-up. Unfortunately this distinction disguises the fact that both types of voluntary liquidation are actually initiated by the company's members, albeit for different reasons. The essential difference is that creditors can exert a degree of control in the case of a voluntary liquidation of an insolvent company. In 1997–98 there were 8121 creditors voluntary liquidations. The Cork Committee suggested[2] that the voluntary liquidation of an insolvent company should be termed a "liquidation of assets," but this recommendation was never implemented.

Declaration of solvency

5-03 Section 90 of the Insolvency Act 1986 provides that a winding-up is a members' voluntary liquidation if the directors have made a statutory declaration of solvency under section 89, but that if not it is a creditors' voluntary liquidation. In a declaration of solvency the company's directors (either unanimously or by majority decision) must vouch that they have made a full enquiry into the company's affairs and, as a result of this, have concluded that the company will be able to pay its debts (including interest) in full within a maximum period of 12 months. This declaration, supported with a statement of the company's assets and liabilities, must be made within the five weeks immediately preceding the day on which the resolution for voluntary liquidation was passed. It can be made at the meeting in question provided it is done before the resolution. The declaration must be registered at the Companies Registry within 15 days of the resolution.

5-04 Directors who negligently make a false declaration of solvency are committing a criminal offence and, moreover, the burden of proof is on them to disprove lack of care if the company eventually turns out to be insolvent.

Inaccurate declaration

5-05 The consequences of an inaccurate declaration of solvency were considered in *De Courcy v. Clements*.[3] Here, it was held that errors in the declaration do not

---

[1] See Cork Report (Cmnd. 8558) Chap. 13.
[2] *op. cit.*
[3] [1971] Ch. 693.

invalidate it and thereby convert a members' voluntary liquidation into a creditors' voluntary liquidation, where it is clear that the declaration overall presents a fair picture and the company is solvent. Megarry J. declared:[4]

> "There must be something which can be reasonably and fairly described as a statement of the company's assets and liabilities; but if there is, then even if it subsequently appears that there are errors and omissions, that will not prevent the statement from being a statement within the subsection. I do not think that I ought to impute to Parliament an intention to require perfection in a provision which contains no words to indicate this super-human standard."

If the error turns out to tip the balance in favour of insolvency, it will be up to the liquidator to convert the winding-up into a creditors' voluntary liquidation by using the procedure described in sections 95, 96 and 102 of the Insolvency Act 1986.

Creditors' meeting

5-06 Section 95 states that the liquidator must call a creditors' meeting within 28 days of his forming the opinion that the company is insolvent.[5] The creditors must be informed by personal notices and newspaper advertisements. Creditors must be furnished with any information which they may reasonably require. The liquidator is obliged to lay a statement of affairs before the creditors' meeting.[6] Section 102 emphasises that the creditors' meeting may appoint a liquidator and establish a committee,[7] as would normally occur under section 98. From the date of the creditors' meeting, according to section 96, the Act applies as if the liquidation had always been a creditors' voluntary winding-up.

INITIATION OF A CREDITORS' VOLUNTARY LIQUIDATION

5-07 This has proved a vexed area of law in recent years. The basic procedure laid down by section 84 is that the company's members can either pass a special resolution in favour of voluntary liquidation, or, more usually, pass an extraordinary resolution on the grounds that "it cannot by reason of its liabilities continue its business, and that it is advisable to wind up." The majority required for both species of resolution is three quarters of those present and voting, but, of course, an extraordinarily resolution can be promoted with greater urgency.[8] The company must, by virtue of section 85, advertise the resolution in the Gazette within 14 days or else criminal sanctions may be imposed on its officers, including its liquidator. Section 86 states that a voluntary liquidation is deemed to commence at the date of the resolution.

"Centrebinding"

5-08 The real problem in this area has been the need to ensure that creditors are involved in the liquidation from an early stage. There have been provisions included

[4] *ibid.*, at 698–9.
[5] See Insolvency Rules 1986, rr. 4.54 and 4.56.
[6] Note r. 4.34, *ibid.*
[7] See *ibid.*, 4.51 (as amended) and 4.53.
[8] Companies Act 1985, s.378.

in successive Companies Acts with this aim in mind, but these were dealt a severe blow in *Re Centrebind Ltd*,[9] where Plowman J. held that failure to comply with the specified procedure did not invalidate the proceedings. This case was quickly exploited and the practice known as "Centrebinding" became widespread. Typically, the company would be placed into voluntary liquidation without notice being given to creditors or anyone else. By the time a creditors' meeting was held, the creditors would often discover that the whole of the company's saleable assets had been sold at an undervalue to a new company, often with a very similar name, common directors and carrying on practically the same business as the old company but without its liabilities. Some refinements of this play are discussed in Chapter 10.

5-09 The Companies Act 1981 made further amendments in the hope of plugging the gaps but these reforms were immediately neutralised by the much criticised decision of Judge Finlay Q.C. in *Saxton & Son v. Miles (Confectioners) Ltd.*[10] The latest attempts at solving this problem is to be found in sections 98, 99, 114 and 166 of the Insolvency Act 1986.

Statutory requirements

5-10 Under section 98 of the Insolvency Act 1986, the company must call a creditors' meeting for a date within 14 days of the meeting at which the resolution for voluntary liquidation is to be proposed.[11] Notices must be posted to creditors, giving them at least seven days warning. The notice of the creditors' meeting has to be advertised in the Gazette, and in two local newspapers. The advertisement must state the name of the insolvency practitioner who is qualified to act in relation to the company as its voluntary liquidator, and must disclose the location where a list of creditors can be consulted.

Key provision

5-11 Section 99 obliges the directors to prepare a statement of affairs in the prescribed form and to lay it before the meeting of creditors. (See also rr. 4.34, 4.34A and 4.38.) The directors must nominate one of themselves to attend the meeting of creditors and to preside over it. Criminal penalties may be imposed on directors who fail to fulfil these obligations. However, in *Re Salcombe Hotel Development Co. Ltd*[12] it was held that failure by the nominated director/chairman to attend the meeting did not invalidate the proceedings, which had been conducted under the chairmanship of a fresh nominee.

5-12 The key provision which it is hoped will curb Centrebinding in the future is section 166. This prevents a liquidator, as a general rule, from exercising any of his powers under section 156 (*e.g.* to dispose of the company's property without the leave of the court) until the creditors' meeting required by section 98 has been held. Exceptions are provided to enable him to take control of or protect assets and to sell perishables. Basically, the effect of this provision is to make the liquidator merely a provisional liquidator, until the creditors' have had an opportunity to express their views. Section 166 also provides that the liquidator must attend the creditors'

---

[9] [1967] 1 W.L.R. 377.
[10] [1983] 1 W.L.R. 952.
[11] Insolvency Rules 1986, rr. 4.51 (as amended), 4.53 and 4.62 relevant here.
[12] [1991] B.C.L.C. 44.

meeting and inform them of any exercise of powers by him, or of any applications made to the court under section 112. The liquidator is further obliged to ensure that the company and its directors comply with their duties under section 98. In the event of them failing in this respect, he must apply to the court within seven days to rectify the matter.

APPOINTMENT OF THE LIQUIDATOR

5-12 The purpose of the creditors' meeting summoned under section 98 is to give them the opportunity of a say in the appointment of the liquidator. The procedure is outlined by section 100 and supplemented by the Insolvency Rules 1986. These provide that the members can nominate a liquidator at their meeting, whilst the creditors can select their nominee at their own section 98 meeting. In the event of the members and creditors choosing a different person, the creditors' choice will prevail. However, this is subject to the requirement that the creditors' appointment was procedurally regular.[13] The company is entitled to challenge the creditors' choice by applying to the court within seven days.[14] These provisions are reinforced by section 114, which freezes the powers of the directors (except for emergency purposes) pending the proper appointment of a liquidator.[15]

Appointment "from the floor"

5-13 Insolvency practitioners commonly offer a service to their commercial clients of attending on their behalf at creditors' meetings of their insolvent debtors and reporting on the proceedings free of charge. Professionals in the field, usually representatives of the larger accountancy firms, are well known to each other, and commonly discussions take place before the meeting to find out which of them commands the most voting power, now measured by value of debt under rule 4.63(1). By arrangement, some of the professionals attend the creditors' meeting, and frequently one of them proposes the appointment of one of the others, either as liquidator in place of the members' nominee, or, more commonly nowadays, as joint liquidator. The proposal often follows lengthy and expert cross examination of the chairman director, and usually commands the support not only of the professionals, but the creditors present. The question then remains whether the chairman holds or claims to hold sufficient proxies from creditors to outvote those present, and, if so, whether he will seek to use them against the clearly expressed will of the meeting. Note that votes at creditors' meetings are now determined by value of debt only, (see r. 4.63) rather than number and value, as was formerly the case. It was galling to creditors for see their nominee defeated by large numbers of proxies for small amounts from employees.

Appointment as liquidator

5-14 However, insolvency practitioners hoping to be appointed liquidators on the strength of their clients' debts still have a delicate path to tread. Rule 4.63(4) pre-

---

[13] See *Re Caston Cushioning Ltd* [1995] 1 All E.R. 508.
[14] See Insolvency Rules 1986, r. 4.103, and also s.100(3) of the Act.
[15] But see here *Re A Company (006341 of 1992) ex p. B Ltd* [1994] B.C.L.C. 225.

vents a person from using his votes (including votes he holds as a general proxy) in favour of his own, or his partner or employee's, appointment. The rule does not apply to a special proxy directing him to vote in his own favour. But if he solicits special proxies, or arranges for his client (or some other proxy for him) to attend and support him, he must beware of rule 4.150. This gives the court power to disallow the remuneration of a liquidator who has procured his appointment by improper solicitation.

5-15 Any person chosen to act as a liquidator in a creditors' voluntary winding-up must under rule 4.101 being a qualified insolvency practitioner. There is no objection to the appointment of joint liquidators. The court has power to appoint an additional liquidator to assist a sole liquidator.[16] Once appointed, he must advertise his appointment in the Gazette, and notify the Companies Registry within 14 days.

Consequences of liquidation

5-16 It is important to appreciate the consequence of the company entering into voluntary liquidation. It is emphasised by section 103 that the powers of the directors cease. However, the directors and other employees are not automatically dismissed.[17] Section 87(2) states that the corporate state and powers of the company continue right up to the time of the dissolution. An instructive authority to note here is *Fargo Ltd v. Godfroy*.[18] In this case, Walton J. held that a minority shareholder's right to bring a derivative action on behalf of his company under one of the exceptions to the rule in *Foss v. Harbottle*[19] terminates once the company goes into voluntary liquidation:[20]

> "But once the company goes into liquidation, the situation is completely changed, because one no longer has a board, or indeed a shareholders' meeting, which in any sense is in control of the activities of the company of any description, let alone its litigation. Here, what has happened is that the liquidator is now the person in whom that right is vested."

The minority shareholder must therefore wait to see if the liquidator is prepared to prosecute the action. He may well only do so if the shareholder is prepared to offer an indemnity against costs. Where the liquidator refuses to act, the shareholder can apply to the court to overrule him and it would also appear that in proper cases a misfeasance claim could be instituted.

THE POWERS OF THE LIQUIDATOR

Sanction required

5-17 These are governed by a combination of sections 165 and Schedule 4 of the Insolvency Act 1986. The drafting of the legislation leaves something to be desired,

---

[16] *Re Sunlight Incandescent Ltd* [1906] 2 Ch. 728.

[17] See *Fowler v. Commercial Timber Co. Ltd* [1930] 2 K.B. 1, *Gerard v. Worth of Paris* [1936] 2 All E.R. 905.

[18] [1986] 3 All E.R. 279.

[19] (1843) 2 Hare 461.

[20] [1986] 3 All E.R. 279 at 281. But the company retains the right to receive bequests—*Re ARMS (Multiple Sclerosis) Research*, *The Times*, November 29, 1996.

but the position appears to be as follows. The liquidator can exercise the first three powers listed immediately below, provided he first obtains the sanction of the liquidation committee, though unauthorised actions may be ratified subsequently. It is stressed by rule 4.184 of the Insolvency Rules 1986 that the permission given by the committee must be specific and not general in nature.

1. To pay any class of creditors in full.
2. To make compromises or arrangements with creditors or alleged creditors.[21]
3. To compromise calls, debts, potential debts, claims and any question relating to the assets or the winding up of the company. Security may be taken for the discharge of any of the above items. It is believed that this power extends to the quantum of claims (*e.g.* unliquidated claims for damages, claims subject to unliquidated counterclaims, and so on). However there is authority to suggest that if a compromise would result in the alteration of the rights of a creditor *vis-à-vis* other creditors, the liquidator should normally apply to the court under section 425 of the Companies Act 1985.[22] Possibly an application under section 112 of the Insolvency Act 1986 would be a prudent first step.

No sanction required

5-18 No sanction is required to enable a liquidator to exercise the following powers.

4. To bring or defend any action or legal proceedings in the name of and on behalf of the company.
5. To carry on the business of the company insofar as it may be necessary for its beneficial winding up. It would appear from *Hire Purchase Co. v. Richens*[23] that the onus here is on a person objecting to the exercise of this power to show that it was not beneficial for the winding up.
6. To sell and transfer any of the company's property by public auction or private contract.
7. To do all acts and execute all deeds on behalf of the company and to use the company's seal.
8. To prove in the insolvency of any contributory and to receiver dividends in that insolvency.
9. To deal with bills of exchange on behalf of the company.
10. To borrow against the security of the company's assets.
11. To take out, in his official name, letters of administration to the estate of any deceased contributory.

---

[21] See *Re BCCI S.A. (No. 2)* [1992] B.C.C. 715—a formal reconstruction under s.425 of the Companies Act 1985 is not always required. Indeed a C.V.A. is also available—see Insolvency Act 1986, s.1(3)(*b*).

[22] This was the conclusion of the court in *Re Trix Ltd* [1970] 1 W.L.R. 1421. But compare *Re BCCI S.A. (No. 2)* [1992] B.C.C. 715.

[23] (1887) 20 Q.B.D. 387.

12. To appoint an agent to perform any business which he is unable to conduct himself.[24]

13. To do all such other things as may be necessary for the winding up of the company's affairs and distribution of its assets.[25]

Enabling provisions

5-19 These general implied powers are supplemented by a number of specific statutory enabling provisions. Thus, the liquidator may apply to the court under section 112 for guidance on questions arising out of the winding up. This provision will be considered in more detail later. An application to the court may be made for the appointment of a special manager under section 177 of the Act.[26]

5-20 Certain powers of a more contentious nature will be discussed in later Chapters. Thus the liquidator may be able to set aside prior transactions at an undervalue or those amounting to preferences (see Chap. 11). He may be able to apply under section 214 of the Insolvency Act 1986 for an order that some directors or former directors make a contribution to the assets (see Chap. 12). He can obtain an order under section 236 for the examination of company officers, etc., to obtain the necessary information.

Power to disclaim onerous property

5-21 A most interesting specialised statutory power is to be found in sections 178–182 of the Insolvency Act 1986—*i.e.*, the power to disclaim onerous property.[27] This power is well established in company law and it may be exercised by all types of liquidator. Until the passing of the 1986 Act it was rarely used successfully, largely because the procedure was cumbersome and involved applications to the court for leave to disclaim.[28] The court was also keen to protect interested parties who would otherwise be injured if leave to disclaim was granted.[29] Furthermore, the range of disclaimable property was unduly restricted. The Cork Committee suggested[30] a number of reforms and many of these found their way into the Insolvency Act 1986.

5-22 The basic starting point is section 178(2), which provides:

> "(2) Subject as follows, the liquidator may, by the giving of the prescribed notice, disclaim any onerous property and may do so notwithstanding that he has taken possession of it, endeavoured to sell it, or otherwise exercised rights of ownership in relation to it."

---

[24] This does not permit a wholesale delegation of duties—*Ah Toy v. Registrar of Companies* (1986) 10 A.C.L.R. 630. See also *Re Great Eastern Electric Co. Ltd* [1941] Ch. 241.

[25] A voluntary liquidator may also petition for compulsory liquidation—*Re Zoedone Co. Ltd* (1884) 49 L.T. 654.

[26] See Insolvency Rules 1986, Part 4, Chap. 18.

[27] See also Insolvency Rules 1986, rr. 4.178–4.194.

[28] For unsuccessful applications to disclaim see *Re Katherine et Cie* [1932] 1 Ch. 70, *Re Madely Homecare* [1983] N.I. 1, and *Re Potters Oil Co.* 1985 P.C.C. 148. Applications were successful in *Re Nottingham General Cemetery Co.* [1955] 2 All E.R. 504, *Tempany v. Royal Liver Trustees* [1984] B.C.L.C. 568, and *Re Distributors and Warehousing Ltd* [1986] B.C.L.C. 129.

[29] *Re Katherine et Cie (supra).*

[30] See Cmnd. 8558 paras. 1191 *et seq.*

The first change to note here is that it is no longer necessary for the liquidator to obtain the leave of the court before exercising his power of disclaimer.[31] In addition, the 12 month deadline for disclaimer has been dropped, in spite of a recommendation (para. 1195) from the Cork Committee that it be retained to prevent protracted uncertainty.

Disclaimable property

5-23 The property which may be disclaimed under this provision is defined by section 178(3), to include any unprofitable contract and any other property of the company which is unsaleable, or not readily saleable, or is such that it may give rise to a liability to pay money or perform any other onerous act.[32] There appears to be some change here, as compared to the position prior to 1985, in that the categories of disclaimable property have been widened. Thus, it is now sufficient if the property is simply unsaleable; it does not, in addition, have to be subject to any onerous requirement. Conversely property subject to onerous burdens may be disclaimed under the new provision, even if it is not actually unsaleable. Worthless leaseholds are obvious candidates for disclaimer.

Effect

5-24 The effect of disclaimer is described by section 178(4). It prospectively terminates the rights and liabilities of the company in the property disclaimed, but does not, over and above this, affect the rights and liabilities of any other person. A disclaimer is presumed to have been validly exercised unless the countrary is proved (rule 4.193). In *Re Hans Place Ltd*[33] the court made it clear that the prospects of a successful challenge to a liquidator's disclaimer were remote—as with the exercise of any other power, the production of evidence of lack of good faith would be necessary.

5-25 The House of Lords in *Hindcastle Ltd v. Barbara Attenborough Associates*[34] considered the impact of disclaimer upon third parties—*e.g.* a surety of a lease. An old established bankruptcy authority[35] indicated that a disclaimer would have the effect of releasing a surety or guarantor. However, when this matter was reviewed in *Hindcastle*[36] the House of Lords took the view that disclaimer should not release a surety or guarantor as that would defeat the whole purpose of a landlord taking such security on the grant of a lease. This modern approach to the consequences of dis-

[31] The notice of disclaimer must be filed in the court—Insolvency Rules 1986, r. 4.187. For further dissemination of the notice, see rr. 4.188–4.190.

[32] In *Environmental Agency v. Stout* [1998] B.P.I.R. 576 (sometimes reported as *Re Mineral Resources Ltd* [1999] 1 All E.R. 746) Neuberger J. concluded that a waste management licence could not be disclaimed by a liquidator. Although clearly falling within the concept of property, environmental policy concerns meant that the power of disclaimer was excluded from being exercised with regard to such a licence. This decision concerned insolvency practitioners greatly. The point was taken to the Court of Appeal which in *Official Receiver v. Environment Agency, The Times*, August 5, 1999, took the opposite view to Neuberger J. and concluded that such licences were disclaimable. The licence could be disclaimed without fear of offending under environmental legislation.

[33] [1992] B.C.C. 737.

[34] [1996] 2 W.L.R. 262.

[35] *Stacey v. Hill* [1910] 1 QB 660—this authority was questioned in *WH Smith Ltd v. Wyndham Investments Ltd* [1994] B.C.C. 699, rejected in Ireland in *Tempany v. Royal Liver Trustees Ltd* (1985) 1 B.C.C. 99,364 and finally overruled in *Hindcastle* (*supra*).

[36] *Supra*.

claimer has been welcomed by commentators because whilst retaining the effectiveness of disclaimer as an option it prevents it being used as an undeserved windfall by third parties.

Limit of the power

5-26 The power of the liquidator to disclaim property is curtailed by section 178(5), which provides that where an interested party has required the liquidator in writing to decide whether he intends to disclaim and the liquidator has within 28 days failed to give a notice of disclaimer, then the liquidator's right to disclaim is lost. This merely repeats the existing law.[37]

Leasehold land

5-27 Persons suffering loss or damage as a result of the liquidator exercising his statutory power of disclaimer can prove as creditors in the winding-up. The House of Lords has clarified the law governing the calculation of the loss of the landlord on a disclaimer with its ruling in *Re Park Air Services plc*.[38] Here it was held that although the landlord is to be compensated for his loss that compensation should take account of the fact that the landlord will in a sense be receiving accelerated payment and therefore the overall amount awarded should be discounted to reflect that fact.

5-28 If the property to be disclaimed is leasehold land then a special procedure outlined in section 179 must be followed. A copy of the notice of disclaimer must be served on every person claiming under the company as underlessee or mortgagee. The disclaimer will not take effect where such a person makes an application under section 181 (see below) within 14 days after the last copy of the disclaimer notice was served on him unless and until the court so orders. Special procedures must be followed in the case of land subject to rentcharges.

Role of Court

5-29 Section 181 is an important provision in that it allows the court a certain degree of control over disclaimers, even though of course its leave is no longer required to effect a disclaimer. Persons having an interest in the disclaimed property or who are subject to a liability not removed by the disclaimer may apply to the court for an order having the disclaimed property vested in them or delivered to them.[39] The court should only do this if it would be a just way of compensating them. Any such order is to be taken into account in assessing loss or damage provable under section 178(6). If the court concludes that the applicant has no such interest it will refuse to grant a vesting order.[40] Thus a vesting order was refused by the court in *Re Spirit Motorsport Ltd*.[41] In this particular instance directors of the company who had

---

[37] See *Boston House Property C. v. Ludgate Finance Co. Ltd* (1966) 110 S.J. 769.

[38] [1999] 2 W.L.R. 397. This was an unusual case in that the disclaimer was effected by a liquidator of a solvent company. There was therefore a real incentive for the landlord to maximise the amount of his unsecured claim.

[39] Insolvency Act 1986, s.181; Insolvency Rules 1986, r. 4.194. See *Re Vedmay Ltd* [1993] E.G.C.S. 167.

[40] On this see *Lloyds Bank SF Nominees v. Aladdin Ltd* [1996] 1 B.C.L.C. 720 and *Sterling Estates v. Pickard (U.K.) Ltd* [1998] B.P.I.R. 402 (reported *sub nom. Re ITM Corp. Ltd* in [1997] B.C.C. 544).

[41] [1996] 1 B.C.L.C. 684.

guaranteed its debts were refused a vesting order by Laddie J. because it could not be said that they had an interest in the disclaimed property.

5-30 Once again special provision is made for leasehold property. The court should not make a vesting order under section 181 in favour of an underlessee or mortgagee without making that person subject to the same obligations as those imposed on the company by the lease. Refusal to accept these obligations may result in his being debarred from all interest in the property. Fine tuning is provided for to deal with the case where only part of the leasehold property is made subject to a section 181 order.

CONTRACTS AND THE LIQUIDATOR

5-31 The position with regard to pre-liquidation contracts is clear. These remain enforceable against the company,[42] unless disclaimed, though not personally against the liquidator. However, the other party can apply to the court under section 186 of the Insolvency Act 1986 to have the contract rescinded. Compensatory payments can be ordered to be paid by either party. Sums ordered to be paid by the company are provable as winding-up debts. A voluntary liquidator may incur personal liability on such a contract if it can be shown that he has actually adopted it, as happened in *Re S. Davis & Co. Ltd.*[43]

5-32 For similar reasons it would appear that a voluntary liquidator is not personally responsible for contracts made by him on behalf of the company during liquidation. He is merely acting as the company's agent in this respect.[44] Thus the company is liable for debts incurred by the liquidator and creditors whose debts arise during this period are entitled to petition for the compulsory winding up of the company.[45]

VOLUNTARY LIQUIDATION AND CREDITOR CONTROL

5-33 It is the degree of control exercised by creditors that distinguishes a creditors' voluntary liquidation from a members' voluntary winding-up. How does this control manifest itself? First, of course, it is in theory the creditors who will have the dominant voice in the appointment of the liquidator. The procedural changes introduced by the Insolvency Act 1986 will reduce the possibility of this influence being pre-empted or neutralised. Creditors also enjoy the right under section 104 to fill casual vacancies in the office of liquidator.

Liquidation committee

5-34 The main instrument of creditor control will be the liquidation committee established under section 101 of the Act.[46] The maximum membership of this committee is fixed at five creditors, and five contributories, although the creditor members have the power under section 101(3) to veto all or any of the contributo-

42 *British Waggon Co. v. Lea & Co.* (1880) 5 Q.B.D. 149.
43 [1945] Ch. 402.
44 Unless the contract is under seal—*Plant (Engineers) Sales Ltd v. Davis* (1969) 113 S.J. 484.
45 *Re Bank of South Australia (No. 2)* [1895] 1 Ch. 578.
46 See also Insolvency Rules 1986, Part 4 Chap. 12.

ries from acting. The contributories have a right of appeal to the court. The quorum is stated to be two committee members.[47] Committee members can be removed by the creditors at large.[48] The liquidator must certify that the committee has been properly constituted before it can exercise any of its powers.

5-35 The liquidator is obliged under rule 4.155 of the Insolvency Rules 1986 to report all relevant matters to the committee. Meetings are generally at the discretion of the liquidator, although machinery exists for committee members to require meetings to be called. The committee has the right to grant or refuse its sanction for the exercise by the liquidator of certain of his powers (see above). It can also ratify unauthorised actions. A crucial point to note is that committee members occupy a fiduciary position *vis-à-vis* the company and its assets. This is well established at common law[49] and is reinforced by rule 4.170 of the Insolvency Rules 1986. Thus either the sanction of the court or of the whole committee will be required before individual committee members can benefit from the administration of the company's estate or any transaction involving its assets. There is some relaxation on the previous law here which imposed an absolute bar on dealings. Transactions are now permitted provided full disclosure has been made and the requisite approval obtained.

5-36 Section 105 of the Insolvency Act 1986 provides an additional opportunity for creditors to participate in the liquidation by attending the annual meeting which it obliges the liquidator to summon.

Rights of creditors

5-37 Creditors have other weapons available in their armoury. Thus, they can apply to the court for directions under section 112. They clearly also enjoy the right to remove liquidators[50] or, alternatively, to apply to the court for the removal of a voluntary liquidator, as occurred in *Re New De Kaap*.[51] As a last resort, they can exploit section 116 and petition the court to have the company compulsorily wound up. It is well settled that the court will do this if the interests of all concerned would be better protected by a compulsory liquidation.[52] It is clear from the judgment of Megarry J. in *Re Lubin, Rosen and Associates Ltd*[53] that the public interest should also be considered here. In *Re Medisco Equipment Ltd*,[54] Harman J. indicated that a voluntary liquidator is entitled to appear on the hearing of a winding-up petition to give evidence but he should act in an impartial and not a partisan manner.

---

[47] *ibid.*, r. 4.158.
[48] *ibid.*, r. 4.162.
[49] Thus in *Re F. T. Hawkins & Co. Ltd* [1952] 2 All E.R. 467 it was held that a liquidator should not employ a firm of solicitors if a member of that firm is on the liquidation committee.
[50] See Insolvency Act 1986, s.171 and Insolvency Rules 1986, rr. 4.114 and 4.117. Note also *Re Inside Sport Ltd*, *The Times*, November 27, 1998.
[51] [1908] 1 Ch. 589. Note also Insolvency Rules 1986, r. 4.120.
[52] See *Re Lowestoft Traffic Services Co. Ltd* (1986) 2 B.C.C. 98, 945. Compare *Re Rhine Film Corp.* (1986) 2 B.C.C. 98, 949, where the court decided that the voluntary liquidation could continue. Note also Chaps. 1 and 6 here for further discussion.
[53] [1975] 1 W.L.R. 122.
[54] [1983] B.C.L.C. 305. The Cork Committee (Cmnd. 8558, para. 809) called for the removal of the bar laid down in *Re Lubin, Rosen and Associates Ltd (supra)* that the voluntary liquidator should not oppose the winding up petition. This recommendation has not been implemented.

THE ROLE OF THE COURT

No day to day involvement

5-38 Obviously, one of the great attractions of the voluntary liquidation procedure is that it does not necessitate the day to day involvement of the court. This point was emphasised by Wynn-Parry J. in *Re Phoenix Oil and Transport Co. Ltd (No. 2)*:[55]

> "A study of the relevant sections . . . dealing with winding up shows clearly that as regards voluntary winding up the legislature has followed . . . a different policy from that laid down in the case of compulsory winding up. The reason is not far to seek."

The learned judge explained:

> "In the case of voluntary winding up, the jurisdiction of the court is not invoked in order to place a company in liquidation. In the case of a creditors' liquidation, the creditors, through their committee of inspection, are in control as against the contributories; while in the case of a members' voluntary winding up, it is the members who are in control. In both cases, the court is given a certain degree of jurisdiction, but I think it can be accurately, though shortly, said that in both forms of voluntary winding up, the court is in the background to be referred to if the necessity should arise. In the case of winding up by the court, however, different considerations arise."

5-39 However, that is not to say that the court is completely shut out of proceedings. Section 112 of the Act, which has been mentioned on a number of occasions in the previous analysis, provides (*inter alia*) as follows:

> "(1) The liquidator or any contributory or creditor may apply to the court to determine any question arising in the winding up of a company, or to exercise, as respects the enforcing of calls or any other matter, all or any of the powers which the court might exercise, if the company were being wound up by the court.
>
> (2) The court, if satisfied that the determination of the question or the required exercise of power will be just and beneficial, may accede wholly or partially to the application on such terms and conditions as it thinks fit, or may make such other order on the application as it thinks just."

Power to stay

5-40 One of the powers which the court might exercise in a compulsory liquidation is the power to stay the winding-up. This facility is imported into voluntary liquidations by section 112.[56]

---

[55] [1958] Ch. 565 at 570.
[56] See *Re Stephen Walters & Co.* [1926] W.N. 236. A stay was refused in *Re Calgary & Edmonton Land Co. Ltd* [1975] 1 W.L.R. 355.

Examples

Late claims

5-41 Let us consider a few examples of section 112 in operation. In *Re Centrifugal Butter Co. Ltd*,[57] Neville J. doubted whether it could be used by the court to set aside company contracts. Even if this is so, it is an unimportant restriction because the liquidator now enjoys express statutory power to disclaim such contracts. In *Re R-R Realisations Ltd*,[58] the liquidator applied to the court for permission to distribute realised funds to the company's shareholders. The creditors had already been paid off. Unfortunately, persons having a possible claim in tort against the company arising out of an aircraft accident, objected to this final distribution. They were late in putting in their claim, because the accident had occurred shortly before the date when the company went into liquidation, and they had waited for the outcome of the official investigation. The liquidator was well advanced in his proposal to make a final distribution and objected to having his plans upset at this late stage. Megarry V.-C., after a careful consideration of the authorities, ruled that in exercising his jurisdiction under the statutory predecessor to section 112, he had to give first consideration to the justice of the case. This consideration pointed to him rejecting the liquidator's application. The late claimants were not blameworthy in submitting their claims late.[59] Megarry V.-C. also indicated that he would look more favourably on late claimants where the proposed distribution was, as in this case, to members (as opposed to creditors). The fact that by refusing the liquidator's application great inconvenience would be caused, did not sway him in his desire to see that justice was done.

Guidelines

5-42 Another useful illustration of the court's attitude towards applications under section 112 is afforded by *Pitman v. Top Business Systems Ltd*.[60] This case involved a creditor applying to the court to restrain a sale of company property by its liquidator. The claim failed but, during the course of his judgment, Nourse J. formulated guidelines as to when the court will interfere with the exercise of powers by a liquidator. Nourse J. referred to "the desirability of a liquidator, whether in a winding-up by the court or a voluntary winding-up, being able to exercise his powers without undue fetters." Bascially, the court would only intervene if the liquidator was acting fraudulently, or in bad faith, or in a totally unreasonable manner. Allegations of mere negligence would not suffice, and, in any case, a liquidator had not necessarily acted negligently merely because he had sold property without first having it valued.

5-43 The other main way in which the courts can interfere in a voluntary liquidation is by acceding to a request to remove a liquidator where good cause has been shown.[61] This possibility has already been considered in Chapter 2.

---

[57] [1913] 1 Ch. 188.
[58] [1980] 1 W.L.R. 805.
[59] Compare the decision of Brightman J. in *Re Sale Continuation Ltd* (1977) unreported, here.
[60] [1984] B.C.L.C. 593.
[61] See *Re Sir John Moore Gold Mining Co.* (1879) 12 Ch.D. 325, and *Re Charterland Gold Fields Ltd* (1909) 26 T.L.R. 132.

THE DUTIES OF THE LIQUIDATOR

Pari passu distribution

5-44 The prime duty of a voluntary liquidator is to ensure the most efficient realisation of the company's assets and subsequent distribution of the proceeds to those entitled. This duty is confirmed by section 107, which establishes the principle of *pari passu* distribution, which, of course, has been much modified in practice.

5-45 The rules as to proof of debts and distribution of assets are substantially contained in rules 4.73 to 4.94 of the Insolvency Rules 1986 (as amended). The liquidator must follow the guidelines in the rules as to the manner in which claims are to be proved, and whether they should be accepted or rejected. A dissatisfied creditor can challenge the liquidator's decision by applying to the court under rule 4.83.[62]

Duties

5-46 The liquidator must pay dividends as and when he can.[63] Furthermore, it is clear from authorities such as *Re Armstrong Whitworth Securities Ltd*,[64] that a liquidator is under a positive duty to contact known creditors to settle their claims. He cannot sit back and wait for them to approach him. The liquidator must not distribute assets without first taking into account all known debts.[65] Conversely, he must not make a distribution to persons who lack an enforceable claim against the company's assets, *e.g.* because their claims are statute-barred. To do so might make him guilty of misfeasance as was explained in Chapter 2.[66]

Proofs and dividends

5-47 Under the old winding-up rule 106, the liquidator could advertise from time to time a date (not less than 14 days distant) by which proofs of debt or claims to priority were to be established, failing which defaulting creditors were barred from objecting to, or participating in, any distribution which took place before they complied. This has apparently been replaced by the liquidator's obligation under rule 4.180(2) to give notice of his intention to declare a dividend, his obligation under rule 4.182, in doing so, to provide (*inter alia*) for the claims of creditors who may not have had time to prove by reason of distance, and the provision that creditors who have not proved when a dividend is declared cannot disturb the dividend. No forms or time limits are prescribed for the liquidator's notice of his intention to declare a dividend, so presumably the liquidator will have to decide what is reasonable in every case—an uncomfortable and unsatisfactory state of affairs. In order to be safe, a liquidator must avail himself of section 153 (presumably via an application under section 112) whereby the court can set a date by which creditors must prove or be debarred from participating in distributions. It seems that the liquidator can accept a claim submitted after this date, if he has sufficient funds[67] but he will not be bound to do so.

---

[62] A disappointed creditor must follow the correct appeals procedure—*Craven v. Blackpool Greyhound Stadium* [1936] 3 All E.R. 513.
[63] *ibid.*, r. 4.180.
[64] [1947] Ch. 673.
[65] *Argylls Ltd v. Coxeter* (1913) 29 T.L.R. 355, *James Smith & Sons (Norwood) Ltd v. Goodman* [1936] Ch. 216.
[66] *Re Home and Colonial Insurance Co. Ltd* [1930] 1 Ch. 102.
[67] *Harrison v. Kirk* [1904] A.C. 1.

5-48 A liquidator is subject to a number of obligations with regard to payments by him into the Insolvency Services Account. These are detailed in the Insolvency Regulations 1994 (S.I. 1994 No. 2507). These regulations also deal with the maintenance of proper accounts, minutes of meetings, and other administrative records. Furthermore, provision is made by these Regulations for the audit of the liquidator's accounts and for the mechanics of payments of dividends to creditors.

Fiduciary position

5-49 In addition to these functional obligations, it must always be remembered that a liquidator occupies a fiduciary position *vis-à-vis* his company. The liquidator should not allow any conflict of interest of interest to arise.[68] Moreover, in *Re Gertzenstein Ltd*[69] it was held by Bennett J. that he must not make a private profit from his position. In this case, it was stated that it was improper for a liquidator (who was a solicitor) to employ himself to do legal work connected with the winding-up. This is extended by rule 4.149 of the Insolvency Rules 1986, which allows the court to set aside dealings between the liquidator and his associates which involve company assets.

5-50 At the moment, there is some uncertainty as to whether the duty to "act honourably" imposed by the rule in *Ex p. James*[70] applies to voluntary liquidators but the better view is that it does not apply.[71]

REMOVAL, RESIGNATION OR VACATION OF OFFICE BY THE LIQUIDATOR

5-51 These matters are all governed by sections 108 and 171 of the Insolvency Act 1986. A liquidator may be removed either by the court[72] or by the creditors. A provisional liquidator can only be removed by the court. A liquidator must vacate office after he has made a return to the registrar of companies concerning the final meeting of creditors.[73] A liquidator can only resign his position for reasons of ill-health, retirement from insolvency practice, or supervening conflict of interest or change in personal circumstances making it impracticable for him to continue (s.171(5) and r. 4.108(4)). A joint liquidator has available the additional ground that he is superfluous. In all cases, the liquidator must, under rule 4.108 (as amended), call a creditors' meeting to accept his resignation, and if it will not do so, he can apply to the court.

---

68 *Re P. Turner (Wilsden) Ltd* [1987] B.C.L.C. 149. See also *Re Charterland Gold Fields Ltd* (1909) 26 T.L.R. 132.

69 [1937] 1 Ch. 115.

70 (1874) L.R. 9 Ch. App. 609.

71 In *Re John Bateson & Co. Ltd* [1985] B.C.L.C. 259, Harman J. indicted that the rule did not apply to voluntary liquidators. For the same conclusion, see *Re T. H. Knitwear Ltd* (1988) 4 B.C.C. 102, where the Court of Appeal overruled *Re Temple Fire and Accident Assurance Co.* (1910) 120 L.T.Jo 115. See also Chap. 2.

72 See here *Re Corbenstoke Ltd (No. 2)* (1989) 5 B.C.C. 767 (conflict of interest). For guidance on *Locus standi* under s.108 see *Deloitte and Touche AG v. Johnson, The Times*, June 16, 1999. In *Re Adams Builders Ltd* [1991] B.C.C. 62 it was held that a voluntary liquidator will automatically cease to hold office if his qualification has lapsed, though presumably an application can be made to the court if the liquidator refuses to give up his position voluntarily. For procedural aspects see rule 4.120 and its counterpoint, for compulsory liquidations, rule 4.119.

73 *ibid.*, section 171(6).

THE CONCLUSION OF THE LIQUIDATION

Release

5-52 In the normal course of events, the creditors' voluntary winding-up will be concluded by the liquidator realising all available assets and then distributing the proceeds to the various persons having claims against the company in the correct priority sequence. Having done this, he must then call final meetings of members and creditors under section 106.[74] Sufficient sums must be retained to fund these meetings, to which the liquidator must present an account of the realisation and distribution process. A copy of this account must be forwarded to the Companies Registry within a week of the meetings. If there was no quorum at either of the meetings, the liquidator's return should disclose this fact. The creditors may release the liquidator at the meeting, but if they do not, he will have to apply for his release to the Secretary of State under rule 4.122.[75]

Dissolution

5-53 The next stage in the procedure is governed by section 201, which provides that the Registrar shall record the liquidator's account and return. After the expiry of three months the company is automatically dissolved. Interested parties can apply to the court to defer this dissolution date. If such an order is obtained, it must be registered at Cardiff within seven days.

5-54 The operation of the dissolution procedure outlined in section 201 was considered by Neuberger J. in *Re Wilmott Trading Ltd.*[76] The insolvent company in this case held a non disclaimable waste management licence and the question before the court was whether this would preclude dissolution. Neuberger J. concluded that a dissolution could go ahead. The dissolution would necessary lead either to the licence being terminated or possibly, though this point was not argued, vesting in the Crown as *bona vacantia*. This latter possibility was the subject of further argument and consideration in *Re Wilmott Trading Ltd (No. 2)*[77] where Neuberger J. on reflection was prepared to accept the contention that the licence did not vest in the Crown in the aforementioned circumstances as it could not be regarded as "property" within the meaning of section 654 of the Companies act 1985.

5-55 Where the company has been dissolved, it ceases to exist, and therefore it can neither be sued nor sue. Thus, in *M. H. Smith (Plant Hire) Ltd v. Mainwaring*,[78] the Court of Appeal held that an insurance company could not institute proceedings in the name of the assured as it was a company that had been dissolved and had lost its personality. The right to subrogation died with the company itself.

Restoration to register

5-56 An application may be made to the court within two years of dissolution to have the company restored to the register.[79] This unusual step may be taken if addi-

[74] 28 days notice is required—see Insolvency Rules 1986, r. 4.126.
[75] See Insolvency Act 1986, s.174(6) for the effect of the liquidator's release.
[76] *The Times*, April 28, 1999. The following discussion may be academic in view of *Official Receiver v. Environment Agency, The Times*, August 5, 1999.
[77] *The Times*, June 17, 1999.
[78] [1986] B.C.L.C. 342.
[79] See Companies Act 1985, s.651 (as amended by Companies Act 1989, s.141 and Sched. 24).

tional assets belonging to the company come to light and a particular unsatisfied creditor wishes to lay claim to them. An application can be made after expiry of the two years period for the purpose of bringing an action for damages in respect of personal injuries or a fatal accident.[80]

[80] Companies Act 1985, s.651(5).

CHAPTER 6
Compulsory Liquidation

INTRODUCTION

6-01 This Chapter will be concerned with what is, procedurally speaking, the most interesting (and expensive) method of winding up an insolvent company. The main differences between compulsory liquidation and creditors' voluntary liquidation are as follows:

1. Compulsory liquidation is normally the result of a hostile process initiated against the company's wishes, whereas the company's shareholders initiate, albeit reluctantly, a voluntary liquidation. This element of antipathy explains why there is considerably more litigation arising out of compulsory liquidations as opposed to voluntary winding up.
2. The court is necessarily more intimately involved in the compulsory winding up procedure.

6-02 The Department of Trade and Industry statistics for 1997–98 show that there were 5103 compulsory liquidations as compared to 8121 cases of creditors' voluntary winding up.

COMPANIES WHICH MAY BE WOUND UP BY THE COURT

6-03 A variety of companies may be subject to the compulsory liquidation procedure. This Chapter will be concerned with those that are insolvent.[1] The fact that some other form of corporate insolvency process may be taking place is no bar to compulsory liquidation. Thus, a company can be liquidated.[2] The courts are regularly invited to decide whether a company in voluntary liquidation should be placed in compulsory liquidation.[3] In so determining the court will clearly have regard to the interests of creditors, though as always the net financial result

[1] Solvent companies can also be wound up under the Insolvency Act 1986, s.122.

[2] *Re Rubber Improvements Co., The Times*, June 5, 1962.

[3] Insolvency Act 1986, s.116. See also *Re Lubin, Rosen and Associates* Companies Act 1985, [1975] 1 W.L.R. 122, *Re Lowestoft Traffic Services Co.* (1986) 2 B.C.C. 98, 945, *Re Palmer Marine Surveys Ltd* [1986] 1 W.L.R. 573, *Re Falcon R. J. Developments Ltd* (1987) 3 B.C.C. 146 and *Re M.C.H. Services Ltd* (1987) B.C.L.C. 535. Compare *Re Medisco Equipment Ltd* [1983] B.C.L.C. 305, *Re Rhine Film Corp* (1986) 2 B.C.C. 98, 949, *Re Fitness Centre (South East) Ltd* [1986] B.C.L.C. 518. *Re Wm Thorpe & Son Ltd* (1989) 5 B.C.C. 156 and *Re Hewitt Brannon (Tools) Co. Ltd* [1991] B.C.L.C. 80. In *Re Lubin, Rosen and Associates Ltd* [1975] 1 W.L.R. 122 it was held that a voluntary liquidator should not attend the hearing and actually oppose the petition. The Cork Committee (Cmnd. 8558, para. 809) called for this restriction to be lifted but no legislative action appears to have been taken with regard to this recommendation.

is not the sole determining factor here.[4] A clinching factor is often the need for a full and independent investigation of the company's affairs, which the court believes can be best undertaken by one of its officers acting in a compulsory liquidation.[5]

Overseas companies and specialised organisations

6-04 Overseas companies registered in other jurisdictions are susceptible to compulsory liquidation under English law. Although it is well settled that the English courts can wind up a foreign company, they may decline jurisdiction if there is already a winding up proceeding in the country of incorporation and in their view the English creditors could gain no additional protection.[6] The normal requirement is that in order to be wound up foreign companies must have assets in this country. This possibility is expressly recognised by sections 221–225 of the Insolvency Act 1986, and indeed it seems that it covers foreign companies that have already been wound up and dissolved in their native jurisdictions. The term "assets" is widely defined in this context and indeed it now appears not to be an essential precondition.[7] A cause of action with a reasonable prospect of success will suffice.[8] Industrial and provident societies may also be wound up as Harman J. recently confirmed in *Re Norse Self Build Association Ltd*.[9] The same is true of building societies[10] and friendly societies.[11]

Company already struck off

6-05 On the other hand, if the company has already been struck off the register of companies, it would appear from the recent decision of Harman J. in *Re Aga Estate Agencies Ltd*[12] that the courts will not restore it to the register simply to enable a winding-up petition to be presented against it by a person who was neither a creditor nor member at the date of dissolution. This restriction however will not operate to frustrate a winding-up petition which was presented before the date of striking off.[13]

---

4 *Re Gordon and Breach Science Publications Ltd* [1995] 2 B.C.L.C. 189.

5 *Re Manlon Trading Ltd* [1995] 3 W.L.R. 271, *Re Leading Guides International Ltd* [1998] 1 B.C.L.C.

6 *New Hampshire Insurance Co. v. Rush and Tompkins* [1998] 2 B.C.L.C. 471. Compare *Re Richbell Information Services Inc*, *The Times*, January 21, 1999.

7 *Re Compania Merabello San Nicholas S.A.* [1973] Ch. 75, *Re Eloc Electro-Optieck and Communicatie B.V.* [1981] 2 All E.R. 1111. See also *Banque des Marchands de Moscou v. Kindersley* [1951] Ch. 112 and *Re Azoff-Don Commercial Bank* [1954] 1 All E.R. 947. The "assets" requirement may not be strictly necessary if the petitioner can show that he would benefit from the winding up and the company has a sufficient link with the jurisdiction—*Re A Company (No. 00359 of 1987)* (1987) 3 B.C.C. 160. See also *IWB v. Okeanos Maritime* [1987] B.C.L.C. 450 and *Re A Company (No. 003102 of 1991) ex parte Nyckeln Finance* [1991] B.C.L.C. 539 and *Re Latreefers Inc* [1999] 1 B.C.L.C. 271. Compare *Re Real Estate Ltd* [1991] B.C.L.C. 210. For a review see *Dawson* [1995] 15 Insolvency Lawyer 3.

8 *Re Allobrogia Steamship Corp.* [1978] 3 All E.R. 423.

9 (1985) 1 B.C.C. 99, 436. The relevant statutory provision is the Industrial and Provident Societies Act 1965, s.55.

10 See Building Societies Act 1986, ss.89 and 90.

11 For incorporated friendly societies see Friendly Societies Act 1992, ss.19 *et seq*.

12 1986 P.C.C. 358, following *Re Timbiqui Gold Mines Ltd* [1961] Ch. 319.

13 *Re Thompson & Riches Ltd* [1981] 1 W.L.R. 682.

COURTS HAVING JURISDICTION TO HEAR WINDING-UP PETITIONS

6-06 In English law insolvency jurisdiction is shared between the county courts and the High Court.[14] The former has concurrent jurisdiction with the High Court over the liquidation of companies whose issued and paid up share capital does not exceed £120,000. The Chancery Division is the appropriate division of the High Court as far as winding-up petitions are concerned and, indeed, within the Chancery Division there is a specialist Companies Court. In Scotland the appropriate courts will either be the Sheriff Courts (subject to the £120,000 share capital limit) or the Court of Session.[15]

Appropriate jurisdiction

6-07 In view of the distinct identities of the English, Scottish and Northern Irish systems of company law, it is essential that the winding-up is instituted in the appropriate jurisdiction, as was emphasised in *Re Baby Moon (UK) Ltd*.[16] The crucial factor is whether the company is registered at Cardiff, Belfast or Edinburgh. In *Re Baby Moon Ltd*,[17] Harman J. held that a company which was registered in England but whose registered office was improperly located in Scotland could be wound up in this country though it would be necessary of course to serve the winding-up petition outside the jurisdiction.

PETITIONERS AND GROUNDS FOR THE PETITION

"Unable to pay its debts"

6-08 According to section 122(1)(*f*) of the Insolvency Act 1986, a winding-up petition may be presented if "the company is unable to pay its debts." This central concept is further explained by section 123, which provides *inter alia* as follows:

"123(1) A company is deemed unable to pay its debts—

(a) if a creditor (by assignment or otherwise) to whom the company is indebted in a sum exceeding £750 then due has served on the company, by leaving it at the company's registered office, a written demand (in the prescribed form) requiring the company to pay the sum so due and the company has for 3 weeks thereafter neglected to pay the sum or to secure or compound for it to the reasonable satisfaction of the creditor, or

(b) if, in England and Wales, execution or other process issued on a judgment, decree or order of any court in favour of a creditor of the company is returned unsatisfied in whole or in part, or

---

[14] Insolvency Act 1986, s.117. For the jurisdiction of a Deputy High Court judge see *Fabric Sales Ltd v. Eratex* (1984) 128 S.J. 330. Provincial district registries lack jurisdiction unless specifically authorised—*Re Pleatfine*, *The Times*, June 15, 1983. The High Court can transfer proceedings to the county court even if the company's share capital exceeds £120,000—see Insolvency Rules 1986, r. 7.11 and *Re Vernon Heaton Co. Ltd* [1936] Ch. 289. For appeal routes see r. 7.47 and *Re Calahurst Ltd* [1989] B.C.L.C. 140.

[15] See Insolvency Act 1986, ss.120 and 121.

[16] 1985 P.C.C. 103. Compare *Re Normandy Marketing Ltd* [1993] B.C.C. 879.

[17] *Supra*.

(c) ....
(d) ....
(e) if it is proved to the satisfaction of the court that the company is unable to pay its debts as they fall due,

(2) A company is also deemed unable to pay its debts if it is proved to the satisfaction of the court that the value of the company's assets is less than the amount of its liabilities, taking into account its contingent and prospective liabilities.

Statutory demand

6-09 Section 123(1)(*a*) will be most commonly relied on to establish inability to pay debts. Guidance as to the form and contents of the statutory demand is to be found in the Insolvency Rules 1986.[18] It should be noted that the courts are fastidious with regard to compliance with the rules relating to the statutory demand. Thus, the three week period of grace must be strictly observed. Again, it was held recently by Nourse J. in *Re A Company*[19] that a demand made by telex will not suffice for the purposes of a statutory demand, for the simple reason that the demand could not be served by leaving it at the company's registered office. Nourse J. declared:[20]

> "It may be that the provisions of the Companies Acts have not yet fully caught up with modern conditions and that there would be a case for allowing a statutory demand to be sent through the post, or indeed to be sent by telex. On the other hand a statutory demand is a solemn document with potentially serious consequences. I can well understand that the legislature might have consciously intended that the service of a document of that character should be carried out in much the same way as the service of a winding-up petition, which cannot be sent through the post and certainly cannot be sent on the telex machine."

6-10 This ruling has been reinforced by the new wording of section 123(1)(*a*) which requires the written demand to be in the "prescribed form," which is explained by rules 4.4–4.6 and Form 4.1 of the Insolvency Rules 1986. Having said that, there is still doubt as to this matter. For in *Re A Company (No. 008790 of 1990)*[21] Morritt J. took a more relaxed view of the required formalities and rejected the above approach of Nourse J. Here, a statutory demand which had been sent through the post and then delivered to the company's registered office was held to have been properly served. Morritt J. denied that this well established method of service of official documents had been ruled out by the draftsman of the 1986 legislation. It would be ludicrous if personal service at the appropriate address was acceptable whilst confirmed service through the post was not permitted.

6-11 Inability to pay debts can be established by an unsatisfied execution or by other means, as section 123(1)(*e*) implies. Indeed it should be stressed that service of a statutory demand is not the exclusive method of establishing that a corporate debtor

[18] See rr. 4.4–4.6 and Form 4.1 (as amended).
[19] [1985] B.C.L.C. 37.
[20] *ibid.*, at 42–43.
[21] [1991] B.C.L.C. 561. See also Civil Procedure Rules 1998 r. 6.2 which permits service by electronic means in general.

is insolvent. This point was made clear by the Court of Appeal in *Taylor's Industrial Flooring v. M. and H. Plant Hire Ltd*.[22] Failure to pay an undisputed debt could provide the basis of a winding-up petition even though the creditor had not served a statutory demand for repayment. An instructive authority here is *Re A Company*,[23] another decision of Nourse J. Here it was held that a company that engages in brinkmanship in settling its debts and which ultimately pays those debts with money borrowed from other sources, is not necessarily unable to pay its debts. On the other hand, in *Cornhill Insurance v. Improvement Services Ltd*,[24] Harman J. held that a company that was apparently solvent but which refused to pay a particular undisputed debt could nevertheless be viewed as unable to pay its debts for these purposes.

Commercial solvency

6-12 Finally, inability to pay debts can now be established under section 123(2) by applying the test for commercial solvency—*i.e.*, a company will not be solvent if the amount of its assets is less than the amount of all its liabilities. This subsection represented a novel departure in corporate insolvency law[25] in 1986, and while there is no actual evidence that it has resulted in the premature liquidation of companies which would formerly have continued to trade, it will certainly have affected the advice given to directors of companies in financial difficulties.

Categories of petitioner

6-13 The categories of petitioner are identified by section 124(1), and these include creditors, directors, contributories, the Secretary of State and also the company itself. Further explanation is required here.

6-14 The term "creditor" includes contingent and prospective creditors.[26] Furthermore, an assignee of a debt owed by the company enjoys locus standi to present a winding-up petition.[27] Where the assignment takes place after the date of a petition presented by the assignor, the court has power to amend the petition and have the assignee substituted as petitioner. This possibility was the subject of much doubt for many years, as a result of the Court of Appeal decision in *Re Paris Skating Rink*.[28] However, this authority was "reinterpreted" by the Privy Council in *Perak Pioneer Ltd and Plessy Investments v. Petroliam Nasional Berhad*,[29] where the possibility of substitution was accepted.

---

[22] [1990] B.C.L.C. 216. However it should be borne in mind that there are risks in proceeding to a winding up petition without the preliminary step of presenting a statutory demand. In *Re A Company (No. 006798 of 1995)* [1996] 1 W.L.R. 491 the court held that a wasted costs order may, in exercise of the jurisdiction conferred under section 51(6) of the Supreme Court Act 1981, be made personally against the solicitor acting for the petitioner if the petition is then dismissed. See also Civil Procedure Rules 1998, r. 48.7.

[23] [1986] B.C.L.C. 261.

[24] 1986 P.C.C. 204. See also *Re World Industrial Bank* [1909] W.N. 148 and *Re A Company* (1950) 94 S.J. 369.

[25] *Hodson v. Blanchards (London) Ltd* (1911) 131 L.T.Jo 9, *Re W.H. Jones & Co., ex p. Frankenburg* (1913) 2 L.J.C.C. 101, *Re Patrick & Lyon Ltd* [1933] Ch. 786 and *Crowley v. Northern Bank Finance Ltd* [1981] I.R. 353.

[26] See *Re Austral Group Investments Ltd* [1993] 2 N.Z.L.R. 692 for a discussion of the differences between these two types of creditor. It should be stressed that a petitioner whose debt is statute barred through expiration of the relevant limitation period loses his right to use the winding-up procedure as a means of recovery—*Re Karnos Property Co. Ltd* [1989] B.C.L.C. 340.

[27] An equitable assignment will suffice—*Re Montgomery Moore Syndicate* [1903] W.N. 121.

[28] (1877) 5 Ch.D. 959.

[29] [1986] 3 W.L.R. 105. On substitution generally see *Re Xyllyx plc* (No. 1) [1992] B.C.L.C. 376.

6-15 It used to be thought, on the basis of *Re Pen-Y-Van Colliery Co.*[30] that a person having a claim in tort for unliquidated damages could not present a winding-up petition against the tortfeasor company. However, this view was questioned by some academics and also by Megarry J. in *Re A Company*,[31] and in view of the changes implemented by the Insolvency Act 1986, with regard to proof of debts by such a claimant,[32] it must surely not represent the law today.

Disputed claims

6-16 One of the most recurrent questions in this area is whether a creditor whose claim to be owed money is disputed by the company can present a winding-up petition. The position here seems to be largely governed by judicial discretion, as the Privy Council emphasised in *Brinds Ltd v. Offshore Oil*.[33] On the other hand, there is a well-established rule of practice dating back to *Re London and Paris Banking Corp.*,[34] that if the company disputes the claim in good faith and on substantial grounds, the court will be unlikely to accede to the petition. In *Re Lympne Investments Ltd*,[35] it was explained that in the case of a genuine dispute the company can hardly be said to have "neglected to pay" the debt in question. In *Re Wisepark Ltd*,[36] Nourse J. indicated that in cases of doubt, less harm would be done by rejecting the petition and forcing the petitioner to first establish his claim in separate proceedings than would be inflicted on the company by allowing the petition to proceed. However, this rule of practice might be departed from in exceptional cases. Thus in *Re Claybridge Shipping Corp. S.A.*,[37] the Court of Appeal allowed a petition based on a disputed debt to proceed where it would be difficult for the petitioner to establish his debt in separate proceedings as the company concerned was an overseas company. Furthermore, where there is no doubt that the company does owe the petitioner a sum in excess of the statutory minimum, the fact that the precise amount of the debt is unclear will not necessarily preclude a winding-up petition.[38] Whether a debt is disputed on reasonable grounds is a matter for the trial judge. The Court of Appeal will be reluctant to interfere with any ruling he may make on this issue.[39]

Cross claims

6-17 Another defence to a winding up petition is to assert that the debtor company has an enforceable cross claim against the petitioner which exceeds the

---

[30] (1877) 6 Ch.D. 477.
[31] [1973] 1 W.L.R. 1566 at 1571.
[32] See Insolvency Rules 1986, r. 13.12 here.
[33] (1986) 2 B.C.C. 98, 916.
[34] (1875) L.R. 19 Eq. 444. See also *Stonegate Securities v. Gregory* [1980] Ch. 576, *Re Laceward Ltd* [1981] 1 W.L.R. 133, *Re A Company (No. 003729 of 1982)* [1984] 1 W.L.R. 1098. *Re A Company (No. 0010656 of 1990)* [1991] B.C.L.C. 464 and compare *Re A Company (No. 001946 of 1991) ex parte Finsoft Holdings S.A.* [1991] B.C.L.C. 737. See also *McDonalds Restaurants Ltd v. Urbandivide Co. Ltd* [1994] 1 B.C.L.C. 306.
[35] [1972] 2 All E.R. 385.
[36] (1984) 134 N.L.J. 203.
[37] [1997] 1 B.C.L.C. 572.
[38] *Re Tweeds Garage Ltd* [1962] Ch. 406, *Re R. A. Faulds Ltd* (1986) 2 B.C.C. 99, 269. Nor will it matter if once the minimum level has been reached there is an excess that is disputed—*Re A Company (No. 008122 of 1989) ex parte Trans Continental Insurance Services Ltd* [1990] B.C.L.C. 697.
[39] *Pentagin Technologies International v. Express Company Securities*, *The Times*, April 7, 1995, *London and Global Ltd v. Sahara Petroleum*, *The Times*, December 3, 1998.

amount of the petitioner debt. In *Re Bayoil SA*[40] the Court of Appeal resurrected a thirty year old decision[41] which it said accurately reflected the correct practice in such cases. According to the Court of Appeal, the court could, in the exercise of its discretion, dismiss or stay the winding up petition, where the debtor company had a genuine cross against the petition, a cross claim which could not be litigated.

6-18 The Secretary of State for Trade and Industry can, under section 124A, (as inserted by the Companies Act 1989) present a winding up petition on various grounds, notably where it is in the public interest to do so. This power has been used extensively recently to wind up insolvent companies which were trading simply in order to defraud the public.[42]

Company directors

6-19 The directors of the company are also identified as potential petitioners by section 124, though it would appear that they may only present a petition if authorised to do so by their shareholders as it was indicated in *Re Emmadart Ltd*[43] that directors cannot present a winding-up petition on their own initiative. The practice that had developed to the contrary must cease, according to Brightman J. This situation is less likely to arise these days for the simple reason that in such a scenario voluntary winding-up would surely be the preferred option. Where a petition emanates from directors, the petition must be presented collectively by all of the directors or be presented by individual directors acting upon a board resolution. In *Re Instrumentation Electrical Services Ltd*[44] it was held that an individual director acting without the authority of his colleagues cannot petition for the winding up of his company.

Receivers

6-20 A receiver can, in the view of Brightman J. in *Re Emmadart Ltd, supra* present a winding-up petition if a liquidation would aid his task of realisation. His wide powers to realise the company's assets would include such an extreme step. An administrator also has the power to petition for winding up (see Insolvency Act 1986, Sched. 1 para. 21). Indeed, he or she may indirectly have an obligation to seek the winding-up in some situations. If the administrator arrives at the opinion that the purposes of the administration cannot be achieved, he must, under section 18 of the Insolvency Act 1986, apply to the court for a discharge. Although the court has wide powers in such a case, it appears[45] that it cannot substitute a winding-up order on

---

[40] [1999] 1 W.L.R. 147. It must be stressed that this is ultimately a matter of discretion and the court might decide that it is in the best interests of all concerned if the cross claim is dealt with in the liquidation—see *Re Richbell Information Systems Inc., The Times*, January 2, 1999. On this difficult area of cross claims see also *Re Greenacre Publishing Ltd, The Times*, December 17, 1998 and *Re Latreefers Inc, The Times*, January 18, 1999.

[41] *Re Portman Provincial Cinemas Ltd (Note)* [1999] 1 W.L.R. 157.

[42] This is a useful facility because it enables companies to be wound up where directors have preyed upon small creditors—*i.e.*, those owed less than £750. In such a case, a winding up petition is unlikely to be forthcoming from the creditors themselves. See *Re Secure and Provide plc* [1992] B.C.C., 405 *SIB v. Lans. and Yorks. Portfolio Management* [1992] B.C.L.C. 281 and *Re Normandy Marketing Ltd* [1993] B.C.C. 879.

[43] [1979] Ch. 540.

[44] [1988] B.C.L.C. 550.

[45] See *Re Brooke Marine Ltd* [1988] B.C.L.C. 546.

such an application. Instead it can postpone the discharge of the administrator and then authorise the administrator, as the company's agent, to present a petition under section 124 of the Insolvency Act 1986.

Contributories

6-21 Contributories are also potential petitioners but are normally precluded from fulfilling this role in insolvency cases. It is an established rule of practice that contributories must be able to show that there would be sufficient funds to repay the shareholders after all debts had been settled, an impossibility, surely, where the company appears to be insolvent.[46] If a contributory is also owed money by the company, it is possible to have the petition amended to a creditor's petition and to have himself substituted as petitioner.[47]

ADVERTISEMENT OF THE PETITION AND GENERAL PROCEDURE

6-22 The form of the petition is scheduled to the Insolvency Rules as Form 4.2, which is to be adapted as circumstances require (r. 12.7(2)). Once again, the courts will demand strict compliance with prescribed formalities, in view of the serious nature of the proceedings. Normally, if the petition gets the name of the company wrong, this will invalidate it, though the courts might be prepared to turn a blind eye in exceptional cases, as was made clear in *Re Vidiofusion Ltd.*[48]

Outstanding petitions

6-23 A person seeking to present a winding-up petition should first check the Gazette to ensure that there are no other petitions outstanding against the company. Failure to consider this possibility could result in the petitioner being unable to claim his petition costs.[49] The court administrator will often make investigations on an *ex gratia* basis, but he is not obliged to do so and the ultimate protection for a petitioner rests in his own hands. The petition must, according to the Insolvency Rules 1986, be advertised in the Gazette and in a local newspaper, and also served by leaving it at the company's registered office.[50] Advertisement must occur at least seven days after service of the petition[51] and at least seven days before the hearing

---

[46] *Re Rica Gold Washing Ltd* (1879) 11 Ch.D. 36, *Re Chesterfield Catering Co. Ltd* [1976] 3 W.L.R. 879. *O'Connor v. Atlantis Fisheries* [1998] S.C.L.R. 401.

[47] *Re Commercial and Industrial Installations* (1986) 2 B.C.C. 98, 901. For a different example of substitution of petitions see *Re Creative Handbook Ltd* [1985] B.C.L.C. 1.

[48] [1974] 1 W.L.R. 1548, following *Re L'Industrie Verriere Ltd* [1974] W.N. 222.

[49] *Re Dramstar Ltd*, *The Times*, October 30, 1980.

[50] Insolvency Rules 1986, r. 4.8. In *Business Computers International Ltd v Registrar of Companies* [1987] B.C.L.C. 621, an action in negligence by a company, which had been ordered to be wound up on a petition served at the wrong address was struck out insofar as it named the petitioner as a defendant. Scott J. held that the petitioner owed no duty of care to ensure that the petition was served at the correct address. The reason why the petition was served at the wrong address was not explained but it may be significant that the Registrar of Companies was named, amongst others, as a defendant.

[51] This delay is to allow the company an opportunity to object. The court will dismiss a petition in the event of premature advertisement—*Re Signland Ltd* [1982] 2 All E.R. 609n but see *Re Garton (Western) Ltd* (1989) 5 B.C.C. 198. The courts will view seriously any failure to comply with the correct advertisement procedure—*Re Shusella Ltd* [1983] B.C.L.C. 505. Minor irregularities might be overlooked—*Re Saul Moss & Sons Ltd* [1906] W.N. 142. But see now *Practice Direction* (No. 1 of 1996) [1996] 1 W.L.R. 1255.

of the petition.[52] As a result of a *Practice Direction* of February 1986, a copy of the advertisement must now also be lodged with the court as soon as possible.[53] This will be required even if the advertisement is defective, or the petitioner decides to abandon his petition.

What is an advertisement?

There has been some dispute as to what constitutes "advertisement" of a petition for winding-up purposes. In *Re A Company (No. 00687 of 1991)*[54] Harman J. construed this term in a wide sense. Thus, in this particular case, a letter by the petitioner's solicitors informing the company's bankers of the existence of a winding-up petition by a contributory was found to be a breach of a court order restraining advertisement of the petition. "Advertisement" of a petition in the context of rule 4.23 simply meant notification. This decision co-existed uneasily with the later ruling of Parker J. in *S.N. Group plc v. Barclays Bank*[55] where it was held that simply notifying a company's bankers of the existence of a petition did not involve a breach of the restriction imposed under rule 4.11 on premature advertisement. "Advertisement" for these purposes meant advertisement in the *Gazette*. The earlier judgment of Harman J. was distinguished on the grounds that in that case, the petition was being presented by a contributory against a solvent company and a different Insolvency Rule was involved. This conflict of authorities was resolved by the Court of Appeal in *Secretary of State v. North West Holdings*.[56] Here a company was served with notice that the DTI intended to present a winding up petition under section 124A of the Insolvency Act 1986. An immediate appointment of a provisional liquidator was also secured. Prior to the elapse of the seven day period set aside for challenging the proposed advertisement the DTI issued a press notice explaining what was happening. The company sought to have the petition struck out under rule 4.11(5) of the Insolvency Rules 1986 on the basis that the rules governing advertisement had not been complied with. The Court of Appeal refused to strike out the petition because what the DTI had done did not constitute "advertisement". The concept was restricted to formal notification in the Gazette. Thus the views of Parker J. were preferred to the earlier approach of Harman J. However, it is clear that the court did not like this way of circumventing the strict procedures on advertisement and indicated that it did have residual jurisdiction to strike out petitions if it felt there had been an abuse of process.[57] In cases of uncertainty a petitioner would be well advised to seek guidance from the court before disseminating information about a pending winding up petition.

Constructive notice

6-24 The effect of advertising the petition is to give constructive notice to the world of its existence.[58] One of the purposes of the advertisement is to give other cred-

[52] Saturdays and Sundays do not figure in this calculation—*Re Yeoland Consols* (1888) 58 L.T. 108, *Re Display Multiples Ltd* [1967] 1 W.L.R. 571.
[53] [1986] 1 All E.R. 704.
[54] [1991] B.C.C. 210.
[55] [1993] B.C.C. 506.
[56] [1998] B.C.C. 997.
[57] Here the court was satisfied with the conduct of the DTI, particularly as a provisional liquidator had been appointed and the public had a right to be made aware of that fact.
[58] *Re London, Hamburg and Continental Exchange Bank* (1866) L.R. 2 Eq. 231 reversed on other grounds see (1866) L.R. 1 Ch. App. 433.

itors a chance to support the petition. Under rule 4.16 of the Insolvency Rules 1986, such creditors must notify the petitioner of their intentions, with certain particulars of their debts, and the petitioner must furnish the court with a list of them. In *Re Wavern Engineering Ltd*[59] the petitioner falsely represented to the court that no other creditor wished to take over the petition, in breach of what is now rule 4.15 of the Insolvency Rules 1986. It was held that he had no right to withdraw his petition.

Restraint on advertisement

6-25 The court has power to restrain the advertisement of a winding-up petition and will do so if it regards the petition as an abuse of process or the debt is disputed. Advertisement of a winding-up petition can of course have a very damaging effect on a company's financial prospects. As we have seen in Chapter 4, advertisement may be restrained if there is an extant administration[60] petition. In *Re A Company*,[61] Hoffmann J. held that the ban on publicising the petition could extend beyond a prohibition on gazetting it, and could apply to any form of publicity.

6-26 A petitioner living outside the jurisdiction (*e.g.* in Scotland or Northern Ireland) may be required to provide security.[62]

6-27 Once the petition has been presented to the court, the Registrar will fix a date for hearing it.[63] The petition must proceed with due despatch, though the court may overlook delays in exceptional cases.[64]

PROTECTING THE ASSETS BETWEEN PETITION AND ORDER

Protective mechanisms

6-28 It is not uncommon for several months to elapse between the date of the presentation of a winding-up petition and its ultimate hearing. This delay can expose both the company and the petitioner to great risks. On the one hand, the company ought not, as a general rule, to be deprived of its power to continue trading by the mere fact that a winding-up petition has been presented against it. To be set against this the petitioner should be protected against the possibility of the directors dissipating the company's assets to frustrate the petitioner's claim. The law has at its call a number of mechanisms designed to balance these competing demands.

1. Provisional liquidators

6-29 In cases where the petitioner can establish that there is a serious risk of the directors disposing of the company's assets, and thereby denying him the remedy

---

[59] (1986) unreported.

[60] *Re A Company (No. 00963 of 1991) ex p. Electrical Engineering Contracts (London) Ltd* [1992] B.C.L.C. 248.

[61] [1986] B.C.L.C. 127.

[62] There is current controversy as to whether an impecunious Northern Irish company should be required to provide security for costs. Compare *Wilson Vehicle Distributors Ltd v. Colt Car Co. Ltd* [1984] B.C.L.C. 93 and *D.S.Q. Property Co. Ltd v. Lotus Cars Ltd* [1987] 1 W.L.R. 127. Bearing in mind Companies Act 1985, s.726, an anomaly could arise if security were not required in such a case. For a full account of this issue see Milman, "Security for Costs: Principles and Pragmatism in Corporate Litigation" in Rider, *The Realm of Company Law: Essays in Honour of Len Sealy* (1998), pp. 167–181.

[63] For the position where the petitioner fails to appear, see *Re A Company (No. 002791 of 1986)*, (1986) 2 B.C.C. 99, 281.

[64] *Re A Company (No. 002791 of 1986)* (1986) 2 B.C.C. 99, 281.

sought, the court can, under section 135 of the Insolvency Act 1986, appoint a provisional or interim liquidator, whose role is to oversee the company's assets on a caretaker basis until the petition is heard.[65] Procedural aspects of the law on provisional liquidators are governed by rules 4.25–4.31 of the Insolvency Rules 1986 (as amended).

Examples

6-30 Normally, the Official Receiver will be appointed to fulfil this delicate role, though section 135(2) makes it clear that a private practitioner may be selected in certain exceptional cases. This occurred in *Re Croftheath Ltd*,[66] where Brightman J. appointed a private practitioner because it would be more cost effective. The provisional liquidator should assume a neutral stance[67] in the dispute between the petitioner and the company, and he should certainly not prejudge the outcome of the petition. A recent illustration of the circumstances under which a provisional liquidator may be appointed is provided by the case of *Re Highfield Commodities Ltd*.[68] Here the Secretary of State had presented a winding-up petition in the public interest against a company which was alleged to be defrauding its American customers. A provisional liquidator had been appointed at an *ex parte* hearing. Two months later, the company sought to have the provisional liquidator discharged. Megarry V.-C. refused either to discharge the provisional liquidator, or to require an undertaking in damages to be given in the event of his appointment proving to be unjustified. Megarry V.-C. also held that although it was not clear in the then current winding-up rules it was possible for the court to appoint a provisional liquidator on a winding-up petition presented by the Secretary of State.

6-31 Normally the provisional liquidator takes no active part in the management of the company. If he feels that it is necessary that trading should continue, he can apply to the court under section 177 of the Insolvency Act 1986 to have a special manager appointed. Thus, in *Re U.S. Ltd*[69] a special manager was appointed to sell certain haute couture clothes whilst they remained in fashion. Delay in selling these items would not have benefited anyone. Further provision on special manager is to be found in rules 4.206–4.210 of the Insolvency Rules 1986.

2. Invalidation of dispositions, etc.[70]

6-32 A crucial element in the strategy of protecting the company's assets during the period of the interregnum is to be found in section 127 of the Insolvency Act 1986:

> "In a winding up by the court, any disposition of the company's property, and any transfer of shares, or alteration in the status of the company's members,

---

[65] The appointment will terminate the authority of the agents—*Pacific and General Insurance v. Hazell* [1997] B.C.C. 400. For costs where the petition is ultimately dismissed see *Re A Company (No. 001951 of 1987)* [1988] B.C.L.C. 182. On procedure note Practice Direction 31 1996, *The Times*, December 5, 1996.

[66] *The Times*, February 18, 1975.

[67] *Re Chateau Hotels Ltd* [1977] 1 N.Z.L.R. 381.

[68] [1984] 3 All E.R. 885. See also *Re Pinstripe Farming Ltd* [1996] B.C.C. 913.

[69] (1984) 1 B.C.C. 98, 985. See also *Re Mawcon Ltd* [1969] 1 All E.R. 188.

[70] For further discussion see Chap. 11 *post*.

made after the commencement of the winding up is, unless the court otherwise orders, void."

6-33 The purpose of this provision was explained by Buckley J. in *Re Levy (Holdings) Ltd* as follows:[71]

> "It was designed to preserve the value of the assets of a company for the benefit of the people interested in the assets, notwithstanding the pendency of winding up proceedings in order that the company might not be unduly hampered in carrying out transactions which might be for the benefit of those interested in the value of its assets."

For the purposes of this provision, it should be noted that if a winding-up order is subsequently made, the liquidation is deemed to commence at the date of the petition.[72]

Transactions covered

6-34 Section 127 is capable of nullifying a wide range of transactions. A transfer of shares falls within its ambit.[73] Clearly, the repayment of debts by the company (whether in whole or in part) would be caught by this provision.[74] It is no excuse that the person receiving the payment was unaware of the winding-up petition.[75] Furthermore, it was held in *Re Western Welsh International Building Systems Ltd*[76] that repayment of the debt claimed by the petitioner himself could also be invalidated by section 127. The sale of company property or the grant of security could also fall foul of this provision.[77] However, it was decided by Goulding J. in *Sowman v. David Samuel Trust Ltd*[78] that the appointment of a receiver to enforce an existing security was not within the scope of section 127.

Advance rulings

6-35 The section is not entirely negative in its impact, for it is clear that it can be exploited by directors who can apply to the court for an advance ruling as to whether a particular transaction occurring after the date of the winding-up petition would be sanctioned by the court.[79]

---

71 [1964] Ch. 19 at 24. See also *Re Wiltshire Iron Co.* (1868) L.R. 3 Ch. 443.
72 Insolvency Act 1986, s.129(2).
73 *Sullivan v. Henderson* [1973] 1 W.L.R. 333.
74 *Peak v. Midland Commercial Services* [1977] C.L.Y. 303, *Re Grays Inn Construction Co.* [1980] 1 All E.R. 814.
75 *Re Civil Service and General Store* (1888) 58 L.T. 220.
76 (1985) 1 B.C.C. 99, 296.
77 See Chap. 11 here. But in *Re French's Wine Bar Ltd* (1987) 3 B.C.C. 173, Vinelott J. held that the completion of an unimpeachable specifically enforceable contract entered into prior to the petition was not a disposition of company property as the company was not beneficially entitled to the property at the date of the petition.
78 [1978] 1 W.L.R. 22.
79 *Re Levy (Holdings) Ltd* [1964] Ch. 19, *Re Operator Control Cabs Ltd* [1970] 3 All E.R. 657. The earlier decision of Vaisey J. in *Re Miles Aircraft Ltd* [1948] Ch. 188 must now be considered as bad law.

Criteria

6-36 Section 127 is silent on the criteria to be applied by the court when deciding whether to exempt transactions from its invalidating effect. Recourse to case law principles is essential here.[80] Thus, in *Re Park, Ward and Co. Ltd*,[81] the company created a charge over its assets to secure a loan which the company required to enable it to continue paying its employees wages. The chargee knew of the petition but the court still validated the charge. Again, in *Re Steane's (Bournemouth) Ltd*,[82] the circumstances were similar but the money was needed to prevent the business being paralysed in the period prior to the hearing of the petition. The lender who took the security acted in good faith and knew nothing of the petition. The court sanctioned the grant of security by the company. Ignorance of the petition is not a ground for the court exercising its discretion to sanction the arrangement for the simple reason that advertisement of the petition constitutes constructive notice of its presentation to the whole world.[83] This proposition must be read in the light of *Denney v. John Hudson & Co. Ltd*[84] where the Court of Appeal sanctioned a payment of money by an insolvent haulage company to its usual supplier of diesel fuel, since failure to maintain this source of fuel would lead to an immediate cessation of the haulage business and this would not have been in the interests of creditors. A key factor behind the sympathetic attitude of the court was the fact that the petition had not yet been advertised at the time of the payment, and the supplier was therefore unaware that liquidation was imminent.

Consequences

6-37 Finally, it should be noted that section 127 does not deal with the consequences of a transaction being invalidated. It specifies no recovery process. The general mechanisms of tracing and voidable preference would instead have to be employed.[85] Alternatively, there is the possibility of instituting misfeasance proceedings against the directors who were responsible for the illicit transaction.[86]

3. The restriction on legal proceedings and execution processes

6.38 It is clear from sections 126 and 128 of the Insolvency Act 1986 that the presentation of the petition will also prevent the pursuit of legal actions or the levying of execution against the company's assets. The principles to be applied here are considered fully in Chapter 8.

---

[80] The transaction must be designed to benefit the company (and not its directors)—*Re Webb Electrical Ltd* [1988] B.C.L.C. 382. In *Re French's Wine Bar Ltd* (1987) 3 B.C.C. 173 Vinelott J. indicated that the court would sanction a valid specifically enforceable contract entered into prior to the petition. See also *Re Sugar Properties (Derisley Wood) Ltd* (1987) 3 B.C.C. 88. If it is a case of a solvent company which is being wound up by the court, sanction is more likely to be forthcoming—*Re Burton & Deakin Ltd* [1977] 1 W.L.R. 390. For a more marginal case see *Re A Company (No. 007523 of 1986)* (1987) 3 B.C.C. 57.

[81] [1926] Ch. 828.

[82] [1950] 1 All E.R. 21.

[83] *Re T.W. Construction Ltd* [1954] 1 W.L.R. 540, *Re Leslie Engineers Co. Ltd* [1976] 1 W.L.R. 292.

[84] [1992] B.C.L.C. 503.

[85] *Re Leslie Engineers Co. Ltd* (*supra*).

[86] *Re Neath Harbour Smelting & Rolling Works Ltd* [1887] W.N. 87.

THE HEARING OF THE PETITION

6-39 The decision whether to grant the winding-up order, or not, is entirely a matter for the discretion of the court. This much is apparent from the language of section 125(1) of the Insolvency Act 1986. The court can accede to the petition notwithstanding the fact that the company's assets are mortgaged to the hilt. A creditor who can show that he is owed in excess of £750[87] and that he has followed the correct procedure is entitled to a winding-up order as of right (*ex debito justitiae*).[88] However, in spite of this, the court might decide to exercise its discretion to reject the petition. If the company is already in voluntary liquidation and the court is satisfied that the interests of creditors are well protected, it might instead prefer to allow that situation to continue.[89]

Creditors opposed

6-40 Clearly, if a majority[90] of the company's other creditors are opposed to liquidation (*e.g.* because they think it could trade its way out of difficulties), that fact might influence the court to refuse a winding-up order. On the other hand, it must be stressed that the court will not be swayed by the pure arithmetic of the situation. To do so would result in its discretion being fettered.[91] Thus, in *Re Flooks of Bristol (Builders) Ltd*,[92] the majority of the creditors who were opposed to the petition enjoyed the protection of security, and could therefore afford to give the company a second chance. Notwithstanding their opposition, Vinelott J. granted the winding up order. The court will also disregard the majority view if the majority has some vested interest in the company over and above its interest as creditors—*e.g.*, as shareholders or directors.[93] The Court of Appeal ignored majority opposition to the petition for this reason in the case of *Re Holiday Stamps Ltd*.[94]

Ulterior motive

6-41 The court will not, on the other hand, grant a winding-up order if the petitioner has some ulterior motive for seeking the liquidation. The court is always alert to the possibility of an abuse of process here.[95] It must be remembered that the granting of a winding-up order is a class remedy designed to benefit all of the company's

---

[87] This figure may be varied by the Secretary of State. The £750 figure is normally regarded as an absolute minimum for a successful petition—*Re Industrial Insurance Association* [1910] W.N. 245. Creditors can combine their debts to qualify—*Re Leyton & Walthamstowe Cycle Co.* [1901] W.N. 275. Debts of less than £750 may suffice if the company is deliberately exploiting the law to avoid paying—*Re World Industrial Bank* [1909] W.N. 148. Debts in a foreign currency can also found a statutory demand—*Re A Debtor (No. 51/SD.1991)* [1992] 1 W.L.R. 1294. The debt must not be statute-barred—*Re Karnos Property Co. Ltd* [1989] B.C.L.C. 340.

[88] *Re Camburn Petroleum Products Ltd* [1979] 3 All E.R. 297.

[89] See *Re Medisco Equipment Ltd* [1983] B.C.L.C. 305, *Re Rhine Film Corp.* (1986) 2 B.C.C. 98, 949 and *Re Fitness Centre (South East) Ltd* [1986] B.C.L.C. 518.

[90] This means a majority in value.

[91] *Re Southard & Co. Ltd* [1979] 1 W.L.R. 1199.

[92] [1982] Com. L.R. 53.

[93] *Re Vuma Ltd* [1960] 1 W.L.R. 1283. Compare *Re A.B.C. Coupler & Engineering Co. Ltd* [1969] 1 All E.R. 354.

[94] *The Times*, July 11, 1985.

[95] *Re A Company* [1894] 2 Ch. 349, *Re A Company (No. 001573 of 1983)*, *The Times*, May 5, 1983. Malicious presentation of a winding up petition is a tort—for discussion see *Partizan Ltd v. Kilkenny & Co Ltd* [1998], 1 B.C.L.C. 157.

creditors, and not to further some ulterior strategem of the petitioner.[96] Thus, in *Re A Company (No. 0013925 of 1991) ex parte Roussel*[97] it was held to be an abuse of process for the petitioner to have notified the company's bank of the petition with the intention of triggering a withdrawal of continued finance from the company. The courts in *Re A Company (No. 001259 of 1991) ex parte Medialite Ltd*[98] indicated that they will frown upon the use of winding-up procedures as an alternative to waiting for cheques to be cleared through normal banking channels, and will strike out petitions in such circumstances.

6-42 The issue of ulterior motive arose again in *Re Leigh Estates Ltd*[99] where a local authority petitioned for the winding up of a company in respect of rates arrears owed by it. It appeared that the local authority preferred this form of insolvency regime to receivership because it will recoup more of its arrears. The court held that this was not in the interests of unsecured creditors at large who would gain more benefit if the company did not go into liquidation.

6-43 The issue of ulterior motive can also be raised when considering opposition to a winding up petition. The court is aware that opposition might relate not to the financial position of the company but may be put forward to block an investigation of its affairs which would be an inevitable consequence of compulsory liquidation.[1]

Costs

6-44 If the petition fails, the petitioner will naturally be expected to meet the costs of the abortive petition.[2] However, this may not be so if the company was, by its behaviour, responsible for the petition being presented in the first place.[3] If the company wrongfully opposes a petition which proves to be successful, the costs of the company are not to be met out of its assets. Therefore, any solicitor acting for a company which is vexatiously opposing a petition should look for an indemnity from the shareholders or directors to meet his bill.[4]

THE EFFECT OF A WINDING-UP ORDER

6-45 Once the court grants a winding-up order, the date of commencement of the compulsory liquidation procedure is fixed. By virtue of section 129(2) of the Insolvency Act 1986, the date of commencement is deemed to be the time when the

---

[96] *Re Greenwood* [1900] 2 Q.B. 306, *Re Chapel House Colliery Co.* (1883) 24 Ch.D. 259, *Re Crigglestone Coal Co.* [1906] 2 Ch. 327, *Re A Company (No. 001573 of 1983)* [1983] Com. L.R. 202.

[97] [1992] B.C.L.C. 562—reported *sub nom. Re Bill Hennessey Associates Ltd* in [1992] B.C.C. 386.

[98] [1991] B.C.L.C. 594.

[99] [1994] B.C.C. 292.

[1] On this see *Bell Group Finance Pty Ltd v. Bell Group U.K. Holdings Ltd* [1996] 1 B.C.L.C. 304.

[2] *Re Fernforest Ltd* [1990] B.C.L.C. 693. But see *Re Edric Audio Visual, The Times*, May 14, 1981. See also *Re A Company (003689 of 1998), The Times*, October 7, 1998. Compare *Re Hayter & Sons (Portchester) Ltd* [1961] 2 All E.R. 676. If the petition succeeds, the petitioner's costs are to be paid out of the company's assets—*Re Bostels Ltd* [1968] Ch. 346.

[3] *Re McCarthy & Co. (Builders) Ltd (No. 2)* [1976] 2 All E.R. 339, *Re Lanaghan Brothers Ltd* [1977] 1 All E.R. 265. Compare *Re Arrow (Leeds) Ltd* [1986] B.C.L.C. 538.

[4] If the petition is dismissed because the company pays up it will be liable for the costs of the petitioner—*Re Nowmost Co. Ltd* [1997] B.C.C. 105. Directors can now be made personally responsible for the company's costs under Supreme Court Act 1981 s.51 and Civil Procedure Rules 1998 r. 48.2—see *Aiden Shipping v. Interbulk* [1986] A.C. 965 and *Re A Company (No. 004055 of 1991) ex p Doe Sport Ltd* [1991] 1 W.L.R. 1003. The type of order used in *Re Bathampton Properties Ltd* [1976] 1 W.L.R. 168 will therefore no longer be used.

successful petition was presented to the courts and not the date of the order.[5] This backdating of the winding-up, so to speak, can have important practical consequences in relation to the avoidance of transactions (*e.g.*, under sections 127, 238–40 and 245 of the Insolvency Act 1986).

6-46 However, this retrospective feature is not universal. Thus it is clear that a floating charge created by the company over its assets will, in the absence of provision to the contrary, crystallise at the latest at the date of the winding-up order, and not the presentation of the petition.[6] Contracts of employment are also only terminated at the date of the order.[7] In the case of debts in a foreign currency the date of conversion into sterling is once again the date of the order.[8]

Grant of order

6-47 If a winding-up order is granted, it should be officially notified in the *Gazette*,[9] and it is also required, by virtue of section 130(1), to be recorded at the Companies Registry.[10] Under rules 4.20 and 4.21, the court must notify the official receiver of its order and he will then communicate the fact of his appointment to the company and deal with the gazetting of the order and notification under section 130(1). The official notification of the order does not, of itself, give constructive notice to the world of the compulsory liquidation,[11] though registration at Cardiff presumably does. Business letters, etc, must also disclose the fact that the company has gone into liquidation.[12]

6-48 The company will not be deprived of the legal title to its assets merely because a compulsory liquidation has commenced, as the House of Lords made clear in *Ayerst v. C. & K. Construction Ltd*,[13] though of course the directors will lose their power to manage its affairs. The prohibition on the commencement or prosecution of actions against the company without the leave of the court is maintained by section 130(2) of the Insolvency Act 1986. One case deserving of special mention in this context is *Re Coregrange Ltd.*[14] Here, Vinelott J. held that the court would normally be prepared to grant leave to bring an action for specific performance of an unimpugnable contract to purchase property from the company, because it would be unfair to condemn the plaintiff in such a case to the vastly inferior remedy of suing the defendant insolvent company for damages for breach of contract.

6-49 Two questions have cropped up with some regularity in recent times, namely what are the consequences of commencing an action without leave, and

---

5 See also *Bank of New South Wales v. Official Assignee* [1982] 1 N.Z.L.R. 427. On the significance for limitation periods see *Re Cases of Taffs Well Ltd* [1992] B.C.L.C. 11.

6 *Hodson v. Tea Co.* (1880) 14 Ch.D. 859, *Wallace v. Automatic Machines* [1894] 2 Ch. 547, *Re Crompton & Co. Ltd* [1914] 1 Ch. 954.

7 *Chapman's Case* (1866) L.R. 1 Eq. 346. Confirmed by the Privy Council in *Commercial Finance Co. Ltd v. Ramsingh—Mahabir* [1994] 1 W.L.R. 1297.

8 Insolvency Rules 1986, r. 4.91. See also *Re Dynamics Corp. of America* [1976] 2 All E.R. 669, *Re Lines Brothers Ltd* [1982] 2 W.L.R. 1010.

9 Companies Act 1985, s.42(1)(*a*).

10 The registrar will in fact place the notice in the *Gazette* and this will constitute official notification—see Companies Act 1985, s.711(1)(ip) and (2).

11 *Official Custodian of Charities v. Parway Express* [1984] 3 W.L.R. 525.

12 Insolvency Act 1986, s.188.

13 [1976] A.C. 167. A trust for the benefit of creditors is activated—*Re Cases of Taffs Well* [1992] B.C.L.C. 11.

14 [1984] B.C.L.C. 453. Note here *Re French's Wine Bar Ltd* (1987) 3 B.C.C. 173 and *Canon v. G.A. Business Systems* [1993] B.C.L.C. 1194.

whether the court can mitigate those consequences by granting retrospective leave. The initial view here was quite draconian. Proceedings instituted without leave were void and that state of affairs could not be altered ex post facto by approaching the court and asking its forgiveness.[15] A more liberal approach was adopted by Lindsay J. in *Re Saunders Ltd*[16]—the court did have the power to rectify matters by granting leave "*nunc pro tunc*", *i.e.* with retrospective effect. That latter approach now appears to be the more favoured solution.[17]

Power to discharge order

6-50 It is sometimes assumed that the making of an order for compulsory liquidation is an irrevocable step; this is not so. The court enjoys the power under section 146 of the Act to discharge or stay winding-up orders.[18] If there is a serious possibility of a rescue scheme being put into effect, this would be a suitable course of action for the court to adopt.[19] In *Re Orthomere Ltd*,[20] Vinelott J. decided to stay a winding-up order in curious circumstances. Here, two petitions had been presented to wind up an insolvent company. The earlier partition had been presented by the Secretary of State, and the later one by the Inland Revenue. For some reason, the winding-up order was made on the basis of the second petition. Unfortunately, this precluded the liquidators from challenging certain alleged fraudulent preferences which could have been impugned had the order been based on the earlier petition. Vinelott J. decided to stay the proceedings and to grant a winding-up order on the first petition. The court can also rescind a winding-up order, the appropriate authority being contained in rule 7.47(1) of the Insolvency Rules 1986.[21]

THE APPOINTMENT OF THE LIQUIDATOR[22]

6-51 In the immediate aftermath of the winding-up order, the court will appoint the Official Receiver to act pending the appointment of a private practitioner by the creditors. Once again, the Official Receiver is described as a "provisional liquidator," though of course his role here is somewhat different to the one already adverted to. A liquidator selected by the creditors under section 139 of the Insolvency Act 1986 must be a qualified insolvency practitioner[23] and must satisfy the other conditions imposed by the 1986 Act. The appointment of joint liquidators is permissible.[24] The creditors can no longer opt to allow the official receiver to continue to act as liquidator by refusing to appoint a liquidator themselves; in such a case the contributories' nominee (if any) will become liquidator.[25] Section 163 states that the official

---

[15] *Re National Employers Mutual General Insurance Association* [1995] B.C.C. 744 (Rattee J.).
[16] [1996] 3 W.L.R. 473.
[17] See for example the decision of Vinelott J. *Re Linkrealm Ltd* [1998] B.C.C. 478.
[18] It will not do so if the conduct of the directors is questionable—*Re Telescriptor Syndicate Ltd* [1903] 2 Ch. 174. Compare *Re Lowston Ltd* [1991] B.C.L.C. 570.
[19] See here *Re Patent Automatic Knitting Machine Co. Ltd* [1882] W.N. 97 and *Re Calgary and Edmonton Land Co. Ltd* [1975] 1 W.L.R. 355.
[20] (1981) 125 S.J. 495.
[21] See here *Re Calmex Ltd* (1988) 4 B.C.C. 761 and *Re Virgo Systems Ltd* (1989) 5 B.C.C. 833.
[22] See Insolvency Rules 1986, rr. 4.100–4.106 (as amended).
[23] See Insolvency Act 1986, Part XIII.
[24] This is less common these days in practice.
[25] S.139(3). *Cf. Re Prime Metal Trading Co. Ltd* [1984] B.C.L.C. 543. But see *Re Manmac Farmers Ltd* [1968] 1 W.L.R. 572.

name to be adopted is either to be "liquidator" or "official receiver and liquidator," where appropriate.

THE POWERS OF A LIQUIDATOR IN A COMPULSORY WINDING-UP

Sanction of committee

6-52 This matter is largely governed by a combination of section 167 and Schedule 4 of the Insolvency Act 1986. The Insolvency Rules 1986 are also relevant here.[26] These powers have already been described in Chapter 5 but it should be noted that a compulsory liquidator's powers are more circumscribed in that he will require the sanction of the court or committee before instituting or defending legal proceedings in the name of the company, and in order to carry on the business of the company (which rarely happens).[27] If a liquidator acts without first obtaining the sanction of the committee (or the court), as required, it is open to the committee (or the court) under rule 4.184(2) to ratify his actions. If a liquidator proposes to act contrary to the wishes of his liquidation committee he should either enlist the support of the general meeting of creditors or the court.[28] The power of ratification only arises where the liquidator acts in a case of urgency and seeks ratification promptly. The liquidator who acts inadvertently without authority may find his remuneration disallowed.

6-53 In addition to the above provisions, the following powers deserve special mention. Under section 144(1), the liquidator must take into possession all property belonging to the company, including that which it appears entitled to. Wrongful seizure of property belonging to a third party may expose the liquidator to liability in conversion.[29] However section 234(3) will protect him from liability for loss of damage not caused by his own negligence.

Statement of affairs

6-54 The liquidator can, under section 131, require a statement of affairs from the company's directors, etc. Additional rules on this statement can be found in the Insolvency Rules 1986, rules 4.32–4.38 (as amended). There is also the power to disclaim onerous property and contracts. This is another aspect of the law which has been dealt with in Chapter 5. A liquidator has power under section 215 of the Insolvency Act 1985 to inspect the Land Register.[30] The powers of the court to settle the list of contributories and to make calls upon them have been delegated to the liquidator as an officer of the court by the Insolvency Rules.[31] The liquidator normally enjoys discretionary power to call meetings of creditors and contributories, however he can be forced to do so under section 168(2) by contributories or creditors having the support of one tenth in value of their fellows.

---

[26] Insolvency Rules 1986, r. 4.184.
[27] See *Re Wreck Recovery and Salvage Co. Ltd* (1880) 15 Ch.D. 353.
[28] *Re Consolidated Diesel Engine Manufacturers Ltd* [1915] 1 Ch. 192, *Re North Eastern Insurance Co.* [1915] W.N. 210.
[29] See *Edwards v. Bendall* (1953) 103 L.J. 351.
[30] This inserts a new s.112AA into the Land Registration Act 1925.
[31] Insolvency Act 1986, s.160 and rr. 4.195–4.201.

Control over liquidator

6-55 The court, of course, will always oversee the exercise of powers by a liquidator in a compulsory winding-up. Persons aggrieved by his decisions can challenge them by applying to the court under section 168(5). The court has been called upon increasingly to review actions by liquidators by using the section 168(5) jurisdiction. In such cases the court is naturally reluctant to intervene however there is a body of precedent which indicates a willingness to make use of this reserve power. Thus, in *Re Greenhaven Motors Ltd*[32] a contributory challenged the action of a liquidator in settling a legal claim. This challenge was unsuccessful at first instance before Harman J., but on appeal the Court of Appeal felt that the liquidator had been unable to show that the company would gain any appreciable benefit from the compromise and it therefore should not be sanctioned. Again in *Re Edennote Ltd*[33] the Court of Appeal upheld a decision of Vinelott J. to set aside an assignment of a cause of action entered into by a liquidator who had failed to evaluate other options. Finally, in *Hamilton v. Official Receiver*[34] a refusal by a liquidator to sell a cause of action for a modest sum of money was successfully impugned. The liquidator did not intend to pursue the proceedings and although the applicant had offered a relatively small price for the claim there were no other persons willing to take a risk on it. The court can also, for example, authorise *ex gratia* payments by the liquidator where these may be necessary to promote the realisation process.[35] Moreover, it would appear from *Re Associated Travel Leisure and Services Ltd*,[36] that it does have the power to indemnify him against any personal liability incurred as a result of his misbehaviour in acting without proper sanction. The court can give guidance to the liquidator on an application to it under section 168(3) for directions.[37]

6-56 The liquidator can take part in a public examination[38] of company officers, etc., applied for by the official receiver under section 133. Only the official receiver can apply for such a public examination but he may be obliged to do so in certain circumstances.[39] The provisions of the Act on this matter are supplemented by rules 4.211–4.217 of the Insolvency Rules 1986.

CONTRACTS AND COMPULSORY LIQUIDATION

6-57 As a general rule, the entry of the company into compulsory liquidation will not terminate company contracts, save for contracts of employment.[40] Specific performance may be available for current contracts in appropriate circumstances.

---

32 [1999] B.C.C. 463.

33 [1996] 2 B.C.L.C. 389. At the end of the day the claim in question was compromised by the liquidator and Lightman J. refused to interfere with that particular decision—see *Re Edennote Ltd (No. 2)* [1997] 2 B.C.L.C. 89.

34 [1998] B.P.I.R. 602.

35 See *Banque des Marchands* [1953] 1 All E.R. 278.

36 [1978] 2 All E.R. 273.

37 See *Ross v. Smith* 1986 S.L.T. (Sh.Ct.) 59. On procedure see *Re Hinckley Island Hotel Ltd* [1998] 2 B.C.L.C. 526.

38 For costs see *Re Avatar Communications* (1988) 4. B.C.C. 473.

39 Under s.133(2) his hand can be forced by creditors owed 50 per cent. in value of the company's debts.

40 *Chapman's Case* (1866) L.R. 1 Eq. 346.

However, such contracts are vulnerable in that they are subject to the liquidator's power of disclaimer under section 178 of the Insolvency Act 1986. As a counterbalance, the court enjoys power under section 186 to rescind contracts made between some person and the company on the application of that person. Such rescission may be on such terms as the court thinks fit, and if it decides to award damages to the applicant, these may be proved for in the liquidation.

Liquidator's contract

6-58 What is the legal position with regard to contracts made by the liquidator on behalf of the company? It was held in *Stead Hazel and Co. v. Cooper*[41] that a liquidator in a compulsory winding-up does not incur personal liability on contracts made in such circumstances. Personal liability may arise, however, if the contract is made under seal.[42]

DUTIES OF THE LIQUIDATOR

Basic duty

6-59 The basic role of the liquidator is outlined by section 143(1), which provides as follows:

> "The functions of the liquidator of a company which is being wound up by the court are to secure that the assets of the company are got in, realised and distributed to the company's creditors and, if there is a surplus, to the persons entitled to it."

Thus, the liquidator is obliged to realise the assets as efficiently as possible and to satisfy all liabilities insofar as the realised assets will allow this. He is not entirely without discretion in performing this duty, as section 168(4) makes clear. A liquidator who fails to fulfil this duty can, of course, be penalised by a misfeasance action[43] under section 212 of the Insolvency Act 1986. He also runs the risk of being deprived of his claim to costs.[44] The fact that the liquidator is an officer of the court does not, apparently, render him immune from an action in negligence.[45] A liquidator who, as part of the realisation process, pursues misfeasance or fraudulent trading actions unsuccessfully, may incur liability for costs, though these could be covered by his indemnity.[46]

6-60 The liquidator must take into account all claims against the company of which he is aware. It is clear from the leading case of *Pulsford v. Devenish*[47] that this may involve him taking the initiative to contact known creditors, including contingent creditors. This might include, for example, the landlord under a lease of which the company in liquidation was the original tenant, but which has been assigned. He

[41] [1933] 1 K.B. 840.
[42] *Cf. Plant Engineers (Sales) Ltd v. Davis* (1969) 113 S.J. 484 (voluntary liquidator).
[43] Note here *Re Mouitex Ltd* [1992] 1 W.L.R. 303.
[44] *Re Silver Valley Mines* (1882) 21 Ch.D. 381.
[45] *I.R.C. v. Hoogstraten* [1985] Q.B. 1077.
[46] *Re Wilson Lovatt & Sons Ltd* [1977] 1 All E.R. 274.
[47] [1903] 2 Ch. 625.

cannot remain passive and simply wait for creditors to get in touch with him. Furthermore, the placement of a general advertisement will not absolve him of his responsibility to contact known creditors.[48]

Proper accounts

6-61 A liquidator must keep proper accounts and lodge any funds realised by him at the Insolvency Services Account at the Bank of England.[49] His accounts must be sent to the Secretary of State for audit. His obligation to file accounts and returns can be enforced under section 170 of the 1986 Act. A liquidator must by virtue of the Insolvency Regulations 1986 (S.I. 1986 No. 1994) also keep minutes of meetings and administrative records.

Officer of the court

6-62 In addition to these basic duties, it must always be remembered that a liquidator in a compulsory winding-up is an officer of the court and, as such, is subject to the strict duties imposed by the rule in *Ex p. James*.[50] In *Re Allebart Pty. Ltd*[51] Street J. felt that this position placed additional responsibilities on him to search out misconduct by company officers and to rectify matters by instituting civil or criminal proceedings. He should also jealously protect his independence. Moreover, under rule 4.149 of the Insolvency Rules 1986, the court can set aside transactions between a liquidator and an "associate" where full value has not been given.

Duties to particular creditors

6-63 In addition to these duties imposed by law a liquidator may in principle undertake additional obligations to particular creditors in contract,[52] though this type of arrangement needs to be carefully monitored to prevent conflicts of interest arising.

THE LIQUIDATION COMMITTEE

6-64 A liquidator in a compulsory winding-up may be answerable to the liquidation committee established by the company's creditors under section 141 of the Insolvency Act 1986. Further details on the constitution and role of this committee are to be found in rules 4.151–4.172 of the Insolvency Rules 1986 (as amended). The committee must consist of between three and five creditors and its quorum must be at least two creditors. Votes are passed by a simple majority and there is no weighting of votes. Under rule 4.170 there are tight restrictions on dealings between committee members and the estate. These matters have been discussed above in Chapter 5.

---

48 *Re Armstrong Whitworth Securities Co. Ltd* [1947] Ch. 673.

49 Note also Insolvency Act 1986, ss.151 and 403–409.

50 (1874) 9 Ch. App. 609. Note also *Re Regent Finance and Guarantee Corp.* [1930] W.N. 84. An official receiver is subject to similar duties—*Re Wyvern Developments Ltd* [1974] 1 W.L.R. 1097. However, moral gestures over and above these duties are not required. Moreover, an estoppel which might bind the company does not bind the liquidator if it were to frustrate his statutory duties—*Re Exchange Securities and Commodities Ltd* [1987] 2 W.L.R. 893.

51 [1971] 1 N.S.W.L.R. 24. Compare *Re South West Car Sales Ltd* [1998] B.C.C. 163.

52 *AJ Fabricators Ltd v. Grant* [1998] 2 B.C.L.C. 227.

PROOF OF DEBTS

6-65 The background law on these matters is similar to that applicable in voluntary liquidations, and the reader should refer to Chapter 5. The special rules relating to compulsory liquidations are referred to in the appropriate footnotes.

REMOVAL, RESIGNATION OR VACATION OF OFFICE BY THE LIQUIDATOR

6-66 These matters have again been dealt with in Chapter 5.

FINAL MEETING OF CREDITORS AND DISSOLUTION

6-67 Once the liquidator has realised all potential assets and distributed all available funds, section 146 of the Insolvency Act 1986 requires him to call a final meeting of creditors.[53] It is important that he retains sufficient sums in hand to fund such a meeting. The liquidator will then make a report to the meeting which may grant him his release.[54] If it does not, the liquidator will have to apply to the Secretary of State for his release under rule 4.121.

Dissolution

6-68 The liquidator must then notify the court and the Companies Registry of the outcome of the meeting. Three months later the company will be automatically dissolved.[55] The effect of this, and how it can be reversed, are dealt with in Chapter 5.

Expedited procedure

6-69 The Insolvency Act 1986 makes a radical change in the procedure leading up to dissolution of a company that has been wound up by the court in that it allows it to be shortcircuited where the company's realisable assets are insufficient to cover the costs of the liquidation, and also where its affairs do not require full investigation. In such circumstances, the official receiver may apply to the Registrar of Companies under section 202 of the Act for an early dissolution order. However, he must give at least 28 days notice of his intention to do so to any creditors, contributories or administrative receiver. Where the official receiver has made such an application, the Registrar must record the fact in his register and after three months the company will be automatically dissolved. It is open to creditors, contributories or an administrative receiver to apply to the Secretary of State to prevent an early dissolution under section 202. The procedure governing such an application is mapped out by section 203 of the Act. Basically, the Secretary of State may give directions on such an application to the effect that the winding up should proceed as normal or alternatively, that the three month period for automatic dissolution be deferred.

---

[53] Insolvency Rules 1986, r. 4.125.
[54] For the effect of a liquidator's release, see Insolvency Act 1986, s.174(6).
[55] *ibid.*, s.205.

CHAPTER 7

Fixed and Floating Charges

7-01 Secured creditors form a somewhat heterogenous group, although they have certain features in common. For example:

(1) Most fixed and floating charges require registration at the Companies Registry in Cardiff if the security is to stand up against the liquidator and other creditors. (See Chapter 11.)

(2) Unless the security can be avoided for non-registration or for some other reason the secured creditor's rights against the charged assets prevail over the claims of unsecured creditors on corporate insolvency.

(3) The secured creditor can take possession of the charged assets (either personally or by a receiver) and ensure the repayment of the debt due to him from the company in various ways depending on the type and terms of the security. Unsecured creditors have no such rights.[1]

7-02 However there are important differences between the two main forms of security recognised by English law, namely fixed and floating charges. The remainder of this chapter is devoted to a consideration of them.

FIXED CHARGES

7-03 If a company wishes to raise money from a bank, it will naturally be expected to give security in return for the loan. The most attractive security which it can offer will consist of the company's land, (*e.g.* factory premises), and fixed plant. Major items like ships,[2] aircraft, etc., owned by the company, will also be an obvious potential source of fixed security. A company can create a number of fixed charges over its assets.[3]

Land

7-04 Where a company creates a fixed charge over its land, details of that charge will have to be registered at the Companies Registry pursuant to sections 395 and 396(1)(*d*) of the Companies Act 1985. In addition, particulars of the security may also have to be recorded at the Land Registry or the Land Charges Registry.[4]

---

[1] *Harris v. Beauchamp Bros.* [1894] 1 Q.B. 801, *Re Swallow Footwear Ltd*, *The Times*, October 23, 1956.

[2] See *e.g. The Pan Oak* [1992] 2 Lloyds Rep. 36.

[3] Where this happens chargees can vary their priority *inter se* without obtaining the consent of the company—*Cheah Theam Swee v. Equiticorp Finance Group* [1992] 2 W.L.R. 108.

[4] All charges over registered land require registration at the Land Registry—Land Registration Act 1925, s.60(1). Specific charges over unregistered land created after 1970 must be registered at the Land Charges Registry. Double registration is not required for unregistered land in the case of a floating charge already registered at the Companies Registry—Land Charges Act 1972, s.3(7).

Ships and aircraft

7-05 Charges over ships and aircraft must not only be registered at the Companies Registry, but also respectively on the Merchant Shipping Register[5] and the Register of Aircraft Mortgages.[6]

Priority

7-06 Where a company creates a fixed charge over property, this may take the form of a legal mortgage or charge, or some form of an equitable security—*e.g.* a charge over land created informally by deposit of title deeds. Such an equitable charge also requires registration at the Companies Registry.[7] Subject to the rules on registration and notice and any agreement between chargees, fixed charges rank in order of date of creation (*qui priori est tempore potior est jure*). However an equitable chargee will lose priority to a later legal chargee if the latter took his security for value and without notice of the earlier equitable charge. This is very unlikely to happen if the rules as to registration are observed, as registration is legally equivalent to notice to subsequent chargees of the existence of the charge.

7-07 Clearly, as a general rule, a fixed charge will take priority over a floating charge covering the same assets (subject to the rules on registration and notice). However, it is possible for a fixed chargee to surrender priority to a floating charge by agreement. Where this is done, the fixed chargee should be aware that he may be giving more away than he initially intended. This danger was perfectly illustrated by *Re Portbase Clothing Ltd*.[8] Here a company had created a fixed charge over book debts in favour of its bank. It later sought finance from the trustees of its pension fund in order to reduce its indebtedness to the bank. This finance was forthcoming but was in return for a charge on book debts, which it was conceded took effect as a floating charge. The bank was persuaded to postpone its rights to those of the trustees. On the liquidation of the company, a question arose as to whether the bank should also be postponed to the claims of the preferential creditors and of the liquidator for his expenses all of which would normally take priority over a floating charge. Chadwick J. answered this question in the affirmative. As the effect of the arrangement was that the fixed charge should be treated as if subject to the floating charge, it followed that it must also be treated as subject to claims having priority over the floating charge. Chadwick J. accepted that the conclusion might have been different had the parties agreed that the trustees should be subrogated to the bank's rights to the extent of the postponement of priority, but no such agreement had been made. The case will have come as a nasty shock to the bank in question, but the main outcome will surely be a revision of the wording of such postponement arrangements so as to incorporate a subrogation solution and thereby to avoid losing priority to other groups having priority over the floating charge.

7-08 Another related and complex priority issue arose in *Griffiths v. Yorkshire Bank*.[9] Here there were two debenture holders enjoying both fixed and floating

---

[5] Merchant Shipping Act 1895, s.31(1).

[6] Mortgaging of Aircraft Order 1972 (S.I. 1972, No. 1268).

[7] *Re Wallis and Simmonds (Builders) Ltd* [1974] 1 All E.R. 561.

[8] [1993] B.C.C. 96—following *Waters v. Widdows* [1984] V.R. 503. There is no objection to chargees altering priority rights as between themselves—*Cheah Theam Swee v. Equiticorp Finance Group Ltd* [1992] 1 A.C. 472.

[9] [1994] 1 W.L.R. 1427. It is curious that this case has never featured in any of the specialist Company Law reports. For analysis see Cooke (1995) 11 I.L. & P. 163 and Waller [1997–98] 3 R.A.L.Q. 131, *Walters* (1995) 16 Co. Law 291. For a Scottish perspective see *Grier* (1998) 19 Co. Law. 56.

charges created over a company's assets and the later floating charge was crystallised by the giving of notice by the second debenture holder. The earlier floating charge holder then appointed a receiver but it was held that the priorities had been determined already on the crystallisation of the later charge even though this might have an adverse effect upon preferentials. Morritt J. felt able to distinguish *Portbase*[10] because in that case there had been an agreement between the chargees as to their respective priorities. Having reached this conclusion, a priority order was drafted which seems to be inconsistent with the reasoning used in the judgment and certainly has created much uncertainty as to the position of preferentials where a complex priority relationship between various floating charge holders is present.

7-09 This question was revisited by Neuberger J. in *Re H & K (Medway) Ltd*[11] where again there were competing floating charges though a deed of priority had been agreed to deal with that context. Neuberger J. held that irrespective of who appoints the receiver and which floating charge prevails the obligation to meet preferential claim endures. In so deciding doubt was cast[12] upon the accuracy of the report of *Griffiths (supra)* and the fact that the preferentials were not represented before Morritt J. was commented upon. As a result the earlier views of Morritt J. were rejected and this rejection has met with broad approval in the world of insolvency practice.

Position of fixed chargee

7-10 A fixed chargee of a limited company is in a relatively strong position. The security attaches to the assets covered by the charge even if the company purports to dispose of them, unless the chargee agrees to release it.[13] So long as the charge is registered, the purchaser of charged property from the company can only take it subject to the charge. Furthermore, in the event of the company going into receivership or liquidation, fixed chargees are entitled to be repaid out of the proceeds of realisation of their security in priority to other claimants on the company's assets. This right of priority enjoyed by fixed chargees extends to giving them pre-eminence over preferential creditors of the company.[14] Despite these strengths the fixed chargee, particularly of book debts, still needs to be careful in appraising his security. This matter will be considered later in this Chapter. Fixed charges cannot improve the quality of the assets charged. Thus book debts of manufacturing companies are particularly likely to be subject to counterclaims for damages. Leasehold property may be liable to forfeiture for non-payment of rent or breach of covenant, or may be disclaimed by the liquidator (see Chapter 10). Intellectual property, increasingly the subject of fixed charges, may be useless without some licence from a third party that terminates automatically on insolvency.

FLOATING CHARGES

Court of Chancery creativity

7-11 Clearly, from the viewpoint of a person lending money to a limited company, it is advisable to be secured by a fixed charge. But what if the company has

---

[10] *Supra.*
[11] [1997] 1 B.C.L.C. 545. For comment see *Bidin* (1997) 18 Co. Law. 290.
[12] See *ibid.*, at 554.
[13] *Re Ind Coope and Co. Ltd* [1911] 2 Ch. 223.
[14] *Re Lewis Merthyr Consolidated Collieries* [1929] 1 Ch. 498.

already granted fixed charges over all available, suitable assets—taking a second or third ranking fixed charge over those same items of property may be futile. In Victorian England the problem of finding security for lenders to limited companies caused difficulties in the economy. The Court of Chancery, ingenious as ever, hit upon the solution. Why not allow a limited company to create a charge over items of property which could not be secured with a fixed charge—*e.g.* stock in trade? Such assets were not suitable subject matter for a fixed security for two reasons. First, they would be constantly changing from day to day, therefore it would be impossible for the chargee to identify his security and unless he kept renewing it with fresh replacement assets, his original security would soon be dissipated by the company. More importantly, from the viewpoint of the borrowing company, it would be impossible for it to conduct business with such "volatile" assets if it had to obtain the permission of the debenture holder before disposing of them.

The solution devised by the Court of Chancery in the celebrated *Panama Case*[15] of 1870 was to permit a limited company to create an equitable floating charge over its undertaking and stock in trade. Without getting too bogged down in metaphysics, this charge "hovered"[16] over the company's assets until the debenture holder decided to enforce the security. During this period, the company could dispose of assets included in the security without requiring the consent of the debenture holder. This solution was brilliant and must rank as one of the great creations of English law, though a similar concept was recognised in Roman law in the form of the hypotheca. The floating charge has been successfully exported throughout the Commonwealth,[17] and, in revised form, to the United States and Japan. However, it is a formulation that has attracted opposition on the Continent, thereby creating problems when questions of harmonising EEC insolvency laws arise.

Characteristics

7-12 Let us now consider in more detail the characteristics of this most enigmatic form of security. The classic analysis is provided by Romer L.J. in *Re Yorkshire Woolcombers Association Ltd*[18]—three basic features are to be noted:

(1) it is an equitable charge over the whole or a class of the company's assets. A floating charge will normally be over the whole assets and undertaking of the company, including uncalled capital, but there is no objection to restricting such a charge to a class of the company's assets such as book debts. This possibility was confirmed by the House of Lords in *Illingworth v. Houldsworth*.[19]

(2) The assets which are the subject of the floating charge are constantly changing. It is this feature of the security which makes a fixed charge impractical.

---

[15] (1870) 5 Ch. App. 318. For a historical survey see *Pennington* (1960) 23 M.L.R. 630 and *Ferran* [1988] C.L.J. 213.

[16] *Illingworth v. Houldsworth* [1904] A.C. 355 at 358 *per* Lord Macnaghten.

[17] Strangely, the floating charge was only accepted in Scotland in 1961. This reticence on the part of Scottish law to accept the notion of a floating charge owes much to the fact that Scottish law has been influenced by civil law systems found on the continent. See now *Sharp v. Woolwich Building Society* [1998] B.C.C. 115.

[18] [1903] 2 Ch. 284 at 295.

[19] [1904] A.C. 355.

Assets vesting in the company after the date of the creation of the floating charge are clearly comprised in the security, as are post-crystallisation assets, unless these are impressed with a trust in favour of other creditors—*e.g.*, where a liquidator has successfully recovered property on the grounds that its disposal by the company constituted a preference.[20] Notwithstanding this, the chargee will hope that the overall value of the security will remain stable and if there is evidence of its value diminishing, the debenture holder will normally be entitled, under the terms of his debenture, to appoint a receiver.

(3) The company will retain freedom to deal with the assets included in the security in the ordinary course of business so long as the charge continues to float. This is sometimes explained in terms of the company having a "licence" to deal with its assets. It is not easy to determine what constitutes a dealing by the company in the ordinary course of business. Clearly it is entitled to dispose of assets subject to the security,[21] but this freedom does not extend to permitting it to dispose of the whole or substantially the whole of its business and undertaking.[22] This freedom to deal with assets is terminated once the floating charge crystallises, whereupon it becomes a fixed equitable charge. The significance of this is that the company can no longer deal with the assets without first obtaining the permission of the debenture holder to whom the assets have been assigned in equity.[23] Crystallisation does not mean that the floating charge is converted into a fixed charge for priority purposes. This is reinforced by section 251 of the Insolvency Act 1986, which provides that whether a charge is to be viewed as a floating charge or otherwise, is to be determined by reference to its status at its date of creation.

These then are the determining characteristics of a floating charge. When the court is asked to determine whether a transaction constitutes such a charge it will concentrate upon the essential substance of the operation of the arrangement; the way in which it is dressed up is less important. In *Re Coslett Contractors Ltd*[24] the Court of Appeal was faced with a curious arrangement under which a company (then in administration) had ceded certain rights over coal washing plant to the owner of the land on which it was conducting a clean up operation. Under the terms of the contract the landowner could realise the plant in the event of the company failing to honour certain obligations under the land reclamation contract. The Court of Appeal

---

20 *Re Yagerphone Ltd* [1935] 1 Ch. 392. Followed in Australia in *Re Quality Camera Co. Pty Ltd* [1965] N.S.W.R. 1330, and *Re Masureik & Allan Pty Ltd* (1982) 6 A.C.L.R. 39. See *Milman* [1979] Conv 138. On the other hand, it appears that the debenture holders can lay claim to the proceeds of a successful misfeasance action—*Re Anglo-Austrian Printing and Publishing Union* [1895] Ch. 152, *Wood v. Woodhouse and Rawson United* [1895] W.N. 4 and *Re Asiatic Electric Co. Pty Ltd* (1970) 92 W.N. (N.S.W.) 361. A controversial issue is whether the proceeds of a successful wrongful trading claim are to be devoted to unsecured creditors, or are available to be claimed by secured creditors. In *Re Produce Marketing Consortium Ltd (No. 2)* [1989] B.C.L.C. 520 at 554 Knox J. supported the latter conclusion. However, this view has attracted criticism—(see *Oditah* [1990] L.M.C.L.Q. 205), and was not followed by Millett J. in *Re MC Bacon Ltd (No. 2)* [1990] 3 W.L.R. 646. The authors favour the latter interpretation.

21 *Re Vivian & Co. Ltd* [1900] 2 Ch. 654.

22 *Hubbuck v. Helms* (1887) 56 L.J. Ch. 536. But see *Re Borax & Co. Ltd* [1901] 1 Ch. 326.

23 *Re Tullow Engineering Holdings Ltd* [1990] I.R. 452.

24 [1997] B.C.C. 724—for comment see Sealy [1998] C.L.J. 22. Compare *Royal Trust Bank v. Nat West Bank* [1995] B.C.C. 128 where the security arrangement was found to have more in common with a fixed rather than a floating charge.

held that on close analysis the rights given to the landowner represented a floating charge which was void for non-registration.

Crystallisation

7-14 Clearly the most important event in the history of the floating charge will be its crystallisation. It is therefore unfortunate that it is still not entirely clear in English law when this metamorphosis will occur. This is a matter that requires further detailed consideration.

Appointment of receiver

7-15 The normal event which precipitates crystallisation will be the appointment of a receiver by debenture holders. In the vast majority of cases this will be effected out of court pursuant to an express power in the debenture. The appointment of receivers has been considered fully in Chapter 4 but a few points are worth repeating in the present context. The power to appoint a receiver can be exercised on the occurrence of certain events specified in the security documents (usually after a formal demand)—*e.g.* failure to pay principal or interest, the company's assets/liabilities ratio falling below a certain level, the levying of execution against the company's assets, or the presentation of a winding-up petition against it. As a last resort, debenture holders secured by a floating charge can always apply to the court for the appointment of a receiver, notably on the grounds of jeopardy to the security, but this facility is rarely exploited these days for the simple reason that jeopardy is often identified in a debenture as an event entitling the chargee to make an out of court appointment. Where the debenture holders appoint a receiver out of court the appointment commences, and therefore the charge crystallises, when the receiver receives the letter of appointment, provided he accepts the appointment within 24 hours.[25]

Liquidation

7-16 If the debenture holders have not acted before the winding-up commences, a floating charge will crystallise without further ado on the company's going into liquidation.[26] The debenture cannot prevent such a crystallisation. In the case of a voluntary liquidation, the key moment will, according to the Insolvency Act 1986, s.86, be the time of the resolution for winding-up. The position in the case of compulsory liquidation is less clear. Normally the date of commencement here would be the time when the successful petition was presented, (Insolvency Act 1986, s.129), but it is possible that, for the purposes of crystallisation, the crucial event will be the date of the winding-up order granted by the court.[27]

Ceasing business

7-17 Another event which will cause the charge to crystallise without intervention by the debenture holder will be the company ceasing to do business. This

[25] Insolvency Act 1986, s.33. See also *Re Gabriel Controls Pty Ltd* (1982) 6 A.C.L.R. 684.
[26] *Hodson v. Tea Co.* (1880) 14 Ch.D. 859, *Wallace v. Automatic Machines Co.* [1894] 2 Ch. 547, *Re Crompton and Co. Ltd* [1914] 1 Ch. 954.
[27] *Wallace v. Automatic Machines Co. (supra).* Contra *Site Preparations Ltd v. Buchan Developments Ltd* 1983 S.L.T. 317.

possibility was confirmed by Nourse J. in *Re Woodroffes (Musical Instruments) Ltd.*[28] Here a company had granted fixed and floating charges in favour of its bankers. In breach of the terms of the security it then granted a second floating charge to its controlling shareholder. Both floating charges provided for crystallisation on notice being given in certain events. The controlling shareholder served notice crystallising her charge and a few days later the bank appointed a receiver. The appointment would have crystallised the bank's charge irrespective of what had already happened. Nourse J. was faced with a complicated priority wrangle both between the two chargees and as between the chargees and the preferential creditors. The rights of the parties hinged on the date when the bank's floating charge crystallised. Nourse J. held that it was possible for a floating charge to crystallise without intervention where the company ceased to do business but there was no evidence that such a cessation had occurred until the bank had appointed its receiver.

7-18 Similar consequences will ensue from the sale of a business. In *Re The Real Meat Co. Ltd*[29] Chadwick J. was faced with a priority contest between various secured creditors, the outcome of which depended upon the question of whether a floating charge had crystallised automatically upon the sale of the company's business. The specific provisions in the debenture required a notice of demand to be served on the company on the cesser of business in order to crystallise the charge but it was held that this specific provision was not sufficiently unequivocal to exclude implied automatic crystallisation by operation of law on such an occurrence. Chadwick J. decided on the facts that such crystallisation had indeed occurred and drew the necessary conclusions from that fact.

Automatic crystallisation

7-19 A most hotly debated question in this area was whether it is possible to identify in the debenture certain events—*e.g.* those catalogued above as entitling the chargee to appoint a receiver—on the occurrence of which the floating charge will crystallise automatically, that is, without a positive act of intervention by the debenture holder, apart, possibly, in some cases, from notifying the company that this has happened. The advantage of the law allowing such a possibility is that it would enable a floating charge to crystallise possibly hours or even days before the receiver is actually appointed, and in priority disputes involving the floating charge such a time interval may prove crucial. Indeed, it also used to be thought that if the floating charge crystallised before the appointment of the receiver, he would then be acting to enforce a charge which was now fixed, therefore he would not have to concern himself with the payment of preferential claims.[30] This possibility has now been ruled out by section 251 of the Insolvency Act 1986, which defines a floating charge according to its status at its date of creation.

Conflict of authority

7-20 Notwithstanding this elimination of many of the practical advantages of automatic crystallisation, the question still remains, does English law recognise such

---

[28] [1985] 3 W.L.R. 543.

[29] [1996] B.C.C. 254. This case progressed to the Court of Appeal but on different grounds relating to the relative priority rights of various secured creditors—see *Mallett v. The Real Meat Producers Ltd* [1997] B.C.C. 537.

[30] *Stein v. Saywell* (1969) 121 C.L.R. 529.

a concept? The answer was doubtful for many years. Basically, a dispute existed as to whether a floating charge was a creature of law with certain immutable characteristics, *e.g.*, it can only crystallise on intervention—or whether it was simply the product of a contract between the company and chargee, and therefore could possess those characteristics which the parties to the contract append. Older authorities such as *Re Manila Railways Co. Ltd*[31] and *Evans v. Rival Granite Quarries Ltd*[32] suggest an underlying hostility towards the concept of automatic crystallisation on the part of the English judiciary. On the other hand, reading between the lines of the judgment of Nourse J. in *Re Woodroffes (Musical Instruments) Ltd*,[33] a more liberal attitude might be detected. In this case, the facts of which are given above, Nourse J. indicated that it would be possible to insert a provision in a debenture to the effect that any floating charge which it conferred would crystallise automatically in the event of another floating charge granted by the company itself crystallising. On the facts of the case before him, Nourse J. could find no evidence that such a clause had been included in the debenture in question. Indeed, the Cork Committee, (Cmnd. 8558 para. 1579) in its report of June 1982, felt that, on balance, the concept of automatic crystallisation was recognised by English law, although at the same time it recommended that Parliament should legislate to outlaw it.

7-21 A similar division of opinion has affected academics on this question. Moreover, the judges of the Commonwealth are split on this issue. The possibility of automatic crystallisation has been clearly accepted in New Zealand, by Speight J. in *Re Manurewa Transport Ltd*,[34] and by the High Court of Australia in *Stein v. Saywell*.[35] On the other hand, fierce opposition has been aroused in Canada.[36]

7-22 The authors are of the opinion that the English courts would uphold an automatic crystallisation clause provided it was explicitly drafted. The clause should state that the charge would crystallise immediately and without intervention by the debenture holder on the occurrence of certain specified events. It is not sufficient merely to state that the security will become enforceable in such circumstances.

Key decision

7-23 This opinion appears to have been confirmed by Hoffmann J. in *Re Brightlife Ltd*.[37] Here, the debenture provided that the chargee could by notice crystallise the floating charge if, for example, he believed that the security was in jeopardy. The company went into voluntary liquidation, and the liquidator sought the guidance of the court as to the efficacy of such a provision. If the provision for automatic crystallisation by notice was effective, under the law then applicable, the debenture holder would not have had to wait until the preferential creditors were satisfied. Hoffmann J. held that the possibility of crystallisation occurring in such

---

[31] [1897] A.C. 81.
[32] [1910] 2 K.B. 979.
[33] [1985] 3 W.L.R. 543.
[34] [1971] N.Z.L.R. 909. Followed by the New Zealand Court of Appeal in *Dovey Enterprises v. Guardian Assurance Publications* [1993] 1 N.Z.L.R. 540.
[35] (1969) 121 C.L.R. 529. But see *Re Bismarck Australia Pty Ltd* [1981] V.R. 527.
[36] *R. v. Churchill Consolidated Copper Corp.* (1979) 90 D.L.R. (3d) 357, *Re Caroma Enterprises Ltd* (1980) 108 D.L.R. 412.
[37] [1986] 3 All E.R. 673. See also *Re Permanent Houses (Holdings) Ltd* [1988] B.C.L.C. 563 and *Re Sperrin Textiles Ltd* [1992] 10 Bull. N.I. Law 12.

circumstances had been implicitly recognised in *Re Griffin Hotel Co. Ltd*[38] and as that decision had not been the subject of statutory reversal it must still be good law.[39] Furthermore, he was not prepared to interfere with the contractual freedom[40] of the parties to a debenture to arrange their own terms for crystallisation. He refused to be drawn on the public policy issues associated with automatic crystallisation, insisting that these were matters for Parliament and not for a judge at first instance.

Advantages of floating charge

7-24 These, then, are the characteristics of the floating charge. What are the pros and cons of this form of security? From the company's viewpoint, it allows it to tap a further source of security in its efforts to obtain finance, without thereby jeopardising its freedom to conduct its trade as it thinks fit. From the bank's standpoint, the floating charge enables it to obtain some security for a loan which would otherwise be unsecured, thereby affording a degree of protection for its investment. Another advantage has become apparent in recent years. A holder of a general floating charge has the right to appoint an administrative receiver over the company's assets, and as such, enjoys an effective veto on the entry of that company into administration (Insolvency Act 1986 section 9(3)). Other categories of secured creditor lack this blocking power. Consequently it has become more common in recent times to find banks who may be well secured by fixed charges also taking floating charges to secure possession of this right of veto. Such floating charges (sometimes termed "lightweight floating charges") often have no commercial value as security, but do carry this valuable legal right. Their validity was upheld by Vinelott J. in *Re Croftbell Ltd*[41] where the argument that they were designed simply to frustrate the will of Parliament to facilitate the administration order, was expressly rejected. Parliament had conferred this blocking power on certain floating charge holders and it was not for the courts to take it away.

Disadvantages

7-25 Unfortunately, in recent years, it has become apparent that the security afforded by the floating charge is less substantial than it once may have appeared. It has always been an inherent risk associated with the floating charge that the company might abuse its "licence" to dissipate the security. This freedom to deal with its assets has long been recognised as permitting the company to create further charges over its assets with priority to the floating charge.[42]

Negative pledge clauses

7-26 To avert this danger, prohibition or negative pledge clauses were devised to preclude the company from creating later charges with priority to, or ranking *pari passu* with, the floating charge. Unfortunately, these clauses which are now standard practice, are largely ineffective. This is because they will only serve to postpone the claims of a later chargee if he has actual notice of the clause. It is not enough that he

---

[38] [1941] Ch. 129.
[39] See *Re Brightlife Ltd* [1986] 3 All E.R. 673 at 678 *per* Hoffmann J.
[40] The contract analysis of the floating charge was favoured in *Fire Nymph Products Ltd v. The Heating Centre Pty Ltd* (1992) 7 A.C.S.R. 365.
[41] [1990] B.C.C. 781. See *Oditah* [1991] J.B.L. 49.
[42] *Wheatley v. Silkstone and Haigh Moor Coal Co.* (1885) 29 Ch.D. 715.

has notice of the existence of the earlier floating charge (registration amounts to constructive notice of it), and he is aware that a floating charge will be invariably accompanied by a negative pledge clause. English law does not permit him to put two and two together here to make four.[43] Furthermore, in English law (but not Scots law), as it is not required to register negative pledge clauses at the Companies Registry, there is no possibility of the doctrine of constructive notice being extended to them.[44] The advantage in gratuitous registration of a negative pledge clause is that it might serve to fix an alert searcher at the Companies Registry with actual notice of the clause but the practical possibility of such gratuitous registration is unclear at the moment. The law here, which clearly penalises the diligent searcher, is open to criticism, and the best solution would be to require negative pledge clauses to be registered at Cardiff.

Preferential creditors

7-27 Another flaw in the floating charge is that a receiver seeking to enforce it must set aside from his proceeds of realisation sufficient funds to meet the demands of the preferential creditors. These are a group of essentially unsecured claimants who have been identified by Parliament as being deserving of specially favourable treatment on corporate insolvency. The categories of preferential claims had grown substantially in the years up to 1985, with the state claiming the lion's share of the funds paid out to preferential creditors. The Cork Committee, in its efforts to redress the balance of priority rights on corporate insolvency, called for a substantial reduction in the number of preferential claims (in para. 1450). The government, for obvious reasons, was reluctant to do this, but eventually it partially conceded the point and the list of preferential claims in reduced form is now to be found in section 386 and Schedule 6 of the Insolvency Act 1986. In spite of this improvement in the position of holders of floating charges, it remains true that they still rank after the surviving preferential claims in priority disputes.[45] A full account of the rules applicable to preferential claims will be found in a later Chapter.[46]

Title retention clauses

7-28 The development of title retention clauses and trust devices over the past decade has further eroded the protection afforded to the holder of a floating charge in that when he takes his security in return for his loan, he cannot be sure that the assets which the company appears to own do in fact belong to it in law. Further discussion of the law relating to these devices and the question of whether they are effective against the claims of the floating chargee will be found in Chapter 9.

Statutory invalidation

7-29 Finally, it must be remembered that the floating charge has a particular vulnerability to attack by a liquidator or administrator seeking to maximise assets

---

[43] *English and Scottish Mercantile Investment Co. v. Brunton* [1892] 2 Q.B. 700.

[44] *Re Standard Rotary Machine Co.* (1906) 95 L.T. 829, *Wilson v. Kelland* [1910] 2 Ch. 306, *Earle Ltd. v. Hemsworth R.D.C.* (1928) 44 T.L.R. 605, *Siebe Gorman & Co. v. Barclays Bank* [1979] 2 Lloyds Rep. 142 at 160 *per* Slade J. and also *Welch v. Bowmaker (Ireland) Ltd* [1980] I.R. 251.

[45] But preferential claims do not rank in priority to fixed charges—*Re Lewis Merthyr Consolidated Collieries Ltd* [1929] 1 Ch. 498 and *Re G. L. Saunders Ltd* [1986] 1 W.L.R. 215.

[46] In Chap. 9.

available to unsecured creditors under section 245 of the Insolvency Act 1986.[47] This unique weakness of floating charges is considered in detail in Chapter 11.

FIXED OR FLOATING CHARGE?

Future book debts

7-30 It is not surprising, given the weaknesses of the floating charge discussed in the previous section, that while it remains of great importance to the positioning of the secured creditor faced with a threatened administration, it is of dubious value as a security. The tendency among lenders has been to extend the scope of the fixed charge into previously uncharted territory. In particular, they have embraced the idea of a fixed charge over future book debts. The validity of such a charge was upheld as long ago as 1888,[48] but the locus classicus in modern times is the judgment of Slade J. in *Siebe Gorman & Co. Ltd v. Barclays Bank*.[49] Here a bank debenture purported to create such a charge and also imposed restrictions on the company's right to deal with the book debts comprised in the security. Slade J. upheld the validity of the fixed charge, which was necessarily equitable in nature. The decision was controversial at the time, as despite the old case law the floating charge had come to be widely regarded as the only effective and proper way of charging future assets. Some Commonwealth judges,[50] for example in Australia and Canada, have been reluctant to give their blessing to this extended form of fixed charge whereas other courts have supported it, most notably the Irish Supreme Court in *Re Keenan Brothers Ltd*.[51]

Fixed charges over book debts: practical considerations

7-31 Although the fixed charge over future assets is now firmly re-established in English law, there are a number of practical matters which have to be taken into account in drafting such a security.

7-32 The first is that it must be apparent from the charge that the security is intended to operate in substance as a fixed and not a floating charge. This is one further application of a basic legal approach (familiar *e.g.* in connection with the distinction between leases and licenses) whereby the nature of a transaction is deduced from the substance of the arrangement between the parties, rather than from the words they have used to describe it. Labels can be ignored when determining substance, as Hutton J. made clear in *Re Armagh Shoes Ltd*[52] where a charge that had

---

[47] *Tudor Heights Ltd v. United Dominions Corp. Finance Ltd* [1977] 1 N.Z.L.R. 532, *Kelly v. McMahon Ltd* [1980] I.R. 347.

[48] *Tailby v. The Official Receiver* (1888) 13 App. Cas. 523.

[49] [1979] 2 Lloyd's Rep. 142.

[50] See *Hart v. Barnes* (1983) 7 A.C.L.R. 310 (Australia) and *Royal Bank of Canada v. Madill* (1981) 120 D.L.R. (3d) 17 (Canada).

[51] [1986] B.C.L.C. 242. See also *Re Masser Ltd* (1987) 5 I.L.T. 43, *Jackson v. Lombard and Ulster Banking* [1992] I.R. 94 and *Re Wogan's (Drogheda) Ltd* (1993) 11 I.L.T. 67. The fixed charge over future book debts had become so widely used in Ireland that the legislature has been forced to intervene to neutralise some of the advantages accruing to debenture holders, and in so doing, to protect the position of the Irish revenue authorities. Under section 115 of the Irish Finance Act 1986 fixed charges over future book debts created after May 27, 1986 cannot be used to defeat the preferential rights of the Revenue Commissioners because this section creates a mechanism under which a debenture holder relying upon such a security becomes liable for any fiscal default of the borrower. The effect of this statutory change has been to reduce the popularity of such forms of corporate security.

[52] [1981] 9 N.I.J.B.

been labelled as "fixed" was nevertheless held to have all the indicia of a floating charge, and was therefore treated as such for legal purposes.

7-33 So far as a charge on book debts is concerned, the crucial question appears to be whether in fact the charging company is left in a position to deal with the charged debts and their proceeds in the ordinary course of its business as it thinks fit. If so, the charge is treated as a floating charge only. The issue has generally revolved around the questions of the degree to which the charge provides for the chargee to control the proceeds of the charged debts, and the degree to which in fact he does so.

7-34 Where the chargee is a bank, and the charge provides in effect that the company may not deal with its debts, and that the proceeds of debts must be paid into the company's account with that bank and not dealt with otherwise than in accordance with the bank's instructions, the charge has invariably been treated as fixed, as in *Siebe Gorman (supra)* itself, even if the bank does nothing particular about giving instructions otherwise than by providing for overdraft limits and repayment on demand in the usual way. However, where the chargee is not a bank, it has generally been thought essential (at least in the case of a purported fixed charge over future debts and their proceeds) not only that the charge itself should provide suitable restrictions on dealings and a suitable mechanism giving the chargee the necessary degree of control, but that the chargee should in fact exercise control.[53] This is in contrast to the approach of the Irish Supreme Court in *Re Wogan's Drogheda Ltd*[54] where failure to set up the designated collection account was held not to be destructive of the genuine intention of the parties to create a fixed charge security.

7-35 An ingenious solution to this problem was found by 3i plc (which is not a bank) in *Re New Bullas Trading Ltd.*[55] In this case the charge was expressed to be fixed as to present and future debts owing to the company, and contained the usual provisions prohibiting dealings with debts and for payment of the proceeds into a bank account specified by the chargee and for drawings only in accordance with its directions. However, until such directions were given, or a demand for repayment was made, the proceeds of debts were to be treated as released from the charge on payment into the designated bank, and thereafter subject only to the residual floating charge created by the same debenture. In fact 3i did not give any directions, but the Court of Appeal held that this did not in any way impair the validity of the fixed charge on unpaid debts. In the receivership of the company, the claim of 3i therefore prevailed over that of the preferential creditors, who would have been able to claim only if the charge had been a floating charge as created.

7-36 In *New Bullas* the Court observed that in *Re Brightlife Ltd*[56] a fixed charge had been held to take effect as a floating charge, and that *Siebe Gorman (supra)* had gone the other way, but expressed no view on the merits of either case. It remains an open question, therefore, in the English Court of Appeal whether the exercise of actual control over proceeds of collection is essential for the validity of a fixed charge over uncollected debts and their proceeds (as opposed to a fixed charge with automatic release into the floating charge, as in *New Bullas supra*). Even if such control

---

[53] This was the approach taken at first instance by Knox J. in *Re New Bullas Trading Ltd* [1993] B.C.C. 251, reversed on other grounds as recorded later in the text, and following *Re Brightlife Ltd* [1986] 3 All E.R. 673. Compare *Re Atlantic Medical Ltd* [1992] B.C.C. 653 and *Re CCG International Enterprises Ltd* [1993] B.C.C. 580.

[54] (1993) 11 I.L.T. 67.

[55] [1994] B.C.C. 36. For comment see *Berg* [1995] J.B.L. 433.

[56] [1986] 3 All E.R. 673.

is necessary, however, following *New Bullas (supra)* it is hard to see why its absence should vitiate the validity of an attempted fixed charge containing the usual express restrictions on dealings with the uncollected debts, in so far only as it relates to the debts which are in fact uncollected at the time of the enforcement of the charge. In this respect, it is beginning to look as though *Brightlife (supra)* was wrongly decided.

7-37 The question of whether a security over future book debts was fixed or floating was the subject of scrutiny by Morritt J. in *William Gaskell Group v. Highley*,[57] where the security was found in substance to contain all of the indicia of a fixed charge over book debts. In view of this finding, the fact that the security had been assigned by the debenture holder to a third party who took over the collection machinery for those book debts, did not affect the standing of the security as a fixed charge.

7-38 In *Re Cimex Tissues*[58] the court again concluded that the security under review took the form of a fixed charge and the fact that the company enjoyed some limited freedom to deal with the assets in question did not militate against that conclusion.

7-39 The borderline (which is by no means a purely academic issue[59]) continues to trouble the courts. In the two most recent cases[60] on the subject the courts have reaffirmed that labels have little bearing on the outcome. The critical issue is the degree of control *which the chargee enjoys by virtue of his security*[61] over the charged asset.

7-40 Even where the security does operate as a fixed charge, it can only bite on assets that have been expressly subjected to it by the terms of the debenture. The courts are quite fussy on this subject, and if there is any doubt, their inclination is to hold that a disputed asset will only be covered by the residual floating charge, and not the primary fixed security—a form of the *contra proferentem* rule is thus employed. For example, in *Re Brightlife Ltd*[62] Hoffmann J. held that a fixed charge over a company's "book debts" was not wide enough to cover sums of money standing to its credit at its bank. Equally, it has been held by Harman J. in *Re Hi-Fi Equipment Ltd*[63] that a charge over "fixed plant and equipment" should be construed so as to be limited to equipment that had become fixtures and could not operate on woodworking machinery that rested on a factory floor by its own weight. A similar approach to the interpretation of bank debentures was taken by Henry J. in the New Zealand case of *National Bank of New Zealand v. Commissioners of the Inland Revenue*[64] where a fixed charge over future "fixed plant and machinery" was held to be insufficiently precise to cover computer source code software owned by the borrowing company. The moral of the tale in all these cases is that standard form

---

[57] [1993] B.C.C. 200.

[58] [1994] B.C.C. 626. See also *Re GE Tunbridge Ltd* [1994] 2 B.C.C. 563 and *Re Pearl Maintenance Services Ltd* [1995] 1 B.C.L.C. 449. For a review of the authorities see *Berg* [1995] J.B.L. 433, Sealy (1997) 21 Insolvency Lawyer 2.

[59] Apart from determining priority between different chargees the distinction is relevant to the rights of preferential creditors—see pp.

[60] *Re Double S Printers Ltd*, *The Times*, June 2, 1998 and *Re Westmaze Ltd*, *The Times*, July 15, 1998.

[61] Rights of control vested in the chargee because he happened to be a director are not relevant—*Re Double S Printers Ltd, (supra)*.

[62] [1986] 3 All E.R. 673. Followed by the Court of Appeal in Northern Ireland in *Northern Bank v. Ross* [1990] B.C.C. 883.

[63] [1988] B.C.L.C. 65.

[64] [1992] 1 N.Z.L.R. 250.

debentures should be treated with caution; it is advisable to specifically tailor the fixed asset security to the peculiar characteristics of the asset portfolio of the borrowing company.

7-41 It emerges from a survey of the relevant case law in this area that the decisions on the fixed charge over future assets all turn on the wording of the particular debenture that was the subject of the litigation, and on the actual operation of the security created by that debenture. This was true of *Siebe Gorman (supra)* itself and remains the case in all subsequent decisions. The courts have flatly refused to take an overt policy stance on the pros and cons of allowing the artificial fixed charge over future assets and all the signs are that this ostensibly neutral approach will be the order of the day for the foreseeable future. Instead, they rest their judgments upon freedom of contract robustly reaffirmed by Nourse L.J. in *Re New Bullas Trading Ltd (supra)*, and in so doing reach decisions that may have a profound effect upon the development of corporate insolvency law as a coherent and just distributional system. Direct legislative action will clearly be necessary with regard to the fixed charge over future assets if the recommendations of the Cork Committee (Cmnd 8558, para. 1586), which called for the statutory reversal of *Siebe Gorman*, are to be implemented.

Conflicting claims to proceeds of book debts

7-42 In practice, the fixed charge on book debts is accepted as valid by insolvency practitioners. It is rare, if not unheard of, for an insolvency practitioner to seek any indemnity from the bank against possible future claims by preferential creditors when paying over the proceeds of charged book debts. Even so, this form of security does give rise to practical problems. These can arise from doubts about the nature of the chargee's interest in the proceeds of the charged debts, and related uncertainty about the status of the realisation account into which the company is normally bound to pay them.

7-43 It appears from *Siebe Gorman*[65] that unless a charge on future debts together with their proceeds imposes limitations on the company's right to deal with both risks being construed as a floating rather than a fixed charge. A contractual obligation on the company to pay the proceeds of debts into an account with the chargee is now a standard feature of all bank fixed charges on debts accordingly. If the company goes into liquidation leaving a credit balance on such an account, or (as sometimes happens in practice) having paid the proceeds of charged debts into some other bank in breach of the debenture, the question arises as to the rights of the chargee bank and the other creditors.

Equitable principles

7-44 Clearly once a debt has been paid it is no longer a debt at all and so falls outside the express scope of a fixed charge on debts. However, on ordinary equitable principles, a bank with such a charge has a specific equitable charge on the money or other property received in settlement of the debt. In the words of Slade J. in *Siebe Gorman*[66] the charge "creates in equity a specific charge on the proceeds of such

---

[65] [1979] 2 Lloyd's Rep. 142.
[66] *Supra.*

debts as soon as they are received, and consequently prevents the mortgagor from disposing of an unencumbered title to the subject matter of such a charge."

Guidelines

7-45 In *Re Keenan Brothers*[67] Walsh J. went out of his way to say (*obiter*) that the proceeds of the company's book and other debts standing to the credit of the special realisations account were not subject to the bank's charge. If this is correct, clearly the credit balance on such an account would be subject to the claims of preferential and possibly (unless there was a floating charge) to those of unsecured creditors. The authors respectfully suggest that such a result would be inconsistent with the general equitable principles alluded to by Slade J. They offer the following points of guidance to assist the practitioner in analysing the type of problem outlined earlier. The points assume that the bank has a fixed charge on book debts in the usual form, expressed to be by way of continuing security, with no obligation on the bank to make future advances but containing the usual clauses prohibiting the company from dealing with charged debts and requiring it to pay their proceeds into the chargee bank.

(1) Until the company effects a legal assignment of any debt (which in practice is extremely rare) it is the legal owner of the debt but holds it on trust for the bank. The company retains the right to redeem the debt and put an end to the trust by repaying what is owed to the bank and discharging the security.

(2) Although the company may be bound contractually not to assign the debt to any third party, it retains the capacity to do so. However so long as the charge is registered the third party can take only subject to the bank's charge, of which he will have constructive notice. This is what happened in *Siebe Gorman*[68] but in that case the bank was owed very little when it received notice of the assignment. The third party was not affected by the bank's subsequent lending, by reason of its having given notice of assignment.

(3) A third party who actually knows that the debenture prohibits the company from dealing with the charged debts will still take a legal title so that he, and not the company, can sue for the debt, but his notice to the bank will be ineffective and he will be in no better position *vis-à-vis* the bank than the company itself. He will therefore be bound by further advances.

(4) If the company pays the proceeds into the chargee bank as it should do, those proceeds remain subject to the bank's equitable charge despite the extinction of the relevant debts and the fact that any credit balance at the bank is not a debt for these purposes.[69]

(5) If the company receives property in settlement of a charged debt, the bank will have a fixed equitable charge over it but a purchaser for value of the property without notice of the bank's interest will take free of it.

---

[67] [1986] B.C.L.C. 242.
[68] [1979] 2 Lloyd's Rep. 142.
[69] *Re Brightlife Ltd* [1986] 3 All E.R. 673.

(6) Where the company pays cheques received in settlement of charged debts into an account with a new bank, the principles of equitable tracing will apply. It was held in *Barclays Bank plc v. Willowbrook International Ltd et alia*[70] that the company holds the debt represented by the account on a constructive trust for the chargee bank in these circumstances. Any transactions made with that money can be set aside at the election of the chargee, even if they result in the chargee receiving the money by a roundabout route[71]—presumably the chargee also adopt the transactions if it so elects. The new bank will not usually have constructive notice of the company's duty to pay proceeds into the chargee bank, so that any claim by the chargee alleging inducement to breach contract would fail, as it did in *Siebe Gorman*.[72] In view of the fact that such a duty is an invariable feature of such a charge, it may one day be held that the duty has come to the knowledge of the new bank if (having regard to its constructive notice of the charge) it had made such enquiries and inspections as it ought reasonably to have made.[73]

(7) If the company acquires property with the proceeds of charged debts without first paying them into the chargee bank, the principles of equitable tracing will apply.

FIXED AND FLOATING CHARGES: PRIORITY RULES

Main rules

7-46 Where a liquidator or receiver finds that there are competing charges over the same assets, how are disputes as to priority to be determined? Outlined below are the main rules to be applied. In formulating these rules, it has been assumed that both charges are registrable.

(1) A registered charge prevails over an unregistered charge, the holder of which will be relegated to the status of an unsecured creditor. Furthermore, the position would not be affected by the fact that the later registered chargee had actual notice of the earlier unregistered charge when he took his security. This statement is supported by *Re Monolithic Building Co. Ltd.*[74]

(2) Where both charges have been properly registered, what might be termed the "common law" rules will govern priority. Thus, if both charges are fixed, normally the first in time will prevail. However in the case of successive fixed charges over receivables (such as book debts) the first chargee to give notice of the charge to the debtor will take priority. In any case, the order in which the charges were registered is irrelevant.[75] Clearly, an earlier registered fixed charge will prevail over a later registered floating charge. But what of the

[70] [1987] B.C.L.C. 717.
[71] *Barclays Bank plc v. Willowbrook International Ltd et alia (supra)*. In that case the money had been used to redeem submortgages on farmland secured to the same bank.
[72] [1979] 2 Lloyd's Rep. 142.
[73] In *Barclays Bank plc v. Willowbrook International Ltd et alia (supra)* the new bank was allowed to deduct its bank charges from the sums paid into it.
[74] [1915] 1 Ch. 643.
[75] *Dearle v. Hall* (1828) 3 Russ. 1.

converse situation? Here it must be remembered that a floating charge by its very nature permits the creation of later fixed charges (whether legal or equitable) with priority.[76] Moreover, a general floating charge may also permit the creation of a subsequent particular floating charge over a class of the company's assets with priority.[77] The only qualification to these rules will arise when the later chargee has actual notice of any prohibition or negative pledge clause which might have been attached to the floating charge.

(3) Effect will be given to an agreement between chargees as to priority.[78] This can have the effect of giving a floating charge priority over a fixed charge affecting the same assets.[79] This in turn has the effect of giving the preferential creditors priority over the fixed charge holder, as regards the proceeds of sale of the assets concerned.[80]

[76] *Wheatley v. Silkstone and Haig Moor Coal Co.* (1885) 29 Ch.D. 715, *Re Valletort Sanitary Stream Laundry Co. Ltd* [1903] 2 Ch. 654.
[77] *Re Automatic Bottlemakers Ltd* [1926] Ch. 412. Contrast *Re Benjamin Cope Ltd* [1941] 1 Ch. 800 *Re Household Products Co. Ltd* (1981) 124 D.L.R. (3d) 325.
[78] *Cheah Theam Swee v. Equiticorp Finance Group Ltd* [1992] 1 A.C. 472.
[79] *Re Portbase Clothing Ltd* [1993] B.C.C. 96.
[80] *Re Portbase Clothing Ltd (supra).*

CHAPTER 8

Unsecured, Subordinated, Judgment and Preferential Creditors

INTRODUCTION

8-01 This Chapter will be concerned initially with the rights of the unsecured creditors of an insolvent company. The position will then be considered of those unsecured creditors who, in an effort to recover their money, have instituted proceedings and issued execution against the company's assets. The Chapter will then conclude with an analysis of the rights of a specially favoured group of unsecured creditors, known as preferential creditors.

UNSECURED CREDITORS

8-02 An unsecured creditor of an insolvent company is in an unenviable position. In the case of a voluntary winding-up it is made clear by section 107 of the Insolvency Act 1986 that unsecured claims are to rank equally on liquidation, subject to secured and preferential claimants. There is no equivalent statutory provision in the case of compulsory liquidation, but the rule is the same, as Brightman L.J. in *Re Lines Brothers Ltd* stressed.[1] The ruling of the House of Lords in *British Eagle International Airlines Ltd v. Compagnie Nationale Air France*,[2] to the effect that contracting out of the statutory regime for repayment of unsecured claims *pari passu* is contrary to public policy and therefore unlawful, ensures equality of misery for unsecured creditors. In spite of some criticism, this three-two majority decision of the House of Lords is now well established in corporate insolvency law.[3]

Trust devices

8-03 In practice, unsecured creditors will be lucky to receive a small proportion of the amounts due to them in the form of a dividend paid by the liquidator. Often they will receive nothing at all. It is hardly surprising therefore to find creditors who are prima facie unsecured contending that they have some superior status. The clearest manifestation of this is to be found in the burgeoning case law arising out of so-called

---

[1] [1983] Ch. 1 at 15. It is often said that on liquidation, the assets of the company are held on statutory trust for the benefit of creditors whose rights in contract against the company are transformed into claims against this trust—*Re Cases of Taff's Well Ltd* [1991] B.C.C. 582.

[2] [1975] 1 W.L.R. 758. See also *B. Mullan & Sons (Contractors) Ltd v. Ross* (1997) 54 Const. L. Reps 163.

[3] It was followed by Mahon J. in the Supreme Court of New Zealand in *Re Orion Sound Ltd* [1979] 2 N.Z.L.R. 574. See also *Re Rafidain Bank* [1992] B.C.L.C. 301 at 303 *per Browne-Wilkinson V.-C.*

trust devices. If a claimant against the company's assets can establish that the company is not merely a debtor in respect of the sums of money advanced to it, but rather a trustee holding those sums on trust for the claimant as a beneficiary, the claimant's priority status on corporate insolvency will be radically transformed. A full account of the law on trust claims is to be found in Chapter 9 of this book.[4]

Shareholders' claims

8-04 Although ordinary unsecured creditors rank low in priority on corporate insolvency, shareholders who are "owed" sums of money in their capacity as shareholders (such as dividends) are even more unhappily placed. By virtue of section 74(1)(*f*) of the Insolvency Act 1986, such as shareholders' claims rank after those of the unsecured creditors. If the company is insolvent, they will, by definition, remain unsatisfied. They have priority only over the same shareholders' claims for the return of their capital. This is a rare example of a deferred debt arising in corporate insolvency law.[5]

8-05 The House of Lords in *Soden v. British and Commonwealth Holdings*[6] considered the scope of this provision. In this case the question arose as to whether sums owed to members were due to them in their capacity as members and so deferred. The sums in this question related to a claim in damages brought against the company for misrepresentation with regard to the acquisition of their shares. Their Lordships laid down the test that a claim was only to be deferred if it arose out of the statutory contract which a shareholder had with the company. This criterion was not satisfied in this case, so the claims ranked *pari passu* with those of ordinary creditors.

8-06 In *Re L. B. Holliday & Co. Ltd*[7] shareholders argued that certain sums of money due to them in respect of unpaid dividends should be regarded as loans. In this case, a subsidiary company declared dividends in favour of its parent company (its main shareholder), but, by mutual agreement, the dividends were not paid over but were retained by the subsidiary and used as working capital. On the liquidation of the subsidiary, the parent company argued that the dividends should be regarded as having been lent by it to its subsidiary. This contention rested on the idea of an implied contract between parent and subsidiary. However, Mervyn Davies J., rejected it on the grounds that there was insufficient evidence to support such an implication.[8] The fact that the amounts owing in respect of dividends had been labelled as loans in the subsidiary company's accounts was not conclusive of the matter, especially as other documents referred to them as unpaid dividends. No interest had been paid on these "loans," and, in any case, had they been loans, the borrowing limits placed on the subsidiary company would have been exceeded.

---

[4] See pp. 153–164.

[5] Another form of deferred debt was abolished by the Insolvency Act 1986. This was the limitation on interest arrears fixed per cent. by section 66 of the Bankruptcy Act 1914. For an illustration of the operation of this rule in company law, see *Re Theo Garvin Ltd* [1969] 1 Ch. 624. See rule 11.3 of the Insolvency Rules 1986 for the current law on interest. However, a form of deferred debt was created by s.215(4) of the 1986 Act. Where a director is found to have traded wrongfully, the court can order that debts owed to him by the company be reduced to deferred status.

[6] [1997] 3 W.L.R. 840.

[7] [1986] 2 All E.R. 367.

[8] In *Re Rural and Veterinary Requisites Pty Ltd* (1978) 3 A.C.L.R. 597, the evidence contained in the company's accounts and tax returns was sufficiently compelling to convince the court that the capitalised dividends had become loans. See also *Re Annamond Park & Co.* [1930] N.I. 47 and *Re Dividend Fund Inc.* [1974] V.R. 451. Note that unpaid dividends owed to former members are treated as deferred debts—*Re Consolidated Gold Fields of New Zealand Ltd* [1953] 1 All E.R. 791.

Redress

8-07 If a person finds himself to be an unsecured creditor of a limited liability company, what means of redress are open to him to recover his money? He may, of course, simply try to sue the company to recover the amount due to him. If the company is of doubtful financial standing, this may well result in him throwing a considerable amount of good money after bad. Even judgment against the debtor company will only represent half of the battle, unless the debtor has paid money into court, in which case the plaintiff will have first claim on it.[9] Otherwise, the plaintiff must enforce the judgment by a completed execution in order to secure his position. This is often easier said than done as we shall see shortly.

8-08 By virtue of the doctrine of separate corporate personality, as a general rule, an unsecured creditor cannot pursue the company directors or shareholders personally for reimbursement.[10] Nor can an unsecured creditor have any right to appoint a receiver over the company's assets.[11] Indeed, until recently, where a receiver was appointed by a secured creditor, the unsecured creditors could exercise no control over him. The receiver owed no duty to unsecured creditors[12] and was not bound to disclose information to them. Now, at least, as a result of the Insolvency Act 1986, unsecured creditors may appoint a committee[13] with a view to extracting information from the receiver. Moreover, an administrative receiver may now be the subject of a misfeasance action[14] at the suit of *inter alia* a creditor, if he is found to have been in breach of duty to the company. Before these provisions came into force the main remedy open to unsecured creditors was to petition the court for the winding up of the debtor company.[15] However, a minimum debt of £750 is required and, even if that amount can be established, the court is still entitled to reject the petition in the exercise of its discretion under section 125 of the Insolvency Act 1986, if other creditors are opposed to the winding up.

Protection of unsecured creditors

8-09 Despite the lowly status of unsecured creditors on corporate insolvency, a number of rules of company law exist solely for their protection. Thus:

- *The system of registration of company charges*,[16] supported by the sanction of invalidity, is designed to protect unsecured creditors, as was stressed by the Court of Appeal in *Re Ashpurton Estates Ltd*.[17]

- *The principle of the maintenance of a company's share capital* is based on the preservation of the company's initial capital as a reserve fund for creditors if

[9] See *W. Sherratt Ltd v. John Bromley (Church Stretton) Ltd* [1985] 2 W.L.R. 742 not following *Peal Furniture Co. Ltd v. Adrian Share Interiors Ltd* [1977] 1 W.L.R. 464.

[10] But see Chap. 12.

[11] See *Harris v. Beauchamp Bros.* [1894] 1 Q.B. 801. See also *Re Swallow Footwear Ltd*, *The Times*, October 23, 1956.

[12] *Re Northern Developments Holdings Ltd* (1978) 128 N.L.J. 86.

[13] See Insolvency Act 1986, s.49 and Chap. 4 generally.

[14] *ibid.*, s.212.

[15] *ibid.*, s.122(1)(*f*).

[16] Companies Act 1985, ss.395–409.

[17] [1982] 3 All E.R. 665.

the business fails.[18] Unfortunately the degree of protection afforded by such a principle can only be limited when it is possible to set up a private limited liability company with a nominal capital of as little as £2 (or £1 if it is a single member private company). Even the £50,000 minimum required[19] for a p.l.c. is hardly a princely sum to divide amongst unsecured creditors when set against the amount of credit readily available to such a company.

- One justification claimed for the *ultra vires rule* was that it protected those who had extended credit to the company by preventing that credit from being used for illegitimate purposes. This alleged justification is difficult to reconcile with the case of *Mills v. Northern Railway Co. of Buenos Ayres*,[20] which is authority for the proposition that unsecured creditors cannot invoke the *ultra vires* rule!
- The statutory provisions relating to the invalidation of floating charges created within a certain period of the onset of insolvency,[21] and to *avoidance of preferences and transactions at an undervalue*,[22] are all intended to aid unsecured creditors by preventing company assets being improperly removed from their grasp. Once again, these rules were considerably strengthened by the Insolvency Act 1986.
- The Insolvency Act 1986 (or rather its predecessor, the Insolvency Act 1985) introduced the concept of *wrongful trading*[23] into corporate insolvency law, and this will enable liquidators to swell the assets available to unsecured creditors at the expense of the personal wealth of company directors, provided the fruits of the action are devoted exclusively to the unsecured creditors.[24]
- It is hoped that the improvements to the *rules on disqualification of directors*, now contained in the Company Directors Disqualification Act 1986, should prevent future generations of unsecured creditors being exposed to exploitation at the hands of fraudulent or persistently incompetent entrepreneurs.[25]
- The rules relating to *judgment and execution creditors*, although they may defeat the claims of particular unsecured creditors, are framed so as to ensure equality of treatment for all unsecured creditors on corporate insolvency, as the House of Lords indicated in *Roberts Petroleum v. Kenny Ltd*.[26] These particular rules are examined in more detail below.

---

[18] This is particularly true where the company decides to create reserve capital out of its uncalled capital. Reserve capital can only be used to pay creditors on liquidation and it cannot be charged as security. See Companies Act 1985, s.120 and *Re Mayfair Property Co. Ltd* [1898] 2 Ch. 28.
[19] Companies Act 1985, s.118.
[20] (1870) 5 Ch. App. 621.
[21] Insolvency Act 1986, s.245. See Chap. 10.
[22] *ibid.*, ss.238–41 and 423–5. See Chap. 10.
[23] *ibid.*, s.214.
[24] In *Re Produce Marketing Consortium Ltd (No. 2)* [1989] B.C.L.C. 520 at 554 Knox J. put forward the view that proceeds of a wrongful trading action can be claimed by secured creditors. This contention, however, has attracted criticism—see *Oditah* [1990] L.M.C.L.Q. 205 and was not followed by Millett J. in *Re MC Bacon Ltd (No. 2)* [1990] 3 W.L.R. 646 where the learned judge favoured the argument that such proceeds should be devoted exclusively to unsecured creditors.
[25] See Chap. 13.
[26] [1983] 2 W.L.R. 305.

- The idea that directors of an insolvent (or doubtfully solvent) company may owe a duty of care to its creditors to thriftily manage its dwindling assets represents a recent common law enhancement of the protection of the rights of unsecured creditors.[27] This idea has found some favour with the Court of Appeal in *West Mercia Safetywear v. Dodd*.[28]

8-10 Notwithstanding these developments and the availability of such protective devices it cannot be denied that the plight of unsecured creditors under English law is a miserable one. The Cork Committee did address this fundamental weakness in the law and offered as a solution the idea of a Ten Per Cent Fund (see Cmnd 8558, paras 1538–49). Under this scheme the holder of the floating charge would be expected to give up 10% of net realisations which would be used to offer some solace to unsecured creditors. This proposal did not meet with the approval of the banking community and it was quietly forgotten, having been rejected the White Paper that followed up the Cork Report (see Cmnd 9175, para. 26). Some 15 years after the Cork Committee reported it has been revisited by a number of commentators it is unlikely that the U.K. legislature will enact it.[29] The argument of the banks that such a reform would result in a compensating rise in interest rates, although untested, appears to hold sway. The fact that the weak status of unsecured creditors may have encouraged them to use techniques (such as title retention clauses) that have economic costs is conveniently forgotten.

Subordinated creditors

8-11 There is one other group of vulnerable creditors who deserve mention. These are subordinated creditors, a category of creditor ranked after the unsecured creditors. This lowly status may in rare cases be imposed by law.[30] More usually it is inherited as a matter of choice through contract. Why might an investor agree to such a relegation? One answer is that subordinated debt is invariably compensated by a high rate of interest. For many years there was doubt as to whether the paternalism that underpins UK insolvency law would permit individuals to leave themselves exposed outside the pari passu stockade. Those doubts have now been resolved and in two cases, *Re British and Commonwealth Holdings plc (No. 3)*[31] and *Re Maxwell Communications (No. 3)*[32] the English courts have bowed to the inevitable and have accepted the legality of subordinated debt. In so doing they have recognised the wishes of the international capital markets and have placed English law in step with a number of comparable jurisdictions.[33]

---

[27] For full discussion of this development see Chap. 12.
[28] [1988] B.C.L.C. 250.
[29] In Germany as part of its general revision of insolvency law effective from January 1 1999 a scheme similar to the 10% Fund has been introduced. For comment see Weiss [1998] (August) *Insolvency Practitioner* 38.
[30] See for example Insolvency Act 1986 s.74(2)(f) which has been considered above.
[31] [1992] B.C.C. 58.
[32] [1993] B.C.C. 369.
[33] See *Re NIAA Corp* (1994) 12 A.C.S.R. 141 (Australia), *Stotter v. Armaru Holdings* [1994] 2 N.Z.L.R. 655. For general discussion see Powell [1993] L.M.C.L.Q. 357, Nolan [1995] J.B.L. 485, Capper (1995) 14 *Insolvency Lawyer* 3.

JUDGMENT CREDITORS

8-12 What of the position of a person who has obtained judgment against a limited liability company but the company has failed to pay the judgment debt? No doubt the judgment creditor will first consider levying execution against the company's assets. Alternatively, if execution looks futile, he can petition for the winding up of the company without making any attempt to enforce judgment.[34] In deciding whether to try levying execution, the judgment creditor will need to consider three distinct situations in which special difficulties can arise.

Possibility of rescue

8-13 First, let us suppose that the judgment debtor company is in financial difficulties and moves are afoot to effect some moratorium or scheme of arrangement (whether formal or informal) with its creditors. If the judgment creditor becomes a party to an informal scheme, he will not be allowed to renege on it because the scheme constitutes a contract between the company and all of the creditors concerned.[35] However, suppose the scheme has not reached the point where it is binding, or in the case of an informal scheme, suppose that the judgment creditor was not a party to it and therefore is not bound. There is a clear stream of authority here to support the proposition that, where there is a possibility of a rescue being implemented, the courts will be most reluctant to help a judgment creditor to obtain execution. Decisions of the Court of Appeal such as *D. Wilson (Birmingham) Ltd v. Metropolitan Property Developments Ltd*[36] and *Rainbow v. Moorgate Properties Ltd*[37] all illustrate cases where the courts have refused to complete garnishee proceedings or charging order processes for fear of upsetting a potential rescue plan.[38] Under the Insolvency Act 1986 the judgment creditor is even less likely to succeed in such circumstances. Thus, as we have seen in Chapter 3, under section 5(2), all creditors will be bound by any voluntary arrangement made in accordance with the Act. No doubt informal schemes will become very rare as a result. Where a petition has been presented for an administration order, the leave of the court will be required[39] in order to levy execution against the company's assets and, *a fortiori*, this protection is continued once an administration order has been granted.[40] In view of the attitudes displayed by the judges in the cases cited above, it is unlikely that such leave would be readily given.

Appointment of receiver

8-14 Secondly, the judgment creditor may find himself in a race against time with debenture holders seeking to appoint a receiver. Under the terms of most debentures the fact that a judgment has been obtained against the company's assets and has not been satisfied, or that execution has been levied, will of itself entitle the debenture

---

[34] *Griggs Engineering Ltd* [1963] Ch. 1. But see *Re William Hockley Ltd* [1962] 1 W.L.R. 555.
[35] *Hirachand Punamchand v. Temple* [1911] 2 K.B. 330. Compare *Re Selectmove Ltd*, [1994] B.C.C. 349, where a creditor who had made a private arrangement with the debtor company was allowed to renege on his promise to accept a lesser sum.
[36] [1975] 2 All E.R. 814.
[37] [1975] 1 W.L.R. 788.
[38] See also *Hudson's Concrete Products v. D. B. Evans (Bilston) Ltd* (1961) 105 S.J. 281 and *Prestige Publications v. Chelsea F.C.* (1978) 122 S.J. 436.
[39] Insolvency Act 1986, s.10(1)(*c*) See Chap. 3.
[40] *ibid.*, s.11(3)(*d*).

holders to appoint a receiver. In any case, the mere threat of execution being levied against the company's assets would surely place the security in "jeopardy". This again will normally trigger the right to appoint a receiver.[41] It is now possible to assert with some confidence that if the debenture so provides, the mere occurrence of such events will cause the automatic crystallisation of a floating charge without the need for the appointment of a receiver.[42] Crystallisation will effectively remove the assets subject to the charge from the scope of an execution.

8-15 How far must an execution have progressed in order for the judgment creditor to be secure from intervention by a receiver? The general rule seems to be that the execution process must have been completed. In order to apply this rule to particular situations, it is necessary to analyse the individual execution processes in the light of the case law. However a preliminary caveat is necessary: certain of the cases dealing with priority disputes between judgment creditors and debenture holders were decided before the modern law of the floating charge had been fully worked out. Both statements of principle and the reasoning employed in some of the cases to produce them must therefore be treated with caution.

Fieri facias

8-16 Under a writ of *fieri facias*, the sheriff is directed to seize chattels and if the judgment remains unsatisfied, to sell them. It seems that mere seizure by the sheriff is not enough. Authority for this proposition can be derived from *Re Standard Manufacturing Co.*[43] and *Re Opera Ltd.*[44] An actual sale is required for the process to be completed. Commonly, however the judgment debtor pays up in order to avoid a forced sale. Where this occurs, it appears that the judgment creditor can retain any moneys received.[45]

Garnishee proceedings

8-17 Garnishee proceedings provide a popular method of enforcing judgment against the company's bank account. The process here consists of two stages. A garnishee order *nisi* attaches the debt and directs the bank (or other debtor) to pay it to the judgment creditor unless it can give reasons for not doing so—perhaps because the debt is disputed. If no reasons are given an order absolute is made. It appears that the order must have been made absolute in order for the garnishee process to be completed.[46]

Charging order

8-18 Judgments are normally enforced against land by means of a charging order, which mirrors the garnishee process in many respects. The law here is governed by

---

[41] In any case, the court can appoint a receiver on the grounds of jeopardy.

[42] This follows from the decision of Hoffmann J. in *Re Brightlife Ltd* [1986] 3 All E.R. 673.

[43] [1891] 1 Ch. 627.

[44] [1891] 3 Ch. 620.

[45] *Robinson v. Burnell's Vienna Bakery* [1904] 2 K.B. 624, *Heaton & Dugard v. Cutting Bros.* [1925] 1 K.B. 655.

[46] *Norton v. Yates* [1906] 1 K.B. 112. See also *Evans v. Rival Granite Quarries Ltd* [1910] 2 K.B. 979 on this point. A garnishee process initiated after the commencement of the receivership is futile—*McKay & Hughes (1973) Ltd v. Martin Potatoes* [1984] 9 D.L.R. (4th) 439 (Ontario Court of Appeal). The position is different in a liquidation where actual receipt of the debt is necessary.

the Charging Orders Act 1979. A charging order *nisi* is made (which may be supported by the appointment of a receiver) followed by an order absolute if no reason to the contrary is shown. It appears that the order must have been made absolute before the debenture holders intervene if the judgment creditor is to be secure in his position.[47]

8-19 Clearly in a priority contest between a judgment creditor and a debenture holder secured by a floating charge, the odds are weighted heavily in favour of the latter, a situation heavily criticised by Buckley J. in *Re London Pressed Hinge Co.*[48]

Company in liquidation

8-20 Finally, how does the judgment creditor stand if the judgment debtor company goes into liquidation? There is a formidable armoury of statutory provisions designed to make it difficult for an individual judgment creditor to pursue an execution process. These barriers have been constructed in the interests of all unsecured creditors. In *Re Aro Co. Ltd*, Brightman L.J. declared:[49]

> "The basic scheme of the companies' legislation is that the unsecured creditors of an insolvent company are to rank pari passu (subject to statutory provisions as to preferential payments). . . . In order to achieve this result, there are provisions which restrict the right of a creditor to make use of procedures outside the liquidation."

Compulsory liquidation

8-21 Firstly, there are some special provisions applying only to compulsory liquidations. Section 126 of the Insolvency Act 1986 deals with any execution process commenced after the date of the winding-up petition. The court has power to restrain any "action or proceeding" and this phrase has been held to apply to execution by *fieri facias*,[50] garnishing proceedings,[51] and any form of distress.[52] This provision is reinforced by section 130(2) of the Insolvency Act 1986, which places a similar bar on execution processes commenced or proceeded with after the winding-up order or, indeed, subsequent to the appointment of a provisional liquidator, though the court can grant leave for them to go ahead. The aim of this provision is to ensure equality of treatment for unsecured creditors as Widgery L.J. intimated in *Langley Constructions (Brixham) Ltd v. Wells*.[53] In *Re Memco Engineering Ltd*,[54] Mervyn Davies J. held that the key phrase "action or proceeding," which is also used in section 130(2), could apply to distress for unpaid VAT. This conclusion was arrived at in spite of the doubts expressed by Oliver J. in *Re Bellaglade Ltd*[55] and by the House of Lords in *Herbert Berry Associates Ltd v. I.R.C.*[56]

---

[47] By analogy with the garnishee procedure.
[48] [1905] 1 Ch. 576 at 593.
[49] [1980] 2 W.L.R. 453 at 593.
[50] *Re Hill Pottery Co.* (1986) L.R. 1 Eq. 649, *Bowkett v. Fuller's Union Electric Works* [1923] 1 K.B. 160.
[51] *Re United English & Scottish Insurance Ltd* (1868) L.R. 5 Eq. 300.
[52] Interpleader proceedings are also covered—*Eastern Holdings Establishment of Vaduz v. Singer & Friedlander* [1967] 1 W.L.R. 1017.
[53] [1969] 1 W.L.R. 503 at 508.
[54] [1985] 3 W.L.R. 875.
[55] [1977] 1 All E.R. 319.
[56] [1977] 1 W.L.R. 1437.

8-22 Section 128 of the Insolvency Act 1986 is framed in much stronger terms. This renders void any attachment, sequestration, distress or execution put into effect after the commencement of the compulsory liquidation.[57] Again it has been held to apply to the *fieri facias* process, garnishee proceedings and arrestment of ships. Section 130(2) has been held in cases like *The Constellation*[58] to prevail over section 128 so that the court can, in its discretion, grant relief from this draconian sanction. However, bearing in mind current judicial attitudes, the prospects of its doing so are not promising, save in an exceptional case.[59]

Voluntary liquidation

8-23 The obstacles in the case of a voluntary liquidation appear on the surface to be less formidable, though this impression is misleading. Certainly in this case there are no statutory counterparts of the barriers constructed by sections 126, 128 and 130(2). However under section 112 of the Insolvency Act 1986, the court can restrain any action or proceeding or allow it to go ahead. In *Westbury v. Twigg & Co.*,[60] for example, the statutory predecessor of section 112 was successfully invoked to restrain a *fieri facias* process commenced after the resolution for the voluntary liquidation.

Completion of execution

8-24 Perhaps the most frustrating barrier for a judgment creditor is established by section 183 of the Insolvency Act 1986. This provides that where execution proceedings[61] have been commenced before the initiation of the winding-up, whether compulsory or voluntary,[62] the judgment creditor will only be allowed to retain the fruits of his execution if that execution has been completed either before the commencement of the liquidation, or (if earlier) before he has received notice of the meeting at which a resolution to wind the company up voluntarily is to be proposed.

8-25 Section 183(3) explains when certain common forms of execution are completed for the purposes of the Act, including those of section 183. Thus, *fieri facias* requires both seizure and sale (or payment to avoid a sale). A charging order made under section 1 of the Charging Orders Act 1979 is sufficient in the case of land. It is not clear whether this refers to a charging order nisi or absolute, but probably the liquidator would be able to "show cause" against the making of an order absolute by reason of the liquidation. However, in the case of garnishee proceedings, the judgment creditor must actually receive the debt. The position thus differs sharply from

---

[57] This will presumably be the date of the winding-up petition.

[58] [1966] 1 W.L.R. 272. See also *Re Lancashire Cotton Co.* (1887) 35 Ch.D. 656, *Re Aro Co. Ltd* [1980] 2 W.L.R. 453.

[59] Leave will not be granted if the issues raised by the action could be more conveniently dealt with in the winding-up—*Re Exchange Securities & Commodities Ltd* [1983] B.C.L.C. 186. The court might grant relief if the judgment creditor was fraudulently induced by the company to refrain from execution—*Armorduct Manufacturing Co. v. General Incandescent Co.* [1911] 2 K.B. 143. In very rare cases the court will sometimes allow an action to proceed rather than force the creditor to have a dispute on liability or quantum decided in the liquidator's own forum—*Cook v. "X" Chair Patents Co. Ltd* [1959] 3 All E.R. 906.

[60] [1892] 1 Q.B. 77. See also *Re Poole Fire Brick & Blue Clay Co.* (1873) L.R. 17 Eq. 268.

[61] This does not apply to arrestment of ships—*The Zafiro* [1960] P. 1. In *Re Bellaglade Ltd* [1977] 1 All E.R. 319 it was held that s.183 also does not apply to distress levied by a landlord. Section 183 does not have extraterritorial effect—*Mitchell v. Carter* [1997] B.C.C. 907.

[62] *Re Aro Co. Ltd* [1980] 2 W.L.R. 453 at 459 *per* Brightman L.J.

that in receivership, where the matter is governed by case law and it is clear that an order absolute suffices.

8-26 Section 183 does have some flexibility built into it that the court can allow an incomplete execution to proceed notwithstanding the intervention of a liquidation. Thus under section 183(1)(*c*) the court has power to set aside the liquidator's rights in favour of the judgment creditor to such an extent and subject to such terms as it thinks fit. In *Re Grosvenor Metal Co.*,[63] Vaisey J. stressed that the court is reluctant to see this discretion fettered. However, it is clear from subsequent authorities such as *Re Redman Builders Ltd*[64] and *Re Caribbean Products (Yam Importers) Ltd*,[65] that it will be unlikely to exercise it for fear of making the plight of the other unsecured creditors even more unfavourable than it already is. An interesting authority here is that of *Roberts Petroleum v. Kenny Ltd*,[66] though it is unsatisfactory in many respects.[67] The charging order *nisi* in that case was granted before the company went into voluntary liquidation. Shortly afterwards the company's members resolved on a voluntary liquidation using the "Centrebinding" ploy.[68] The question facing the courts was whether the charging order should now be made absolute even though the liquidation had commenced. The House of Lords ruled that bearing in mind the statutory scheme for payment of creditors, and the interest of the creditors as a whole, the charging order should not be made absolute. Lord Brightman explained:[69]

> "If, therefore, the statutory scheme for dealing with the assets of the company has been irrevocably imposed on the company, by resolution or winding-up order, before the court has irrevocably determined to give the creditor the benefit of the charging order, I would have thought that the statutory scheme should prevail."

It would appear from *Re Suidair International Airways Ltd*[70] that the court's discretion might be exercised in favour of the judgment creditor if he can show that the company induced him to stay his hand by misrepresentation.

Goods seized

8-27 Section 184 of the Insolvency Act 1986 deals with the situation where the sheriff has seized goods and has been told that a provisional liquidator has been appointed, a winding up petition presented (or order made) or that a meeting has been called for the passing of a winding up resolution. In this situation, provided proper notice has been given to the sheriff, the goods seized must be handed over to the provisional liquidator. Moreover, by virtue of section 184(3) if the judgment exceeds a statutory minimum, and if the sheriff has sold the goods or has received money paid to him to avoid a sale,[71] he must retain the proceeds of sale (or money

---

[63] [1950] Ch. 63.
[64] [1964] 1 W.L.R. 541.
[65] [1966] Ch. 331.
[66] [1983] 2 W.L.R. 305.
[67] There was no real discussion of what is now section 183 of the Insolvency Act 1986 until the case got to the House of Lords and even there the analysis was tenuous.
[68] See Chap. 5.
[69] [1983] 2 W.L.R. 305 at 315.
[70] [1951] Ch. 165.
[71] See *Marley Tile Co. Ltd v. Burrows* [1978] Q.B. 241 here. The judgment must exceed £500 for the purposes of section 184(3)—this figure was increased from £250 by the Insolvency Proceedings (Monetary Limits) Order 1986 (S.I. 1986 No. 1996).

received) for at least 14 days before handing them over to the judgment creditor. If within that period he is notified that (in effect) a winding up may have commenced, the proceeds must instead go to the liquidator, if one is appointed. The sheriff (but not the judgment creditor) can claim priority treatment for his costs incurred.[72] It should be noted that the courts will insist that proper notice has been given to the sheriff; the reason for this severe attitude is that section 184 divests persons of vested rights.[73] Finally, it was made clear in *Bluston & Bramley Ltd v. Leigh*[74] that the judgment creditor might overcome the hurdles constructed by section 184 only to find himself toppled by section 183.

PREFERENTIAL CLAIMS

8-28 Preferential claims originated in the late 19th century. They were introduced by Parliament in the Preferential Payments in Bankruptcy Act 1897 in order to promote certain favoured unsecured creditors to a priority status superior to that enjoyed by a holder of a floating charge. They were to rank *pari passu inter se*. Preferential claims multiplied in the following hundred years at the instigation of Parliament (but not of the courts)[75] to such an extent that they began to threaten seriously the security afforded by the floating charge. The state was the main beneficiary of this proliferation.

8-29 It became common for banks to create artificial fixed charges over future assets to avert the dangers presented by preferential claims. Automatic crystallisation clauses were inserted in bank debentures in the hope that they would achieve the same result by converting the floating charge into a fixed charge before preferential claims arose. The growth in preferential claims began to attract criticism, not merely from the banks, but also from ordinary unsecured creditors whose position was progressively eroded as the number and quantity of preferential claims grew.

Cork proposals

8-30 The Cork Committee received numerous representations calling for constraints to be placed on preferential claims, and in its final report it agreed (in para. 1450) that reform in this area was essential. The Government was initially hostile to the Cork proposals, largely because it was invariably the main preferential creditor. However, as a result of public pressure, the Government conceded in part and in the late stages of the passage of the Insolvency Bill 1985 through Parliament, it introduced proposals to reduce the number of preferential claims. The Crown preference

---

[72] [1931] 2 Ch. 320.

[73] *Re T. D. Walton Ltd* [1966] 2 All E.R. 157, *Hellyer v. Sheriff of Yorks* [1974] 2 W.L.R. 844. Compare *Engineering Industry Training Board v. Samuel Talbot (Engineers) Ltd* [1969] 1 All E.R. 480. It seems that entry in the Gazette under s.42(1)(*a*) of the Companies Act 1985 of the fact that the company has gone into liquidation will not suffice—see *Official Custodian of Charities v. Parway Estates Ltd* (1984) 1 B.C.C. 99, 253.

[74] [1950] 2 K.B. 458. Both hurdles were overcome in *Re Walkden Sheet Metal Co.* [1960] Ch. 170.

[75] For the hostility of the courts towards attempts to widen the scope of preferential claims, see *Food Controller v. Cork* [1923] A.C. 647 and, more recently, Nourse J. in *Re Rudd & Son Ltd* [1984] Ch. 237. In *E.C.S.C. v. Liquidator of Ferriere Sant' Anna SpA* [1983] E.C.R. 1681 the European Court of Justice held that there was no preferential treatment automatically afforded to Community institutions but see now the Insolvency (E.C.S.C. Levy Debts) Regulations 1987 (S.I. 1987/2093).

in respect of a large number of unpaid taxes[76] and the favourable treatment afforded to rates arrears were sacrificed.[77] The current stance of the law towards new preferential claims is hostile.[78]

8-31 The law on preferential claims is now contained in sections 40, 175, 386 and 387 of the Insolvency Act 1986, together with Schedule 6 of that Act. Section 196 of the Companies Act 1985 is also relevant, though this is now to be found, as amended, in Schedule 13 of the Insolvency Act 1986.

Priority status

8-32 A preferential claim is a claim that must be satisfied by either the receiver or the liquidator of an insolvent company in priority to the claims of a holder of a floating charge[79] and in priority to any other creditor who does not have a fixed charge. Where a receiver, or (rarely) chargee in possession pays off the preferential creditors, he is entitled to recoup an equivalent amount of money from the general assets of the company.[80] Thus it is the ordinary unsecured creditors of the company who, in effect, subsidise the preferential claimants. It must be stressed that preferential creditors only enjoy priority over debenture holders in relation to assets within the floating, and not the fixed, charges. This important point has been emphasised by the judiciary on a number of occasions, notably by the Court of Appeal in *Re Lewis Merthyr Consolidated Collieries Ltd*[81] and, more recently, by Nourse J. in *Re Saunders Ltd.*[82]

Controversy before 1986 re automatic crystallisation

8-33 Before the Insolvency Act 1986 came into force, there was much controversy over whether a bank could circumvent the requirement that preferential claims had to be satisfied in priority to the floating charge by means of an automatic crystallisation clause in the debenture creating the charge. The automatic crystallisation clause was so drafted that the floating charge crystallised on the happening of specified events (*e.g.*, failure by the debtor company to meet a demand for repayment). Crystallisation converted the charge *eo instanti* into a fixed charge. Any receiver then appointed was enforcing a security which (so the argument ran) had become a fixed charge and had ceased to float prior to his appointment. It was arguable therefore that he was not concerned with preferential claims.

8-34 This argument had been upheld in the courts in Australia,[83] where correc-

---

[76] See *Gowers v. Walker* [1930] 1 Ch. 262. The Crown was given considerable flexibility in opting for the most favourable year of taxation arrears—*Lord Advocate v. Liquidator of Purvis Industries* 1958 S.C. 338.

[77] For an example of the preferential treatment of rates, see *Re Piccadilly Estate Hotels Ltd* (1978) 20 R.R.C. 268. Preferential treatment was not extended to arrears of water rates—*Re Baker* [1954] 1 W.L.R. 1144.

[78] *Re Rafidain Bank* [1992] B.C.C. 376. See also *Lindop v. Stuart Noble & Sons Ltd*, *The Times Scots Law Report*, June 25, 1998.

[79] Insolvency Act 1986, ss.40 and 175. See Chap. 10 for the status of preferential claims as against winding-up costs.

[80] See Companies Act 1985, s.196(4), now to be found in Schedule 13 of the Insolvency Act 1986, and Insolvency Act 1986, s.40(3). See also *Re Mannesmann Tube Co. Ltd* [1901] 2 Ch. 93.

[81] [1929] 1 Ch. 498.

[82] [1986] 1 W.L.R. 215. See also *Re Griffin Hotel Co. Ltd* [1941] Ch. 129 *Bank of New South Wales v. Federal Commissioner of Taxation* (179) 145 C.L.R. 438 at 447 *per* Gibbs J. and *United Bars Ltd v. Revenue Commissioners* [1991] 1 I.R. 396.

[83] *Stein v. Saywell* (1969) 121 C.L.R. 529.

tive legislative action was required. The point was never directly tested in English law until recently.[84] However, in *Re Brightlife Ltd*,[85] Hoffmann J. approved the concept of automatic crystallisation in exactly such a scenario. The point is now academic because sections 40(1) and 251 of the Insolvency Act 1986 taken together make it clear that preferential claims are to be satisfied in priority to any security which was a floating charge at its date of creation.[86] The combination of sections 175 and 251 of the Act applies the same rule to liquidations.

8-35 A difficult question with regard to the interpretation of section 40 arises where there are several floating charge holders in competition with each other. In *Griffiths v. Yorkshire Bank*[87] Morritt J. held that a receiver who has been appointed under a floating charge which had crystallised after an earlier floating charge was not subjected to the obligation to pay preferential claims because he was not a receiver appointed in respect of "the debentures" within the meaning of section 40(2) has by Neuberger J fortunately rejected this odd interpretation in *Re H & K (Medway) Ltd*[88] taking the view that *any* receiver appointed to realise a floating charge was under an obligation to satisfy preferential claims before making distributions to any of the debenture holders, including those with the benefit of floating charges ranking in priority to the charge under which he was appointed. To have held otherwise would surely have led to the preferential claims regime being undermined.

Schedule 6 categories

8-36 The current list of preferential claims is introduced into the law by virtue of a combination of section 386 and Schedule 6 of the Insolvency Act 1986. Schedule 6 lists six categories of preferential debts.

CATEGORY 1: DEBTS DUE TO THE INLAND REVENUE

8-37 This category comprises sums due from the debtor company in respect of PAYE deductions (under section 203 of the Income and Corporation Taxes Act 1988) from employees' wages paid in the 12 month period before "the relevant date" also included in this category are sums due from the debtor company in respect of deductions which it should have made under section 559 of the Income and Corporation Taxes Act 1988. This legislation applies to subcontractors in the construction industry.

CATEGORY 2: DEBTS DUE TO THE CUSTOMS AND EXCISE

8-38 This grouping includes any VAT which is referable to the six month period prior to "the relevant date." In *Re Nadler Enterprises Ltd*,[89] Dillon J. held that where a group of companies has opted for group treatment for the purposes of VAT, if one of those companies is insolvent, but has sufficient assets, the Customs and Excise is

---

[84] This conclusion was implicit in the judgment of Bennett J. in *Re Griffin Hotel Co. Ltd* [1941] Ch. 129.
[85] [1986] 3 All E.R. 673.
[86] See *Re Brightlife Ltd (supra)* on this point. See also *Re Portbase Ltd* [1993] 3 W.L.R. 14.
[87] [1994] 1 W.L.R. 1427. See also para. 7-08 above.
[88] [1997] 1 B.C.L.C. 545.
[89] [1981] 1 W.L.R. 23.

entitled to rank as a preferential creditor for the whole amount of VAT owed by the group. The category also includes certain amounts due at the "relevant date" and those which became due within the period of 12 months immediately before that date, including car tax, generally betting duty, bingo duty, gaming licence duty and amounts collectable in respect of general betting duty or pool betting duty from agents who collect stakes.

CATEGORY 3: SOCIAL SECURITY CONTRIBUTIONS

8-39 This category consists of all contributions due from the debtor company in respect of Class 1 or Class 2 contributions under the Social Security (Contributions and Benefits) Act 1992, which became due in the 12 months next before "the relevant date." Also mentioned here are Class 4 contributions which are assessed on the debtor up to April 5 next before "the relevant date." However, the maximum amount here is one year's assessment.

CATEGORY 4: CONTRIBUTIONS TO OCCUPATIONAL PENSION SCHEMES

8-40 Preferential treatment is to be given to any sum which is owed by the debtor company and represents either a contribution to an occupational pension scheme or a state scheme premium.

CATEGORY 5: REMUNERATION AND HOLIDAY REMUNERATION OWED TO EMPLOYEES[90]

8-41 This category has survived in spite of recommendations (see para. 1433) from the Cork Committee that it be abandoned. The main items listed in this group are accrued remuneration payable to employees in respect of the four month period next before "the relevant date" (subject to an upper limit to be prescribed by the Secretary of State),[91] and any accrued holiday remuneration. This latter item is not subject to any temporal cut-off point. Remuneration for these purposes is defined by paragraphs 13 and 15 of Schedule 6 to include wages, guarantee payments, medical

[90] It must be remembered that employees also enjoy guarantee rights as against the Redundancy Fund in respect of certain entitlements due to them from an insolvent employer. The Secretary of State may then claim to be subrogated to the employees' claim against the insolvent employer. For the legal problems that can arise here see *Re Urethane Engineering Products Ltd* (1989) 5 B.C.C. 614. The issue of the Crown's right of subrogation in cases where money has been paid out of the Redundancy Fund has featured in a National Audit Office report, *The Department of Trade and Industry Redundancy Payments Service: Management and Recovery of Debt* (HCP 1995–96 No. 695, 17 October 1996). In this report it is alleged that the public exchequer is being deprived of recoveries through the propensity of certain insolvency practitioners to treat charges as fixed when they are in fact floating charges. Another criticism is that realisation costs are disproportionately piled up against the floating charge element of a hybrid security thereby reducing the residual balance of funds available to meet preferential claims. Similar criticisms were made by the House of Commons Public Accounts Committee in its 18th Report (1998). The profession has reacted to these criticisms by introducing SIP 14 which reminds insolvency practitioners of their responsibilities with regard to preferential claims. For discussion of these issues see Keay and Walton [1999] *Insolvency Lawyer* 112.

[91] The figure of £800 has been fixed by the Insolvency Proceedings (Monetary Limits) Order 1986 (S.I. 1986 No. 1996).

suspension payments, payments in respect of time off work, statutory sick pay, remuneration under protective awards, holiday and sick pay. However, it must be stressed that only employees working under contracts of service will benefit from this preferential treatment.[92]

8-42 Category 5 also includes[93] so much of any sum owed in respect of money advanced for the purpose as had been applied for the payment of a debt which, if it had not been paid, would have been a debt falling within this category. This right of subrogation is well recognised by case law. For example, in *Re Rampgill Mill Ltd*,[94] the bank was able to take the benefit of this provision by allowing the company to run up its overdraft to pay its employees' wages.[95] It is fair to say that the courts have been generous in their treatment of claims by banks under this provision. Thus, it would appear from *Re Primrose Builders Ltd*[96] that it is not necessary to establish the existence of an express agreement to the effect that the money advanced was to be used to pay employees' wages. All that is required is that it was clearly intended for that purpose.[97] Furthermore, it was held in *Re William Hall (Contractors) Ltd*[98] that if some of the money advanced is protected by security, the bank is allowed considerable flexibility in apportioning amounts between the secured and preferential claims in order to achieve the maximum advantage for itself. On the other hand, it must be reiterated that this subrogated preferential claim is only available if the money advanced is used to pay the wages of employees (as opposed to independent contractors).[99]

CATEGORY 6: LEVIES ON COAL AND STEEL PRODUCTION

8-43 Levies due from the debtor company in respect of levies arising on coal and steel production under the European Coal and Steel Community were given preferential status in 1987—see Insolvency (ECSC Levy Debts) Regulations 1987 (S.I. 1987, No. 2093).

"The relevant date"

8-44 The recurrent and crucial phrase, "the relevant date," is fully explained by section 387 of the Insolvency Act 1986. For example, where the company is subject to an administration order the relevant date will be the date of that order. If the company is in the process of seeking a voluntary arrangement, the relevant date is the date of the court's approval of that arrangement. In cases of winding-up, the relevant date is either the date of the winding-up order (or appointment of a provisional

---

[92] *Re General Radio Co. Ltd* [1929] W.N. 172, *Cairney v. Back* [1906] 2 K.B. 246, *Re Sunday Tribune Ltd* [1984] I.R. 505. If the person is truly an employee, the fact that his salary takes the form of commission is irrelevant—*Re Earl's Shipbuilding Co.* [1901] W.N. 78.

[93] The Cork Committee by a narrow majority recommended the retention of this category of preferential claim—Cmnd. 8558, para. 1440.

[94] [1967] Ch. 1138. For a liberal interpretation of the word "advanced" which is sued in Sched. 6, para. 11 of the Insolvency Act 1986 see *Waikato Savings Bank v. Andrews Furniture Ltd* [1982] 2 N.Z.L.R. 520.

[95] For the rules applicable to bank accounts, see *Re E. J. Morel (1934) Ltd* [1961] 1 All E.R. 796 and *Re Rutherford & Sons Ltd* [1964] 3 All E.R. 137.

[96] [1950] Ch. 561.

[97] See Insolvency Act 1986, Sched. 6 para. 11.

[98] [1967] 1 W.L.R. 948.

[99] *Re C. W. & A. L. Hughes Ltd* [1966] 1 W.L.R. 1369.

liquidator), where the company is in compulsory liquidation, or the date of the resolution for winding-up in the case of voluntary liquidation. On receivership, the relevant date is the date of the appointment of the receiver.

8-45 Where a claim falls within the statutory list of preferential claims, any receiver or liquidator will be under a positive statutory obligation to ensure that it is met;[1] so far as assets permit, or if the assets are insufficient, met to the same extent as the other preferential debts. If a receivership is followed by a liquidation, there may well be two sets of preferential creditors, reflecting the different relevant dates appropriate to the two procedures.

Distress

8-46 Under section 176 of the Insolvency Act 1986, preferential creditors have a first charge on goods distrained upon within the three months before an order for winding-up by the court. In *Re Memco Engineering Ltd*,[2] Mervyn Davies J. ruled that the date of distress for this purpose is the date when the distress procedure was completed by sale of the goods distrained upon. It is interesting that section 176 only applies to compulsory liquidations in spite of its location within the statute. This is made clear by its wording and, indeed, this point was stressed by the House of Lords in *Herbert Berry Associates Ltd v. I.R.C.*[3]

---

[1] *Woods v. Winskill* [1913] 2 Ch. 303, *Westminster C.C. v. Haste* [1950] Ch. 442, *I.R.C. v. Goldblatt* [1972] Ch. 498. Where liquidation and receivership coincide, the onus of paying preferential claims falls primarily on the receiver—*Manley Petitioner* 1985 S.L.T. 42.

[2] [1985] 3 W.L.R. 875.

[3] [1977] 1 W.L.R. 1437.

CHAPTER 9

Non-registrable Proprietary Claims to the Assets

SECURITY AND ARTIFICIALITY

Claim in rem

9-01 An ordinary unsecured creditor is in a very poor position on corporate insolvency, unless he has been fortunate enough to be promoted to preferential status, or has been persistent enough to survive the obstacle course of securing judgment and completing execution against the company before the debenture holders intervene or liquidation commences. It is hardly surprising that he will be inclined to exploit any ploy which will improve his plight. The English law of security, with its love of fictions and artificiality, has in recent years offered two devices which promise great rewards for a person who would otherwise rank as an unsecured creditor on corporate insolvency. It is now settled that such a person may have a claim *in rem* against goods in a limited company's possession, without that claim resting on a registrable security, if he exploits either the mechanism of title retention or the concept of a trust device.

9-02 Banks have criticised these artificial devices on the ground that they are mere shams designed to subvert the generally accepted rules governing priority on corporate insolvency. This has aroused some scepticism on the part of the English judiciary, notably the Court of Appeal in *Clough Mill Ltd v. Martin*,[1] where it was pointed out that much the same allegation could be levelled against that artificial and invisible form of security much beloved of banks, namely the floating charge![2] It is interesting to note, by way of comparison, that the Scottish courts have in the past been more sympathetic to the fundamentalist argument raised by banks opposed to title retention clauses but their approach now mirrors that taken by their English counterparts.[3]

TITLE RETENTION CLAUSES

9-03 In the years before 1976 the task facing the courts when resolving a priority dispute between a receiver or liquidator on the one hand and a person who had

---

[1] [1985] 1 W.L.R. 111.

[2] See Cork Report Comnd. 8558 para. 107.

[3] *Armour v. Thyssen Edelstahlwerke A.G.* [1990] 3 W.L.R. 810. For the earlier antipathy towards title retention in Scotland see *Clarke Taylor & Co. Ltd v. Quality Site Developments* 1981 S.L.T. 309, *Ladbroke Leasing Ltd v. Reekie* 1983 S.L.T. 155, *Emerald Stainless Steel Ltd v. South Side Distributors* 1983 S.L.T. 162, *Deutz Engines v. Terex Ltd* 1984 S.L.T. 273, *Hammer and Sohne v. H. W. T. Realisations Ltd* 1985 S.L.T. (Sh. Ct.) 21, *Zahnrad Fabrik Passau GmbH v. Terex Ltd* 1986 S.L.T. (OH) 84—many of these authorities must now be open to question.

supplied goods to the company on credit on the other was not unduly difficult. The supplier who had supplied goods on credit to the company would, in the event of the company going into receivership or liquidation, be treated merely as an unsecured creditor. He would have no claim *in rem* against the goods, or their proceeds (where they had been sold on by the company). The property in the goods would have passed to the purchasing company under the contract of sale by virtue of what is now section 18 of the Sale of Goods Act 1979.[4] The clear winner in the priority battle would be the bank secured by a floating charge, unless that charge could be challenged on the grounds of non-registration or under what is now section 245 of the Insolvency Act 1986.[5]

Romalpa

9-04 However, the position was revolutionised by the case of *Aluminium Industrie Vaassen B.V. v. Romalpa Aluminium Ltd* (hereafter *Romalpa*).[6] Here, a Dutch supplier had sold aluminium foil to an English company. Under the terms of supply the Dutch company had retained title to the foil until it was fully paid for. The English purchaser went into liquidation and the question arose as to whether the Dutch suppliers were entitled to recover the foil then in the hands of the liquidator. If this claim were permitted, it would have the effect of converting the Dutch suppliers from being mere unsecured creditors into persons who had a claim *in rem* against valuable assets in priority to all other claimants. Both Mocatta J. and the Court of Appeal upheld the claim of the Dutch suppliers. The English purchaser under the terms of supply held the aluminium foil in a fiduciary capacity and as the foil was clearly identifiable, it could be recovered. Moreover, it would appear, at least from the judgment of Mocatta J. at first instance, that this arrangement did not give rise to a registrable charge on the company's assets within the meaning of sections 395 and 396 of the Companies Act 1985.

9-05 The authors would like to make a few preliminary observations about this decision. In some senses, it was almost an accident that the point ever came before the English courts.[7] Title retention clauses were widespread on the continent but rare in this country and, had it not been for the fact that the plaintiff here was a Dutch company which was using its standard terms of supply, the ghost of the *Romalpa* clause might never have arisen to haunt corporate insolvency law in England. Moreover, the fact that there was a foreign element at work in the case may well have caused problems with the ultimate judgment. Difficulties arose in translating the clause and certain concepts of English law were used by the Dutch suppliers in an unorthodox context.

---

[4] The passing of property problem was not entirely new in corporate insolvency law—see *Carlos Federspiel v. Twigg* [1957] 1 Lloyd's Rep. 240. See also *Re Goldcorp Exchange Ltd* [1995] 1 A.C. 74 where the Privy Council held that buyers of unallocated bullion had no proprietary claim on the selling company's assets when it went into receivership prior to delivery of the bullion. This interface between the law on sale of goods and insolvency has been modified as a result of the enactment of the Sale of Goods (Amendment) Act 1995 which deals with the passing of title in goods forming part of an identified bulk and with the sale of undivided shares in goods. This legislation could be of particular importance in insolvencies in the commodity trades, but it only operates prospectively to contracts made after September 19 1995. For consideration of the 1995 Act and its relevance to a number of trust cases see Worthington [1999] J.B.L. 1.

[5] See Chap. 10.

[6] [1976] 1 W.L.R. 676. Compare *Pfeiffer W.W. GmbH v. Arbuthnot Factors*, [1987] B.C.L.C. 522.

[7] Title retention surfaced in Ireland at about the same time—*Re Interview Ltd* [1975] I.R. 382.

Judgment unsatisfying

9-06 Certainly the judgment of the Court of Appeal is unsatisfying in a number of respects—key policy issues for corporate insolvency law, including the practical implications for insolvency practitioners, were never properly addressed. It is interesting to note that there appeared to be some reluctance initially to report the case, possibly because it was realised that this decision, which has been described as the most important commercial law case decided this century,[8] would cause grave upheaval in business practices.

Romalpa confirmed

9-07 Whatever early doubts may have existed about the authority of the principle embodied in the *Romalpa* case, it has been confirmed impliedly by the Court of Appeal on a number of occasions[9] since 1976. Most recently the House of Lords has lent its support to the basic concept of simple title retention in *Armour v. Thyssen Edelstahlwerke A.G.*[10] This case is significant for a number of reasons. First it is the only instance of a title retention case going to the House of Lords, albeit on a Scottish appeal. Secondly it dispels the suggestion that the Scottish courts would not uphold the efficacy of title retention. This is a welcome development in that it will help to harmonise commercial practice throughout Great Britain. Finally, this case involved the controversial "all sums due" species of title retention clause under which the supplier retains title not only until the price of the particular goods supplied has been met, but also until all sums due from the purchasing company (*e.g.* in respect of previous supplies) have been satisfied. This latter extension of title retention was in doubt before 1990, but their Lordships found no objection to it. Parliament has also tacitly given the green light to the general concept (see s.15 Insolvency Act 1986). A more explicit recognition of the practice is to be found in section 39 of the Finance Act 1997 where the concession of bad debt relief is extended to persons who supply goods on credit subject to title retention.[11]

9-08 How should a lawyer in practice approach a legal dispute involving goods supplied to a limited company on a reservation of title basis? There are five broad issues that have to be confronted. Before embarking on the following survey, the reader should note the warning given by Staughton J. in *Hendy Lennox v. Grahame Puttick Ltd*, that this area of law could be described as "a maze, if not a minefield."[12]

9-09 The rules discussed below apply not merely to title retention clauses

---

[8] Its importance can be gauged from the fact that there have been dozens of articles devoted both to it and its succeeding authorities. It has also attracted the attention of textbook writers. For an illuminating survey see de Lacy (1995) Anglo Am. L. Rev. 327.

[9] *Borden (U.K.) Ltd v. Scottish Timber Products Ltd* [1979] 3 W.L.R. 672, *Clough Mill v. Martin* [1985] 1 W.L.R. 111. Note also in this context the Court of Appeal's judgment in *Leyland DAF Ltd v. Automotive Products plc* [1993] B.C.C. 389. Here it was decided that it was not an abuse of a dominant position (contrary to Article 86 E.E.C. Treaty) for a specialist supplier of components to a company now in receivership to insist that pre-receivership supplies (made subject to title retention) be paid for in full before new supplies will be delivered.

[10] [1990] 3 W.L.R. 810. See also *Accurist Watches v. King* [1990] F.S.R. 80 for strong support for title retention where the goods supplied are branded items.

[11] This relief is designed to encourage creditors to participate in business rescue arrangements by offering them tax incentives in return for surrendering claims rather than pursuing them to the detriment of the stakeholders in general.

[12] [1984] 1 W.L.R. 485 at 493.

adopted by suppliers in this country, but also to foreign suppliers delivering goods to U.K. purchasers. The fact that a choice of law clause may have been included in the contract of supply does not prevent the English courts from deciding that a particular clause may constitute a registrable security, a point emphasised by Hoffmann J. in *Re Weldtech Ltd.*[13]

1. Incorporation of title retention clauses into the contract

9-10 Many companies in the wake of the *Romalpa* case amended their standard terms of supply in order to take the benefit of the decision, though the methods used by them to do so varied greatly. Some lawyers, in their eagerness to exploit this authority, may have lost sight of the basic principle that, in order for such a clause to be effective, it must first be incorporated into the contract. This was particularly important where the supply relationship pre-dated the *Romalpa* case.

Rules

9-11 The rules governing the question whether a title retention clause has been incorporated into a particular contract of supply or not are the same as those which the courts have evolved when dealing with exclusion clauses in contracts. Clearly, a title retention clause cannot be added unilaterally to a supply contract after that contract has been made.[14] Normally such a clause will not be incorporated unless the buyer's attention is drawn to it before the contract is concluded. Title retention clauses can be incorporated as the result of "a course of dealing" between the parties.[15]

9-12 The argument that a *Romalpa* clause has not been incorporated into the contract has been raised on a number of occasions but has rarely proved successful.[16] In earlier editions of this book the view was expressed that it was likely to succeed even less as time went on and judges became aware of the high frequency of such terms in commercial contracts.[17] However it has proved highly robust in practice, and insolvency practitioners are sophisticated in the issues involved and astute in putting creditors to proof of incorporation.

Difficulties of incorporation

9-13 The case of *Sauter Automation Ltd v. Goodman Mechanical Services Ltd*[18] affords an interesting illustration of some of the difficulties which can arise in incorporating a title retention clause into a contract. In that case, the plaintiffs supplied a control panel for a boiler system to be manufactured by the defendants. The boiler was to be delivered by the defendants to the Property Services Agency for installa-

---

[13] [1991] B.C.C. 16.
[14] See, *e.g.*, *Olley v. Marlborough Court Ltd* [1949] 1 K.B. 532.
[15] See here *Spurling v. Bradshaw* [1956] 1 W.L.R. 461. Contrast *McCutcheon v. MacBrayne Ltd* [1964] 1 W.L.R. 125.
[16] See, *e.g.*, *Romalpa* itself, *Re Bond Worth Ltd* [1980] Ch. 228, *John Snow & C. v. Woodcroft Ltd* [1985] B.C.L.C. 54. See also the Irish case of *Sugar Distributors Ltd v. Monaghan Cash & Carry Ltd* [1982] I.L.R.M. 399. The argument succeeded in *Wavin Nederland B.V. v. Excomb Ltd* (1983) 133 N.L.J. 937.
[17] See the comments of Tudor Evans J. in *Rob. Horne Paper v. Rioprint* (1978) unreported.
[18] [1986] 2 F.T.L.R. 239. This basic *Romalpa* principle was recently applied by Boreham J. in *John Snow & Co. Ltd v. Woodcraft Ltd* [1985] B.C.L.C. 54. For an Australian perspective on incorporation see *Associated Alloys Pty Ltd v. Metro Engineers and Fabrics Pty Ltd* (1996) 20 A.C.S.R. 205.

tion in Windsor Castle. The plaintiffs stipulated in their subcontract with the defendants that the plaintiffs were to retain title to the control panel until it was paid for. However, the defendants' terms of acceptance were inconsistent with such a provision, and the main contract between the defendants and the Property Services Agency provided that the ownership of any goods delivered on site was to pass to the Property Services Agency. The defendants went into liquidation, and the plaintiffs as unpaid sellers under the subcontract sought a declaration that they were still the owners of the control panel. Mervyn Davies J. held that under the "battle of forms" which had taken place the defendants' terms had prevailed. The title retention clause had therefore not been incorporated into the subcontract. The court also decided that even if it had been incorporated the plaintiffs could not have relied on it. The clause was inconsistent with the express terms of the main contract of which the plaintiffs were aware.

2. Title retention and unmixed goods

Basic principle

9-14 There is now clear authority that a properly drafted and incorporated simple title retention clause will be effective to reserve the title to the goods in the supplier until they have been fully paid for.[19] Such an arrangement is clearly envisaged by the Sale of Goods Act 1979. The effects of this principle are fourfold. First, the supplier may rely on his proprietary rights to recover his goods. Next, the arrangement does not constitute a registrable charge on the company's assets (*i.e.* the goods supplied) because they have never formed part of the company's assets. Thirdly, a floating charge over the company's assets given to a bank will not, when it crystallises, attach to goods belonging to the supplier—the concept of reputed ownership never applied in corporate insolvency law.[20] Fourthly, an insolvency practitioner who wrongfully disposes of goods subject to a title retention restriction may incur personal liability for conversion.[21] Certain limited powers of disposal are conferred on administrators by the Insolvency Act 1986,[22] but neither an administrative receiver nor a liquidator has any such power.

9-15 The key case of *Clough Mill Ltd v. Martin*[23] affords a useful illustration of these principles at work. Here a manufacturer supplied yarn on terms that the manufacturer retained title to the yarn until it and other parcels of yarn had been paid for. The purchasing company went into receivership, but a quantity of yarn remained on its premises. The manufacturer sought to exercise its right under the contract of

---

[19] The clearest support for this proposition was provided by the Court of Appeal in *Clough Mill v. Martin* [1985] 1 W.L.R. 111.

[20] *Gorringe v. Irwell India Rubber Works* (1888) 34 Ch.D. 128. Reputed ownership has now been abolished in bankruptcy law—see now Insolvency Act 1986, s.283.

[21] See *Len Vigden Ski & Leisure Ltd v. Timaru Marine Supplies Ltd* (1985) 2 N.Z.C.L.C. 99, 438. *Cf. Bryanston Leasings v. Principality Finance* [1977] R.T.R. 45 and *Schott Sohne v. Radford* [1987] 6 C.L. 372 (Willesden County Court). Where the legal effectiveness of a title retention device is the subject of litigation, it will be a sufficient protection for the unpaid supplier if the insolvency practitioner personally undertakes to recompense him for the value of the goods in the event of his claim being upheld. In such disputed cases the court will be reluctant to grant an interlocutory injunction to restrain the insolvency practitioner from dealing with the goods (or mixtures containing those goods)—see *Lipe Ltd v. Leyland DAF Ltd* [1993] B.C.C. 385.

[22] Insolvency Act 1986, s.15.

[23] [1985] 1 W.L.R. 111.

supply to repossess the yarn but the receiver refused to allow this on the grounds that the title retention provisions amounted to a charge on the company's assets. The manufacturer accordingly sued the receiver for conversion.

9-16 At first instance Judge O'Donoghue rejected the manufacturer's claim on the grounds that a title retention clause was necessarily a disguised security device which was ineffective for want of registration. The manufacturer's appeal to the Court of Appeal was successful. There was nothing wrong in principle with the concept of title retention and it was clearly intended by the parties that the ownership of any unused yarn should remain with the supplier. The fact that title retention agreements might be intended to operate as security devices did not mean that they were registrable at Cardiff.

Limitations

9-17 Although a simple title retention clause can be effective it has a number of limitations. It is of paramount importance that the clause is properly drafted. In the aftermath of *Romalpa*, there was a scramble to have title retention clauses drawn up and it must be conceded that some of the resultant efforts left a lot to be desired. The curious wording of the clause in *Romalpa* itself, and the translation difficulties associated with it, cannot have helped would-be draftsmen. In *Re Bond Worth Ltd*[24] the clause in question purported to retain only the equitable and beneficial title of the property in question (acrilan yarn). Slade J. held that this departure from the successful *Romalpa* formula was fatal. As the suppliers had only retained the equitable title it followed that the legal title had passed to the purchasing company. The equitable interest which the suppliers claimed had been given by way of security and amounted to an equitable charge over the company's assets, which was void for want of registration. In the light of this decision, title retention clauses must clearly retain the full legal title to the goods supplied in order to be effective.

9-18 Even if the clause is properly formulated, the supplier can be deprived of the goods in certain circumstances. If the goods have been converted into fixtures, they are treated as being part of the land and will, accordingly, pass with the land—*quicquid plantatur solo, solo cedit*. This limitation on title retention was revealed by the pre-*Romalpa* case of *Re Yorkshire Joinery Co. Ltd.*[25] Whether an item of property becomes a fixture in English law or not depends both on the intention of the parties and the degree of annexation to the land.[26] Clearly, the suppliers of building materials and heavy fixed plant should be alerted to this problem.

9.19 Certain dealings with the goods may defeat the suppliers' claim, but it has been held in *Pongakawa Sawmills v. Forest Products*[27] that cutting logs into planks did not destroy the efficacy of title retention. This case is to be compared with the more recent English authority of *Chaigley Farms Ltd v. Crawford, Kaye and Grayshire.*[28] Here a supplier of cattle to an abattoir included in correspondence (which was held to be part of the contract) an assertion that the livestock was only

---

[24] [1980] Ch. 228. Followed in *Stroud Architectural Systems v. John Laing Construction* [1994] B.C.C. 18.

[25] (1967) 111 S.J. 701. See also the analogous case of *Gough v. Wood & Co.* [1984] 1 Q.B. 713.

[26] *D'Eyncourt v Gregory* (1866) L.R. Eq, 382, *Holland v. Hodgson* (1872) L.R. 7 C.P. 327, *Leigh v. Taylor* [1902] A.C. 157. For a similar unreported county court ruling see *Aircool Installations v. British Telecom*—noted in Current Law Week, May 19, 1995.

[27] [1992] 3 N.Z.L.R. 304.

[28] [1996] B.C.C. 957. For comment see de Lacy [1997] (November) *Palmer's In Company* 1.

being supplied on terms that title to the goods was retained until payment. When the abattoir became insolvent the question arose as to whether this clause was effective to retain title to those animals which had been slaughtered and whose carcasses remained on the premises. Garland J. held that the claim was not effective in these circumstances, though it seems likely that had it been drafted in such a way as to encompass slaughtered livestock the court might have reached a different conclusion.

Operation of section 25, S.G.A. 1979

9-20 The supplier may also be divested of his title to goods by virtue of the operation of section 25 of the Sale of Goods Act 1979. Under this provision the company can, by reselling the goods to a bona fide purchaser as a "buyer in possession," pass a good title even though the company itself lacked legal title at the time.[29] This is a recognised exception to the general rule of *nemo dat quod ille non habet*, which is embodied in section 21 of the Sale of Goods Act 1979. The operation of this statutory provision in the context of title retention was recently illustrated in *Four Point Garage v. Carter*.[30] In order for section 25 of the Sale of Goods Act 1979 to operate the delivery must be with the assent of the buyer.[31] Moreover, a delivery on a sale or return basis will also preclude the operation of the statutory transfer of title under section 25.[32]

9-21 Section 25 may pose an even more potent threat to title retention clauses. The section provides in effect that a third party will get a good title to the goods in the event of a delivery of them under "any sale, pledge, or other disposition" thereof by the company to a bona fide purchaser without notice of the unpaid seller's rights. It might well be argued that on the appointment of a receiver pursuant to a floating charge, his taking possession of all assets in the company's hands amounts to a delivery under a "disposition" for the purposes of section 25. The point has been accepted in Kenya[33] but, rather surprisingly, does not seem to have been argued before the English courts. There is authority to support the view that the grant of a floating charge (and not its subsequent enforcement by the appointment of a receiver) constitutes a disposition of the company's assets.[34] Clearly, the acceptance of such an argument would do much to return the advantage to the banks at the expense of trade creditors. The weakness in it may be the suggested of delivery of the goods on the receiver's taking possession. No doubt an administrative receiver will in most cases obtain *de facto* possession of the goods on exercising his right under the charge to assume control of the company's premises. However, as no act of the company is involved in transferring that possession to him (and he is normally the agent of the

---

[29] For title to pass to the sub-purchaser, the goods in question must be in "deliverable state"—*see Hendy Lennox (Industrial Engines) Ltd v. Grahame Puttick Ltd* [1984] 1 W.L.R. 485.

[30] [1985] 3 All E.R. 12. See also the Scots decision in *Archivent Sales & Development Ltd v. Strathclyde Regional Council* 1985 S.L.T. 154.

[31] *Forsythe International (UK) Ltd v. Silver Shipping* Co. [1994] 1 W.L.R. 1334.

[32] *Re Highway Foods International Ltd* [1995] B.C.C. 271.

[33] *G.A. Schmittsches Weingut v. Leslie* 1967 (2) A.L.R. Comm. 34

[34] *Sowman v. David Samuel Trust Ltd* [1978] 1 W.L.R. 22 at 30 *per* Goulding J. In *Re Margart Pty Ltd* [1985] B.C.L.C. 314 it was held that the realisation of the floating charge is not a disposition within the N.S.W. counterpart of the Insolvency Act 1986, s.127. But in *Site Preparations Ltd v. Buchan Developments* 1983 S.L.T. 317, it was held that the grant of the floating charge is not a disposition within the meaning of the statutory predecessor of Insolvency Act 1986, s.127.

company anyway) it is hard to see how the assumption of control can be sufficient of itself to effect a delivery.[35]

3. Title retention and mixed goods[36]

9-22 The position of the supplier is much more precarious where the purchasing company has mixed the goods with others belonging either to itself or to some other supplier. It is submitted that three situations have to be distinguished.

Goods of the same nature

9-23

(a) The company mixes goods with others of exactly the same nature making it impossible for the supplier to say which are his goods. Here, the supplier will normally fail as the recovery of the goods *in specie* depends upon identification both at law and in equity. It has been known for certain unscrupulous insolvency practitioners to exploit this weakness in the supplier's position by mixing up goods in the company's possession so as to make it impossible for individual suppliers to identify their goods. However, this is a precarious strategy for two reasons. Firstly, it could (if detected) expose a receiver or liquidator to an action in conversion. Secondly, there may be special risks where the buyer has a contractual obligation to keep the goods in such a way that they can be distinguished from other goods. According to Lord Eldon in *Lupton v. White*[37] there is a principle both at law and in equity that "if a man, having undertaken to keep the property of another distinct, mixes it with his own, the whole must both at law and in equity be taken to be the property of the other, until the former puts the subject under such circumstances, that it may be distinguished as satisfactorily, as it might have been before that unauthorised mixture upon his part." On the other hand a different solution to this problem was proposed by Staughton J. in *Greenstone Shipping Co. S.A. v. Indian Oil Corp. Ltd.*[38] Here it was held that the mixture should be held in common and that the supplier was entitled to the return of a quantity of crude oil equivalent to that he had supplied. The role of the court was to do justice and to determine rights over the mixture; it was not their function to punish those engaged in wrongful mixing. It may be that in practice the major problem is not the dishonest mixing of the similar goods of different suppliers, but the innocent mixing of goods which are paid for, with identical goods of the same supplier but which are not paid for. Even so, there may well yet be scope for some imaginative drafting. Where there has been innocent mixing in the absence of an express or implies obligation to keep the goods unmixed, but it is possible to say that a given proportion of the mixture belongs to the supplier, it may be that the court will be prepared to cut the Gordian knot and adopt the solution of joint ownership of the mixture.

---

[35] This counter argument is supported by *Wilkinson* in (1985) 1 I.L. & P. 172. See also *Lyford v. Commercial Bank of Australia* (1995) 17 A.C.S.R. 211.

[36] For discussion see de Lacy (1995) Anglo Am. L. Rev. 327.

[37] (1808) 15 Ves. 432 at 436–7.

[38] [1988] Q.B. 345.

Goods retain identity

9-24

(b) The company mixes the supplier's goods with others to form a composite item within which the supplier's goods retain their physical identity. This was the very situation that arose in *Hendy Lennox v. Grahame Puttick Ltd.*[39] Here the plaintiffs had supplied engines (subject to a title retention clause) which had been used as components in generators. The engines remained physically identifiable within the generating sets though clearly it would take some time to dismantle them. Staughton J. held that the plaintiffs were entitled to recover their goods in such circumstances.

Goods have lost identity

9-25

(c) The company mixes the supplier's goods with others to form a composite amalgam in which the supplier's goods have lost their distinct identity.[40] Again the supplier's claim fails. The supplier's goods are no longer identifiable; indeed, the property in them has ceased to exist. This in *Borden (U.K.) Ltd v. Scottish Timber Products Ltd*[41] resin was supplied by the plaintiffs to the defendant company for the manufacture of chipboard. The resin was mixed with other chemicals and reacted with them to form a new chemical in the chipboard. The Court of Appeal held that the suppliers had no proprietary claim on the company's assets once their goods had been used in this chemical process. Their resin had completely lost its identity and, moreover, they could not claim a notional share of the value of the chipboard. Can a supplier do anything to prevent his claim being defeated by the purchasing company mixing his goods with others? Two strategies may at first sight appear attractive. The supplier may require that his goods are stored separately. This will only reduce the risk of the first type of mixing outlined above. If the goods are to be used in a manufacturing process, they will inevitably be mixed at some time. In the case of wrongful mixing, an action for damages against the insolvent company for breach of the separate storage provisions is unlikely to offer much comfort, though a personal action against the company officers responsible might be worth further consideration. It may also be possible to make a claim *in rem* against the whole of the mixture based on *Lupton v. White*.[42]

Rights over mixed product

9-26 Despite the *Borden case*,[43] it is still common for suppliers to adopt the alternative strategy of trying to extend their rights into the mixed product. The *Borden* case[44] suggests that where the supplier's goods lose their identity, the property in them

[39] [1984] 1 W.L.R. 485.
[40] Similar issues arise where goods are processed (rather than mixed). Fine distinctions abound—compare *Pongakawa Sawmills v. N.Z. Forest Products* [1992] 3 N.Z.L.R. 304 with *Modelboard v. Outer Box* [1992] B.C.C. 845.
[41] [1979] 3 W.L.R. 672.
[42] (1808) 15 Ves. 440.
[43] [1979] 3 W.L.R. 672.
[44] *Supra.*

ceases to exist and a new property springs up in the composite goods which is vested in their manufacturer. Any contract term by which the seller acquires ownership of the composite goods involves a transfer of this property by way of security. This amounts to the creation of a charge over the company's assets requiring registration under sections 395 and 396 of the Companies Act 1985.[45] Indeed, unless the supplier's goods are recoverable intact from the composite goods (like the engines in a generator), it appears that the same applies, even though the supplier's goods are identifiable and even though they form the vast proportion of the composite product. In *Re Peachdart Ltd*[46] the plaintiff suppliers had provided the leather which was used by the defendants to manufacture handbags. The handbags consisted almost exclusively of the plaintiffs' leather, but also included buckles and fittings not supplied by the plaintiffs. Vinelott J. held that it was not possible for the plaintiffs to retain the ownership of the leather in the manufactured handbags, nor the handbags themselves. It remains to be seen how this principle applies to the common case of goods such as cloth which have undergone some process such as bleaching, dyeing, or even printing after delivery to the buyer. It is usual in the textile trade for such processes to be carried out by "finishers" on customers' cloth, and although the finisher may claim a lien for the price of his work the cloth is regarded as belonging to the customers throughout. If the customers can retain ownership of cloth despite its being treated in this way, it might be expected that a supplier who delivers cloth to a customer's finisher on retention of title terms would be in the same position. However, to the extent that these finishing processes involve irreversible alterations in the chemical or physical state of the cloth, it may be that the cases discussed immediately above give the supplier grounds for disquiet.

Suppliers as joint owners

9-27 Another point that does not yet appear to have been tested in the English courts is whether title retention would succeed where the mixed product consists entirely of assets delivered by different suppliers subject to reservation of title. Could the suppliers be regarded as joint owners of the composite product, or would the company's efforts in mixing together the goods (*e.g.* its energy costs) mean that each of the suppliers could only be viewed as having a registrable interest in the amalgam?

9-28 To the extent that the individual components of the mixture were both severable and identifiable, no doubt their suppliers could sever and reclaim them under the *Hendy Lennox*[47] principle. To the extent that they were not identifiable, or (pos-

---

[45] *Borden (U.K.) Ltd v. Scottish Timber Products Ltd* [1979] 3 W.L.R. 672 at 686–7 *per* Templeman L.J. at 688 *per* Buckley L.J. *Kruppstahl v. Quitman* [1982] I.L.R.M. 551. *John Snow & Co. Ltd v. Woodcroft Ltd* [1985] B.C.L.C. 54 at 63 *per* Boreham J.

[46] [1983] 3 All E.R. 485. This decision was followed by the Court of Appeal in *Specialist Plant Services Ltd v. Braithwaite Ltd* [1987] B.C.L.C. 1. In this case, a contract for the repair of machinery provided that if the repair involved the supply of parts which were incorporated into the customer's machinery, then the entire ownership of the machinery should pass to the repairer as surety for the payment of the repair bill. On the receivership of a customer, the repairer obtained an injunction to restrain the sale of the machinery by the receiver, pending the determination of his proprietary claim to it. The conclusion of the Court of Appeal that this arrangement constituted a charge over the customer's assets, which was void for non-registration, was so predictable that it was surprising that it was felt necessary to take the case to court, let alone to the Court of Appeal.

[47] [1984] 1 W.L.R. 485.

sibly) not severable, the principles in *Peachdart*[48] and *Borden*[49] would bar some suppliers from any claim in the resulting composite product. However, the authors suspect that in this type of case (*i.e.* mixtures of the first and third kinds discussed above), the insolvent buyer will only acquire title to the composite product if either:

(i) the product is one in which the elements lose their identity as in a mixture of chemicals which react together, or

(ii) the product is one in which the elements retain their identity, but are no longer attributable with certainty to any particular supplier.

In the second type of case it may matter whether the company has expended appreciable resources (*e.g.* energy costs) in effecting the mixture. If not, joint ownership of the mixture by the suppliers might recommend itself to a court as a fair solution to the problem.

9-29 Clearly any clause which purports to retain or transfer to the supplier the ownership of a mixture which has become vested in a buyer will be void unless registered as a charge.

4. The supplier's claim to the proceeds of sub-sales

9-30 A tightly drafted title retention clause will often seek to extend the supplier's claim to any proceeds of subsales received by the company. This would be a desirable result to achieve as the supplier's claim to the goods themselves will usually be defeated on a subsale by the operation of section 25 of the Sale of Goods Act 1979 (the company will be regarded as a "buyer in possession"). Although there have been reported instances in which the unpaid supplier of goods has succeeded in recovering their proceeds under an extended title retention clause, it seems that any such claim is now doomed to failure. The reason is that in most circumstances, the clause will be found to create a registrable charge over the purchasing company's book debts, which is therefore void unless registered. An analysis of recent judicial decisions confirms that gloomy (from the unpaid supplier's viewpoint) prognostication.[50]

9-31 Generally, the claim will fail if the buyer is free to pay the proceeds of sale into the same bank account as the company's own funds. In most cases such an arrangement will be held incompatible with the existence of the fiduciary relationship between the buyer and seller[51] necessary to justify tracing into a mixed fund under the rule in *Re Hallet's Estate*.[52] In *Re Andrabell Ltd*[53] Peter Gibson J. made the point that such a relationship does not necessarily exist, even where the buyer is a bailee or agent of the seller, and distinguished *Romalpa (supra)*, in which a fidu-

[48] [1983] 3 All E.R. 485.
[49] [1979] 3 W.L.R. 672.
[50] For unsuccessful attempts at title retention in this area see *E Pfeiffer Weinkellerei-Weineinkauf GmbH v. Arbuthnot Factors* [1987] B.C.L.C. 522, *Tatung (U.K.) Ltd v. Galex Telesure Ltd* (1989) 5 B.C.C. 325 and *Carroll Group Distributors v. Bourke Ltd* [1990] I.L.R.M. 285. The exceptions (which prove the rule) are the Commonwealth authorities of *Len Vigden Ski and Leisure Ltd v. Timaru Marine Supplies Ltd* (1985) 2 N.Z.C.L.C. 99, 438 and *Puma Australia Ltd v. Sportsman's Australia Ltd* (1990) (unreported, but noted by *de Lacy* in [1993] Conv. 375).
[51] See *Re Bond Worth Ltd* [1980] Ch. 228 at 260–1 *per* Slade J. citing with approval *Henry v. Hammond* [1913] 2 K.B. 515 at 521.
[52] (1880) 13 Ch.D. 696.
[53] [1984] 3 All E.R. 407.

ciary relationship was expressly provided for, in this respect. Clearly, to have any hope of success, an extended title retention clause should expressly create a fiduciary relationship and provide for subsale proceeds to be paid into a separate bank account. Such an arrangement will rarely be commercially acceptable, but even if the seller's clause enables him to take identifiable proceeds of sale, he will face formidable difficulties in extending his claim to the contract debts under which they arise.

9-32 In *Re Weldtech Ltd*[54] a German supplier used terms of supply which stated that the proper law of the contract was to be German law, and the unpaid seller was to be the assignee of all rights of the company against a subpurchaser in the event of a resale by the company. Hoffmann J. held that notwithstanding the choice of law clause, this case was governed by the English law of security and the particular clause relating to proceeds of subsales created a registrable charge over those proceeds, a charge which was void for non-registration. Section 395 of the Companies Act 1985 applies to all charges created by a company registered in England, whatever the proper law of the contract under which they arise.

9-33 The decision of Mummery J. in *Compaq Computers v. Abercorn Group*[55] reveals a final hurdle for the unpaid supplier. Even if no registrable charge over the buyer's book debts has been created (which was not the case here) the interest given to the unpaid supplier in the proceeds of sale will probably be equitable in nature, and where other equitable claims on the same fund are found to exist (*e.g.* because the company has assigned its book debts to a factoring company) priority will be determined according to the rule in *Dearle v. Hall*[56] which gives precedence to the claimant who first gives notice to the debtors of the company under the subsale arrangement.

5. Severability of provisions in a title retention agreement

One element void

9-34 What is the position where the court finds that one of the elements in a title retention agreement is void (*e.g.* for non-registration at the Companies Registry), but the remainder of the provisions are unobjectionable? Do the general principles of contract law governing severability of tainted provisions apply in this context? The matter has not yet been fully aired in the English courts but it has recently arisen in Scotland. In *Glen v. Gilbey Vintners Ltd*[57] Lord Clyde in the Court of Session (Outer House) ruled that the invalid element in a particular title retention agreement could be severed, thereby preserving the enforceability of the remainder of the provisions. Lord Clyde was certainly assisted in reaching this conclusion by the fact that the title retention agreement under scrutiny actually anticipated this possibility and contained an express clause providing for the independent treatment of each element in the title retention agreement and also for severability in the event of any particular clause falling foul of the law. Such a provision would clearly be a useful addition to any title retention agreement.

---

[54] [1991] B.C.C. 16.
[55] [1991] B.C.C. 484.
[56] (1823–8) 3 Russ 1. For analysis see de Lacy (1999) 28 Anglo American L. Rev. 87 and 197.
[57] 1986 S.L.T. 553.

TRUST DEVICES

Claim in rem

9-35 Until recently a person who had lent money to a limited company would, in the event of that company becoming insolvent, merely rank as an unsecured creditor with very little, or no, chance of recovering his cash. However, things would be radically different if the lender could be placed in the position of a beneficiary of a trust imposed on the company. In that case, once again, the lender would have a claim *in rem* against that money in priority to all other persons claiming against the company's assets.

9-36 Conceptually, this idea has an unimpeachable pedigree, but once again in practice it can cause great difficulties for banks and insolvency practitioners. In the following section of this book the authors will first identify some situations where the courts have recognised that such a trust device might be effective. Following this the nature of these trusts and their effectiveness *vis-à-vis* third parties will be considered.

1. Creditor trust situations

9.37 **(a) Funds supplied for an exclusive purpose.** If a company encourages investors to provide it with finance for its general business activities, or even for particular projects, then as a general rule no trust in favour of the investor will arise. However, is the position any different where the person advancing the money to the company stipulates that it is only to be used for a particular purpose and that purpose has subsequently been rendered unattainable?

Advance to trustees

9-38 Towards the end of the last century British companies were clamouring for funds to finance speculative projects in the four corners of the world. Financiers were naturally reluctant to supply the cash unless special precautions were taken to protect their interests. One method commonly adopted was for the financier to advance the money not directly to the company but to trustees, who would release portions of it to the company as it completed various predetermined stages of the project. In *National Bolivian Navigation Co. v. Wilson*[58] the House of Lords held that if the scheme was frustrated but funds remained in the hands of the trustees the investors could recover those funds.

9-39 This case indicated a method involving a trust by which a financier could protect his investment and prevent his money from being swallowed up with the general funds of the company. On the other hand, the method was cumbersome in that it required the money to be held *in medio*.[59]

Advance to company

9-40 In *Barclays Bank Ltd v. Quistclose Investments Ltd*[60] the question arose of whether such a trust could be established where funds were paid direct to the

---

[58] (1880) 5 App. Cas. 176.

[59] *National Bolivian Navigation Co. v. Wilson* (1880) 5 App. Cas. 176 at 180–181 *per* Earl Cairns L.C.

[60] [1968] 3 All E.R. 651. Followed by the Court of Appeal in *Re E.V.T.R. Ltd*, [1987] B.C.L.C. 646. Here it was held that the partial failure of a scheme under which money had been advanced to the company to buy equipment meant that a resulting trust arose in favour of the financier in respect of moneys returned to the receiver by the proposed seller of the equipment. See also *General Communications Ltd v. Development Finance Corp. of New Zealand* [1990] 3 N.Z.L.R. 406.

company. The respondents advanced money to a company stipulating that it was to be used for the sole purpose of paying a dividend which had already been declared by the company. The money was actually paid in the form of a cheque given to the company's bank and credited to a special account in the company's name. The dividend was never paid and the company went into liquidation. The House of Lords held that the respondents were entitled to the money in the special account. It was the intention of all the parties that it should not become part of the general funds of the company—it was held on primary trust to pay the dividend and as this could not be achieved, a resulting trust arose in favour of the respondents. Furthermore, the bank, having been told of the specific purpose for which the payment was made, actually had notice of the trust and was thus a constructive trustee.

9-41 This decision was recently followed by Peter Gibson J. in *Carreras Rothmans Ltd v. Freeman Mathews Treasure Ltd.*[61] Here, C.R., a tobacco manufacturer, employed F.M.T., an advertising agency, to place advertisements for it in the media. In so doing, F.M.T. incurred debts to the media for advertising charges, which it recharged to C.R. with its own fees. F.M.T. got into financial difficulties, and C.R. became concerned that the media creditors would not be paid, and that its reputation would thereby suffer. Accordingly, at C.R.'s request, F.M.T. set up a special client account into which C.R. paid sums to be used by F.M.T. to pay creditors with whom advertisements had been placed. A few months later F.M.T. went into voluntary liquidation, and the question arose as to whom was entitled to the money in F.M.T.'s client account. It was held that the scheme effectively created a primary trust in favour of particular creditors of F.M.T., which they could enforce as beneficiaries. A resulting trust in favour of C.R. arose in respect of unclaimed sums.

9-42 Another exception to the general rule that a person who invests in a company does not become the beneficiary of a trust is illustrated by the decision of Harman J. in *Re Nanwa Gold Mines Ltd.*[62] Here, a company invited subscriptions for new shares which were to be issued as part of a scheme to alter its capital structure. It promised to hold any subscription moneys so received in a separate account and to return them if the scheme proved abortive. The scheme did indeed fail and the company went into receivership. Harman J. held that the promise to keep the money in a separate account (as the company was required to do by what was section 86(6) of the Companies Act 1985), coupled with the undertaking to refund indicated that the moneys were to be held on trust for the subscribers. However, the judge did stress that he was induced to reach this conclusion by the combination of promises and he would not have supported a trust had there been a mere undertaking to refund.[63]

9-43 **(b) Funds earmarked to repay investors.** If a company establishes a special fund to repay a group of its investors, whether they be shareholders or debenture holders, a trust may arise for their benefit so that on the company going into receivership or liquidation the fund cannot be treated as part of the general assets of the company. It was made clear in *Elkins v. Capital Guarantee Society*[64] that the liq-

[61] [1984] 3 W.L.R. 1016.
[62] [1955] 3 All E.R. 219.
[63] See here *Moseley v. Cresseys Co.* (1865) L.R. 1 Eq. 405.
[64] (1900) 16 T.L.R. 423. *Cf. Re Eastern Capital Futures Ltd* (1989) 5 B.C.C. 223.

uidator cannot touch such a fund. In that case the company had set up a "Redemption Fund" to repay its bondholders. When the company went into liquidation there was only sufficient cash in the trust fund to pay a dividend to each bondholder and not the full amount due. Some of the bondholders claimed their share of this fund but others failed to contact the company. The Court of Appeal refused to allow the liquidator to distribute the unclaimed amounts among the general creditors or to permit the identified bondholders to share in the residue—the fund had to be kept intact for 50 years and the liquidator could only claim it when that time had elapsed.

9-44 (c) **Trusts to benefit employees.** It is quite common for receivers to be confronted with claims by the employees of an insolvent company to the effect that moneys in possession of the company are in fact held on trust for their benefit. Apparently these claims normally relate to sick funds, trade union subscriptions collected by the company but not handed over to the union and collections for the firm's outing. There is some judicial authority to support these claims.

9-45 In *Re Independent Air Travel Ltd*[65] the company had, as it was contractually obliged to do, insured the lives of its employees some of whom later died in an air crash. The insurers had paid over money to the company to be distributed amongst the families of the deceased but the company went into receivership before this could be done. Although it was not expressly provided that any insurance moneys would be held on trust, Plowman J. held that a trust arose when the company received these moneys so that the receiver had no right to them. Similarly, in *Smith v. Liquidator of James Birrell Ltd*,[66] on the company going into liquidation, it had moneys in a separate bank account representing sums received from an insurance company in respect of various employee pension and insurance schemes which the company had decided to discontinue. Lord Fraser, in the Court of Session, held that these moneys had clearly been received on behalf of its employees and therefore the liquidator was not entitled to treat them as part of the general funds of the company.

9-46 (d) **Returnable deposits received by the company.** If a company receives a sum of money from a person dealing with it and is under an obligation to return that money in certain circumstances, that person will, as a general rule, rank as a mere unsecured creditor of the company. However, if the company wishes to protect him, it can create a trust for his benefit.

9-47 In *Re Kayford Ltd*,[67] a mail order company, realising that it was in financial difficulties, took advice on how best to protect deposits which its customers were sending in to the company, in anticipation of being supplied with goods. The company was advised to open a special Customers Trust Deposit Account, into which all future deposits received should be paid, but instead it simply paid them into an existing bank account which was empty at the time. On the company going into liquidation, Megarry J. held that a trust had been created in favour of the customers. Although there was a lack of formality, the "three certainties" were present and the company clearly intended to isolate these deposits from its general funds:[68]

---

[65] [1961] 1 Lloyd's Rep. 604.
[66] 1968 S.L.T. 174.
[67] [1975] 1 All E.R. 604. See generally Belcher and Beglan [1997] J.B.L. 1.
[68] *ibid.*, at 607.

> "No doubt the general rule is that if you send money to a company for goods which are not delivered, you are merely a creditor of the company unless a trust has been created. The sender may create a trust by using appropriate words when he sends the money . . . or the company may do it by taking suitable steps on or before receiving the money."

9-48 In spite of some criticism this case has now been followed by the Court of Appeal in *Re Chelsea Cloisters Ltd.*[69] Here, a company which was the underlessee of a block of flats granted numerous tenancies in similar terms. Clause 1 of the tenancy agreement ran as follows:

> "The tenant shall, on the signing of this agreement, pay to the landlord, the sum of (x) pounds as and by way of a deposit against any such sum which may be due from or payable by the tenant at the end of the tenancy for damage, breakages, compensation etc., any balance to be credited to the tenant at the termination of the tenancy."

9-49 The deposits were not initially segregated from the company's funds. The company was part of the Stern Group, which ran into financial difficulties and in June 1974 a "supervisor" was appointed to manage the company's affairs. In order to protect tenants' deposits he set up in August a special "Tenants' Deposit Account," into which were paid all deposits received since the date of his appointment and all new deposits On the subsequent liquidation of the company a dispute arose as to who was entitled to the deposits. Slade J. held that they must be treated as part of the general assets of the company but the Court of Appeal decided that they were held by the company on trust for their tenants. The Court of Appeal doubted whether a trust had been created initially by Clause 1 of the tenancy agreement but the act of the supervisor in opening the separate account did indicate an intention to create a trust. Lord Denning M.R. declared:[70]

> "To my mind it is plain as can be that Mr Iredale realised that the company was in a hopeless position, it had no money to pay anybody and there was a danger that these deposits might fall into the hands of the other creditors of the company contrary to the justice of the case. So, he thought that all these deposits, which the tenants had paid, and which they were entitled to have back under the terms of their agreements, ought to be kept as a separate fund to be secure against the other creditors and to be made available only to the tenants."

Debt factors

9-50 (e) **Trusts and factoring agreements.** One way in which a company can raise money is to assign its book debts to a financier in exchange for an immediate cash payment. Finance companies which specialise in this type of arrangement are known as debt factors. A factoring agreement will sometimes provide for the debts to be paid directly to the factor or alternatively it may authorise the company to collect them on behalf of the factor. Where the latter method of collection is adopted the agreement may additional provide that any debts collected by the company are

[69] (1981) 41 P. & C.R. 98. Compare *Re Holiday Promotions (Europe) Ltd* [1996] B.C.C. 671.
[70] *ibid.*, at 102.

to be held on trust for the factor. In *International Factors Ltd v. Rodriguez*[71] the Court of Appeal confirmed that such a provision indeed creates a valid trust in favour of the factor. Thus in the event of the collecting company going into receivership or liquidation the finance company can assert its title to the proceeds of the debts in priority to any other claimant.

Construction industry

09-51 (f) Retention moneys. It is standard practice in the construction industry either for the employer or the contractor to be in possession of retention moneys payable ultimately either to the contractor (if held by the employer) or to a subcontractor. Normally it is provided that these moneys are to be held on trust for the ultimate recipient; but there used to be doubt as to whether such a trust was effective to achieve its aim of protecting the intended beneficiary in the event of the insolvency of the party holding the fund.[72] The question was answered in the affirmative in 1954 in *Re Tout & Finch Ltd*[73] and this decision has since been confirmed. Of course a retention fund will only be effective if it has actually been set up: a mere promise to establish one will achieve nothing, a point exemplified by *Macjordan Construction v. Brookmount Erostin Ltd.*[74]

Money paid by mistake

9-52 (g) Accidental trusts. A trust can arise unintentionally on corporate insolvency. A classic example is provided by the case of *Chase Manhattan Bank v. Israel-British Bank (London) Ltd.*[75] Here the plaintiff bank paid a sum of money in error through an intermediary to the defendant, and in fact paid twice. The defendant must have been aware of the error shortly after receiving the second payment. Goulding J. held that a trust arose for the benefit of the plaintiff bank and this trust prevailed over the statutory scheme for payment of general creditors.

Clients' trust accounts

9-53 (h) Statutory trusts. Parliament has encouraged the trend towards the use of trusts to guard various groups against the dangers posed by the insolvency of their debtors. An early protective provision was what later became section 86(6) of the Companies Act 1985, which seeks to safeguard investors who advance money to a public company for securities which are never issued. This provision is repealed by the Financial Services Act 1986. Under section 55 of that Act, the Secretary of State is to make regulations providing for the establishment of clients' trust accounts to protect investors' funds. Clients of an estate agent who becomes insolvent are in theory protected by section 13 of the Estate Agents Act 1979 and where a broker

---

[71] [1979] 1 All E.R. 17. See also the Scottish decision in *Tay Valley Joinery Ltd v. C.F. Financial Services Ltd* (1987) 3 B.C.C. 71.

[72] *Rayack Construction Co. Ltd v. Lampeter Meat Co. Ltd* (1979) 12 Build. Law Reps. 30 at 38 *per* Vinelott J.

[73] [1954] 1 All E.R. 127. See also *Rayack Construction Co. Ltd v. Lampeter Meat Co. Ltd (supra)*, *Re Saunders Ltd* (1981) 17 Build. Law Reps. 125. Contrast *Re Jartay Developments Ltd* (1983) 22 Build. Law Reps. 134. See also *Glow Heating Ltd v. Eastern Health Board* [1988] I.R. 111.

[74] [1992] B.C.L.C. 350.

[75] [1979] 3 All E.R. 1025. For a similar case based on different reasoning see *Barclays Bank Ltd v. Simms* [1980] 2 W.L.R. 218. See also *Re Irish Shipping Ltd* [1986] I.L.R.M. 518.

handles investors' funds, the clients' money is protected by being kept in special trust accounts.[76] Similar requirements are contained in many professional codes of conduct.[77]

2. Nature and constitution of the trust

9-54 In the cases discussed above, three distinct types of trust were involved. In some cases, the arrangement was perceived by the courts as an express trust, in others, as a resulting or even a constructive trust. The criteria which determine their effectiveness on corporate insolvency vary from type to type.

9-55 **(a) Express trusts.** Where an express trust is alleged, it is essential that the "three certainties" of a trust are shown to be present. These are certainty of intention, certainty of subject matter (*i.e.* trust property) and certainty of objects.

Certainty of intention

9-56 It is often the issue of certainty of intention which causes the greatest difficulty. In the first place, it was made clear by Megarry J. in *Re Kayford Ltd*[78] that the intention need not be expressed in written form unless the subject matter of the trust is land. Obviously where the arrangement is not documented, there can be daunting evidential problems. Whether the arrangement is in writing or is to be gauged from overt conduct, the question whether a trust has arisen is essentially one of interpretation for the court to unravel. It also follows that a trust can arise even though the transaction is not framed in terms of a trust; the crucial factor, as always, is the substantive operation of the arrangement. Thus, trusts were found to exist in *Re English and American Insurance Co*[79] and *Re Fleet Disposal Services Ltd*,[80] notwithstanding the inappropriate terminology employed. In *Swiss Bank Corp. v. Lloyds Bank Ltd*,[81] the plaintiff bank lent money to a company, I.F.T., to buy securities which were to be kept with an identified depositary, and the proceeds of sale were to be used for the repayment of the loan. Subsequently, the defendant bank took an equitable charge over the same securities and a priority dispute arose as to the respective claims of the plaintiff and defendant to the proceeds of sale of the securities. Browne-Wilkinson J. held that the arrangement was sufficiently clear to give the plaintiff an equitable interest in the proceeds, which took priority over the defendant's subsequent equitable charge. The Court of Appeal and House of Lords disagreed. In the latter forum, Lord Wilberforce concluded that although the proceeds were intended to be used to repay the plaintiff bank, that fund could, in practical terms, have been used by I.F.T. for other purposes.

9-57 Another trust claim failed in *Re Multi Guarantee Co. Ltd*,[82] where the

---

[76] See Financial Services Act 1986 s.55 and regulations passed thereunder. See also *Re Branston and Gothard Ltd* [1999] B.P.I.R. 466.

[77] See, *e.g.*, the rules made under s.32 of the Solicitors Act 1974.

[78] [1975] 1 All E.R. 604 at 607.

[79] [1994] 1 B.C.L.C. 649.

[80] [1995] 1 B.C.L.C. 345.

[81] [1979] 3 W.L.R. 201 (Browne-Wilkinson J.), [1980] 3 W.L.R. 457 (Court of Appeal), [1981] 2 W.L.R. 893 (House of Lords).

[82] [1987] B.C.L.C. 257. Expressing a preferred use for money is not unequivocal—*Lord v. Australia Elizabethan Trust* (1991) 5 A.C.S.R. 587.

Court of Appeal was unable to establish the presence of certainty of intention. Here, M.G. Ltd was in dispute with V. Ltd over a sum of money which M.G. Ltd was holding. Pending resolution of the dispute the sum of money was paid into a joint deposit account, withdrawal from which required the signatures of both parties' solicitors. M.G. Ltd then went into liquidation. The Court of Appeal held that there was no sufficiently unequivocal manifestation of an intention to create a trust in favour of V Ltd. The money may well have been intended to benefit other parties, who were also connected with the dispute. Therefore, as the express trust claim had failed, the solicitors held the money on resulting trust for M.G. Ltd and it should be paid over to the liquidator.

9-58 When interpreting the parties' actions and documents in order to discern their intention, the court will look at the substance of the arrangement and will disregard labels if these fail to reflect reality.[83] On general principles, the terms of any written agreement will also carry little weight if they have not been observed in practice, though in *Re Saunders Ltd*[84] Nourse J. was prepared to invoke the maxim "Equity regards as done that which ought to be done" in order to validate a trust.

9-59 Finally, the cases show that certainty of intention may exist whether the trust is set up in the usual way by the creditor advancing the money on certain terms which the company accepts, or by the unilateral actions of the company, as in *Re Kayford Ltd.*[85]

Certainty of subject matter

9-60 It is no good having a clear intention to create a trust if the property which is the subject matter of the trust cannot be identified. This problem is particularly acute in the case of money advanced to a company; in practice here a claim based upon a trust will only succeed if the money is kept in a separate bank account. A good example of a trust claim failing for want of certainty of subject matter is afforded by the case of *Re London Wine Shippers Ltd.*[86] Here, a wine merchant sold wine to its customers but its practice was to appropriate part of its general stock to the order only when the customer came to collect it. It was held that, on the receivership of the wine merchant, customers who had paid for wine which had not been delivered could not claim to be beneficiaries of a trust as the element of certainty of subject matter was absent.

9-61 An equally instructive authority is that of *Export Credits Guarantee Dept. v. Turner.*[87] Here, the E.C.G.D. had guaranteed a loan made by a bank to a company to finance the latter's exporting business. In return for the guarantee, the company entered into a recourse agreement in September 1971 under which it declared a trust in favour of the E.C.G.D. in respect of sums received by it on export invoices. The company went into voluntary liquidation in February 1972 and subsequently its

---

[83] *Re Kayford Ltd* [1975] 1 All E.R. 604 at 607 *per* Megarry J.

[84] (1981) 17 Build. Law Reps. 125. Contrast *Bank of Scotland v. Liquidators of Hutchinson, Main and Co.* 1914 S.C. 1, *E.C.G.D. v. Turner* 1981 S.L.T. 286, *Re Jartay Developments Ltd* (1983) 22 Build. Law Reps. 134 and *Re E. Dibbens & Sons Ltd* [1990] B.C.L.C. 577.

[85] [1975] 1 All E.R. 604. But the company's receiver or liquidator has no right to set up such a trust—*Re Associated Securities Ltd* [1981] 1 N.S.W.L.R. 742, *E.C.G.D. v. Turner* 1981 S.L.T. 286, *Re Jartay Developments Ltd* (1983) 22 Build. Law Reps. 134. A third party can assert his rights as beneficiary of such a trust even though he was not a party to the arrangement which established it—*Johns-Manville Canada Inc. v. John Carlo Ltd* (1981) 113 D.L.R. (3d) 286.

[86] 1986 P.C.C. 121. See also *Re Ellis, Son and Vidler Ltd* [1994] B.C.C. 532.

[87] 1981 S.L.T. 286.

liquidator collected certain export debts. The question was whether he held sums collected on trust for the E.C.G.D. or whether they could be regarded as part of the general assets of the company. The Scottish Court of Session held that the trust had not come into being in September 1971 as at that time the subject matter of the trust—*i.e.* sums "received" by the company in respect of exports—did not exist. The receipts came after liquidation, by which stage it was too late to declare any new trust. The liquidator was not bound by the company's contractual obligation to set up a trust. However, the court did suggest that it might have reached the opposite conclusion had the company purported to declare a trust in respect of the debts arising out of export transactions, and the decision seems to have turned on the parties' failure to refer to sums "to be" received.

9-62 (b) Resulting trusts. A resulting trust is essentially an implied trust based on the presumed intentions of the settlor. It is in a sense a "parasitic" or "secondary" trust.[88] Perhaps the best example in the cases discussed above is the arrangement in *Barclays Bank v. Quistclose Investments Ltd*,[89] where the trust arose on the failure of the scheme under which the money was paid to the company. Peter Gibson J. reached a similar conclusion in *Carerras Rothmans Ltd v. Freeman Mathews Treasure Ltd*,[90] the facts of which are given above. A resulting trust also arose in *Re Multi Guarantee Co Ltd*[91] where the alleged express trust could not be proved because there was insufficient evidence of certainty of intention.

9-63 (c) Constructive trusts. A constructive trust arises independently of the intention of the parties and in effect is imposed by the courts as a device for securing justice, although the English judiciary seems markedly reluctant to admit this, as appears from the judgment of Browne-Wilkinson J. in *Re Sharpe*.[92] This coyness was again very much to the fore in *Chase Manhattan Bank v. Israel-British Bank (London) Ltd*[93] where Goulding J. held that the recipient of money which he knew had been paid under mistake of fact held it on trust. Rather than view this as a case for a constructive trust, the learned judge preferred a more fictional approach, involving a continuing equitable interest on the part of the bank which paid the money by mistake. Bingham J. approached the matter more adventurously in *Neste Oy v. Lloyds Bank Ltd*.[94] Here the plaintiff shipowners appointed a United Kingdom agent, P.S.L., to handle its business in this country. Often payments were made by the plaintiffs to P.S.L. to settle port fees, etc. These payments were made into a special account which P.S.L. kept at Lloyds Bank. Five large payments were made into the account in January and February 1980, to enable P.S.L. to settle harbour dues. The directors of the group to which P.S.L. belonged resolved at 11.30 a.m. on February 22, to seek the appointment of a receiver for the whole group. Unaware of this, the plaintiffs made a sixth payment into the account later the same day.

9-64 The question then arose whether Lloyds Bank could set off the six sums of money in the P.S.L. account against P.S.L.'s indebtedness to the bank. It could not do

[88] See Lord Wilberforce in *Barclays Bank v. Quistclose Investments Ltd* [1968] 3 All E.R. 651 at 656.
[89] *Supra*.
[90] [1984] 3 W.L.R. 1016.
[91] [1987] B.C.L.C. 257.
[92] [1981] 1 W.L.R. 219 at 225.
[93] [1979] 3 All E.R. 1025.
[94] [1983] 2 Lloyd's Law Rep. 658.

this if the money was held by P.S.L. on trust for the plaintiffs. Bingham J. held that the first five sums were not held on trust; payments by a principal to his agent to be used for a specified purpose do not necessarily give rise to a trust. However, P.S.L. did hold the sixth payment on constructive trust because at that time the directors knew the group would be going into receivership and it would be unconscionable for them not to return this sum to the plaintiff. Bingham J. thus applied the general principle laid down by that famous American judge, Cardozo J., in *Beatty v. Guggenheim Exploration Co.*[95] As Lloyds Bank knew, at the time the last payment was credited to P.S.L.'s account, and certainly by the time they sought to exercise the set-off, that P.S.L. was on the verge of receivership, their claim was secondary to that of the plaintiffs.

3. Rival claims to the assets in trust cases

9-65 The case law does not lay down any convenient general set of rules for determining questions of priority between the claims of beneficiaries and third parties, but the authors offer the following principles by way of a toolkit for the practitioner confronted with a problem of this kind.

Precedence of beneficiary

(a) Where the trust property is clearly identifiable and the company has not purported to create any charge over it, the beneficiary will generally take precedence over the unsecured creditors of the company, so long as the trust was effectively constituted before the commencement of winding up. However the trust may be voidable under sections 238–241 of the Insolvency Act 1986.[96] The trust will survive if and to the extent that it was set up as part of a scheme under which money was advanced to the company, for in that case the beneficiary would not have been a creditor for the money before the transaction occurred.[97]

Voidable trust

(b) If the company or its receiver attempts to set up the trust to protect existing creditors, it is submitted that prima facie the trust is voidable under sections 238–241.[98] The case of *Re Chelsea Cloisters Ltd*[99] is not, the authors submit, inconsistent with this view. In that case the establishment of the trust *ex post facto* was not a fraudulent preference under the old law because the supervisor acted without any intent to prefer but in the mistaken belief that he was obliged to protect the tenants' deposits. In any event had he not done so he might well have found himself a constructive trustee for the money on the principle of *Neste Oy v. Lloyds Bank Ltd.*[1] He might now be obliged to

---

[95] (1919) 225 N.Y. 380 at 386.
[96] See Chap. 10.
[97] See Insolvency Act 1986, s.239(4) and *Re Kayford Ltd* [1975] 1 All E.R. 604 at 606 *per* Megarry J. However the courts are reluctant to reach this conclusion—*Re Lewis's of Leicester* [1995], B.C.L.C. 428 and *Re Branston and Gothard Ltd* [1999] B.P.I.R. 466.
[98] See Chap. 11.
[99] (1981) 41 P. & C.R. 98 especially at 105 *per* Oliver L.J.
[1] [1983] 2 Lloyd's Law Rep. 658.

take similar steps to avoid liability under section 214 of the Insolvency Act 1986[2] even though they would apparently amount to a preference under section 239.

Priority over judgment creditor

(c) The beneficiary will take priority over a judgment creditor who levies execution against the company's assets because the latter can assert no better claim to those assets than the company itself.[3] It is submitted that the position should be the same where a third party is seeking to assert a set-off against the trust fund. It appears from *Neste Oy v. Lloyds Bank Ltd*[4] that the person asserting the set-off can take priority if he has no notice of the trust, but this view is open to question.

Assets dissipated

(d) The beneficiary's claim will fail, however well constituted the trust, if the trust assets have been dissipated—*e.g.*, by payment into an overdrawn bank account or otherwise in settlement of unsecured debts.

Mixed fund

(e) Where trust money has been paid into a bank account and mixed (whether then or later) with the company's own funds, it may be possible to claim any funds remaining as trust money under the rule in *Re Hallett's Estate*.[5] That rule presumes payments out of the mixed fund to have been made so far as possible out of the company's own money, leaving trust money intact.

Identifiable property

(f) In the rare cases where the company has used the trust money to purchase identifiable property, the beneficiaries may claim that property or any other property purchased with the proceeds of its sale.[6]

Acquired with mixed funds

(g) Where property has been acquired partly with trust money and partly with the company's own money, the beneficiaries can claim a charge on the property for the amount of trust money expended on it. Alternatively they can claim a pro-rata share of its value. This rule applies despite *Re Hallett's Estate*,[7] even if on that rule the property would be deemed to have been bought with the company's own money, if the purchase money came from a mixed fund which was later dissipated.[8]

---

[2] See Chap. 12.
[3] For the general priority status of judgment creditors on corporate insolvency, see Chap. 8.
[4] [1983] 2 Lloyd's Law Rep. 658.
[5] (1880) 13 Ch.D. 696.
[6] *Re Hallett's Estate (supra).*
[7] *Supra.*
[8] *Re Oatway, Herslet v. Oatway* [1903] 2 Ch. 356.

Legal charge

(h) Where the company has granted a legal charge over the trust fund (or property representing it), the legal chargee will take priority if he had no notice of the beneficiaries' rights.[9] The courts have a marked reluctance to extend the doctrine of constructive notice into the commercial arena,[10] so that actual notice is probably required. It is not always easy to predict who will be found to have had notice of a constructive trust.

Equitable charge

(i) Where the company has granted an equitable charge (*e.g.* a floating charge) over the fund or property representing it, the earliest equitable interest prevails—"*qui prior est tempore potior est jure*"—as in *Swiss Bank Ltd v. Lloyds Bank Ltd.*[11] For this purpose a floating chargee only acquires an equitable interest in specific property when the charge crystallises.

Registrable charge

(j) Finally, if the would-be trust arrangement is shown to constitute a registrable charge over the company's assets, it may be void against the company's liquidator and creditors for non-registration under sections 395 and 396(1)(*e*). However, in *Carerras Rothmans Ltd v. Freeman Mathews Treasure Ltd*,[12] Peter Gibson J. held that a transaction which amounts to a genuine trust device does not constitute a registrable charge.

Costs

(k) If the liquidator has incurred costs investigating whether assets apparently belonging to the company are impressed with a trust the court might authorise these expenses to be treated as a charge on the relevant trust assets.[13]

---

[9] In *Barclays Bank v. Quistclose Investments Ltd* [1968] 3 All E.R. 651 at 656. Lord Wilberforce seemed prepared to assume that notice was required.
[10] *Manchester Trust v. Furness* [1895] 2 Q.B. 539 at 545 *per* Lindley L.J., *Welch v. Bowmaker Ltd.* [1980] I.R. 251.
[11] [1981] 2 W.L.R. 893.
[12] [1984] 3 W.L.R. 1016.
[13] See *Re Berkeley Applegate (Investment Consultants) Ltd (No. 2)* (1988) 4 B.C.C. 279 and *Re Telesure Ltd* 1997 B.C.C. 580. But compare *Tom Wise Ltd v. Fillimore* [1999] B.C.C. 129 where it could not be established that the relevant expenses had been incurred in connection with the trust assets and therefore the general creditors had to foot the bill.

CHAPTER 10

Miscellaneous Claims Against the Company's Assets

10-01 This Chapter deals with a variety of more or less disparate claims to the insolvent company's assets. Unlike the priority systems analysed in Chapter 7–9, no particular common element unites these claims, which stand as isolated groups of hazards requiring to be recognised and negotiated by the insolvency practitioner according to their peculiar characteristics.

COSTS AND EXPENSES OF RECEIVERSHIP, LIQUIDATION AND ADMINISTRATION

10-02 On corporate insolvency the law has traditionally granted a high priority status to costs and expenses incurred by insolvency practitioners. These costs and expenses would include both remuneration and disbursements. The law relating to the remuneration of insolvency practitioners has been considered above in Chapter 2. As a general rule, this priority claim can only be satisfied out of assets belonging to the company (and not to some other third party).[1]

Receivers

10-03 In the case of receivership, the priority status of the receiver's costs and expenses was determined by the case of *Re Glyncorrwg Colliery Co. Ltd.*[2] Here, it was stressed that these items ranked before both the claims of the preferential creditors and also those of the debenture holders on whose behalf the receiver was acting. Of all costs, realisation expenses enjoy the highest priority. However, these are narrowly defined and do not include the expense incurred in preserving an asset prior to its sale.[3]

Liquidators

10-04 A similar priority regime operates on liquidation. Section 115 of the Insolvency Act 1986 states that all expenses properly incurred in a voluntary winding-up, including the remuneration of the liquidator, are payable out of the company's assets in priority to all other claims. There is no comparable unqualified provision in the case of compulsory liquidation, but section 156 allows the court to

[1] *Taylor, Petitioner* 1976 S.L.T. (Sh. Ct.) 82. See further *Re Exchange Securities and Commodities Ltd (No. 2)* (1986) 2 B.C.C. 98, 932.
[2] [1926] Ch. 951.
[3] *Lathom v. Greenwich Ferry* (1895) 72 L.T. 790. But the cost of an earlier abortive sale may be included—*Batten v. Wedgewood Coal and Iron Co.* (1884) 28 Ch.D. 317.

give various expenses of winding-up such priority as it thinks fit where the company's assets are insufficient to meet all of its liabilities. Presumably in this section also "expenses" include the remuneration of the liquidator, but it does not say so. Section 175(2)(*a*) makes it clear that winding up "expenses" are to be satisfied in priority in the preferential claims. (See also r. 4.128 of the Insolvency Rules 1986.)

10-05 If the liquidator continues the business of the company in order to effect the most beneficial winding up, it is clear from *Re Great Eastern Electric Co. Ltd*[4] that any debts incurred by the liquidator whilst conducting the business will rank as winding up costs and that the post-liquidation creditors are to be paid first out of the company's assets.

Administration

10-06 The priority of the costs and expenses of an administrator is governed by section 19 of the Insolvency Act 1986. Under subsection (4), his remuneration and expenses are to be charged on the company's assets in priority to any floating charge. Subsection (5) then provides that where the administrator has incurred debts and liabilities arising under new contracts or contracts of employment adopted by him, they in turn rank in priority to his own claim under subsection (4). Further consideration of this issue is to be found in Chapter 3.[5]

Concurrent insolvency regimes

10-07 Difficult priority issues arise where receivership and liquidation overlap. The rules governing priority of a liquidator's costs in such a case can be derived from two modern authorities. In *Re Barleycorn Enterprises Ltd*[6] the Court of Appeal held that where a floating charge held by a debenture holder has not crystallised prior to the making of the winding-up order, the winding-up costs will rank before both the preferential creditors and the claims of the debenture holders secured by the floating charge. However, Vinelott J. felt able to distinguish this authority in *Re Christonette International Ltd*,[7] in which a receiver was appointed under the terms of a floating charge after a winding-up petition had been presented but before the order was made. The liquidator incurred costs in bringing an unsuccessful action challenging the validity of the debentures. The question was whether these costs incurred by the liquidator were to be paid in priority to the floating charge. Vinelott J. answered this question in the negative. The floating charge had crystallised prior to the making of the winding-up order, so that under the law then in force the debenture holder's security had become a fixed charge. Therefore it followed that the priority which the law granted to winding-up costs did not operate in such a case.

10-08 It is clear that the decision of Vinelott J. in the above case turned both on the particular 1949 company winding-up rules then in force, and the view that a floating charge ceases to be such for the purposes of the companies' legislation on crystallisation.

10-09 Section 251 of the Insolvency Act 1986 carried away a major pillar of

---

[4] [1941] Ch. 241. Corporation tax payable on the making of a capital gain by the liquidator when corporate assets are sold, ranks as a disbursement and is therefore a winding-up cost—*Re Mesco Properties Ltd* [1980] 1 W.L.R. 96.

[5] See here para. 3–43 above.

[6] [1970] Ch. 465. See also *Westminster Corp v United Travellers Club* [1916] 1 Ch. 161.

[7] [1982] 1 W.L.R. 1245.

Vinelott J.'s analysis by providing in effect that for priority purposes, once a floating charge, always a floating charge. Chadwick J. held on these grounds in *Re Portbase Ltd*,[8] a case that has been considered in Chapter 7, that *Re Christonette International Ltd*[9] is no longer good law. It is submitted that the case is to be welcomed because it removes an anomalous distinction in this area of corporate insolvency law.

10-10 A parallel dispute arose more recently in *Re V. V. Sorge & Co. Ltd*,[10] where the company had gone into voluntary liquidation after the date of the presentation of a winding-up petition to the court. The court had made a winding-up order several months later. In the intervening period the voluntary liquidator incurred expenses and after being replaced on compulsory liquidation, he sought to have these expenses treated as part of the costs of the winding up. The liquidator in the compulsory liquidation objected to this. He would have been prepared to allow the claim of his fellow insolvency practitioner had the voluntary liquidation preceded the winding-up petition, but in view of the actual sequence of events, he felt justified in rejecting the claim. The court held that the date that mattered was that of the winding up order, not the petition, and that therefore the voluntary liquidator's claim should be allowed.

LANDLORD

10-11 Landlords, although not technically ranking as preferential creditors, do enjoy a specially favoured position in English law in general, and on corporate insolvency in particular. This elevated position owes much to the continued survival[11] of the anomalous self-help remedy of distress for rent arrears, and the commonly available contractual remedy of forfeiture. Both are of venerable antiquity and hedged about accordingly with qualifications and exceptions, both by statute and at common law. The following section deals only with certain aspects of these remedies as they affect, and are affected by, corporate insolvency. The insolvency practitioner must remember that these areas of law abound in detail and technicality, so it is wise to take legal advice in most cases in practice.

Distress

10-12 Distress allows a landlord whose rent is in arrear to enter a tenant's premises peaceably, and to seize, and ultimately sell, any of the tenant's goods which are to be found there[12] in order to satisfy his claim. In certain circumstances the goods of persons other than the tenant may be taken.[13] The question of the effectiveness of distress as against third parties has been reviewed in two recent cases. Thus in *Cunliffe Engineering v. English Industrial Estates*[14] the High Court held that the

[8] [1993] B.C.C. 96.
[9] [1982] 1 W.L.R. 1245.
[10] [1986] 2 B.C.C. 99, 306. See also *Re Sandwell Copiers* (1988) 4 B.C.C. 227.
[11] The Law Commission Working Paper No. 97 (1986) calls for the abolition of this remedy. On the rights of landlords in general see Milman and Davey [1996] J.B.L. 541.
[12] Distress cannot be levied on premises not included in the lease—*Re Oak Pits Colliery Co. Ltd* (1882) 21 Ch.D. 322 at 328 *per* Lindley L.J.
[13] At common law any goods on the premises could be taken, but numerous exceptions to this rule have been introduced by statute, particularly the Law of Distress Amendment Act 1908.
[14] [1994] B.C.C. 972.

landlord's distress on goods held subject to a chattel mortgage in favour of a bank, which had appointed a receiver under a general debenture the day before the distress was levied, was effective. This odd conclusion was reached because although the goods were subject to a chattel mortgage the company was deemed to be the reputed owner of them under section 4 of the Law of Distress Amendment Act 1908. The bank could not take advantage of section 1(c) of the Act to nullify the distress as it was deemed to have a beneficial interest in the land as a result of its charge over the company's property. In *Salford Van Hire Contracts Ltd v. Bocholt Developments*[15] the Court of Appeal held that a landlord could not distrain upon vehicles which had been hired out to the tenant under a commercial leasing agreement. In modern commercial conditions a landlord must anticipate that a whole range of goods in the possession of a tenant will not be owned by him and the reputed ownership provision in section 4 of the 1908 Act must take account of that fact. This case is inconsistent with *Cunliffe (supra)*, which was not cited to the court, and it is submitted that it reflects a more satisfactory approach to this particular priority conundrum. Incidentally, both Hirst L.J. and Sir Ralph Gibson L.J. urged the government to abolish a landlord's right of distress for rent, an opinion with which we heartily agree. The remedy of distress extends only to rent, and will not normally apply to other amounts due under the lease (such as insurance premiums), unless they have been agreed to be payable by way of extra rent. A landlord needs no help from the court in levying distress, and faces many fewer obstacles than a judgment creditor embarking on an execution.[16]

Forfeiture

10-13 Forfeiture is a right normally (but not always) conferred on a landlord by a lease or tenancy agreement, entitling him to re-enter his premises and bring the lease to an end in certain events. Those events normally include non-payment of rent for a given period and the liquidation[17] receivership or entry into administration of a corporate tenant. Once the right has arisen it is exercisable either by action for forfeiture or by the landlord simply re-entering the premises and changing the locks (so long as he can do so peaceably). In either case the tenant can apply to the court for relief. This can be granted under section 146 of the Law of Property Act 1925, if the landlord has not re-entered, but probably only under the court's inherent jurisdiction if re-entry is complete.[18] It will always be a condition of relief that rent arrears and costs be paid.

Other remedies

10-14 Where the tenant has become insolvent but has sublet the premises, the landlord can serve a notice on the subtenant under section 6 of the Law of Distress Amendment Act 1908 requiring him to pay rent directly to the principal landlord.[19]

---

[15] [1996] R.T.R. 103.
[16] See Chap. 7.
[17] If the parties wish to exclude winding up for the purposes of reconstruction they must do so expressly—*Fryer v. Ewart* [1902] A.C. 187.
[18] *Lovelock v. Margo* [1963] 2 All E.R. 13. But see *Billson v. Residential Apartments* [1992] 2 W.L.R. 15. The Law Commission in Report 142 called for the abolition of forfeiture and its replacement by "landlord's termination orders."
[19] On this and the priority conflicts that can arise, see *Re Offshore Ventilation Ltd* (1989) 5 B.C.C. 160.

Where the insolvent tenant is an assignee of the lease, the landlord may be able to collect the rent from the original tenant if he is still solvent.[20]

Receivership and landlords

10-15 The position of insolvency practitioners holding different offices will now be examined against this background.

10-16 The favourable position enjoyed by landlords in the event of a tenant going into receivership was clearly established by the case of *Re Roundwod Colliery Ltd*,[21] where it was held that a landlord could levy distress after receivership for rent arrears arising in the period before the receiver was appointed. It would also appear that distress may be exercised in respect of rent arrears incurred after the appointment of a receiver. The fact that a receiver is in possession of the company's premises does not normally prevent distress from being levied,[22] though, of course, if the receiver has already disposed of the company's goods as part of the realisation process, the landlord will be stymied. It follows from *Hand v. Blow*[23] that the lessor has no legal grounds for complaint against the receiver in such circumstances, though it has been suggested that if the receiver moves goods simply in order to frustrate the distress, he might be liable for double damages under section 3 of the Distress for Rent Act 1737.[24]

10-17 It is open to a receiver to pay arrears of rent incurred prior to his appointment, or, indeed, arising during the receivership,[25] and indeed he may feel constrained to do this if there are goods on the premises which it is commercially necessary to protect from distraint, or the landlord threatens to forfeit the lease. In the latter case much may depend upon the difference (if any) between the rent under the lease and market rents, but often a receiver will wish to pay rent to avoid the upheaval of moving when he was trying to achieve an advantageous "hive down" or other sale. Where the lease is within the security, the landlord may also put pressure on the receiver to pay rent arrears by refusing consent to any assignment of the lease.

10-18 It should be noted that where the receiver enters into a new lease with the landlord the receiver may become personally liable for the payment of rent and observance of repairing and other convenants.[26] Mere continuance of the existing lease by the receiver will not result in a personal liability.[27] A receiver has no power to disclaim a lease.

---

[20] *Warnford Investments v. Duckworth* [1979] 1 Ch. 127. But see *City of London v. Fell* [1993] 3 W.L.R. 1164 for the position where the assignee renews the lease. For another exception to the general rule see *Deanplan Ltd v. Mahmoud, The Times*, March 3, 1992. See also the note by *Lewis* in (1992) 142 N.L.J. 392.

[21] [1897] 1 Ch. 373. Followed in Canada in *Bank of Montreal v. Woodtown Developments* (1979) 99 D.L.R. (3d) 739.

[22] *Purcell v. Public Curator of Queensland* (1922) 31 C.L.R. 220. Leave may be required if the receiver was appointed by the court, *General Share and Trust Co. v. Wetley Brick and Pottery Co.* (1882) 20 Ch.D. 260, *Engel v. South Metropolitan Brewing and Bottling Co.* [1891] W.N. 31.

[23] [1901] 2 Ch. 721.

[24] It is perhaps worth remembering in this context that the receiver in *Hand v. Blow (supra)* was appointed by the court and sold the goods under the court's direction.

[25] Section 109(8) of the Law of Property Act 1925 confers a power on receivers to do this. However, it imposes no obligation to this effect—*Liverpool Corporation v. Hope* [1938] 1 K.B. 751.

[26] *Re Westminster Motor Garage* (1914) 84 L.J. Ch. 753, *Consolidated Entertainments Ltd v. Taylor*[1937] 4 All E.R. 432.

[27] *Re Abbott & Co. Ltd* (1913) 30 T.L.R. 13.

Liquidation and landlords

10-19 The position of the landlord whose tenant goes into liquidation, whether compulsory or voluntary, is more complex and involves a consideration of different issues.

Distress on winding-up

10-20 In this case if is necessary to distinguish between distress levied before and after the commencement of liquidation,[28] between rent due in respect of periods before and after that time, and between voluntary and compulsory liquidation.

10-21 Although there are superficial resemblances between distress and execution (*e.g.* under a writ of *fieri facias*), it is clear from *Re Bellaglade Ltd.*[29] that the two are quite distinct. So long as goods have been seized before the commencement of liquidation[30] there is no room for section 183 of the Insolvency Act 1986[31] to deprive the landlord of the fruits of the distress, whether or not the goods have been removed from the premises, let alone sold.

Distress stayed

10-22 The liquidator has the right under sections 112 and 126 of the Insolvency Act 1986 to apply to the court for the distress to be stayed,[32] but the court will not grant such an application in the case of a distress levied before liquidation, unless there are special circumstances making it unconscionable for the landlord to proceed.[33] It is clear that the landlord must be guilty of some misconduct such as fraud or misrepresentation for this to apply.[34] However, in the case of a compulsory liquidation, section 176 of the Insolvency Act 1986 gives the preferential creditors a first charge on the process of a distress levied within three months before the commencement of the liquidation, the landlord being subrogated in turn to the status of the preferential creditors to the extent of the amount paid over. Again so long as seizure was completed more than three months before the liquidation commenced, it is immaterial that the goods were neither removed nor sold.

Pre-liquidation arrears

10-23 Once the liquidation has commenced, the landlord will not normally be allowed to levy distress in respect of pre-liquidation rent arrears. The cases on the subject are extremely confusing, for two reasons. First, most of them were decided before the passing of the Law of Distress Amendment Act 1908, which operates to exempt from distress certain goods which do not belong to the tenant. Secondly some were decided before Parliament had invented the preferential creditor. The results of

---

[28] See Chapters 5 and 6 for the commencement of liquidation in cases of voluntary and compulsory winding-up.
[29] [1977] 1 All E.R. 319.
[30] Seizure under a walking possession agreement will do. See also *Re Winterbottom (Leeds) Ltd* [1937] 2 All E.R. 232.
[31] See Chap. 8 for the effect of s.183 on goods seized under an execution.
[32] Under section 126 the court can stay proceedings against a company in compulsory liquidation and section 112 applies to the court's powers in a compulsory liquidation to voluntary liquidations.
[33] *Re Roundwood Colliery Co. Ltd* [1897] 1 Ch. 373.
[34] *Venners Electrical Cooking and Heating Appliances Ltd v. Thorpe* [1915] 2 Ch. 404 at 408.

the cases are therefore often surprising from today's standpoint, but certain enduring principles do emerge.

10-24 The main principle is that once the statutory scheme of liquidation has been imposed on the company's assets, unsecured creditors are to be treated *pari passu*, and a landlord who has not distrained is an unsecured creditor.[35] So long as he is in fact a creditor he will therefore be left to his right of proof.[36]

10-25 However if the landlord is not a creditor (*e.g.* because the insolvent company is not the tenant, though occupying the landlord's premises), or if for some reason the goods concerned are not available to unsecured creditors anyway, the reason for the rule no longer applies and the landlord will be allowed to distrain (as was noted above). This principle is however subject to all the general common law and statutory qualifications of the right of distress.

10-26 As most of the old cases would have a different result today, a few imaginary examples based on circumstances encountered in decided cases and in practice may help to illustrate the principles, and to give a glimpse of the way in which they are affected by the background law of distress.

EXAMPLES

10-27 (a) Suppose a Company, C, occupies industrial premises as tenant of a landlord, L. C uses three valuable machines for the purposes of its business as a garment manufacturer, of which one is subject to a hire purchase agreement and another to a chattel mortgage securing a loan taken out for its acquisition. The third belongs to the company absolutely but is within the scope of a floating charge to the bank securing all the remainder of the company's moveable assets. The shareholders put the company into a rather sudden liquidation and emigrate at a time when there are substantial rent arrears. L finds out about it when he receives notice of the creditors' meeting called under section 98 of the Insolvency Act 1986. On the advice of his solicitor he instructs a bailiff to distrain for rent, and the bailiff takes walking possession of the three machines and some stock. The liquidator applies to the court under section 112 to set aside the distress.

10-28 In these circumstances the liquidator has the problem that the machines do not belong to the company at all. The machine subject to the chattel mortgage belongs to the mortgagee, subject to the company's right to have it assigned back on payment of the secured debt.[37] The mortgagee will probably get away with serving a notice on the landlord claiming the protection on the 1908 Act, but it is questionable whether he is entitled to do so as a matter of strict law.[38]

10-29 The protection of the 1908 Act does not apply to goods comprised in a

---

[35] *Re Harpur's Cycle Fittings Co.* [1900] 2 Ch. 731. See also *Re New City Constitutional Club* (1887) 34 Ch.D. 646.

[36] *Re Harpur's Cycle Fittings Co. (supra).*

[37] *Santley v. Wilde* [1899] 2 Ch. 474, *per* Lindley M.R.; *London County and Westminster Bank Ltd v. Tompkins* [1918] 1 K.B. 515.

[38] See *Goode*, [1981] J.B.L. 396 at 398. The right of a landlord to levy distress on goods not belonging to the tenant was considered by the New Zealand Court of Appeal in *Metropolitan Life Assurance of New Zealand v. Essere Print Ltd* [1991] 3 N.Z.L.R. 170. The case involved legislation framed in terms similar to those of our Law of Distress Amendment Act 1908. Here it was held that a landlord could levy distress on goods subject to a floating charge, but this was not possible in respect of items covered by a fixed security, because these were specifically excluded from the possibility of distress by the relevant legislation.

bill of sale (except in some consumer cases)—section 4A(2). Although the formal and registration requirements of the Bills of Sale Acts do not apply to company charges, a chattel mortgage granted by a company may nevertheless be a bill of sale for the purposes of the 1908 Act. Furthermore, the machine may be (but probably is not) in the reputed ownership of the company, and this again would disqualify it from the protection of the Act.[39] The hire purchase creditor can claim protection, but will have to show that the agreement has terminated.[40] If either claim fails, it is submitted that L will be entitled to sell the machine concerned, as at the date of liquidation it did not form part of the assets available to unsecured creditors anyway. No question therefore arises of L stealing a march on his fellows, and the liquidator's application should fail to that extent.

10-30 The goods subject to the floating charge are of course not vested in the company either, as a result of the crystallisation of the floating charge.[41] They are vested in the bank, which can apply for the protection of the Act, although the position may depend on whether the floating charge assets are worth more than is owing to the chargee.[42] If the company has an equity of redemption in the machine (and if it matters) it is an open question whether in any event the existence of preferential creditors, to whom the liquidator has a statuory duty to account, would be inconsistent with the exercise of any rights of distress anyway;[43] on general principles L should not be allowed to upset the statutory scheme of priorities. Again it is an open question whether a crystallised floating charge is a bill of sale for the purposes of the 1908 Act, or the doctrine of reputed ownership has any relevance.

10-31 (b) Suppose now that although C pays the rent (if anyone does), L's actual tenant is in fact one of the shareholders. In this case L is not a creditor of C at all, so there is no reason why he should be treated *pari passu* with those who are. Therefore only the 1908 Act stands between L and the goods. The liquidator can now serve notice in respect of all the goods, on the grounds that they do not belong to the tenant and either they do belong to the company or they are in its lawful possession.[44] There may be difficulties if the company's registered office is at the premises.[45] However the position of the chattel mortgagee and the hire-purchase creditor (and possibly the bank) may be subject to the same weaknesses as before; since the 1908 Act was amended by the Consumer Credit Act 1974 it appears that bill of sale and hire purchase goods are now excluded from protection whether or not the tenant gave the bill or made the hire purchase agreement.[46]

10-32 (c) Suppose finally that the situation is as in (b) but that one of the cheques for rent given by C was dishonoured before liquidation. In this case L is a creditor of

---

[39] *Cunliffe Engineering v. English Industrial Estates* [1994] B.C.C. 972, *supra*, p. xxx.

[40] A question fraught with technicality—Law of Distress Amendment Act 1908 s.4A(1)(*a*). Difficulties may also arise with reputed ownership, which survives for this purpose only under s.4(1) although *Cunliffe Engineering v. English Industrial Estates* [1994] B.C.C. 972, *supra*, para. 10–12 suggests that this hoary doctrine may fade at last into the shade so far as rental and finance agreements are concerned.

[41] *Re ELS Limited* [1994] B.C.C. 449. See *Feetham* (1994) 15 Co. Law 113.

[42] The reasoning in *New City Constitutional Club Ltd* (1887) 34 Ch.D. 646 suggests this, but its relevance is doubtful, particularly since *Re ELS Limited*, which was a case of distress for rates.

[43] This point was left open both in *Taggs Island Casino Hotel Ltd v. Richmond upon Thames B.C.* [1967] R.A. 70 and in *Re ELS Limited, supra*.

[44] Law of Distress Amendment Act 1908, s.1. Whether or not the liquidator can serve such a notice in respect of the machine on hire purchase will depend on the terms of the agreement.

[45] Under *ibid.*, s.4(2)(*d*). These are murky waters.

[46] Law of Distress Amendment Act 1908, s.4A.

the company, even though the company is not the tenant. The liquidator can again claim protection under the 1908 Act for all the goods, and the positions of the chattel mortgagee and the hire purchase creditor are as in (b). However the liquidator's position is as in (a), and may depend on the value of the preferential creditors and the debt due to the floating chargee.

Rent accruing after liquidation

10-33 Different rules apply to rent accruing after the commencement of liquidation. Here the same principles apply to both voluntary and compulsory liquidations. A first look at section 128 of the Insolvency Act 1986 might suggest that distress is impossible in a compulsory liquidation, but this is not so. It has been held that what is now section 130(2) gives the court a discretion to allow distress to be levied on the landlord's application.[47] In a voluntary liquidation the boot is on the other foot in that the court has a discretion whether to restrain a distress on the application of the liquidator, but in both types of procedure the court will allow the distress to proceed in the same circumstances. In *Re Oak Pits Colliery Co. Ltd*, Lindley L.J. described those circumstances as follows:[48]

> "When the liquidator retains the property for the purpose of advantageously disposing of it, or when he continues to use it, the rent ought to be regarded as a debt contracted for the purpose of winding up the company, and ought to be paid in full like any other debt or expense properly incurred by the liquidator for the same purpose."

The lessor's position here hinges upon the true intention of the liquidator, as was emphasised in *Re A.B.C. Coupler and Engineering Ltd (No. 3)*.[49] Where these circumstances exist, the liquidator will be obliged to pay the rent as an expense of the winding up in priority to his own remuneration, even though the landlord does not distrain.[50]

Possession for mutual benefit

10-34 The statement of principle in *Re Oak Pits Colliery Co. Ltd*[51] is subject to the important qualification, expressed in that case and others before it,[52] that where the liquidator has kept possession by arrangement with the landlord and for his benefit, as well as for the benefit of the company, and the liquidator has not agreed to pay rent, the liquidator will not be liable for the rent (and the landlord will not be allowed to distrain). Unfortunately it is not entirely clear from the case what constitutes an arrangement with and for the benefit of the landlord[53] and no doubt each case

---

[47] *Re Lundy Granite Co. Ltd* (1871) 6 Ch. App. 462, *Re North Yorkshire Iron Co. Ltd* (1878) 7 Ch.D. 661.

[48] (1882) 21 Ch.D. 322 at 330–31.

[49] [1970] 1 W.L.R. 702.

[50] *Shackell & Co. v. Chorlton & Sons* [1895] 1 Ch.378, *Re Downer Enterprises Ltd* [1974] 1 W.L.R. 1460.

[51] *Supra*, n. 4.

[52] *Re Progress Assurance Co.* (1870) L.R. 9 Eq. 370, *Re Bridgewater Engineering Co. Ltd* (1879) 12 Ch.D. 181.

[53] The facts of *Re Progress Assurance Co.* (*supra*) are scantily reported. *Re Bridgewater Engineering Co. Ltd* (*supra*) it seems that the aution sale held on the leased premises was conducted on behalf of both landlord and tenant.

turns on its own facts. However it seems that the liquidator must do something more than merely leave things as he finds them for the question to arise at all. In the situation often encountered in practice in which the liquidator leaves the company's goods on the premises for a while after the commencement of liquidation and then sells them, without doing anything further in relation to the land, it appears that the liquidator is not liable for the rent, even though he takes no steps to surrender the lease.[54]

Covenants to repair

10-35 Where the liquidator becomes liable for rent as an expense of the winding-up under the principles discussed above, he will normally become liable also under the other covenants of the lease including the covenant to repair.[55] As most commercial repairing covenants these days amount to covenants to put the property in repair and keep it that way, this liability could be onerous indeed, requiring the liquidator to put the property in a better condition than he found it in. A liquidator when faced with such a situation may well seek to exercise his power to disclaim the lease under section 179 of the Insolvency Act 1986. The law on such disclaimers has been considered above.[56]

Forefeiture

10-36 A landlord may seek to influence a liquidator who is considering his position *vis-à-vis* the rent obligations under the lease by threatening to refuse his consent to an assignment of the tenancy[57] or to forfeit the lease.

Relief from forfeiture

10-37 However, the tenant may, if the lease has not been disposed of within a year of the liquidation, seek relief from forfeiture under section 146(10) of the Law of Property Act 1925, though rent arrears will have to be paid and the court must be convinced that future rent obligations will be met. Presumably repairing and other covenants will also have to be observed. It was made clear by the Court of Appeal in *Official Custodian of Charities v. Parway Estates Development Ltd*[58] that the one-year limitation period during which the tenant can apply for relief from forfeiture will not be extended. Dillon L.J. declared:[59]

> "The duty, however, of a liquidator . . . is to realise the assets of the insolvent company . . . in order to meet the liabilities; ordinarily, it would not be appropriate for a liquidator . . . to retain a property unsold for many years in the hope of taking advantage of some future rise in property values. It is necessary that justice should be done to the landlords also, who have no wish to be saddled

---

[54] *Re Oak Pits Colliery Co. Ltd* (1882) 21 Ch.D. 322.
[55] *Re Levi & Co. Ltd* [1919] 1 Ch. 416.
[56] See Chap. 5.
[57] If the liquidator pays rent arrears in order to secure the landlord's consent to an assignment of a lease, this expenditure is not to be viewed as enhancing the asset for capital gains tax purposes—*Emmerson v. Computer Time International* [1977] 1 W.L.R. 734.
[58] [1984] 3 W.L.R. 525. If the application to the court is made within the one-year period, the fact that it is not heard until after that period has elapsed is irrelevant—*Pearson v. Gee* [1934] A.C. 272. On forfeiture generally see *Billson v. Residential Apartments Ltd* [1992] 2 W.L.R. 15.
[59] *ibid.*, at 536–7.

with an insolvent tenant, and who have stipulated in the lease for a right of re-entry in the event of . . . liquidation of the tenant."

If the landlord accepts rent with the knowledge that the tenant has gone into liquidation, he may be deemed to have waived his right to forfeit the lease. However, actual notice of the liquidation is required here. It was decided unanimously by the Court of Appeal in this case that there is no room for the liquidator to employ the argument that the landlord is fixed with constructive notice merely because notice of the liquidation has been recorded in the Gazette, as is required by section 42(1)(*a*) of the Companies Act 1985. This statutory provision was originally introduced to protect outsiders dealing with the company, and not to prejudice their position.

Administration

10-38 The rights of landlords of corporate tenants that go into administration are less than clear. It seems likely that a provision in a lease permitting a landlord to forfeit the lease on the entry of the tenant into administration will be upheld by the courts.[60] However, it is beginning to look as though the protective moratorium provided by sections 10 and 11 of the Insolvency Act 1986 does not prevent a landlord from re-entering peaceably for non payment of rent.[61] By parity of reasoning one might naturally infer that a similar freedom was extended to the levying of distress for unpaid rent but a closer consideration of ss.10(1)(c) and 11(3)(d) indicates that such action is expressly forbidden without leave. Fuller consideration of these issues is to be found in Chapter 3.

SET-OFF RIGHTS[62]

10-39 When considering the rules governing the right of debtors of insolvent companies to set-off sums of money owed to them by the creditor companies, it is again necessary to consider the rules on receivership and liquidation separately.

Receivership

10-40 Where a company goes into receivership, the general principle is that a right of set-off can be exercised provided it arises before the date of receipt of notice of the crystallisation of the floating charge. Thus, in *Rother Iron Works Ltd v. Canterbury Precision Engineers Ltd*,[63] a corporate seller of goods went into receivership, having earlier agreed to sell goods to the defendant to whom it already owed a sum of money. Even though the goods were delivered to the defendant after the appointment of the receiver, the Court of Appeal held that the right of set-off had arisen at the date of the contract and therefore it could be exercised against the

---

60 *Re Olympia & York Canary Wharf Ltd* [1993] B.C.C. 154. This issue was not argued to conclusion in *Scottish Exhibition Centre v. Mirestop* [1993] B.C.C. 529.

61 See above at para. 3-15.

62 In Scotland the comparable principle is known as *compensation*. For its application in the liquidation context see *Powdrill v. Murrayhead Ltd* 1997 S.L.T. 1223.

63 [1974] Q.B. 1. See also Mocatta J. in *Handley Page v. Rockwell Machine Tool Co.* [1970] 2 Lloyds Rep. 459 at 464, *Tony Lee Motors v. Macdonald and Son* [1981] 2 N.Z.L.R. 281 Note also *John Dee Group Ltd v. WMH (21) Ltd* [1998] B.C.C. 972.

receiver who could stand in no better position than the company itself. The opposite conclusion was arrived at by Templeman J. in *Business Computers Ltd v. Anglo-African Leasing Ltd.*[64] Here, the plaintiffs, who were owed a sum of money by the defendants in respect of the sale of a computer, were in turn indebted to the defendants in respect of the hire of another computer. The defendants went into receivership. The sums owed to the defendants represented arrears of hiring instalments due to periods both before and after the plaintiffs had been notified of the receiver's appointment. Templeman J. refused to allow the latter amounts to be set-off. These sums did not arise out of the contract under which the defendants owed money to the plaintiffs, and, moreover, they did not accrue until the plaintiffs had in effect received notice of assignment of the defendant's assets to the debenture holder.

10-41 On the same principle, it is thought that a debt which is wholly contingent at the date when the contingent creditor receives notice of the receivership of the contingent debtor cannot be set-off against a debt due from the contingent creditor to the company in receivership. This is certainly the case in liquidations, and an example of how it works in practice is given below.

Liquidation

10-42 Once again, the set-off rules on liquidation are more complex and raise more difficult issues of law. The starting point here is what is now rule 4.90 of the Insolvency Rules 1986:[65]

> "(1) This Rule applies where, before the company goes into liquidation there have been mutual credits, mutual debts or other mutual dealings between the company and any creditor of the company proving or claiming to prove for a debt in the liquidation.
>
> (2) An account shall be taken of what is due from each party to the other in respect of the mutual dealings, and the sums due from one party shall be set off against the sums due from the other.
>
> (3) Sums due from the company to another party shall not be included in the account taken under paragraph (2) if that other party had notice at the time they became due that a meeting of creditors had been summoned under section 98 or (as the case may be) a petition for the winding up of the company was pending.
>
> (4) Only the balance (if any) of the account is provable in the liquidation. Alternatively (as the case may be) the amount shall be paid to the liquidator as part of the assets."

10-43 This rule of English bankruptcy law can trace its origins back to Elizabethan times.[66] It has variously been described as a mere accounting exercise,[67]

[64] [1977] 1 W.L.R. 578. See also *Robbie & Co. v. Witney Warehouse Co. Ltd* [1963] 1 W.L.R. 1324.

[65] Derived from s.31 of the Bankruptcy Act 1914. Insolvency Act 1986, s.323 (relating to bankruptcy) is in similar terms.

[66] *Farley v. Housing and Commercial Development* [1984] B.C.L.C. 442 at 449 *per* Neill J. This case, notwithstanding the accuracy of the above comment, is no longer good law—*Stein v. Blake* [1993] 3 W.L.R. 718.

[67] *Re Unit 2 Windows Ltd* [1985] 1 W.L.R. 1383 at 1333 *per* Walton J.

and a provision designed to do substantial justice between the parties.[68] It was clear from the House of Lords decision in *Mersey Steel and Iron Co. v. Naylor, Benzon & Co*[69] that it applied on corporate insolvency. However section 612 of the Companies Act 1985, which applied to the winding up of companies the rules applicable in bankruptcy as to debts provable and the valuation of liabilities, was repealed by the Insolvency Act 1986 and has not been replaced. It appears that the matter is now entirely governed by the rules applicable to corporate insolvency made under the powers conferred by section 411 and Schedule 8,[70] which presumbly are intended to provide a complete code. Presumably, in view of the close similarity between the words of rule 4.90 and the old bankruptcy provision,[71] the old case law on their meaning will be taken to apply.

10-44 Crucially, the rule has been held to be mandatory; it was confirmed by the House of Lords in *National Westminster Bank v. Halesowen Presswork and Assemblies Ltd*[72] that parties cannot contract out of its operation on corporate insolvency.

"Mutuality"

10-45 Many cases show the need for "mutuality" between the debts to be set off under the rule. Thus:

(a) A company cannot be set-off sums due to it against money which it holds on trust for another, or which was paid to it for a specific purpose.[73]

(b) A set-off cannot be invoked by a director ordered to pay damages for misfeasance, in order to reduce the net amount he has to contribute to the company's assets.[74]

(c) A salesman can set-off against any money due to him from the company any proceeds of sale he is holding, and even the value of any of the company's goods he has in his possession for sale on the company's behalf, but not the value of goods he holds purely for demonstration purposes or for any purpose other than that of turning them into money.[75]

---

[68] *Farley v. Housing and Commercial Developments* [1984] B.C.L.C. 442 at 450 *per* Neill J. See also *Forster v. Wilson* (1843) 12 M. & W., 191 *per* Parke B.
[69] (1884) 9 App. Cas. 434. Followed in *Re H. E. Thorne & Son Ltd* [1914] 2 Ch. 438.
[70] Para. 12 of Sched. 8 provides for the rules to cover (*inter alia*) the debts that may be proved in a winding up and the manner of proving them and establishing their value.
[71] Bankruptcy Act 1914, s.31.
[72] [1972] A.C. 785, See also *Rolls Razor Ltd v. Cox* [1967] 1 Q.B. 553, *British Eagle International Airlines v. Compagnie Nationale Air France* [1975] 1 W.L.R. 758. For the rule with regard to secured debts owed by the company see *Re Norman Holding Co. Ltd* [1991] B.C.L.C. 1.
[73] *Re Mid-Kent Fruit Factory* [1896] 1 Ch. 567 at 572 *per* Vaughan Williams J. *Re City Equitable Fire Insurance Co. (No. 2)* [1930] 1 Ch. 293.
[74] *Re Anglo-French Cooperative Society, ex p. Pelly* (1882) 21 Ch. D. 492, *Flitcroft's Case, ibid.*, at 519, *Zemco v. Jerrom-Pugh* [1993] B.C.C. 280, *Manson v. Smith* [1997] 2 B.C.L.C. 161.
[75] *Rolls Razor Ltd v. Cox* [1967] 1 Q.B. 553.

(d) A holding company cannot set-off its contingent liability on a guarantee of its insolvent subsidiary's bank account against a debt due from the holding company to the subsidiary.[76]

10-46 Rule 4.90 was considered by the Court of Appeal in *M.S. Fashions Ltd v. Bank of Credit and Commerce International S.A. (No. 2)*[77] Here, directors of a company had guaranteed the repayment of the company's overdraft with B.C.C.I. The bank guarantee was framed as an indemnity rather than a simple guarantee, so that the directors were described and treated as principal debtors having primary liability for the company's borrowings. The directors in their personal capacity also held accounts with B.C.C.I. which were in credit, (these accounts being charged in favour of the bank with repayment of the company's overdraft). On the collapse of B.C.C.I. in 1990 the directors sought to set-off their liabilities under the guarantees against the sums owed to them as depositors of an insolvent bank. The Court of Appeal held that as under the terms of the guarantee the liability of the guarantors was primary (and not contingent upon failure of the company to repay the overdraft) sufficient mutuality existed for the purposes of rule 4.90, and a set-off could be allowed to operate. The operation of rule 4.90 was not precluded by the fact that the right of one of the directors (who owed more under the guarantee than was owing to him as a depositor) to prove in the liquidation of the insolvent bank would be extinguished by the set-off.

The fall out from the B.C.C.I. collapse has added further to the jurisprudence on set off rights. In *Re B.C.C.I. (No. 8)*[78] the House of Lords stressed the need for mutuality for the mechanism of set off to work. If set off is available it is mandatory and the courts will not disapply it, a point stressed in *Re B.C.C.I. (No. 10)*.[79]

10-47 This following example drawn from practice, provides a further illustration of this very important aspect of mutuality:

EXAMPLE

10-48 A director owes the company money on a so-called "loan account," perhaps as a result of the director having paid personal debts through the company. The director has guaranteed the bank overdraft. The bank has no valid fixed charge on debts. The director is selling off his house to pay off the bank.

10-49 If, according to the usual practice, the bank makes no demand under the guarantee before the liquidation commences, it is submitted that the director will not be able to set off his claim as a guarantor who was paid the guaranteed debt against the company's claim against him under the loan account, as there was nothing due from the guarantor to the bank at the date of the liquidation. The guarantor director's claim against the company was therefore wholly contingent at the date of liquidation and accordingly there was no "mutuality" in the cross debts. The result is that the director has to pay both the company's debt to the bank and his own debt to the company.

---

[76] *Re Vinyl Compositions (Holdings) Ltd et alia* (1984) unreported, *Re Fenton* [1931] 1 Ch. 85, *Re A Debtor (No. 66 of 1955)* [1956] 1 W.L.R. 226.
[77] [1993] 3 W.L.R. 220.
[78] [1997] 3 W.L.R. 909.
[79] [1997] 2 W.L.R. 172.

10-50 Even if a demand is made before liquidation, the position may well be the same unless the guarantor has satisfied the demand and the bank has transferred the money to the company's account. However if the bank has an effective fixed charge on debts the position is quite different. In such a case once the director has paid the bank he will be subrogated to the bank's security over the debts due from himself and others to the extent of his payment.[80]

Government departments

10-51 Another important feature of the set-off rules in practice is that government departments can and do exploit them to great advantage. This is because the departments are not treated as separate entities so that, for example, if a government department owes money to the insolvent company, and that company in turn is indebted to another department, the debts can be set-off.[81] This possibility was confirmed by Brightman J. in *Re D. H. Curtis (Builders) Ltd*,[82] whose views were accepted by Vinelott J. in *Re Cushla Ltd.*[83] This principle was further extended in favour of the Crown in *R. A. Cullen Ltd v. Nottingham Health Authority*,[84] where the Court of Appeal ruled that a set-off could be enforced against an insolvent company which was indebted to the DHSS and, in turn, was owed money by a health authority. The latter could, in reality, be regarded as an agent of the Crown, therefore the principle of mutuality was satisfied.

10-52 In this context, the decision of Walton J. in *Re Unit 2 Windows Ltd*[85] requires consideration. Here, a company which was in voluntary liquidation was owed a sum of money by the Customs and Excise in respect of a V.A.T. refund. On the other hand, the company owed a larger sum to the DHSS, part of this amount ranking as a preferential debt against its assets. The question was whether the DHSS could appropriate the V.A.T. to which the company was entitled to set off to the non-preferential element in the debt owed to it, thereby preserving its preferential claim. Walton J., rejecting the earlier decision of Buckley J. in *Re E. J. Morel (1934) Ltd*,[86] held that what is now Rule 4.90 of the Insolvency Rules 1986 had not anticipated such a "conundrum." Justice required the DHSS to exercise its set-off rateably against the preferential and non-preferential elements of its debt.

Set-off in V.A.T. groups

10-53 A frequent set-off problem arises in practice where an insolvent group of companies opts for group treatment for V.A.T. In such a case, all members of the group are jointly and severally liable for the V.A.T. due from the group, and the

---

[80] See note 76 *supra*. If tax has been paid on the director's loan under s.419 of the Income and Corporation Taxes Act 1988, there may be advantage to the liquidator in persuading the director and the bank to let part of the proceeds of sale of the director's house be paid to the company in satisfaction of the director's debt to the company. As the bank has not been paid the debt falls within its charge. The liquidator therefore has to account to the bank for the money, but because the debt has been paid off, he can claim a return of s.419 tax from the Inland Revenue s.419(4).

[81] This position was criticised by the Cork Committee Cmnd. 8558 para. 1347.

[82] [1978] Ch. 162.

[83] [1979] 3 All E.R. 415. For the position in Scotland see *Smith v. Lord Advocate (No. 2)* 1980 S.L.T. 105.

[84] (1986) 2 B.C.C. 99, 368.

[85] [1985] 1 W.L.R. 1383. For another recent authority on set-off see *Willment Brothers v. N. W. Thames R.H.A.* (1984) 26 Build. L. Rep. 51.

[86] [1962] Ch. 21.

Commissioners of Customs and Excise are entitled to prove for the whole of the amount in the liquidation of each member of the group.[87] As V.A.T. is a preferential debt[88] it is common for one group member to end up, despite its insolvency, paying more than the full amount of the V.A.T. attributable to its own trading.

Rule against double proof

10-54 On normal principles, the paying company would be entitled in these circumstances to claim indemnity from other members of the group for the amounts paid in respect of other group members' trading, and to be subrogated to the creditor's preferential rights.[89] However this will not be allowed in the case of another group member in liquidation, unless Customs and Excise have been paid in full, because otherwise there might be two proofs in the liquidation for the same debt. This is called the rule against double proof.

Guarantor

10-55 Where one member has paid in full, it might be thought that an amount paid in respect of the trading of another group member in liquidation could be set off against any debt due from the paying member to the other. However, this is unlikely to be so. The paying member is in the position of a guarantor of the debt due from the other. Unless the paying member has made the payment by the date on which the other goes into liquidation, the debt due from that other to the paying member will be wholly contingent. Such a debt cannot be set off in liquidation. In these circumstances the paying member may well be able to prove in the liquidation of the other as a preferential creditor[90] for all sums due from all group members, but the other will be entitled to claim payment of the debt due to it *pari passu* with the other unsecured creditors of the paying member.

Claims in tort

10-56 The Insolvency Act 1986 effects a change in the law of set-off. The old rule that a claim for unliquidated damages in tort cannot be used as the basis of a set-off no longer seems to be good law in view of the fact that such a claim now ranks as a provable liquidation debt (see Insolvency rules 1986, rr. 12.3 and 13.12).

CLAIMS BY UTILITY SUPPLIERS

Former powerful position

10-57 For many years there was a great difference between the *de jure* and the *de facto* rights enjoyed by suppliers of utility services (such as gas, electricity or telephone facilities) in the event of a corporate customer becoming insolvent. Technically, any claim they had in respect of arrears for such services would merely be regarded as an unsecured claim. However, in practice, such monopoly suppliers were in a peculiarly powerful position because they could threaten to cut off essential services unless the

---

[87] *Re Nadler Enterprises Ltd* [1981] 1 W.L.R. 23.
[88] But only in part—see Chap. 8.
[89] Mercantile Law Amendment Act 1856, s.5.
[90] *ibid.*

receiver or liquidator agreed to pay existing arrears.[91] A receiver or liquidator wishing to continue trading to effect a beneficial realisation of the company's assets, had to accede to the suppliers' demands to avoid the potentially disastrous consequences of a termination of supply.

Change in occupation?

10-58 In the case of a receiver appointed out of court, the utility supplier could lawfully make such a threat for the simple reason that such a receiver was invariably installed as the agent of the company so that there was no change in occupation when he took over the premises on the company's behalf. This reasoning recently commended itself to the Canadian courts in *Peat Marwick Ltd v. Consumers Gas Co.*[92]

10-59 The position in the case of a receiver appointed by the court was less clear. On the one hand, a receiver is an officer of the court and not an agent of the company so that an appointment arguably brought about a change of occupier, obliging the supplier to make a supply.[93] To be set against this was the argument that as an officer of the court it would be inequitable for him to insist that the supplier honour its contract with the company whilst refusing to pay arrears arising under that contract.[94]

10-60 The position in the case of liquidation was very similar.[95] Thus, in *Wellworth Cash & Carry (North Shields) Ltd v. North Eastern Electricity Board*,[96] the liquidator offered to pay for future supplies of electricity, but refused to settle existing arrears. The Electricity Board refused to accept this state of affairs and threatened to cut of supplies which, in this case, would have led to the destruction of large quantities of frozen food contained in the company's refrigerators. The court held that the Electricity Board was entitled to issue such a threat. An analogy with those cases where the courts had restrained the levy of a distress against the company's premises could not be drawn as this was a totally different situation.

Reform

10-61 Not surprisingly, such commercial blackmail by public utilities, invariably possessing monopoly rights, attracted criticism, and the Cork Committee called for a change in the law.[97] Section 233 (as amended) of the Insolvency Act 1986 prevents a supplier of gas, electricity, water, or public telecommunications from requiring an "office holder' to pay arrears incurred prior to his appointment as a precondition of receiving a continued supply. Office holders include administrators, CVA supervisors, administrative receivers, liquidators in both compulsory and voluntary liquidations and also provisional liquidators.[98] In any case it does not protect receivers unless they qualify as administrative receivers.[99]

---

[91] Private suppliers of strategic raw materials also enjoy such a powerful bargaining position—see here *Leyland DAF v. Automotive Products* [1993] B.C.C. 389.

[92] (1981) 113 D.L.R. (3d) 754. See also *Waitemata Electric Power Board v. Mills* [1971] N.Z.L.R. 630.

[93] *Corporation of Bacup v. Smith* (1890) 44 Ch.D. 395 at 398 *per* Chitty J.

[94] See *Paterson v. Gas Light & Coke Co.* [1896] 2 Ch. 476, *Husey v. London Electric Supply Corp.* [1902] 1 Ch. 411, *McClintock v. Westminster Electric Supply Corp., The Times*, May 2, 1931.

[95] A liquidator might be viewed as a new occupier where the court had vested the premises in him under the Insolvency Act 1986, s.145. See also *Re Fir View Furniture Co., The Times*, February 9, 1976.

[96] (1986) 2 B.C.C., 265.

[97] Cmnd. 8558 para. 1462.

[98] Insolvency Act 1986 s.233(1).

[99] See Insolvency Act 1986, s.29(2).

RATES ARREARS OWED TO LOCAL AUTHORITIES

10-62 Prior to the Insolvency Act 1986 a certain proportion of rates arrears ranked as a preferential claim on corporate insolvency. This favourable treatment has now been abandoned, and local authorities have been reduced to the ranks of ordinary unsecured creditors,[1] though they do retain certain statutory powers of distress which have survived unscathed the repeal of the General Rates Act 1967 by Part IX of the Local Government Finance Act 1988. The relevant provisions are now to be found in regulations made under Schedule 9 of the 1988 Act, namely the Non-Domestic Rating (Collection and Enforcement) (Local Lists) Regulations 1989 (S.I. 1989/1058).

Practitioner's personal liability

10-63 A local authority may seek to improve its position by arguing that the insolvency practitioner has incurred personal liability for unpaid rates falling due during his period of occupation,[2] thereby rendering him liable for liability order and distress under regulation 12 of the Non-Domestic Rating (Collection and Enforcement) (Local Lists) Regulations 1989 (S.I. 1989/1058) but a reminder must be served before liability proceedings can be commenced. This is unlikely to succeed in the case of a receiver. In the test case of *Ratford and Hayward v. Northavon D.C.*,[3] the Court of Appeal held that joint receivers and managers who had been appointed out of court as the agents of the company were not personally liable for rates which had become payable during their period of occupation of the company's premises as there had been no change of rateable occupation. It was held that once the local authority had established that the rate had been duly demanded, the onus of proof switched to the receivers to show that they were not liable. This they could do by establishing that they had been appointed as the company's agents, in which case the burden would then revert to the local authority to establish that their occupation was not in reality that of agents. The local authority had failed to satisfy the court as to this latter point. Slade L.J. reasoned:[4]

> "Any occupation of the relevant premises enjoyed by a receiver will normally be enjoyed by him solely in his capacity as agent for some other party. Though it is possible for him, to take independent possession of the premises as principal, such cases I suspect may be comparatively rare."

Therefore the summons issued against the receivers by the local authority was misconceived. This conclusion was followed by Arden J. in *Re Sobam BV*,[5] where it was confirmed that receivers occupy the premises not in a personal capacity but rather on behalf of the company. Moreover these rates could not be treated as an expense of

---

[1] An unpaid rates demand can form the basis of a winding up position—see *Re North Bucks Furniture Depositories Ltd* [1939] Ch. 690 and *Re McGreavy* [1950] Ch. 269.

[2] Rates falling due during this period might also be regarded as expenses of the winding-up—*Re National Arms and Ammunition Co.* (1885) 28 Ch.D. 474.

[3] [1987] Q.B. 357, 268. The earlier and apparently inconsistent decisions in *Taggs Island Casino Hotel Ltd v. Richmond upon Thames L.B.C.* (1967) 201 E.G. 201 and *Banister v. Islington L.B.C.* (1973) 235 E.G. 2301 must now be viewed with scepticism.

[4] [1987] Q.B. 357 at 379. Followed in Scotland—*McKillop and Walters, Petitioners* [1994] B.C.C. 677.

[5] [1996] B.C.C. 351—reported *sub nom. Brown v. City of London Corporation* [1996] 1 W.L.R. 1070.

the receivership and accorded the high priority that such claims attract. An attempt to argue that, receivers, who remain in occupation allowing rates arrears to build up knowing that the company would be unlikely to satisfy the obligations thereby incurred, might be guilty of fraudulent trading, was firmly rejected by Arden J. The receivers were merely fulfilling their proper role to realise the security and were not acting dishonestly. To put it mildly, this decision came as a disappointment to local authorities.

10-64 It would appear that the courts would arrive at a similar conclusion in the case of occupancy of premises by receivers appointed by the court[6] and by liquidators, whether acting in a voluntary or compulsory liquidation.[7] Once a liquidation commences, a receiver's agency for the company ceases, so that he or his appointor (if the receiver is his agent) may then become personally liable for rates.

10-65 However a liquidator who has taken possession of the property for the beneficial winding up of the company may become liable to pay rates as an expense of the liquidation in priority to his own remuneration. This will apply if the circumstances are such that the liquidator would be liable for rent, if the company were a tenant. No doubt the local authority's rights could be enforced by application under section 112 of the Insolvency Act 1986. The relevant principles here were reviewed by Judge Weeks, Q.C. in the High Court in *Re Nolton Business Centres Ltd*[8] where it was held that non domestic rates falling due after the commencement of a winding up could be treated as liquidation expenses where the liquidator had retained use of the premises in order to trade.

Distress against company

10-66 Whether or not the local authority has any right of distress against the receiver or liquidator personally, there remains the question of whether it can obtain a distress warrant against the company. It is thought that a distraint set in motion before the commencement of liquidation will be allowed to proceed, but generally speaking, one commenced after that date will be restrained, on the principles outlined in relation to distress by a landlord above. In the case of a receiver, there would seem to be no reason why distress should not proceed, so long as goods can be found which are liable to be seized for rates.

10-67 This leads however, to an important difference between distress for rates (and other taxes) and distress for rent, arising from the fact that distress for rates (and Crown taxes) is, and distress for rent is not, a creature of statute. The relevant provision[9] entitles the local authority to levy the appropriate amount[10] by distress and sale of goods "of the debtor against whom the order was made". The common law rules which bring the goods of strangers into the scope of distress for rent do not apply.

---

[6] *Re Marriage, Neave & Co.* [1896] 2 Ch. 663 (where the result might have been different if the order had directed the company to give up possession to the receiver), *Gyton v. Palmour* [1945] K.B. 426.

[7] *Re Wearmouth Crown Glass Co.* (1882) 19 Ch. D. 640 at 642 *per* Kay J. See also *Re Briant Colour Printing Ltd* [1977] 1 W.L.R. 942—wrongful exclusion of insolvency practitioner from premises by sit in.

[8] [1996] B.C.C. 500—applying *Re National Arms and Ammunition Co.* (1885) 28 Ch. D. 474.

[9] Regulation 14(1) of the Non-Domestic Rating (Collection and Enforcement) (Local Lists) Regulations 1989, S.I. 1989/1058.

[10] Excessive distress for rates is a wrongful interference with goods, giving rise to an action for an injunction and damages: *Steel Linings v. Bibby & Co.* [1933] R.A. 27, CA.

Floating Charge Goods

10-68 It was held in *Re ELS Limited*,[11] that as the crystallisation of a floating charge effects an assignment of the property to which it applies, any goods comprised in the charge are not the property of the charging company after crystallisation. They are not therefore liable to distress for rates due from the company.

10-69 *Re ELS Limited*[12] also suggests that any goods comprised in a fixed equitable charge will escape distress on the same ground, unless the charge neither operates by way of assignment nor confers power to appoint a receiver, take possession or sell without the assistance of the court. It may be readily accepted that a charge which has none of these characteristics will not be proof against distress. On the other hand, it is hard to see why a contractual provision for the appointment of a receiver or a right to possession in a charge which does not take effect as an assignment should have the effect of changing the ownership of the goods, at least until such a right is enforced. Generally a charge which is not expressed to be by way of assignment merely makes the goods liable for the amount charged upon them, and must be distinguished from an equitable mortgage, whereby the goods are assigned subject to a covenant for re-assignment or redemption.[13] This *obiter* part of the judgment may perhaps be doubted.

COMMUNITY CHARGE AND COUNCIL TAX

10-70 Since the repeal of the General Rates Act 1967 (by Part IX of the Local Government Finance Act 1988), a company which owns domestic property which is not occupied by an individual may be liable for community charge in respect of the period April 1, 1989 to March 31, 1993 and for council tax in respect of periods after that. These liabilities can be enforced by a liability order and distress warrant under the Community Charges (Administration and Enforcement) Regulations 1989[14] but will rank as unsecured in corporate insolvency.

10-71 A distress commenced before the start of winding up will probably be allowed to proceed, but thereafter the local authority will be left to its right of proof. Community charge which arises after the commencement of the winding-up does not count as a debt provable in liquidation at all.[15] Nor will the court exercise its discretion to order that charges incurred after the commencement of liquidation be paid as an expense of the winding-up.

10-72 A company in the course of winding up cannot be made liable for business rates under the Local Government Finance Act 1988, as the owner of unoccupied non-residential property, as is made clear by the Non Domestic Rating (Unoccupied Property) Regulations 1989.[16]

---

[11] [1994] 1 B.C.L.C. 743 not following *Re Marriage, Neave & Co.* [1896] 2 Ch. 663, doubted in the last edition of this book. See *Feetham* (1994) 15 Co. Law 113.

[12] See *supra*.

[13] *London County and Westminster Bank Ltd v. Tompkins* [1918] 1 K.B. 515; *Santley v. Wilde* [1899] 2 Ch. 474 *per* Lindley M.R.

[14] S.I. 1989 No. 438.

[15] *Re Kentish Homes Ltd* [1993] B.C.C. 212.

[16] (S.I. 1989 No. 2261.)

THE ENFORCEMENT OF LIENS ON CORPORATE INSOLVENCY

10-73 A lien is basically a right to retain possession of property until a debt has been paid. Liens may be of a general nature: for example, a solicitor is entitled to retain possession of any of his client's property until his bill has been paid.[17] Alternatively, liens may be particular—*i.e.*, the person exercising the lien may only be entitled to retain property associated with the transaction out of which the debt arose. A repairer's lien is a good example of this genre. Liens can arise at common law, by statute,[18] or under contract,[19] and may be legal or equitable. Such liens are particularly frustrating for the insolvency practitioner in that it is clear they they do not require registration at the Companies Registry under sections 395–6 of the Companies Act 1985.[20]

Liens and the receiver

10-74 What is the position with regard to the enforcement of liens against the receiver acting on behalf of a debenture holder? In some situations a lien, such as an unpaid vendor's lien in respect of the purchase price of property, will prevail over a charge subsequently granted to a debenture holder over that same property.[21] In other cases, a lien arising by operation of law takes priority over a floating charge, and the fact that a prohibition clause or negative pledge provision is attached to that floating charge makes no difference.[22]

10-75 The best analysis of the problems posed for receivers by liens is to be found in the Court of Appeal judgment in *George Baker (Transport) Ltd v. Eynon*.[23] In this case, a haulier sought to assert a contractual lien in respect of unpaid carriage costs over the goods of the company in receivership. The Court of Appeal held that the receiver would be bound by such a contractual lien where it had originated from a contract entered into by the company prior to the appointment of the receiver. As the company would have been bound by such a contractual lien it followed that the receiver who was a mere assignee of the company's rights and obligations could be in no better position. This principle was developed further in *De Lorean Motor Cars Ltd v. Northern Irish Carriers*,[24] where it was stressed that the crucial date to establish priorities was the date of the contract under which the lien arose and not the date of its exercise. Astute insolvency practitioners often engage in a new firm of hauliers for post-receivership transactions in order to avert the danger of being caught by contractual liens in this way.

---

[17] See *Re Rapid Road Transit Co.* [1909] 1 Ch. 96. For an unusual case, involving solicitors who had lent money to a client to assist in the purchase of property, asserting an unpaid vendor's lien, by subrogation, see *Boodle, Hatfield & Co. v. British Films Ltd* 1986 P.C.C. 176.

[18] See, *e.g.*, the Sale of Goods Act 1979, s.41. Note also *Channel Airways Ltd v. Manchester Corporation* [1974] 1 Lloyd's Rep. 457 and Civil Aviation Act 1982, s.88.

[19] Conversely, a right to a lien can be excluded by contract—*Rolls Razor Ltd v. Cox* [1967] 1 Q.B. 553.

[20] *Capital Finance Ltd v. Stokes* [1969] 1 Ch. 261, *London and Cheshire Insurance Co. v. Laplagrene Properties* [1971] Ch. 499, *Burston Finance v. Speirway* [1974] 1 W.L.R. 1648, *Waitomo Wools (N.Z.) Ltd v. Nelsons (N.Z.) Ltd* [1974] 1 N.Z.L.R. 484.

[21] *Security Trust Co. v. Royal Bank of Canada* [1976] 1 All E.R. 381.

[22] *Brunton v. Electrical Engineering Corp.* [1892] 1 Ch. 434.

[23] [1974] 1 All E.R. 900. Followed in Australia in *Re Diesels & Components Pty. Ltd* (1985) 9 A.C.L.R. 825.

[24] [1982] N.I. 163.

Liquidators

10-76 The rules governing the priority of liens on the liquidation of the company are presumably of a similar nature, though there is a dearth of authority here. However, it should be noted that by virtue of section 246 of the Insolvency Act 1986 a lien over the company's books, papers, or records cannot be exercised so as to deny possession of these items to, *inter alia*, the company liquidator or provisional liquidator.[25] This invalidation of liens does not apply to liens on documents of title to property held as such (section 246(3)). This curiously worded excluding provision was considered by Morritt J. in *Re SEIL Trade Finance Ltd*[26] who held that the section did not operate to entitle a liquidator to call for title documents belonging to the insolvent company held by its solicitors, in circumstances in which they were entitled to exercise their common law lien for their unpaid costs.[27] So long as the documents conferred a title to property (as do title deeds to land, share certificates, and charges), it was only necessary that the holder should hold them by way of lien. It was not necessary that he should also have some interest in the property to which the documents related. Morritt J. noted that "property" was extremely widely defined in section 436 to include every description of property, including *inter alia*, choses in action, obligations, and every description of interest, present or future, vested or contingent, arising out of or incidental to property.

Administrators

10-77 Where a company goes into administration any person wishing to exercise a lien, whether that lien be based upon contract or statute, will be confronted with the protective moratorium set up on presentation of the petition and cemented further once the order is granted (see Insolvency Act 1986 ss.10 and 11). Except in the cases where section 246(3) applies (see above), enforcement of liens in such cases is not permitted[28] unless the administrator or the court grants leave. This matter has been fully dealt with in Chapter 3.

PROVABLE DEBTS

10-78 The question of provable debts does not arise in the event of receivership, because the receiver is solely concerned with meeting the claims of the preferential creditors and also the debenture holders. However, it is a topic of some importance for liquidators.

Insolvency Rules

10-79 In order to describe the present law governing provable debts on a winding-up, it is necessary to delve into the Insolvency Rules 1986. Formerly, one had to examine bankruptcy law principles in this context. However, the need to do

---

[25] The position at common law was much the same—*Re Capital Fire Insurance Association* (1883) 24 Ch. D. 408.

[26] [1992] B.C.C. 538.

[27] As to the nature of the solicitor's lien see *Barratt v. Gough-Thomas* [1951] Ch. 242 at 250 *per* Evershed M.R.

[28] See *Bristol Airport v. Powdrill* [1990] 2 W.L.R. 1362 and *Re Sabre International Products Ltd* [1991] B.C.L.C. 470.

this has been removed by the abandonment of the rule (formerly contained in section 612 of the Companies Act 1985) providing for the application of bankruptcy law principles to company liquidation.

10-80 The procedure for proving a debt on liquidation is explained by rules 4.73–4.85 of the Insolvency Rules 1986. The liquidator decides whether a proof of debt is to be admitted, and for how much. A disgruntled creditor may challenge his decision by applying to the court under rule 4.83.[29] The basic rule governing those debts which may be proved in a winding-up is now to be found in rule 12.3; all debts or liabilities, including future debts, contingent debts, claims for unliquidated damages in tort, and for arrears of interest accruing before the commencement of the liquidation may be proved. Some further comment is required here.

10-81 Rule 4.93 (as amended) allows for proof in respect of arrears of interest,[30] though presumably this must be read subject to section 244 of the Insolvency Act 1986.[31] Payments of a periodical nature such as rent are provable under rule 4.92. Future debts are also, by virtue of rule 4.94, regarded as being provable, though the claim here is liable to be reduced by reference to the formula set out in rule 11.13 (as amended). Unpaid fines are now apparently provable on liquidation (but strangely not in the case of bankruptcy).[32] The question as to whether a claim for unliquidated damages in tort could be admitted to proof on the winding-up of a company did cause some difficulty formerly[33] but this doubt has now been dispelled by a combination of rules 12.3 and 13.12 which render such a claim provable.

Restrictions on proof

10-82 Having examined those debts which are provable on the liquidation of the company, it is worth mentioning claims that are not so regarded. These restrictions are preserved by rule 12.3(3) of the Insolvency Rules 1986. First, there is a well-established principle of law that a foreign government will not be allowed to prove in respect of a foreign tax debt. Thus, in *Government of India v. Taylor*[34] the court explained that it would not allow proof because this would constitute the enforcement of foreign revenue laws. This principle may well be abandoned in the future between EEC members, but for the present it still stands. In addition, the rule

---

[29] See also Chaps. 5 and 6 here.

[30] For the confusion that existed previously on whether the bankruptcy rule formerly found in s.66 of the Bankruptcy Act 1914 applied to liquidations see *Re Agricultural Wholesale Society* [1929] 2 Ch. 261 which criticised in *Re Bush* [1930] 2 Ch. 202, and *Re Theo Garvin Ltd* [1969] 1 Ch. 624. In *Re Amalgamated Investments and Property Co. Ltd* (1984) 1 B.C.C. 99, 104 Vinelott J., although making it clear that interest accruing after the date of the commencement of the winding up could not be proved, nevertheless severely criticised the basic restrictive strategy contained in section 66 of the Bankruptcy Act 1914. This restriction was also abandoned for bankruptcy situations by the Insolvency Act 1986 on the recommendation of the Cork Committee (Cmnd. 8558 para. 1380).

[31] See Chap. 10.

[32] See Insolvency Rules 1986, r. 12.3(2)(*a*). For the common law position see *Re Pascoe (No. 2)* [1944] Ch. 310. The Cork Committee argued that unpaid fines should not be regarded as provable debts (Cmnd. 8558 para. 1330).

[33] Compare *Re Berkeley Securities (Property) Ltd* [1980] 1 W.L.R. 1589 with *Re Islington Metal and Plating Works* [1984] 1 W.L.R. 14. A claim for liquidated damages for breach of contract always was provable—*Mersey Steel and Iron Co. v. Naylor, Benzon & Co.* (1884) 9 App. Cas. 434, *Telsen Electric Co. v. Eastick & Sons* [1936] 3 All E.R. 266.

[34] [1955] A.C. 491. See also *Clyde Marine Insurance v. Renwick & Co.* 1924 S.C. 113, *U.S.A. v. Hardern* (1963) 41 D.L.R. (2d) 721, *Re Norway's Application* [1986] 3 W.L.R. 452 and *QRS 1 Aps v. Frandsen*, *The Times*, May 27, 1999. Debts in a foreign currency are provable provided they are converted into sterling at the date of the commencement of the liquidation—Insolvency Rules 1986, r. 4.91.

against double proof, which disqualifies two proofs in respect of the same debt, still applies.[35]

10-83 *Re Kentish Homes Ltd*[36] illustrates a general lacuna in the class of provable debts, arising from the definition of "debt" in rule 13.12. This included debts or liabilities to which the company may become subject after the commencement of winding up only to the extent that they relate to an obligation incurred before that date. This case was concerned with the status of unpaid community charges on the liquidation of a housebuilding company. Here the company had gone into receivership (under the Law of Property Act 1925) and the receiver had begun the completion of various dwellings under construction and encompassed within the security. Under the relevant community charge legislation, if a dwelling remains unoccupied for six months after construction the builder becomes liable for the charge. By the time the specified six months had elapsed, the company had also gone into liquidation and the dwellings were not completed by the receiver until after the liquidation had commenced. Nicholls V.-C. held that the unpaid community charge could not be regarded as an expense of the winding-up as it was the receiver who had completed the dwellings and who was responsible for them. The dwellings were not being used for the benefit of the liquidation. Nor could it rank as a provable debt because it was not a debt as defined by rule 13.12 at all, having arisen after the liquidation but not in respect of an obligation incurred before winding up commenced. Section 109 of the Law of Property Act 1925 did not enable the local authority to enforce the obligation to pay against the receiver, and although the liquidator would have had a right of recourse against the receiver if he had been made to pay as an expense of the winding-up, the court would not exercise its discretion to order the liquidator to pay on that basis. To do so would have gone from one extreme to the other by giving the local authority priority over all other unsecured creditors. Nicholls V.-C. admitted that he had little enthusiasm for this conclusion but he felt that he had no choice under the law as it then stood. This case will continue to apply in the wake of the abolition of the community charge because Nicholls V.-C. made it clear that he would have reached the same conclusion with respects to the new council tax.

10-84 Finally, the possibility has to be borne in mind that a creditor may be barred from proving because his debt has become statute-barred through expiry of the relevant limitation period prior to the commencement of the liquidation.[37] The normal limitation period for unsecured debts would be six years.[38] In *Re Art Reproduction Co. Ltd*[39] the claim to prove in respect of a particular debt failed because the limitation period had expired; the court would not lend its assistance in such a case.

[35] See *Re Oriental and Commercial Bank* (1871) LR 7 Ch. App. 99, *Re Polly Peck International* [1996] B.C.C. 486 and *Re Parkfield Group plc* [1997] B.C.C. 778. It is clear from the modern cases that the courts are adept at circumventing this utilitarian rule.

[36] [1993] B.C.C. 212.

[37] The limitation period ceases to run at the date of a winding up order—*Re General Rolling Stock Co.* (1872) 7 Ch. App. 646. A statute barred debt cannot form the basis of a winding-up petition—*Re Karnos Property Co. Ltd* [1989] B.C.L.C. 340.

[38] Limitation Act 1980, s.5 (simple contract debts). The limitation period for speciality debts is 12 years—*ibid.*, s.8.

[39] [1952] Ch. 89. See also *Re Fleetwood & District Electric Light and Power Syndicate Ltd* [1915] 1 Ch. 486.

CHAPTER 11

Avoidance of Transactions

11-01 The aim of this Chapter is to consider various provisions in the Companies Act 1985 and the Insolvency Act 1986, which may be used either to invalidate the grant of security by a company or, indeed, to impugn a wider range of transactions entered into by an insolvent company.[1] Normally, these statutory avoidance mechanisms will be exploited by a liquidator or in some cases, an administrator in order to reduce the number of priority claims existing against the company's assets in the interests of the unsecured creditors as a whole.

NON-REGISTRATION OF SECURITY

11-02 It may be necessary for a lawyer advising an insolvency practitioner to consider the registration rules contained in Part XII of the Companies Act 1985 for a number of reasons. He may, for instance, have been approached by a person, who has been asked to accept an appointment as a company receiver, seeking advice on the validity of the security which he will be expected to enforce. If a receiver accepts appointment and the charge conferred by the debenture turns out to be registrable but not registered then he may incur liability for trespass.[2] Alternatively, a liquidator, seeking to maximise the assets available for unsecured creditors, may seek a legal opinion as to the vulnerability of the security in the light of the registration laws. A consideration of these rules will also be a necessity when determining priority rankings between competing charges on the company's assets. These rules will be substantially amended if Part IV of the Companies Act 1989 is ever brought into force. As there is some uncertainty as to the fate of Part IV the following commentary will disregard it and will concentrate instead upon the current rules in the 1985 Act.

11-03 All charges created by a company over its assets and all instruments of charge must by virtue of sections 406 and 407 of the Companies Act 1985 be registered at the company's own registered office. However, if a chargee fails to ensure compliance with this requirement, his position will not be unduly prejudiced, for the only sanction which the law imposes will be the possibility of a fine for the responsible company officer.[3] Of much more practical importance is the requirement imposed by section 395 of the Companies Act 1985 that prescribed details of certain charges listed in section 396 be submitted for registration at the Companies Registry at Cardiff within 21 days of the creation of the charge. The stakes are

[1] For general reviews of the subject see Milman [1997] (Special Issue) *Insolvency Lawyer* 2, Milman and Parry (1997) 48 N.I.L.Q. 24 and Keay [1998] J.B.L. 515 (for an Anglo-Australian comparison).
[2] The court can order the appointor to indemnify the receiver under the Insolvency Act 1986, s.34.
[3] Companies Act 1985, s.407(3). The security remains unaffected—*Wright v. Horton* (1887) 12 App. Cas. 371.

much higher here in the case of non-compliance for the law will impose the draconian sanction of invalidating the security and, in the case of an insolvent company, the consequences of such a sanction being imposed hardly require further elaboration.[4]

Categories of registrable charge

11-04 The categories of charge which must be submitted for registration at Cardiff have developed in a piecemeal fashion since the introduction of the public registration system for company charges in 1900. The list of registrable charges is now embodied in section 396(1) of the Companies Act 1985 and each head of registrable charge is considered individually below.

11-05 (a) **"A charge for the purpose of securing any issue of debentures"** If the remaining categories of s.396(1) are to have any utility at all, it is generally accepted that this paragraph must be interpreted to mean debentures in the nature of loan stock, normally secured by a charge of the company's assets to trustees.

11-06 (b) **"A charge on uncalled share capital of the company"** The charging provisions of most debentures expressly refer to uncalled capital when creating a floating charge. As uncalled share capital is not technically regarded as an "asset" of the company, it would not be covered by a charge within paragraph. (f).[5]

11-07 (c) **"A charge created or evidenced by an instrument which, if executed by an individual, would require registration as a bill of sale"** This cumbersome category of registrable charge is necessary because limited companies are exempt from the requirements of the Bills of Sale Acts 1878 and 1882.[6] In *Re Sugar Properties (Derisley) Ltd* a charge over a share in a racehorse was held not to come within this category.[7]

11-08 (d) **"A charge on land (wherever situated) or any interest in it, but not including a charge for any rent or periodical sum issuing out of the land"** In spite of the exclusion of rent charges this category is still broad. Thus, it includes equitable charges created by simple deposit of title deeds as was confirmed in *Re Wallis & Simmonds Ltd*[8] and also equitable sub-mortgages.[9] It should also be noted that the requirements of the Land Registration Act 1925 and the Land Charges Act 1972 may also need to be complied with. Thus a legal charge of registered land takes effect only in equity until it is registered,[10] and equitable and puisne mortgages are vulnerable to loss of priority unless protected in the appropriate way under these Acts.

---

[4] A liquidator or administrator can challenge security for lack of registration but an individual creditor cannot—*Re Ayala Holdings Ltd* [1993] B.C.L.C. 256.
[5] *Re British Provident Life and Fire Assurance Society, Stanley's case* (1864) 4 De G.J. & Sm. 407.
[6] *Re Standard Manufacturing Co.* [1891] Ch. 627.
[7] [1988] B.C.L.C. 146.
[8] [1974] 1 All E.R. 561. This type of charge now requires written documentation—*United Bank of Kuwait v. Sahib, The Times*, February 13, 1996.
[9] [1968] Ch. 325.
[10] *Grace Rymer Investments Ltd v. Waite* [1958] Ch. 831.

11-09 (e) **"A charge on the book debts of the company"**[11] This paragraph has posed severe difficulties of interpretation for the courts. Erle C.J. defined book debts in *Shipley v. Marshall*[12] as debts arising out of the ordinary course of the company's business whether actually entered in its books or not. The fact that as a matter of commercial practice the arrangement was assumed not to create a registrable charge is irrelevant.[13] One difficulty here has been to distinguish a charge over a company's book debts from an absolute assignment of book debts which is not registrable. A charge over future book debts does require registration,[14] as does a charge over selected book debts.[15] In *Re Brightlife Ltd*[16] Hoffmann J. held that a charge over sums standing to the credit of the company's bank account was not a charge over book debts. Again, in *Re Charge Card Services Ltd (No. 2)*[17] Millett J. ruled that a company cannot create a charge over book debts owed to it by the chargee—this was a conceptual impossibility. The "chargeback" debate rumbled on for many years amongst city practitioners. Attempts were made to combat this apparent *lacuna* in the law of corporate lending.[18] The Legal Risks Review Committee,[19] concerned about damage to business confidence, called in 1992 for a clarification of the law and this clarification was effected through legislation in a number of jurisdictions.[20] Legislation proved unnecessary in this country for in *Re B.C.C.I. (No. 8)*[21] the House of Lords rejected the view of Millett J. and ruled that a chargeback was indeed effective as security under English law. Unfortunately, the question of registrability was left unanswered and it is thus uncertain whether a bank taking security over a customer's deposit would be creating a charge over that customer's book debts.

11-10 (f) **"A floating charge on the company's undertaking or property"** This category would include floating charges over the totality of the company's assets as well as floating charges over selected items of its property.[22]

---

[11] Note here the exception provided by s.396(2) for deposits of negotiable instruments and see *Chase Manhattan v. F.B.C.F.* [1990] 1 W.L.R. 1181.

[12] (1863) 14 C.B.N.S. 566 at 571.

[13] *Re Welsh Irish Ferries Ltd* [1985] 3 W.L.R. 610.

[14] *Independent Automatic Sales v. Knowles and Foster* [1962] 3 All E.R. 27, *Contemporary Cottages (N.Z.) Ltd v. Margin Traders Ltd* [1981] 2 N.Z.L.R. 114 and *Re Brush Aggregates Ltd* [1983] B.C.L.C. 320. But compare *Paul and Frank Ltd v. Discount Bank Overseas Ltd* [1967] Ch. 348.

[15] *Timbar Pty. Ltd v. W.T. and N.E. Peterie Pty. Ltd* (1983) 7 A.C.L.R. 111.

[16] [1986] 3 All E.R. 673. This decision was anticipated by the Companies Registry which in a notice dated March 13, 1985 indicated that charges over a company's credit balance at its bank would no longer be accepted for registration. See now the letter of May 1987 from the Assistant Registrar (1987) 137 N.L.J. 548. See also *Northern Bank v. Ross* [1990] B.C.C. 883.

[17] [1986] 3 W.L.R. 697. This decision was confirmed on appeal in [1988] 3 All E.R. 702.

[18] The "triple cocktail" using a "flawed asset" being one such attempt—for its *modus operandi* see Rajani (1997) 13 I.L. & P. 180.

[19] The concern here is that the resulting uncertainty undermines the competitive position of the U.K. as a leading bank centre.

[20] This was the strategy adopted in Bermuda, Cayman Islands, Hong Kong and Singapore. For judicial comment on the Hong Kong reform see *Tam Wing Chuen v. Bank of Credit and Commerce Hong Kong Ltd* [1996] 2 B.C.L.C. 69.

[21] [1997] 3 W.L.R. 909—this case is sometimes referred to as *Morris v. Agrichemicals Ltd* as in [1997] B.C.C. 965. For comment see Rajani (*supra*) de Lacy [1998] (May) *Palmer's In Company* 1, and Rotherham [1998] C.L.J. 260.

[22] *Hoare v. British Columbia Development Association* (1912) 107 L.T. 602.

11-11 (g) "A charge on calls made but not paid" A shareholder only becomes indebted to a company in respect of sums of money due on his shares once a call in respect of those sums has been made by the directors. However, as this liability cannot be characterised as a book debt, it does not fall under paragraph (e) above, therefore a separate grouping is provided for.

11-12 (h) "A charge on a ship or aircraft or any share in a ship" This category was extended in 1972 to cover charges on aircraft.

11-13 (i) "A charge on goodwill, on a patent or a licence under a patent, on a trademark or on a copyright or a licence under a copyright"

Devices not requiring registration

11-14 These then are the charges requiring registration at the Companies Registry at Cardiff. Unfortunately, it has become increasingly apparent that there are a large number of what are essentially security devices which do not have to be notified to Cardiff. In the first place, any charge over the company's assets arising by operation of law, such as an unpaid vendor's lien, is excluded from the public registration system, presumably because it is not technically "created by a company" within the meaning of section 395.[23] Moreover, even where it is accepted that a charge has been created by the company, it does not necessarily follow that it will fall in the list contained in section 396. There are notable *lacunae*. Thus, a possessory charge created by way of pledge does not have to be registered.[24]

Pledges

11-15 This seems fair enough in the vast majority of cases because there is no danger of a false impression being given of the company's creditworthiness by details of the security not appearing at Cardiff because the asset used as security would not be in the company's possession. But what if a person dealing with the company would expect certain corporate assets, such as a company car, to be in the possession of a third party in any case? In *Barrett & Co. v. Livesey*[25] it was held that a pledge of a company car to a director who had lent money to the company, and who was already using that car, did not fall within sections 395–6 of the Companies Act 1985.

Specific charges over shares

11-16 Moreover, specific charges created by limited companies over their shareholdings in other companies also escape the registration net. This is a notable omission because, in the case of holding companies, such shareholdings will often represent the major assets of the companies concerned.[26] In recent years it has become common for the courts to rule that a number of widespread corporate financing transactions also fall outside the registration pale, so to speak. Thus a genuine

---

[23] *London and Cheshire Insurance Co. v. Laplagrene Property Co.* [1971] Ch. 499.

[24] *Wrightson v. McArthur and Hutchinsons Ltd* [1921] 2 K.B. 807. The same is true of a possessory lien—*Re Hamlet International plc*, *The Times*, March 13, 1998.

[25] (1981) 131 N.L.J. 1213.

[26] This lacuna was criticised both by the Jenkins Committee (Cmnd. 1749, para. 301), and by the Cork Committee (Cmnd. 8558, para. 1520).

assignment of book debts entered into by the company as part of a block discounting agreement with a factoring company would not, on the basis of *Lloyds and Scottish Finance Ltd v. Cyril Lord Carpet Sales*,[27] require registration. Similarly, a carefully drafted reservation of title agreement does not involve the creation of a registrable charge within the meaning of sections 395 and 396 of the Companies Act 1985.[28]

The need for reform

11-17 In *Carreras Rothmans Ltd v. Freeman Mathews Treasure Ltd*,[29] it was held that an effective trust device arrangement does not result in the trustee company creating a registrable security over its assets. The range of novel financing transactions is unlimited and as English law currently stands, each one has to be individually analysed by the courts to see if a registrable charge is thereby created.[30] This generates unnecessary, unpredictable litigation and creates confusion within the business community.

11-18 This question of registration of security interests has been reviewed in recent years by the Diamond Committee, which in 1989 recommended in the long term a move towards a comprehensive filing system for security interests in personal property similar to that which operates in the U.S.A. This radical proposal, which mirrored the conclusions of the Crowther Committee some two decades previously, did not find favour with the government, which quietly ditched it.[31] Provisions in the 1989 Companies Act to radically overhaul the charge registration system have been dropped.

Procedural matters

11-19 Further flaws in the registration system arise from procedural matters. For instance, on closer examination, section 395 only requires that details of registrable charges be submitted for registration—it does not state that they must actually be registered.[32] Thus, if a chargee can prove that the prescribed details were submitted to the Companies Registry, the security will not be invalidated even if the Registrar refuses to register the charge. Furthermore, even where the submitted particulars are registered, they may well give an inaccurate impression of the extent of the loan or the security granted by the company. Even so, provided the chargee has received his certificate from the Registrar to the effect that the requirements of the Act as to registration have been complied with, the certificate will be viewed as conclusive.[33] The chargee can rely on the full extent of his rights under the debenture, even though they are not disclosed in the public register.[34] The strong line of authority to support this

[27] [1992] B.C.L.C. 609. See also *Re George Inglefield Ltd* [1933] Ch. 1.
[28] See Chap. 8.
[29] [1984] 3 W.L.R. 1016.
[30] Compare *Welsh Development Agency v. Export Finance Co. Ltd* [1992] B.C.C. 270, *Re Curtain Dream plc* [1990] B.C.L.C. 925 and *Re Marwalt plc* [1992] B.C.C. 32.
[31] See Written Answer, Hansard (H.C.), Vol. 189, col. 482 (April 24, 1991). For a review of the Diamond Committee proposals see *Lawson* [1989] J.B.L. 287.
[32] *N.V. Slavenburg's Bank v. Intercontinental Natural Resources Ltd* [1980] 1 All E.R. 955.
[33] Companies Act 1985, s.401(2)(*b*). This is true also of certificates of late registration—*Exeter Trust v. Screenways Ltd* [1991] B.C.C. 477.
[34] *National Provincial Bank v. Charnley* [1924] 1 K.B. 431, *Re Eric Holmes Property Ltd* [1965] Ch. 1052, *Re Mechanisations (Eaglescliffe) Ltd* [1966] Ch. 20 and *Re Nye Ltd* [1971] Ch. 442.

strange proposition was reinforced by the Court of Appeal in *R. v. Registrar of Companies ex p. Esal Commodities Ltd*,[35] where it was held that the Registrar's certificate cannot be challenged by way of application for judicial review as a prelude to circumventing these authorities.

Discretion to rectify

11-20 If a lawyer or insolvency practitioner inspects the register and finds that the details of the charge held by the person he is representing have not been registered, is there anything that can be done to salvage the situation? The court does enjoy discretion under section 404 of the Companies Act 1985 to rectify the register if it is satisfied that the omission to register was accidental,[36] due to inadvertance,[37] or due to some other sufficient cause[38] or was not of a nature to prejudice shareholders or creditors, or that it would be just and equitable to grant relief. This provision would cover situations where the initial failure to register was due to an administrative error at the solicitor's office,[39] or where there had been a loss of documents, etc., and even a conscious decision not to register the charge. The onus is on the applicant to adduce evidence to support a plea for late registration; a bare request without more will not find favour.[40] Moreover, it seems that the court will not permit late registration if the company is in liquidation receivership or administration, and even if things have not got this far, it will be reluctant to grant registration out of time if it is insolvent. This latter restriction was emphasised by the Court of Appeal in *Re Ashpurton Estates Ltd.*[41] Furthermore, even where late registration is allowed, it will only be permitted subject to the proviso that those persons who had acquired rights against the company's assets in the period between the end of the 21-day registration deadline and the date of actual late registration will be protected.[42] The court enjoys discretion to withdraw protection from undeserving cases.[43] An unsecured creditor would not be protected by this proviso unless the company goes into liquidation.[44]

INVALIDATING FLOATING CHARGES[45]

11-21 Section 245 of the Insolvency Act 1986, which can trace its ancestry back to 1907, will be of interest to insolvency practitioners for a number of reasons. A potential receiver might wish to investigate whether the floating charge under which he has been appointed can be set aside for breach of section 245 because, if it can,

---

35 [1986] 2 W.L.R. 177. For Companies Registry practice in the wake of this decision see the notice dated August 28, 1985. Particulars of charge submitted outside the 21 day deadline will not normally be accepted and an application for late registration under s.404 must be made.
36 *Re Joplin Brewery Co.* [1902] 1 Ch. 79.
37 *Re Mendip Press Ltd* (1901) 18 T.L.R. 38.
38 *Re S. Abrahams and Sons Ltd* [1902] 1 Ch. 695.
39 See *Re Braemar Investments Ltd* [1988] B.C.L.C. 556.
40 *Re Telomatic Ltd* [1993] B.C.C. 34.
41 [1982] 3 W.L.R. 964. For the position on late registration in cases of administration see *Re Barrow Borough Transport Ltd* [1990] Ch. 227.
42 *Watson v. Duff, Morgan and Vermont Holdings Ltd* [1974] 1 W.L.R. 450.
43 *Re Fablehill Ltd* [1991] B.C.L.C. 830.
44 *Re S. Abrahams and Sons Ltd* [1902] 1 Ch. 695, *Re Anglo Oriental Carpet Co.* [1903] 1 Ch. 914. For a novel type of order see *Re Chantry House Development Co. Ltd* [1990] B.C.L.C. 813.
45 For a historical review of this provision see *Milman* (1980) 31 N.I.L.Q. 255.

he, the receiver, might incur liability for trespass.[46] Alternatively, a liquidator might wish to exploit this provision to nullify a floating charge and thereby make more assets available for the unsecured creditors.

11-22 Bearing in mind the potential importance of this provision, which was substantially amended by the now repealed section 104 of the Insolvency Act 1985 as a result of the recommendations of the Cork Committee, it is a pity that it is obscurely drafted and creates important difficulties of interpretation for practitioners.

Only floating charges

11-23 The first thing to note about section 245 is that it can only operate against floating charges. Fixed charges, even those covering future assets, are not prejudiced by its existence. Hence, the importance of distinguishing between these two types of security in marginal cases.[47] At one time, it was felt that if a floating charge crystallised before the commencement of the liquidation, it could not be viewed as a "floating charge" for the purposes of this provision.[48] Parliament has now decreed *ex abundanti cautela* in section 251 of the Insolvency Act 1986 that the crucial date for determining whether a charge is or is not a floating charge is its date of creation. So section 245 only works against floating charges. Moreover, it cannot operate where the company has paid off the debenture holder secured by the floating charge or where a receiver has taken possession and dissipated the company's assets in payment of the debenture holder.[49]

"Relevant time"

11-24 If it can be shown that the charge in question is a floating charge, another hurdle must be surmounted before the security can fall within the orbit of this statutory invalidating provision. The floating charge must have been created at a "relevant time." Normally, this means either within the 12 months ending with the "commencement date" or within the period between the presentation of the petition for an administration order and the date of the granting of that order. The commencement date is defined by section 245(5) to mean, in effect, either the date of the presentation of a successful petition for an administration or winding-up order[50] or the date of the resolution for voluntary liquidation.[51] The question of timing is further complicated by the substitution of a two-year period prior to the commencement date where the chargee is a "connected person." This phrase is defined by sections 249 and 435 of the Insolvency Act 1986 to include directors and shadow directors of the company, "associates" of directors or shadow directors, and "associates" of the company. It would appear[52] that "associates" include spouses, relatives, partners, employers, employees, trustees and associated companies. Suffice it to say that the net is cast wide.

---

46 The court can order the appointor to indemnify the receiver under the Insolvency Act 1986, s.34.
47 *Kelly v. McMahon* [1980] I.R. 347.
48 This point was argued unsuccessfully in *Re Port Supermarket Ltd* [1978] 1 N.Z.L.R. 330 and *Re Eastern Retreads Wholesale Pty. Ltd* (1979) 4 A.C.L.R. 136.
49 *Re Parkes Garage (Swadlincote) Ltd* [1929] 1 Ch. 139 and *Mace Builders (Glasgow) Ltd v. Lunn* [1987] B.C.L.C. 55. But note here *Power v. Sharp Investments* [1993] B.C.C. 609.
50 *ibid.*, s.129. See also *Bank of New South Wales v. Official Assignee* [1982] 1 N.Z.L.R. 427.
51 Insolvency Act 1986, s.86.
52 See the Insolvency Act 1986, s.435.

Company insolvent

11-25 Finally, where it can be shown that a floating charge in favour of a person unconnected with the company was created within any of the periods mentioned above, the liquidator will have to show that the company was then unable to pay its debts within the meaning of section 123 of the Insolvency Act 1986. The classic definition of this state of affairs was provided by Maugham J. in *Re Patrick and Lyon Ltd*[53]—inability to pay debts as they fall due. This definition is preserved by section 123(1)(*e*), along with the established statutory deeming provisions relating to failure to comply with a statutory demand for three weeks after service and failure of execution. A company is now also deemed unable to pay its debts if its liabilities exceed its assets.[54] This additional test for insolvency was grafted on to the orthodox definition as a result of the recommendations of the Cork Committee. It should be noted that when applying any of these tests, the effect of the loan transaction under which the floating charge was granted has to be taken into account.

Burden of proof

11-26 The Cork Committee promoted a further change in the law in this area. Formerly, the onus was on the chargee seeking to protect his security to show that the company was solvent at the time when he took his charge. It is now clear from section 245(4) that the burden of proof has been reversed, with the onus now being imposed on the person seeking to impugn the charge to show that the company was insolvent. Despite the wider meaning now attributed to insolvency, this change has made it more difficult to invalidate bank and other charges in favour of outsiders under the statutory provisions. On the other hand, the onus of proving insolvency is removed from the shoulders of the liquidator where the chargee is connected with the company. It is not necessary to show that the directors of the company had any fraudulent motive when granting the charge. This point was emphasised by Nourse J. in *Re G. T. Whyte Ltd*,[55] where it was stressed that what is now section 245 is a purely objective provision.

Consideration

11-27 If the liquidator can show that the floating charge was created within the relevant period and (where necessary) that the company was insolvent at the time, the floating charge will be vulnerable to invalidation. However, the security will be valid as to "so much of the consideration for the creation of the charge" as consists of goods or services supplied to the company, or the discharge of any of the company's indebtedness. Interest payable under the agreement conferring the charge is also protected. The wording of section 245 differs strikingly from that of its statutory predecessor,[56] and the question arises whether the law has been changed. Unfortunately the answer is far from clear.

11-28 The earlier section provided that a floating charge was void in the defined circumstances "except as to the amount of any cash paid to the company

[53] [1933] Ch. 786.
[54] Insolvency Act 1986, s.123(2). See Chap. 1.
[55] [1983] B.C.L.C. 311.
[56] Companies Act 1985, s.617.

. . . in consideration for the charge." Clearly section 245 is wider in scope in that it is no longer limited to cash. However, it may be more restricted in another respect. The expression "in consideration for the charge" in the old section was liberally interpreted in *Re Yeovil Glove Co. Ltd.*[57] In that case, money advanced by a bank several months after the creation of a floating charge was held to have been advanced "in consideration for" the charge, even though the charge did not refer to new money and did not require the bank to make further advances. Thus the phrase "in consideration for" was interpreted to mean "as a result of." It may be that the wording of the new section will give less scope for liberality. The question used to be whether any particular cash could be shown to have been advanced in consideration for the charge. The new wording, which requires the consideration for the creation of the charge to be identified and evaluated, may indicate an intention to return to a more strictly contractual notion of consideration.

Time of consideration

11-29 A second significant difference in wording relates to the time at which any money or other consideration has to be provided in order to be secured by the charge. The old section referred to cash paid "at the time of or subsequent to the creation of the charge." These words were again very liberally interpreted in the past, to cover cash supplied by the chargee to the company some considerable time before the charge was created.[58] Section 245, on the other hand, refers to supplies of money, goods and services "at the same time as or after" the creation of the charge. The legislature could well have left the established wording alone but it did not.

11-30 The significance of this change in the law has been illustrated by the Court of Appeal ruling in *Re Shoe Lace Ltd.*[59] Here a parent company had loaned money to its insolvent subsidiary after the board of the subsidiary had resolved to issue a debenture to the parent in return for this loan. This resolution was not sufficiently precise to constitute an immediate agreement to grant security, thereby creating an equitable interest from that moment. Unfortunately the debenture was not executed until several months after the loan had been provided. When the subsidiary went into liquidation shortly afterwards, a question arose as to whether the loan had been provided at the same time as or after the creation of the floating charge. Both Hoffmann J.[60] and the Court of Appeal, spurning the old authorities mentioned above, decided that the security was not valid to the extent of the advances made by the parent company. The saving formula had to be strictly interpreted and, subject to a very limited *de minimis rule*, advances made at any time before the floating charge was created would no longer be regarded as protected. Sir Christopher Slade held in the Court of Appeal that although there was little or no difference in the wording of section 245(2) of the 1986 Act and its predecessors, the correct rule was (and always had been) that no moneys paid before the execution of the debenture will qualify for the exemption, unless the interval between payment and execution is so short that it

---

[57] [1965] Ch. 148.
[58] See *Re Colombian Fire Proofing* [1910] 1 Ch. 758 and [1910] 2 Ch. 120, *Re F. and E. Stanton Ltd* [1929] 1 Ch. 180.
[59] [1993] B.C.C. 609. Sometimes cited as *Power v. Sharp Investments*.
[60] Reported in [1992] B.C.C. 636. It is interesting to note that a more relaxed view of the temporal restriction was adopted at first instance by Mummery J. in *Re Fairway Magazines Ltd* [1992] B.C.C. 924 but this case must now be regarded as overruled by the Court of Appeal in *Shoe Lace (supra)* in which it was cited on behalf of the debenture holder (see [1993] B.C.C. at 618).

can be regarded as minimal, and payment and execution can be regarded as contemporaneous.

11-31 Subsection (2)(*b*) is something of a mystery. Does it validate the floating charge to the extent of cash paid to the company which is then immediately used by the company to pay off an unsecured debt owed to the chargee? In view of the purpose of section 245 this would appear a surprising result,[61] though perhaps no more surprising than that of the much criticised case of *Re Yeovil Glove Co. Ltd.*[62] In that case, the company had overdrawn bank accounts and gave its bankers a floating charge. It was held that receipts into the bank after the date of the charge were applicable to the oldest debits on the account by application of the rule in *Clayton's Case*[63] by which the first credits to an unbroken account are to be set against the oldest debits, even though those debits predated the charge and were not secured by it. The bank provided "new money" only by meeting cheques drawn by the company after the charge was given, and it was held that the aggregate of the drawings was covered by the charge. This strengthening of the security provided by a floating charge by the progressive extinction of unsecured debits is known in banking circles as the "hardening" of the floating charge.

Payments to third party

11-32 It is not clear whether section 245(2)(*b*) would cover payments to a third party which are used to pay off existing debts owed by the company. Here the money never goes through the company's hands. The Scottish courts ruled in the case of *Libertas Kommerz GmbH*[64] that such a transaction was not protected by the former proviso, but the position may not be the same under the new wording of subsection (2)(*b*).

PREFERENCES AND TRANSACTIONS AT AN UNDERVALUE

11-33 Sections 238–241 of the Insolvency Act 1986 give much wider scope for transactions to be set aside.[65] Grants of fixed and floating charges, repayments of debts, transfers of property, gifts, *etc.*, can all be set aside by a liquidator or administrator if they take place within the period defined by the sections and at a time when the company was insolvent.

11-34 These provisions represented a substantial change from the former law which was embodied in section 615 of the Companies Act 1985. The former provision allowed a liquidator to challenge transactions voluntarily entered into by an

---

[61] For the approach of the courts to the question of whether there has been a genuine cash payment, etc., to the company see *Re Matthew Ellis Ltd* [1933] Ch. 458, *Re Destone Fabrics Ltd* [1941] Ch. 319 and *Re Fairway Magazines Ltd* [1992] B.C.C. 924.

[62] [1965] Ch. 148.

[63] (1816) 1 Mer 572.

[64] 1978 S.L.T. 222. A payment to a third party is covered if the company benefits—see *Pennywise Smart Shopping v. Sommer Ltd* (1992) 6 A.C.S.R. 435.

[65] These statutory rules do not exclude the possibility of recovery of company property under common law principles, such as by exploiting the concept of a constructive trust. See here Insolvency Act 1986, s.241(4) and *Re Clasper Group Services* [1989] B.C.L.C. 143. Note that the Scots have their own specific statutory avoidance rules in ss.242 and 243 of the Insolvency Act 1986. For discussion see *Nicholl v. Steelpress* 1993 S.L.T. 533 *McLuckie Bros. v. Newhouse Contracts* 1993 S.L.T. 641 *Secretary of State v. Burn* 1998 S.L.T. 1009.

insolvent company within six months of the commencement of its liquidation. The transaction in question had to have been carried out with an intention to prefer—if there were bona fide commercial reasons for it, and it merely resulted in a preference, it was not within the scope of the section.[66] The classic type of so called "fraudulent preference" occurred where directors, having guaranteed the company's overdraft, ensured that it was paid off with the few remaining funds belonging to the insolvent company, thereby protecting their position under the guarantee.[67] The Cork Committee felt that this statutory power of avoidance should be strengthened in a number of respects and some of its recommendations are now reflected in the current sections.

11-35 What type of transactions are covered by this group of provisions? Basically, they fall into two categories: transactions at an undervalue as defined by section 238, and preferences as described by section 239.

Transaction at undervalue

11-36 The concept of a transaction at an undervalue is explained fully by section 238(4):

> "For the purposes of this section and section 241, a company enters into a transaction with a person at an undervalue if—
>
> (a) the company makes a gift to that person or otherwise enters into a transaction with that person on terms that provide for the company to receive no consideration, or
>
> (b) the company enters into a transaction with that person for a consideration the value of which, in money or money's worth, is significantly less than the value, in money or money's worth, of the consideration provided by the company."

This definition is qualified by section 238(5), which excludes from the invalidating net transactions entered into by a company in good faith for the purpose of carrying on its business, where there were reasonable grounds for believing that the transaction would benefit the company.[68] It is doubtful whether this provision could protect a sale of the company's business at an undervalue, as such a transaction could rarely be said to be entered into "for the purpose of carrying on" the company's business. The same objection might be made if sub-section 238(5) were prayed in aid to protect an upstream guarantee granted by a subsidiary of its parent's banking facility, without consideration, although the applicability of section 238 to such a transaction is itself in doubt in view of *Re M.C. Bacon Ltd.*[69] In that case Millett J. held that it was not appropriate to use section 238 to challenge the grant of security, because such a grant did not diminish the value of the company's assets (as was in effect

---

[66] *Re Inns of Court Hotel Co.* (1868) L.R. 6 Eq. 82.

[67] See here *Re Industrial Design and Manufacture Ltd* [1984] 10 N.I.J.B. 1 noted by *McCormack* in (1986) 37 N.I.L.Q. 86 where such a transaction was held by Carswell J. to be a fraudulent preference.

[68] This provision would appear to be in line with the case of *Re Matthews Ltd* [1982] 2 W.L.R. 495 which rejected the idea that a transaction could not be treated as a fraudulent preference if the directors honestly believed that the company would retrieve its financial position at some time in the future, when they realised that at the moment it was insolvent.

[69] [1991] Ch. 127.

required by section 238(4)(*b*). In such a case the transaction should be reviewed under section 239 if it appeared objectionable. A useful illustration of section 238 at work is afforded by *Phillips v. Brewin Dolphin Bell Lawrie Ltd*[70] where the sale of a company's business was found by the Court of Appeal to have been entered into at an undervalue with the consequence that difference in consideration had to paid over to the liquidator. The case is instructive in that it shows a robust approach towards the application of section 238 to a complex commercial transaction.

Preferences

11-37 Turning to preferences, the key provision here is section 239(4):

> "For the purposes of this section and section 241, a company gives a preference to a person if—
>
> (a) that person is one of the company's creditors or a surety or guarantor for any of the company's debts or other liabilities, and
> (b) the company does anything or suffers anything to be done which (in either case) has the effect of putting that person into a position, which, in the event of the company going into insolvent liquidation, will be better than the position he would have been in if that thing had not been done."

The provision is refined by subsections (5)–(7). It is implicit in the provision that the preference must actually have resulted from the action under scrutiny. An intention to give a preference without more does not breach section 239, as is implicit in the Privy Council ruling in *Lewis v. Hyde*.[71] It seems that this is a common law requirement that has survived the statutory formulation with regard to preferences and thereby operates to supplement the legislative provision. As before, an intention to prefer will be required, though such an intention will be inferred where the recipient of the preference was connected with the company (as defined by s.249). The test is slightly less onerous here in that it needs only to be shown that the company was "influenced" by a desire to produce a preferential effect. The former requirement of an intention to prefer has been replaced with a requirement that the company which gave the preference was "influenced in deciding to give it by a desire to produce" the preferential effect. Such a desire will be presumed where the beneficiary of the preference was connected with the company (as defined by section 249). The introduction of this presumption of preference in the case of transactions entered into in favour of connected persons is beginning to have an impact. Thus in a series of decisions[72] the courts have found that payments made to directors within the prohibited period must be regarded as presumed preferences and the directors in question have been unable to rebut that presumption. An act can be a preference for the purpose of these provisions even if it was done, or allowed to be done, under a court order.

---

[70] *The Times*, March 30, 1999.
[71] [1998] 1 W.L.R. 94.
[72] See *Weisgard v. Pilkington* [1995] B.C.C. 1108, *Re Exchange Travel* [1996] 2 B.C.L.C. 524, *Re Corfe Joinery Ltd* [1997] B.C.C. 511, *Re Agriplant Ltd* [1997] B.C.C. 842, *Re Barton Manufacturing Ltd* [1998] B.C.C. 827 and *Re Brian D Pierson Contractors Ltd* [1999] B.C.C. 26. But the presumption is rebuttable—see *Re Beacon Leisure* [1990] B.C.C. 213 and *Re Fairway Magazines Ltd* [1992] B.C.C. 924.

Intent and desire

11-38 The early hopes that this reformulation might lead to increased usage in practice have been severely dented by the judgment of Millett J. in *Re M.C. Bacon Ltd.*[73] Here, after warning of the dangers of resurrecting authorities decided under the fraudulent preference provision, the learned judge held that in order to invoke section 239 it was still necessary to establish that the act was influenced by some desire to prefer. "Desire was a subjective concept, and if all the directors were seeking to do when granting security to a creditor was to buy time for their company, then, even though they realised that they were preferring the said creditor, that in itself did not establish "desire". In this respect section 239 is narrower than its predecessor; actions which are intended are not necessarily desired. Section 239 has increased the range of transactions which are open to attack as preferences, as the example on page 205 shows, but has merely substituted a new burden for an old one as regards the liquidator's burden of proof. The radical solution would be to make all transactions voidable if they take place at a relevant time and have preferential effect, regardless of intention or desire.

"Onset of insolvency"

11-39 Transactions are prima facie vulnerable if they were carried out within the periods specified in section 240(1), which are measured from "the onset of insolvency." This phrase is defined by section 241(3) to mean (in effect) the date of a resolution for voluntary winding-up, or the date of presentation of a petition on which a winding-up order is eventually made. The basic period of vulnerability for preferences is six months ending with the onset of insolvency (section 241(1)(*b*)). However this is extended by section 240(1)(*a*) to two years in the cases of preferences given to persons connected with the company,[74] and transactions with anybody at an undervalue—this seems reasonable as the recipient will invariably be a connected person. A further extension is provided by section 240(1)(*c*) to protect the period between the presentation of a petition for an administration order and the making of the order. Transactions occurring within the periods mentioned above can only be set aside if the company was unable to pay its debts (within the extended meaning given by section 123) when the transaction took place or became so as a result of the transaction. However, where the beneficiary is connected with the company, the onus will, by virtue of section 240(2) be on him to show that the company was not insolvent at the time in issue.

11-40 If a transaction satisfied the above criteria, who may challenge it?[75] According to sections 238 and 239, office holders may take advantage of this facility. However, there is a trap to be avoided here. It is clear from section 238(1) that the term "office holder" is restricted in this context to liquidators and administrators, and does not carry the wider meaning attributed to it by section 230 of the Act—*i.e.* neither administrative receivers nor provisional liquidators can exploit sections 238–41.

---

[73] [1991] Ch. 127. See also *Re Ledingham-Smith* [1993] B.C.L.C. 635.

[74] The issue of whether a person is connected with the company or is an associate can get technical. For a good illustration of this issue in the context of a failed preference action see *Re Thirty Eight Building Ltd* [1999] B.P.I.R. 620 where the failure to establish the necessary connection meant that the transaction in question fell outside the period of challenge.

[75] Action can be taken even though the defendant is resident abroad—*Re Paramount Airways* [1992] 3 W.L.R. 690.

Options open to the court

11-41 Where an action is brought under these provisions, what options are open to the court? It is apparent that the court enjoys general discretion[76] in order to retrieve the status quo, but some particular examples of the avenues open to it are listed in section 241(1). Special protection is afforded by section 241(2) to persons dealing in good faith, for value, and without notice of the relevant circumstances (as defined by subsection (3)), but it does not extend to persons dealing with the company nor parties to "the transaction" under attack. The Insolvency (No. 2) Act 1994 makes certain amendments to the power of the court to deal with the consequences of a breach of the aforementioned provisions. This short piece of legislation is designed to reassure bona fide third parties[77] who take a transfer of property after July 26, 1994 which earlier up the chain may have been part of a transaction susceptible to avoidance under ss.238 or 239. Provided the transfer was taken in good faith and for value the title cannot be impugned.[78] As far as the authors are aware this new legislation has not attracted judicial attention since its enactment.

11-42 An example drawn from practice will serve to illustrate the very different workings of the new and the old regime.

EXAMPLE

11-43 Suppose an insolvent company has an overdraft which has been personally guaranteed by the directors. The bank has a valid fixed charge on book debts, but the debts are insufficient to cover the overdraft. There is a floating charge on other assets. Debts due to preferential creditors exceed the value of the floating charge assets.

11-44 The directors arrange for a professional valuation of (say) the plant and machinery. They then enter into an agreement with a third party—say a company controlled by the directors or their nominees—whereby the insolvent company agrees to sell those assets at the valuation at a future date. The insolvent company then goes into creditors' voluntary liquidation.

11-45 Clearly the effect of the transaction is to convert assets which are either free of any charge or subject only to a floating charge into a book debt, which is within the bank's fixed charge. On liquidation the liquidator is bound to account to the bank for the amount received from the third party.

11-46 It was very uncertain whether this familiar ploy could be set aside by the liquidator under section 615 of the Companies Act 1985. That section applied only to voidable preferences as defined by section 44 of the Bankruptcy Act 1914, *i.e.* to "every payment made . . . by (an insolvent) in favour of any creditor" with an intent to prefer. It is very doubtful whether an agreement to sell assets at a fair valuation to a third party could be said to be a transaction "in favour of" the bank. It is doubtful even whether it was "in favour" the guarantors, where they controlled the third party. The onus was on the liquidator to prove an intention to prefer.

---

[76] A Mareva injunction is available to preserve the status quo pending trial—*Aiglon and l'Aiglon S.A. v. Gau Shan Co.* [1993] 1 Lloyds Rep. 164.

[77] Apparently, prior to the passage of this legislation insurance was being taken out to guard against this risk.

[78] In such a case the office holder who becomes aware of the suspect transaction will more than likely bring a personal claim against the directors responsible seeking compensation for misfeasance.

Prima facie voidable

11-47 It seems clear, however, that this type of transaction would be prima facie voidable as a section 239 preference. Both the bank (a creditor) and the directors (guarantors) are put in a better position than they would have been in if the sale had not been made. It will be presumed under section 239(6) that the company was influenced by a desire to prefer the directors unless the contrary is shown. The court can revest the assets sold in the company (s.241(1)(*a*)) or recover the proceeds of their sale (s.241(1)(*d*)). It may be that the court will leave the transaction alone, and merely release the bank's fixed charge over the book debt under section 241(1)(*c*).

11-48 Even if the third party to whom the assets are sold is a truly independent outsider acting in good faith the transaction is still vulnerable under the new rules. The saving provisions in favour of such persons in section 241(2) do not apply to a party to the transaction. However, in such a case the directors may be able to show that they were not influenced by the requisite desire. Suppose the company has the benefit of substantial contracts which it may be impracticable for a liquidator to carry out. The directors know that the company will have to go into insolvent liquidation. Before that happens competitors might be prepared to pay something for the contracts, whereas afterwards they might hope to pick them up for nothing.

11-49 In these circumstances the directors have a duty under s.214 of the Insolvency Act 1986 to take every step to minimise the loss to creditors and sell the contracts with the other assets as best they may; the preference is incidental.

Fruits of the action

11-50 If a transaction at an undervalue or a preference is set aside under these new provisions, it would appear from the decision in *Re Yagerphone Ltd*[79] that any proceeds recovered either by the liquidator or administrator cannot be claimed by the secured creditors: rather, they are impressed with a statutory trust in favour of the unsecured creditors. In spite of some criticism this case was followed by Millett J. in *Re M.C. Bacon Ltd (No. 2)*.[80]

11-51 The practical considerations involved in the pursuit of a preference claim were reviewed by the Court of Appeal in *Katz v. McNally*.[81] Here office holders had instituted a preference action against the directors of a failed company in order to recoup payments made by the company to those directors shortly before the onset of insolvency. At first instance[82] it was held that these payments were indeed preferences contrary to section 239. On an appeal against this ruling the directors raised a number of additional procedural points. In particular, they objected to the way that the liquidator had been able to finance the action by securing funding from a major creditor (a company in the same group as the failed company) in return for a promise that that creditor would be allowed to recover its funding before the other creditors were paid out of any eventual proceeds. The cause of action was not assigned and control of the action remained vested with the office holder. The Court of Appeal[83]

[79] [1935] 1 Ch. 392. Followed in *Re Quality Camera Co. Pty Ltd* [1965] N.S.W.R. 1330 and *Re Masureik & Allan Pty Ltd* (1982) 6 A.C.L.R. 39. For discussion see (1997) 13 I.L. & P. 48.

[80] [1990] 3 W.L.R. 646. See also *Bibra Lake Holdings Pty Ltd v. Firmadoor Australia Pty Ltd* (1992) 7 A.C.S.R. 380.

[81] [1997] B.C.C. 784.

[82] [1996] 2 B.C.L.C. 524.

[83] *Supra.*

could find nothing objectionable with this arrangement. There was nothing champertous about the agreement, particularly as the funding party was a major creditor who had a legitimate interest in maximising recoveries.

Changes made in pre-1986 law

11-52 Bearing in mind the complex nature of the drafting of sections 238–41, perhaps a resumé is in order, with particular stress being laid on the changes that have been effected in the law.

(i) The time limit has been extended to two years to deal with transactions in favour of connected persons.

(ii) Modifications have been implemented to cater for the introduction of the administration order procedure.

(iii) A new, wider meaning has been attributed to the concept of insolvency.

(iv) The burden of proving insolvency is reversed where the beneficiary of the transaction or preference is connected with the company—*i.e.*, he must prove that the company was solvent at the time in question.

(v) The leading cases of *Sharp v. Jackson*[84] and *Peat v. Gresham Trust*[85] are no longer of general application, as the principles laid down in them have been partially eroded by the Insolvency Act 1986.

AVOIDANCE OF TRANSACTIONS AFTER WINDING-UP PETITIONS

11-53 The provisions considered above relate to transactions entered into by a company in the period prior to the commencement of the winding-up. However, other statutory invalidating mechanisms may be invoked in respect of transactions occurring in the interval between presentation of a winding-up petition and the making of the winding-up order by the court. We have explained in Chapter 6 that one of the great dangers facing an unsecured creditor of a company who has presented a winding-up petition against it is that the directors, realising that liquidation is inevitable, will attempt to dissipate its assets. The law affords some protection here, through the medium of a provisional liquidator (appointed under section 135 of the Insolvency Act 1986), who will take control of the company's assets out of the hands of its directors. In cases where no provisional liquidator is appointed, section 127 of the Insolvency Act 1986, which repeats a well established provision in company law, may offer the last line of defence:[86]

> "In a winding up by the court, any disposition of the company's property, and any transfer of shares, or alteration in the status of the company's members, made after the commencement of the winding up is, unless the court otherwise orders, void."

---

[84] [1899] A.C. 419.

[85] [1934] A.C. 252.

[86] This provision is in addition to the rules on preferences, etc. In other words, these avoidance mechnisms are cumulative—*Re Omnico Ltd* (1976) 1 A.C.L.R. 381.

Disposition of property

11-54 For present purposes, the key phrase is "any disposition of the company's property." It is clear that this phrase will embrace the sale of company property, the repayment of debts,[87] payments out of its bank account,[88] the grant of security or payments for goods supplied.[89] However, it seems that it does not cover the situation where a chargee enforces his security in the period in question by appointing a receiver, nor where the receiver realises company property in order to raise money to pay the debenture holder. This was certainly the view of Goulding J. in *Sowman v. David Samuel Trust Ltd*,[90] and this approach has been adopted more recently in Australia in *Re Margart Pty Ltd*.[91] However, a transfer of property under a court order may well be viewed as a disposition.[92]

11-55 The fact that a disposition in breach of section 127 is void exercised the mind of the court in *Mond v. Hammond Suddards*.[93] Here it was argued successfully before Judge Kolbert that as the disposition is void the property in question is deemed never to have left the ownership of the company and therefore can be claimed by a creditor enjoying security over the assets. In this sense a successful claim under section 127 produces consequences that are abnormal in that these recoveries are not held exclusively for the benefit of unsecured creditors. In spite of some raised eyebrows this conclusion has attracted support in Australia.[94]

11-56 If a transaction falls within the ambit of section 127, it is void unless the court decides to validate it. Under what circumstances might the court be prepared to grant such a dispensation?[95] It has been held that the grant of security in order to obtain finance to maintain the company's business in the period after the petition may well justify the court intervening to waive section 127,[96] as may the grant of a charge in return for money to pay employees' wages.[97] The power is often exercised in practice where a petition on the "just and equitable" ground under section 122(1)(*g*) cannot for some reason be heard at once, but is less common in insolvency cases.[98]

Avoidance of executions

11-57 Another provision which is relevant to the period between the presentation of the winding-up petition and the making of the order is section 128, which

---

[87] *Re Leslie Engineers Co. Ltd* [1976] 1 W.L.R. 292. *Re Ashmark Ltd (No. 1)* [1990] 2 I.R. 10. See Chap. 6 here.

[88] *Re Gray's Inn Construction Co. Ltd* [1980] 1 W.L.R. 711. Drawing a cheque is not a disposition—this occurs when the cheque is paid—*Re Ashmark Ltd (No. 2)* [1990] I.L.R.M. 455. Payments into the company's account are not covered—*Re Barn Crown Ltd* [1994] 2 B.C.L.C. 186.

[89] *Re Civil Service and General Store Ltd* (1887) 57 L.J. Ch. 119.

[90] [1978] 1 W.L.R. 22.

[91] [1985] B.C.L.C. 314. See also *Re French's Wine Bar Ltd* (1987) 3 B.C.C. 173 where it was held that there is no disposition of property unless the company is beneficially entitled to the asset in question.

[92] See here the bankruptcy case of *Re Flint* [1992] 3 W.L.R. 537.

[93] [1996] 2 B.C.L.C. 470. For later proceedings see *The Times*, June 18, 1999.

[94] *Bayley v. National Australia Bank* (1995) 16 A.C.S.R. 38 and *Campbell v. Michael Mount* (1995) 16 A.C.S.R. 296.

[95] The general aim of the court seems to be to prevent the sudden paralysis of the business which would benefit no one. See Cairns L.J. in *Re Wiltshire Iron Co.* (1868) L.R. 3 Ch. App. 443 at 447. See generally *Re Tramway Building Co. Ltd* [1987] B.C.L.C. 632, *Re Fairway Graphics Ltd* [1991] B.C.L.C. 468.

[96] *Re Steane's (Bournemouth) Ltd* [1950] 1 All E.R. 21. *Denney v. John Hudson & Co. Ltd* [1992] B.C.C. 503.

[97] *Re Park Ward & Co. Ltd* [1926] Ch. 828.

[98] See Chap. 6 again here.

avoids any execution against the company's assets, etc., put into effect during this period. The scope for such an execution these days is limited because it follows from the House of Lords decision in *Roberts Petroleum v. Kenny*[99] that if the company is insolvent, and on the verge of liquidation, the court will not lend its assistance to any execution process.

MISCELLANEOUS AVOIDANCE PROVISIONS

Extortionate credit bargain

11-58 In practice, most attempts to avoid security, etc., will rest on non-registration or invalidation under sections 127, 238–241 or 245. However, there are other options to note. Thus, under section 244, where the company has entered into an extortionate credit bargain, an office holder may apply to the court to have its terms varied, or indeed, to have the transaction set aside.[1] An extortionate credit bargain is defined by section 244(3) to cover a credit transaction where

> "(a) the terms are or were such as to require grossly exorbitant payments to be made (whether unconditionally or in certain contingencies) in respect of the provision of the credit, or
> (b) it otherwise grossly contravened ordinary principles of fair dealing
>
> and it shall be presumed, unless the contrary is proved, that a transaction with respect to which an application is made under this section is or, as the case may be, was extortionate."[2]

Furthermore, office holders (which for these purposes includes liquidators, administrators and provisional liquidators, but not administrative receivers) can use section 246 to recover possession of the company's books where they have been made the subject of a lien, etc.

General avoidance provision

11-59 Finally, the general provision in the Insolvency Act 1986 dealing with the avoidance of transactions at an undervalue on corporate or personal insolvency must not be forgotten. This is section 423, which is derived from section 172 of the Law of Property Act 1925, and, indeed, can trace its origins back much further. The main attraction of section 423 of the Insolvency Act 1986 is that, unlike sections 238–41 of the 1986 Act, it imposes no time limits on the invalidation process. This can be crucial, bearing in mind the aptitude of some directors to stave off liquidation in order to "protect" certain dubious transactions. For these purposes, a transaction at an undervalue covers gifts, or arrangements where the consideration to be received by the company is significantly less than the value of the consideration provided by it. If a transaction can be so characterised, it can be challenged under section 423,

---

[99] [1983] 2 W.L.R. 305.

[1] This provision is modelled on ss.137–9 of the Consumer Credit Act 1974, which did not apply to corporate debtors—see s.189.

[2] For some instructive authorities on the meaning of "extortionate" in this context see *Ketley v. Scott* [1981] I.C.R. 241, *Wills v. Woods* (1984) 128 S.J. 222 and *Davies v. Directloans Ltd* [1986] 1 W.L.R. 823.

provided it can be established that it was entered into with the intention of putting assets outside the reach of potential applicants under section 423 or prejudicing their interests. All that is required is that the dominant intention behind the transaction was improper; the fact that there might be other subsidiary motives that are unimpeachable is irrelevant.[3] The range of applicants for a section 423 order is wide—it covers liquidators, administrators, supervisors of voluntary arrangements and "victims" (persons capable of being prejudiced by the transaction in question).[4]

11-60 The majority of successful section 423 cases are found in the arena of personal insolvency where transactions tend to be less complicated and therefore more susceptible to unravelling.[5] However, section 423 can operate in a corporate context. In *Jyske Bank (Gibraltar) Ltd v. Spjeldnaes (No. 2)*[6] Evans-Lombe J. went to the lengths of giving it extra territorial effect to unravel a property transaction entered into in Ireland, a transaction that was linked to funds ultimately derived from a substantial commercial fraud.

11-61 In determining whether a transaction was entered into with an improper motive the court does have the power, as it indicated in *Barclays Bank v. Eustice*,[7] to set aside professional privilege and to examine correspondence between a client and his solicitor. This facility will greatly assist the process of transactional avoidance by enabling the court to gain a full insight into the motivation behind a suspect transaction.

11-62 Where an application is made to court under section 423, the court enjoys general discretion to restore the status quo[8] and to protect the interests of "victims." Possible courses of action are mapped out by subsection (1) The operation of these provisions was considered in *Chohan v. Saggar*.[9] Here it was held that the aim of a section 425 order was to try and restore the position as it was before the improper transaction occurred, though this aim might not be fully attainable as the rights of innocent third parties had to be taken into account. Partial invalidation of transactions might therefore be required. Protection is provided by subsection (2) for persons dealing bona fide with the company for value and without notice of a possible breach of section 423.

POSTSCRIPT

11-63 Where transactions avoidable under the rules discussed above arise from the deliberate acts of the directors, the company is often very short of assets by the

---

[3] *Chohan v. Saggar* [1992] B.C.C. 306. See also *Arbuthnot Leasing International v. Havelet Leasing Ltd (No. 2)* [1990] B.C.C. 636 where Scott J. held that simply because the transaction was entered into on legal advice does not place it beyond the purview of s.423.

[4] A creditor can be a victim—See *Re Ayala Holdings Ltd* [1993] B.C.L.C. 256.

[5] See for example *Chohan v. Saggar* [1994] B.C.L.C. 706, *AMC v. Woodward* [1994] B.C.C. 688, *Moon v. Franklin* [1996] B.P.I.R. 288.

[6] [1999] B.P.I.R. 525—in earlier proceedings in this case (see *The Times*, October 10, 1998) it was indicated that an application under section 423 does not technically constitute a form of "insolvency proceedings" under Insolvency Rules 1986, rule 13.7 as the provision can be invoked in non insolvency cases. The provision was invoked without success in the following "commercial" cases—*National Bank of Kuwait v. Menzies* [1994] 2 B.C.L.C. 306 and *Pinewood Joinery v. Starelm Properties* [1994] 2 B.C.L.C. 412. The commercial potential of s.423 is not always recognised—see *Ogowewo* [1999] Insolvency Lawyer 106.

[7] [1995] 1 W.L.R. 1238.

[8] A Mareva injunction can be granted as pre-trial relief—*Aiglon and l'Aiglon S.A. v. Gau Shan* Co. [1993] 1 Lloyds Rep. 164.

[9] [1994] B.C.C. 134. For earlier proceedings in this case see [1992] B.C.C. 306.

time the liquidator is appointed. In practice therefore the liquidator may not be in a position to avail himself of the sections unless someone is willing to finance the litigation.[10] Very often the only creditors likely to benefit will be the preferential creditors—invariably Government departments. Unfortunately it has usually been impossible in the past to persuade preferential creditors to take any interest in the matter, even in clear cases where the probable benefit to them is substantial.

[10] These funding issues have been fully outlined above at para. 1–30 *et seq*. For empirical research on the practical difficulties faced by insolvency practitioners wishing to pursue avoidance proceedings see Milman and Parry, "A Study of the Operation of Transactional Avoidance Mechanisms in Corporate Insolvency Practice" (ILA Research Report, 1998) (GTI Publishing).

CHAPTER 12

Directors of Insolvent Companies

12-01 The aim of this Chapter is to consider the position of a director whose company goes into administration, liquidation or receivership. What are the immediate consequences in terms of his managerial responsibilities and continued employment? Will he have to answer in any way for his conduct as a director? Might he be liable for his company's debts?

MANAGERIAL RESPONSIBILITIES: NEGATIVE ASPECTS

Receivership

12-02 Where a company goes into receivership, the directors' managerial powers as directors (as distinct from any contractual functions they have as employees) are, for the most part, suspended. In effect the directors become *functus officio*. As a general rule, they have no control over the receiver, but, rather, they must obey his instructions, as was emphasised in *Meigh v. Wickenden*.[1] However, it may be that they retain some powers in relation to the company. In *Newhart Developments Ltd v. Cooperative Commercial Bank Ltd*,[2] it was held that after the appointment of a receiver the directors retain the power to bring actions in the name of the company, provided such litigation does not interfere with the conduct of the receivership. Here, the directors were permitted to bring an action for breach of contract against the bank which had appointed the receiver. This decision has had a mixed reception, particularly in Scotland,[3] but it appears to have been confirmed and indeed taken further by Peter Gibson J. in *Watts v. Midland Bank*,[4] where it was accepted in principle that directors might bring a derivative action against the receiver himself. On the other hand, in *Gomba Holdings Ltd v. Homan*,[5] Hoffmann J. refused to accept the possibility of a general diarchy over the assets of a company in receivership. This issue was most recently reviewed in *Tudor Grange Holdings*

---

[1] [1942] 2 K.B. 160. See also *Re Emmadart Ltd* [1979] Ch. 540 at 544 *per* Brightman J. The directors certainly lose their powers if the receiver is appointed by the court—*Federal Business Development Bank v. Shearwater Marine* (1979) 102 D.L.R. (3d) 257. A receiver does not need the permission of the directors before exercising his powers—*Re Scottish Properties Pty. Ltd* (1977) 2 A.C.L.R. 264.

[2] [1978] 2 W.L.R. 636. For instructive reviews see *Doyle* (1996) 17 Co. Law 131 and *Hemsworth* [1999] Insolvency Lawyer 92.

[3] See, for example, *Imperial Hotel (Aberdeen) Ltd v. Vaux Breweries* 1978 S.L.T. 113. But see *Taylor Petitioner* 1982 S.L.T. 172 and *Ross v. Taylor* 1985 S.L.T. 387 for a more favourable reception. The *Newhart* case has been followed in the New Zealand Court of Appeal—see *Paramount Acceptance Co. Ltd v. Souster et alia* (1981) unreported, but noted in (1982) 3 Co. Law 46. In this case the directors were allowed to challenge both the debenture and the appointment of the receiver. For Irish support see *Lascomme v. U.D.T.* [1994] I.L.R.M. 227.

[4] [1986] B.C.L.C. 15.

[5] [1986] 1 W.L.R. 1301.

v. Citibank N.A.[6] In this case, Browne-Wilkinson V.-C. bluntly doubted the correctness of the Court of Appeal ruling in *Newhart (supra)*. He pointed out that the causes of action alleged by the directors on behalf of the company were the property of the company, and therefore formed part of the property charged to the appointing creditors, which the receivers had power to collect. He dismissed the argument that the receivers were in an invidious position as regards proceedings against the appointing creditor, on the basis that the receiver could always apply for directions under section 35 of the Insolvency Act 1986, and suggested that serious difficulties might arise as to who might have the conduct of any counterclaim by the appointing creditors. However, he was able to dispose of the case before him (which was an application by the secured creditor to strike out the directors' proceedings) on the merits, as there was no prospect of success on the facts.

12-03 Clearly, the Vice-Chancellor was right about the availability of section 35 to a receiver contemplating proceedings against his appointing creditor, and indeed, that section may be a welcome refuge if the receiver is beset by the aggrieved clamourings of directors and guarantors. Nevertheless, the receiver is likely to be a reluctant party to any such proceedings. He has a real, if not theoretical, conflict of interest, and it would be unfortunate if there were no independent remedy. There is no particular reason why the receiver should be better placed than interested directors and guarantors to pursue such a claim, or to defend a counterclaim—as any recovery will fall within the charge, he will not be prejudiced by it, regardless of who pursues it. If the company loses, the appointing creditor's claim for costs will be an unsecured claim against the company, which again will not concern the receiver or interfere with him in the realisation of the assets under his control. In any event, as the case makes clear, the director's claim will not normally be allowed without an indemnity in favour of the company (as opposed to security in favour of the defendants) from outside sources, in anticipation of any costs which might be awarded against it.

12-04 The issue of directors' residual powers in receivership is clearly far from being resolved.

Liquidation

12-05 The picture in the case of liquidation is rather clearer. Section 103 of the Insolvency Act 1986 emphasises that the powers of directors cease on the commencement of a voluntary liquidation. Although there is no statutory equivalent in the case of compulsory liquidation, there is a firm stream of authority to support the cessation of directors' powers.[7] In *Fowler v. Broads Patent Night Light Co. Ltd*[8] it was decided that the power to make calls on shareholders passes from the directors to the liquidator from the commencement of the winding-up.

12-06 Normally, a director would not lose his managerial powers merely because a petition has been presented for the winding-up of the company, but if the

---

[6] [1991] 3 W.L.R. 750. For an Irish attempt to reconcile the authorities here see *Lascomme Ltd v. U.D.T.* [1994] I.L.R.M. 227. See also *Independent Pension Trustee v. LAW Construction*, *The Times*, *Scots Law Report*, November 1, 1996.

[7] *Re Farrows Bank Ltd* [1921] 2 Ch. 162 at 173 *per* Lord Sterndale M.R. However, directors do retain the power to challenge the appointment—*Re Diamond Fuel Co.* (1879) 13 Ch.D. 400.

[8] [1893] 1 Ch. 724. *Re Country Traders Distributors Ltd* [1974] 2 N.S.W.L.R. 135 at 138.

petitioner has persuaded the court to appoint a provisional liquidator,[9] the provisional liquidator's powers (which are such as the court may confer on him under section 135(4) of the Insolvency Act 1986) will supersede those of the directors to the extent that they are inconsistent or co-extensive with them.

Administrators

12-07 The appointment of an administrator under Part II of the Insolvency Act 1986, has the effect of making the directors' powers exercisable only with the administrator's consent, in so far as they might otherwise interfere with his functions (s.14(4)). The administrator has an express power under section 14(2)(*a*) to appoint or remove directors.[10]

Duties of directors

12-08 Where a company is in receivership or liquidation (or an administration order has been granted), and there is an "office holder" within the meaning of section 230 of the Insolvency Act 1986 in charge of its affairs, the directors are, by virtue of section 235 of the Insolvency Act 1986, under a positive obligation to assist him in the performance of his duties. This matter has been discussed in Chapter 2. The directors' fiduciary duties continue in any kind of insolvency, despite the divestment or suspension of their powers.

12-09 A major responsibility facing company officers will be to prepare a statement of affairs for the administrator, receiver, or liquidator, under section 22, 47 or 131 of the Insolvency Act 1986. Although the Insolvency Rules make provision for an allowance to be made out of the assets for the expenses of preparation of the statement of affairs, the amount of the allowance is limited to what the office holder considers to be reasonable.[11] In the case of a liquidation, directors will also have to bear in mind that an insolvency practitioner will usually require a substantial deposit from them to cover the expenses of calling and advertising the statutory meetings at a time when there must be doubt as to whether the creditors will confirm the liquidator's appointment, and whether the company will prove to have sufficient uncharged assets to cover these expenses.

Right to employment

12-10 Turning to more personal matters, what effect does receivership or liquidation have on a director's right to employment and remuneration? First, it must be remembered that a company director is not *ipso facto* an employee of the company.[12] A director who cannot show that he has a contract of service will indeed be in a precarious position. If he cannot be regarded as an employee, he will enjoy no preferen-

[9] Insolvency Act 1986, s.135. For authority in favour of the cessation of directors' powers on the appointment of a provisional liquidator, see *Re Mawcon Ltd* [1969] 1 W.L.R. 78 at 82 *per* Pennycuick J. However, it is open to directors in such a case to instruct solicitors to oppose the winding-up order—*Re Union Accident Insurance Co. Ltd* [1972] 1 W.L.R. 640.

[10] Directors who interfere with an administrator can be liable for contempt—*Re Exchange Travel Holdings Ltd* [1991] B.C.L.C. 728.

[11] Insolvency Rules 1986, rr. 2.15, 3.7 and 4.38.

[12] A company director is not *ipso facto* an employee of the company—*Hutton v. West Cork Railway Co.* (1883) 23 Ch.D. 654 at 672 *per* Bowen L.J. See also *Parsons v. Parsons Ltd* [1979] I.R.L.R. 1117.

tial claim to unpaid salary,[13] nor will he be entitled to a redundancy payment. An executive director with a service contract making him an employee of the company will be in a much stronger position,[14] and it will not matter that he controls the company,[15] though even he will not be allowed to claim unpaid director's fees not amounting to salary as a preferential debt. The fact that the directors may have assented to the company going into receivership or liquidation will not jeopardise their rights as employees.[16]

Receivership

12-11 As a general rule, where a debenture holder appoints a receiver out of court to take control of the company's business and assets, the appointment does not terminate contracts of employment of company employees.[17] However, it can result in such termination[18] if the receiver deliberately dismisses an employee, or closes down the company's business, or if the employee's role becomes otiose with the appointment of the receiver and manager. This third possibility could well arise in the case of an employed managing director, who would surely be superfluous on the appointment of an administrative receiver. It was held in *Reid v. Explosives Co.*[19] that the appointment of a receiver by the court automatically terminates contracts of employment of company servants. Despite criticism,[20] this decision was cited with approval by the Court of Appeal in *Nicoll v. Cutts*.[21]

12-12 If a director is dismissed from employment, any claim for compensation he may have will normally have to be pursued against the assets of the insolvent company. A prescribed amount of any arrears of salary will be treated as a preferential debt,[22] this type of claim having survived the reduction in preferential claims by Part XII of the Insolvency Act 1986. Details of the payments that can be regarded as salary for this purpose will be found in Chapter 8.

12-13 A receiver who has offered the director of a new contract of employment, or has adopted his old contract of employment, will become personally liable under the contract. The rules governing adoption of contracts of employment (now contained in ss.37 and 44 of the Insolvency Act 1986) were specifically introduced to iron out the problems exposed by the case of *Nicoll v. Cutts*,[23] where it was held that the receiver was not personally liable to pay the salaries of company employees he had retained. It would appear from *Re Paramount Airways Ltd (No. 3)*,[24] a case on

---

[13] *Re Newspaper Proprietary Syndicate Ltd* [1900] 2 Ch. 349. In *Stakelum v. Canning* [1976] I.R. 314 a director was found to be an employee for the purposes of a preferential claim in spite of the lack of a formal service contract.

[14] *Re Beeton & Co. Ltd* [1913] 2 Ch. 279.

[15] *Lee v. Lee's Air Farming Ltd* [1961] A.C. 12.

[16] *Fowler v. Commercial Timber Co.* [1930] 2 K.B. 1, *Re T. N. Farrer Ltd* [1937] 1 Ch. 352 at 359.

[17] See Chap. 4.

[18] The following three exceptions to the general rule are derived from *Griffiths v. Secretary of State for Employment* [1973] 3 All E.R. 1184.

[19] (1887) 19 Q.B.D. 264.

[20] See the Australian decision of *International Harvester Export Co. v. International Harvester (Australia) Ltd* (1983) 7 A.C.L.R. 391.

[21] (1985) 1 B.C.C. 99, 427.

[22] The amount is prescribed by regulations made under para. 9 of Sched. 6 to the Insolvency Act 1986. The current maximum is £800 (Insolvency Proceedings (Monetary Limits) Order 1986 S.I. 1986 No. 1996).

[23] (1985) 1 B.C.C. 99, 427.

[24] Reported *sub nom. Powdrill v. Watson* [1995] 2 W.L.R. 312.

administrators but equally applicable to receivers, that it is not possible for an administrative receiver to adopt a contract of employment whilst excluding any personal liability thereunder. Liability can be excluded if bona fide new arrangements are made.

Liquidation

12-14 What is the position with regard to a director's contract of employment when his company goes into liquidation, as opposed to receivership? It was laid down in *Re General Rolling Stock Co., Chapman's Case*,[25] that the granting of a winding-up order automatically dismisses employees. The position in the case of voluntary liquidation is confused. There are judicial dicta in favour of automatic dismissal on the passing of the resolution for voluntary liquidation,[26] and dicta to the contrary.[27] Some judges reject a rigid rule either way, preferring a flexible approach geared to the circumstances of each individual case.[28] What is clear, however, is that where dismissal has occurred, it is open to the liquidator to re-engage the dismissed employee.[29] Where the liquidation of the company operates to dismiss the director before the end of a fixed term contract, or without the notice to which his contract entitles him, the dismissal will be wrongful at common law, and he will be entitled to damages for breach of contract.[30] The usual rules on mitigation apply.[31] An award of damages does not rank as a preferential debt,[32] and in practice the right to damages may well be worthless against an insolvent company, unless the director can exercise some right of set-off against money owed by him to the company or goods in his possession for sale on the company's behalf.[33] It may be more important to the director that if his dismissal is wrongful, he is released from his covenants under his contract of service.[34] An employee cannot claim compensation for unfair dismissal merely because his employer has gone into liquidation.[35]

PERSONAL LIABILITY OF DIRECTORS[36]

12-15 The general rule is that on corporate insolvency a director cannot be made liable for financial obligations which are essentially those of his company. Under the doctrine consecrated by the House of Lords in *Salomon v. Salomon & Co. Ltd*,[37] the company is a separate person which must meet its debts out of its own corporate assets. The conventional wisdom of a few years ago was to the effect that if the assets proved insufficient, an aggrieved third party could not pursue the

---

[25] (1866) L.R. 1 Eq. 346.
[26] *Fowler v. Commercial Timber Co. Ltd* [1930] 2 K.B. 1 at 6 *per* Greer L.J.
[27] *Midland Counties Bank v. Attwood* [1905] 1 Ch. 357.
[28] *Reigate v. Union Manufacturing Co.* [1918] 1 K.B. 592 at 606 *per* Scrutton L.J.
[29] *McDowall's Case* (1886) 32 Ch.D. 366.
[30] *General Billposting Co. v. Atkinson* [1909] A.C. 118. See also *Currie v. Consolidated Kent Collieries* [1906] 1 K.B. 134, *Cook v. "X" Chair Patents Co.* [1960] 1 W.L.R. 60. This assumes that the director can establish the existence of a contract of service—*Re T. N. Farrer Ltd* [1937] 1 Ch. 352.
[31] *Re Gramophone Records Ltd* [1930] W.N. 42.
[32] *Re Leeds 20th Century Decorators* [1962] C.L.Y. 365 (Pennycuick J.).
[33] *Rolls Razor v. Cox* [1967] 1 Q.B. 553. See Chap. 9 for set-off rights.
[34] *Measures Bros. Ltd v. Measures* [1910] 2 Ch. 248.
[35] *Fox Bros. Cloths Ltd v. Bryant* [1979] I.C.R. 64.
[36] For discussion see *Milman* (1992) 43 N.I.L.Q. 1.
[37] [1897] A.C. 22. Followed in *Rayner v. D.T.I.* [1990] 2 A.C. 418.

personal wealth of the company directors. This was unfortunate as well as galling for unsecured creditors, whose rights against the insolvent company were invariably worthless, although they could often see directors displaying substantial personal wealth while walking away from the company's ruin without a scratch, so to speak.

12-16 However, it became increasingly apparent that directors could, by one means or another, be made personally liable for corporate obligations. There was a clear trend in the common law to this effect, and the Insolvency Act 1986 contains a number of provisions which increased the risk of personal liability being imposed on company directors from then on. One crumb of comfort extended to company directors was the repeal of section 152(4) of the Social Security Act 1975, under which directors were personally liable for unpaid national insurance contributions collected by the company from employees' wages but not forwarded to the DHSS.

12-17 Unfortunately for company directors, however, government policy appears to have turned full circle and under the Social Security Act 1998 where a company becomes insolvent and is in default in payment of sums to the Contributions Agency those directors deemed responsible for the default can be made personally liable by the authorities for any shortfall. This reversion to the pre-1985 position is effected by section 64 of the 1998 Act (inserting section 121C into the Social Security Administration Act 1992), which took effect from April 6, 1999 (see Commencement Order No. 4, S.I. 1999 No. 526, c.10).

CONTRACTUAL LIABILITY

Assumption of personal responsibility

12-18 It is clear from cases such as *Henry Brown & Sons v. Smith*[38] that a company director is not generally liable on the contracts of the company. However, the position may be radically altered if he permits the impression to be created that he is somehow assuming personal responsibility for the performance of the contract. Thus, in *The Swan*,[39] it was held that, taking into account the overall circumstances of the case, and, in particular, the manner in which the contract had been signed, the director had assumed personal responsibility. Again, in *Rolfe Lubell & Co. v. Keith*,[40] a director was found to have undertaken personal responsibility for the honouring of a bill of exchange issued by his company. On the other hand, in the case of *Bondina Ltd v. Rollaway Shower Blinds Ltd*,[41] the Court of Appeal ruled that a company officer who signs a cheque bearing the printed name of the company without using the magic formula "for and on behalf of" to indicate that he is signing merely in a representative capacity, will not necessary incur personal liability under section 26(1) of the Bills of Exchange Act 1882.

---

[38] [1964] 2 Lloyd's Rep. 476.

[39] [1968] 1 Lloyd's Rep. 5. See also *Mitton, Butler, Priest & Co. v. Ross, The Times*, December 22, 1976.

[40] [1979] 1 All E.R. 860.

[41] [1986] 1 W.L.R. 517. The opposite conclusion was arrived at in the Canadian case of *Holtz v. Parkdale Refrigeration Ltd* (1981) 117 D.L.R. (3d) 185.

Error in company name

12-19 A rather similar type of liability can arise under section 349(4) of the Companies Act 1985. By that section, where a company officer signs a bill of exchange, promissory note, endorsement, cheque or order for money or goods[42] in which the company's name is not accurately and legibly mentioned, he will incur personal liability for payment if the company defaults. This is a foolish trap to fall into but it does ensnare a number of company directors each year. The courts are prepared to accept abbreviations like "Co.," or "Ltd," or "plc,"[43] but any other departure, no matter how slight, from the registered name of the company may trigger personal liability under section 349. A classic example is provided by the case of *Hendon v. Adelman*,[44] where an ampersand was missed out of the company's name, with disastrous consequences for the officer who had signed the cheque. Once section 349(4) entraps a company officer there is little that can be done to escape liability. In *Rafsanjani Pistachio Producers v. Reiss*[45] a novel attempt by directors to wriggle out of the consequences of a breach of section 349 by invoking the equitable remedy of rectification to modify the relevant documentation containing the erroneous reference to the company's name, was scotched by Potter J. The clear intention of Parliament was not to be frustrated by the courts' exercising of their equitable jurisdiction.

12-20 Section 349(4) can impose personal liability not merely on the officer who signs, but also on any officer who authorises the signing of a cheque, etc., on which the company's name is illegibly or inaccurately shown. It is not a prerequisite to liability that the officer signs in some representative capacity.[46] However, the Court of Appeal emphasised recently in *John Wilkes (Footwear) Ltd v. Lee International (Footwear) Ltd*[47] that the defendant in such a case must have been aware that the proper name of the company was not being used. The defendant was a director of a private company and authorised his son, a fellow director, to sign orders for goods. The company's name had been changed, but the son placed an order on stationery bearing the old name. The father was not aware that the old order forms were being used, and therefore was not liable under this provision. Moreover, the officer will not be liable under section 349(4) if the other party to the transaction was responsible for the error on the document with regard to the company's name. The Court of Appeal ruled in *Durham Fancy Goods Ltd v. Michael Jackson (Fancy Goods) Ltd*[48] that the company officer will be protected by the doctrine of estoppel in such circumstances.

---

[42] It would appear from the county court decision in *East Midlands Electricity Board v. Grantham* [1980] C.L.Y. 271 that an order for services is not covered by this provision.

[43] *Banque de L'Indochine et de Suez v. Euroseas Group Finance* [1981] 3 All E.R. 198. On the other hand, liability will arise where Ltd is omitted—*Penrose v. Martyr* (1858) E, B & E 499, *Atkins & Co. v. Wardle* (1890) 5 T.L.R. 734.

[44] (1973) 123 N.L.J. 859. To omit "Ltd" is equally disastrous—*Penrose v. Martyr* (1858) E, B & E 499, *Atkins & Co. v. Wardle* (1890) 5 T.L.R. 734, *Lindholst v. Fowler* [1988] B.C.L.C. 166, *Blum v. O.C.P. Repartition* [1988] B.C.L.C. 170. See also *Barber & Nicholls Ltd v. R. & G. Associates (London) Ltd* (1982) 132 N.L.J. 1076, where "London" was omitted from the company's name and liability therefore arose. Note also *B.A.B. v Parish* [1979] 2 Lloyd's Rep. 361. It is difficult to reconcile *Jenice Ltd v. Dan* [1993] B.C.L.C. 1349 with the aforementioned cases and its authority is open to question.

[45] [1990] B.C.C. 708.

[46] *Maxform SpA v. Mariani & Goodville Ltd* [1981] 2 Lloyd's Rep. 54.

[47] [1985] B.C.L.C. 444.

[48] [1968] 2 Q.B. 839. See *Griffin* [1997] J.B.L. 438.

Guarantees

12-21 It is of course very common for a company director expressly to underwrite obligations which are primarily those of the company. It is important here to note that so-called "letters of comfort" are not normally binding guarantees unless so drafted as to indicate that a legally binding obligation is being undertaken. The director's guarantee of the company's bank overdraft is the most common species of the guarantee genus.[49] It is standard practice for banks to demand such guarantees from directors of private companies seeking overdraft facilities. There is a trap to avoid here, which was graphically illustrated in *Goodman v. First National Finance Corporation Ltd.*[50] In that case a director of p.l.c. had guaranteed the company's overdraft. On leaving the company, he failed to obtain a release from his obligations as guarantor. It was held that he remained liable on the guarantee and, moreover, this liability extended to increases in the overdraft run up after his departure. Another danger commonly encountered with guarantees occurs in the context of a group of companies. Where a director of one of the companies in the group signs a guarantee of his company's indebtedness he must be careful to ensure that he is not guaranteeing the debts of the whole group, either directly or indirectly (because there is a network of cross guarantees within that group). This point was stressed by Brooke J. in *Bank of Scotland v. Wright.*[51]

TORTIOUS LIABILITY

Claim in negligence

12-22 There are two broad situations where a company director may be faced with a claim for damages alleging tortious behaviour on his part. One possibility is a claim in negligence by creditors of the company who have suffered financially in the wake of the company's collapse. It is clear from the judgment of Dillon L.J. in the Court of Appeal in *Multinational Gas and Petroleum Co. Ltd v. Multinational Gas and Petroleum Services Ltd*[52] that a director owes no duty of care to company creditors whilst the company is solvent. However, it would appear from Commonwealth authorities[53] that such a duty may arise if debts are incurred when the company is insolvent or nearly insolvent. This view found favour with Lord Templeman in *Winkworth v. Baron Developments:*[54]

---

[49] Guarantees can arise informally—see *Paulger v. Butland Industries* [1989] 3 N.Z.L.R. 549.

[50] [1983] B.C.L.C. 203. See also *N.H.B.C. v. Fraser* [1983] 1 All E.R. 1090 for an unusual case of liability arising under a guarantee, and *Calsil Ltd v. Seimon* (1983) 7 A.C.L.R. 418 for an abortive attempt to escape liability under a guarantee. For the liability of directors under a group cross guarantee see *Coghlan v. S.H. Lock (Australia) Ltd* (1987) 3 B.C.C. 183. See also *D.F.C. Financial Services v. Caffey* [1991] B.C.C. 218.

[51] [1990] B.C.C. 663.

[52] [1983] 3 W.L.R. 492 at 519. A similar point was made by Hobhouse J. in *Berg Sons & Co. v. Mervyn Hampton Adams* [1993] B.C.L.C. 1045 at 1066–7.

[53] *Walker v. Wimborne* (1976) 50 A.L.J.R. 446, *Nicholson v. Permakraft Ltd* (1985) 2 N.Z.C.L.C. 99, 264 and *Kinsela v. Russell Kinsela Pty. Ltd* (1986) 10 A.C.L.R. 215 and *Jeffree v. NCSC* (1989) 15 A.C.L.R. 217.

[54] [1986] 1 W.L.R. 1512 at 1516. It is interesting to compare the aforementioned judicial pronouncement with the more relaxed view of Dillon, L.J. in the *Multinational* case [1983] 2 All E.R. 563 only a few years earlier.

> "But a company owes a duty to its creditors, present and future. The company is not bound to pay off every debt as soon as it is incurred and the company is not obliged to avoid all ventures which involve an element of risk, but the company owes a duty to its creditors to keep its property inviolate and available for the repayment of its debts. . . . A duty is owed by the directors to the company and to the creditors of the company to ensure that the affairs of the company are properly administered and that its property is not dissipated or exploited for the benefit of the directors themselves to the prejudice of the creditors."

12-23 The Court of Appeal put this principle into practice in *West Mercia Safetywear v. Dodd*,[55] where misfeasance proceedings were successfully instituted by a liquidator against a director who had allowed corporate funds to be diverted for the benefit of a parent company notwithstanding instructions from the liquidator-elect that its remaining funds were not to be touched. This was held both to be a fraudulent preference of the parent and an act of misfeasance by the director. According to the Court of Appeal, the well established duty to act in the company's best interests encompasses the legitimate expectations of creditors to have corporate assets protected once the company has become insolvent. This protective attitude manifested itself in *Re Purpoint Ltd*[56] where Vinelott J. indicated that it was misfeasance for a director of a failing company to waste its dwindling resources on purchasing unnecessary assets. To be contrasted with this is the decision of Hoffmann J. in *Re Welfab Engineers Ltd*[57] where it was suggested that directors of an insolvent company would not necessarily be in breach of a duty to creditors in selling off assets (such as a factory) at a marginal undervalue if in so doing they were motivated by a desire to protect the jobs of employees who were to be re-engaged by that particular purchaser.[58]

Enforcement

12-24 Formerly, it was unclear[59] as to whether an individual creditor could exploit this principle, *e.g.* by taking advantage of misfeasance proceedings under section 212 of the Insolvency Act 1986. In *Yukong Line Ltd of Korea v. Rendsburg Investment Corp. of Liberia (No. 2)*[60] the position appears to have been clarified in favour of a restrictive interpretation of the new principle. Here Toulson J. refused to accept the possibility of a creditor invoking what was in essence a breach of a fiduciary duty owed to the company for his own personal benefit. Thus, even if directors are found to have broken their duty of good husbandry to creditors it will be the liquidator who initiates any proceedings for misfeasance. This approach is understandable in view of judicial concerns about the risks of multiplicity of actions, nevertheless for those commenta-

---

[55] [1988] B.C.L.C. 250.

[56] [1991] B.C.C. 121.

[57] [1990] B.C.L.C. 833. Had there been misfeasance Hoffmann J. indicated that he would have granted relief under s.727 of the Companies Act 1985.

[58] Directors are of course now obliged to have regard to employees' interests—see s.309 of the Companies Act 1985.

[59] For discussion of the problems raised by this development see *Riley* (1989) 10 Co. Law 87 and *Grantham* [1991] J.B.L. 1. For an Irish perspective see *MacCann* (1991) 2 I.L.T. 30 and *Linnane* (1995) 16 Co. Law 319. One obstacle which might prove fatal is the hardening of judicial attitudes towards actions designed to recover purely economic loss. For an indication of current judicial thinking in this context see *Nordic Oil Services Ltd v. Berman* 1993 S.L.T. 1164.

[60] [1998] 1 W.L.R. 294. For comment see *Ogowewo* [1999] *Insolvency Lawyer* 106.

tors who believed that the *West Mercia* case[61] represented a major advance in the law it does come as a disappointment. Any doubts which may have existed[62] as to whether the former provision covered acts of negligence must have been dispelled by the modified wording of section 212, which covers breaches of duty other than simply fiduciary duties. As to the question of who can claim the fruits of a successful misfeasance action, it seems clear that the normal result would be the award of a sum of money to swell the pool of company assets[63] and it is submitted that the wording of section 212 is not sufficiently elastic to leave open the possibility of direct payments to creditors.

Primary tortfeasor

12-25 A second type of liability can arise where prima facie the company was the primary tortfeasor. Normally, of course, it is pointless to pursue a claim for unliquidated damages in tort against an insolvent company, and generally the directors and members are not personally liable for the company's tort because they can hide behind the fiction of separate personality of the company.[64] However, it was made clear by the Court of Appeal recently in *Evans (C.) & Sons Ltd v. Spritebrand Ltd and Sullivan*,[65] that if a director authorises the commission of a tortious act, such as an infringement of copyright, he may incur personal liability for it.

12-26 A further instance where a company director was held personally responsible for a tort committed by his company was found in the case of *Mancetter Developments Ltd v. Garmanson Ltd et alia*.[66] Here, the defendant company went into occupation of a factory which had been leased by another company from the plaintiffs. The defendant company was not the lessee of the premises, though the plaintiffs accepted rent from it as negotiations for a lease were in progress. The factory contained various extractor fans and pipes which had become tenant's fixtures prior to the occupation of the defendant company. On leaving occupation of the factory, G., the sole director of the defendant company, ordered these fixtures to be removed, and, as a result, damage was done to the factory walls, etc. No lease had been granted, therefore the plaintiffs' claim was necessarily founded in tort. The Court of Appeal, by a majority decision, held that the failure to make good this damage constituted an act of waste for which the defendant company was liable. More importantly for our purposes, G., who had authorised the removal, was personally liable for the tort committed by the defendant company.

12-27 Another example of liability founded in tort arose more recently in *Thomas Saunders Partnership v. Harvey*[67] where a director, (who, in his efforts to secure business for his company had made statements about its products which turned out to be inaccurate), was held to have incurred liability either for negligent misstatement or in the tort of deceit. The fact that he made the relevant statements

---

[61] *Supra*.

[62] As reflected in *Re B. Johnson & Co. (Builders) Ltd.* [1955] 1 Ch. 634.

[63] Secured creditors can claim the benefit of proceeds of a misfeasance action—*Re Anglo Austrian Printing and Publishing Union Ltd* [1896] W.N. 4. For further discussion see *Milman* [1979] Conv. 138 at 142.

[64] *British Thomson-Houston Co. v. Sterling Accessories* [1924] 2 Ch. 33.

[65] [1985] 1 W.L.R. 317. See also *Rainham Chemical Works v. Belvedere Fish Guano Co.* [1921] 2 A.C. 465 at 476 *per* Lord Buckmaster, *Performing Right Society v. Ciryl Theatrical Syndicate* [1924] 1 K.B. 1 at 14–15 *per* Atkin L.J. This line of authority was followed in *Wah Tat Bank Ltd v. Chan Cheung Kum* [1975] A.C. 507 at 514–15 *per* Lord Salmon. For the most recent discussion of this subject see *P.L.G. Research Ltd v. Ardon International Ltd* [1993] F.S.R. 197.

[66] [1986] 2 W.L.R. 871. See also *Fairline Shipping Corp. v. Adamson* [1974] 2 All E.R. 967.

[67] (1990) 9 Trad. L.R. 78.

whilst acting in his capacity as a company director conferred no immunity in tort. These cases must all now be viewed in the light of the latest pronouncement from the House of Lords in *Williams v. Natural Life Health Foods*.[68] In this case M, the director of a "one man company", was sued personally for negligent misstatement in respect of information contained in the company's promotional literature. The company specialised in selling franchises to prospective franchisees and made much of M's personal expertise in such matters. The House of Lords, rejecting the majority view of the Court of Appeal, held that there was no evidence that M had personally vouched for the accuracy of such statements and therefore no duty of care arose. The disappointed franchisee was therefore left with a worthless claim against an insolvent company. In reaching this decision there is no doubt that the judges were influenced by policy considerations, and in particular the need to protect the advantages of limited liability for small entrepreneurs.

FRAUDULENT TRADING

12-28 It is, of course, open to Parliament to create exceptions to the general rule that a director is not responsible for the company's debts. A longstanding example applies where the director has been a party to fraudulent trading by the company. If fraudulent trading is proved, the director may have to compensate creditors who have been cheated. Criminal sanctions may also be imposed.

12-29 The concept of fraudulent trading has now been supplemented by the Insolvency Act 1986, which implemented the recommendation of the Cork Committee[69] that the new concept of wrongful trading should be introduced into the law to cover cases where no fraud has been committed, but creditors have suffered loss through the culpable incompetence of the company's officers.

Definition

12-30 Under what circumstances may a company officer be made personally liable for fraudulent trading? The answer is provided by section 213 of the Insolvency Act 1986, which provides:

> "(1) If in the course of the winding up of a company it appears that any business of the company has been carried on with intent to defraud creditors of the company or creditors of any other person, or for any fraudulent purpose, the following has effect.
>
> (2) The court, on the application of the liquidator may declare that any persons who were knowingly parties to the carrying on of the business in the manner above-mentioned are to be liable to make such contributions (if any) to the company's assets as the court thinks proper."

Case law

12-31 To understand the effect of this provision the practitioner must have recourse to the wealth of case law dealing with its statutory predecessors. Before

[68] [1998] 1 W.L.R. 830. For comment see *Grantham and Rickett* (1999) 62 M.L.R. 133.
[69] Cmnd. 8558 Chap. 44.

embarking on a survey, it has to be said that the judges have not been entirely consistent in their approach to fraudulent trading. Some judges view the provision as penal, and therefore feel obliged to interpret it conservatively. Others, (possibly inspired by a lack of sympathy for directors of insolvent companies) have relied on the general drafting of the provision, and have therefore extended its scope as far as it will legitimately go.[70]

12-32 It appears from *Re Maidstone Buildings Provisions Ltd*[71] that positive and active involvement in the fraudulent trading on the part of the officer concerned is a precondition to liability. Mere failure by the secretary/financial adviser to warn the other directors to cease trading will not suffice. This authority was reinforced recently by the decision of Deemster Luft in the Isle of Man High Court in *Re Peake and Hall Ltd*,[72] where it was held that the defendant, who was a director in a company that was effectively run by his parents, had not participated in the fraudulent trading. The fact that he had not carried out his responsibilities as a company director could be criticised, but did not render him liable for fraudulent trading.

12-33 On the other hand, it was decided by Templeman J. in *Re Gerald Cooper Chemicals Ltd*[73] that a single transaction designed to cheat an individual creditor can amount to fraudulent trading. This decision was recently followed by the Court of Appeal in *R. v. Lockwood*[74] though the proviso was added that the element of dishonesty must be established. These cases must be contrasted with the decision of Oliver J. in *Re Sarflax Ltd*,[75] where it was held that merely entering into a transaction intended to give one creditor an unfair preference over his fellows did not constitute fraudulent trading.

State of mind

12-34 The greatest difficulty associated with the concept of fraudulent trading has concerned the requisite state of mind of the officer in question. To put it in a nutshell, must he be aware that the company is trading fraudulently,[76] or is it sufficient that a reasonable man in his position would have drawn such a conclusion from the circumstances? The bulk of authority[77] has always favoured a subjective test (*i.e.* is concerned with the state of mind of the particular director and not some

---

[70] Authorities like *Re Maidstone Buildings Provisions Ltd* [1971] 3 All E.R. 363 and *Re Sarflax Ltd* [1979] Ch. 592 reflect the more conservative approach, whereas the more adventurous judicial spirits were behind the decisions in *Re Gerald Cooper Chemicals Ltd* [1978] Ch. 262 and *Re Cyona Distributors Ltd* [1967] Ch. 889.

[71] [1971] 3 All E.R. 363.

[72] 1985 P.C.C. 87.

[73] [1978] Ch. 262. See also the New Zealand authority of *Re Nimbus Trawling Co. Ltd* (1983) 1 N.Z.C.L.C. 98, 762 and the South African decision in *Gordon and Rennie v. Standard Merchant Bank* [1984] 2 S.A. 519. In the unreported decision of Oliver J. in *Re Murray-Watson Ltd*, (1977), the view was taken that a single transaction could not form the basis of fraudulent trading. However, this view was rejected by Templeman J. in *Re Gerald Cooper Chemicals (supra)* and, indeed, Oliver J. himself appeared to have second thoughts on the matter in *Re Sarflax Ltd* [1979] Ch. 592.

[74] [1986] Crim. L. Rev. 244. Fraudulent trading can also arise out of transactions that are not part of the normal business for that particular company—*Re Nimbus Trawling Co. Ltd* (1983) 1 N.Z.C.L.C. 99, 762. See also *R. v. Phillipou* (1989) 5 B.C.C. 665.

[75] [1979] Ch. 592. See also *Dorklerk Investments Pty. Ltd v. Bhyat* [1980] 1 S.A. 443, *Rossleigh Ltd v. Carlaw* (1985) 1 B.C.C. 99, 537.

[76] See *R. v. Miles* [1992] Crim. L. Rev. 657.

[77] See *Re Patrick & Lyon Ltd* [1933] Ch. 78, *Re William Leitch Brothers (No. 1)* [1932] Ch. 7, *Hardie v. Hanson* (1960) 105 C.L.R. 451, *Norcross Ltd v. Amos* (1981) 131 N.L.J. 1213, and *Rossleigh Ltd v. Carlaw* (1985) 1 B.C.C. 99, 537.

hypothetical counterpart). The mere fact of being a director of a company does not imply knowledge of any fraudulent trading. Despite this, some of the authorities suggest that fraudulent intention can be inferred from a combination of the defendant's knowledge that the company was insolvent plus a deliberate decision to continue trading. This line of authority appears to be supported by the wording of section 213(1) of the Insolvency Act 1986, but the matter has been relegated in importance with the advent of the objective concept of wrongful trading.

Courses of action open to court

12-35 Where fraudulent trading has been established, what courses of action are open to the court? Clearly, it can order a guilty director to contribute funds to the company's assets, to be distributed among its general creditors:[78] this is reinforced by section 213(2). Formerly, it appeared from the judgments of Lord Denning M.R. and Danckwerts L.J. in *Re Cyona Distributors Ltd*[79] that it could direct that compensatory payments be made to particular creditors who have been defrauded, though this possibility was doubted by Russell L.J. However, it now seems clear that this option has been ruled out by section 213(2) which only allows for contributions to be made to the company's assets. Indeed, individual creditors have lost their right to bring an action for fraudulent trading. A punitive or exemplary award against a director who has knowingly participated in fraudulent trading is also a possibility, as was recognised by Lord Denning M.R. in *Re Cyona Distributors*.[80]

12-36 Section 215 provides for ancillary orders to be made to facilitate the main aim of section 213. Thus, any liability imposed on a director for fraudulent trading can be made a charge on debts owed by the company to him or, indeed, it can be used to reduce any claim he may have against the company to a deferred claim.

WRONGFUL TRADING[81]

12-37 In view of the difficulty of proving the existence of fraudulent trading, in 1982 the Cork Committee[82] recommended the introduction of an additional form of personal liability aimed at the incompetent company director. This recommendation was implemented in English law by section 15 of the Insolvency Act 1985 (see now I.A. 1986 s.214), which created a new form of civil liability for directors. It was ironic that this long overdue change in the law came at a time when the courts were beginning to recognise that directors of a company in financial difficulties may owe a duty

---

[78] *Re William Leitch Brothers (No. 2)* [1933] Ch. 261.

[79] [1967] Ch. 889. But see a reconsideration of this issue by Lindsay J. in *Re Esal Commodities Ltd* [1993] B.C.C. 782.

[80] *ibid.*, at 902.

[81] For articles on wrongful trading see *Rajak* (1989) 139 N.L.J. 1458, *Goode* [1989] J.B.L. 436, *Oditah* [1990] L.M.C.L.Q. 205, *Prentice* (1990) 10 O.J.L.S. 265, *Cooke and Hicks* [1993] J.B.L. 338, *Williams and McGee* [1993] *Insolvency Lawyer* (February) 2. *Hoey* (1995) 11 I.L. & P. 50, Doyle [1996] 18 *Insolvency Lawyer* 10, *Cook* [1999] *Insolvency Lawyer* 99, *Schulte* (1999) 20 Co. Law 80.

[82] Cmnd. 8558 Chap. 44. It is interesting to note that in 1962 the Jenkins Committee recommended a somewhat similar concept, to be known as "reckless trading," as the basis for liability—see Comnd. 1749 para. 503. Reckless trading has been introduced in the Republic of Ireland and is now governed by s.138 of the Companies Act 1990. See *Flynn* (1991) 9 I.L.T. 186 and *McCormack*, "The New Companies Legislation," (1991) p. 211 *et seq.*

of care at common law to the company's creditors to preserve the dwindling assets of the company.

12-38 "Wrongful Trading" is the heading of section 214 of the Insolvency Act 1986. It is one of those pithy titles which passes a more or less definite notion into the popular conception of the law, but unfortunately has no particularly close connection with the subject matter it is supposed to cover. The section really imposes a kind of retrospective duty on the directors of a company which in fact goes into insolvent liquidation, to mitigate the loss occasioned to creditors. The section can be invoked only by the liquidator,[83] and requires the identification of a date on which the directors knew or ought to have known[84] that the insolvent liquidation was inevitable. From that date, directors who in fact failed to take every step which ought to have been taken to minimise the loss to creditors, can be ordered under section 214(3) to contribute personally to the assets.

12-39 The identification of the relevant date is in practice often an extremely difficult task. There are few situations in business which are intrinsically irreversible, and many in which there is good reason to suppose that quite heavy and prolonged losses can be recovered with interest if only the wherewithal can be found to survive the storm. Where a company has the backing of a parent company, or a financier such as a bank, which has been kept fully informed of the worsening trading situation, the directors may have no reason to suppose that there is even a remote possibility of insolvent liquidation, despite a long period of technical insolvency, until such time as that support is actually withdrawn. In a climate in which banks are under pressure to maintain support where they can, and a culture in which it is not customary to give warning of unwelcome decisions, the withdrawal of support often comes as a genuine surprise to the directors of the insolvent company, without any negligence on their part.

12-40 It seems from section 214(4) that "every step . . . as (sic) he ought to have taken" is roughly equivalent to "every step which could reasonably be regarded as open to him, knowing what he knew or in his position should have known," although the matter is not free from doubt.[85] The standard of competence expected of directors for this purpose is discussed further below. It is clear, however, that the duty to take steps applies to the directors individually, and not merely as a body. A director who objects to continuing trading, or to any other particular activity (or lack of it), cannot necessarily protect himself merely by resigning, and should at least ensure that his dissenting voice is heard and minuted at key board meetings. Presumably, he should also consider the steps open to him, perhaps as a creditor or shareholder of the company.

12-41 Depending on the nature of the company's business there may be a number of options open to the directors, including (of course) liquidation and a request to the bank for the appointment of a receiver. It could be, however, that a cessation of trading would merely crystallise and maximise the creditors' loss, and that

---

[83] A reading of *Nordic Oil Services Ltd v. Berman* 1993 S.L.T. 1164 may prove instructive here. In Ireland there are other permutations available as to potential prosecutors of a reckless trading action.

[84] The court clearly enjoys some power to "impute" knowledge; for example in *Re Produce Marketing Consortium Ltd (No. 2)* [1989] B.C.L.C. 520 directors were deemed to be in possession of information of which they would have been aware had the company's accounts been prepared on time.

[85] Apparently an attempt to introduce the word "reasonable" into the statutory provision as it went through the parliamentary process failed—see Sealy and Milman, *An Annotated Guide to the 1986 Insolvency Legislation*, 5th ed., at p. 248.

continued trading would be the better course, possibly in the context of an administration or voluntary arrangement. It may be necessary to protect customers paying advance deposits for goods and services to be supplied in the future.[86] The directors will need, and will probably be expected to seek and follow, suitable professional advice. The company's accountants and solicitors are likely to be the first port of call, but the conventional wisdom is that the directors should seek early advice from an insolvency practitioner, who may well act as a management consultant to a company in intensive care. Unfortunately there is no possibility of seeking the reassurance of an anticipatory declaration under section 727 of the Companies Act 1985.[87]

Objective test

12-42 In assessing standards of behaviour expected of directors, an objective test is imposed, though subjective factors are not entirely irrelevant, as section 214(4)(*b*) makes clear.[88] Section 214 provides in effect that what a director ought to know or do, is that which be known or done by a reasonably diligent person having not only that particular director's actual skill and knowledge, but also that skill and knowledge which a person doing his job may reasonably be expected to have. One suspects that subjective factors will be used by the courts to upgrade the required managerial standards rather than to dilute them. The significance of the legislative drift towards objectivity was stressed by Knox J. in *Re Produce Marketing Consortium Ltd (No. 1)*[89] in holding that the power to grant a judicial pardon under section 727 of the Companies Act 1985, which is largely governed by subjective criteria, is not appropriate in the objective climate of wrongful trading. The language of the two statutory provisions was essentially so different that it precluded them from operating in tandem.

12-43 An important departure from the old law is that inactivity is no longer an excuse when a director is being used for wrongful trading.[90] Thus, section 214(5) stresses the fact that for the purposes of setting the scope of the skill and knowledge imputed to a director under section 214(4), his job is to be regarded as including all functions entrusted to him, whether or not he was in fact carrying them out at the relevant time. Presumably, by applying this "functional" test, less exertion will be expected of a non-executive, though even such an appointee will be required to reach a certain minimum level of activity.[91]

12-44 An instructive illustration of the wrongful trading jurisdiction at work is provided by the recent High Court ruling in *Re Brian D Pierson Contractors Ltd*.[92] Here a golf construction company suffered a decline in its business fortunes in the

---

[86] By exploiting the type of trust recognised as effective in *Re Kayford Ltd* [1975] 1 W.L.R. 279.

[87] See *Re Produce Marketing Consortium Ltd (No. 1)* [1989] 1 W.L.R. 745 at 751 *per* Knox J. It is interesting to note that the Cork Committee favoured the availability of an anticiptory declaration on an application to the court in chambers—see Cmnd. 8558 para. 1798.

[88] See here *Norman v. Theodore Goddard* [1991] B.C.L.C. 1028.

[89] [1989] 1 W.L.R. 745. For a similar ruling based upon comparable provisions in New Zealand see *Vinyl Processors v. Cant* [1991] 2 N.Z.L.R. 416. In *Re D.K.G. Contractors Ltd* [1990] B.C.C. 903 the possibility in principle of using this relieving provision seems to have been accepted without argument, though it was found not to be of assistance on the facts.

[90] Thus we have a departure not merely from the law on fraudulent trading, but also from the old authorities on the duty of care owed by a director to his company.

[91] Such as the simple precaution of reading the documents one signs—*Dorchester Finance v. Stebbing* [1989] B.C.L.C. 498.

[92] [1999] B.C.C. 26.

1990s. To some extent this was due to adverse weather conditions, but there were also managerial shortcomings involving unwise investments and an inability to recognise the need for corrective action when difficulties arose. P controlled the company and his wife acted as director/secretary, though her role was rather limited. After a decline in fortunes for a few years the company went into liquidation in 1996 and the liquidator sought to recover from the directors a substantial sum by way of contribution to the company's assets. Therefore various claims were brought against them for misfeasance,[93] preferences[94] and wrongful trading. The former claims were for the most part established and the directors were ordered to pay compensation and to return money to the company where the payment to them by the company was found to be a preference. The wrongful trading claim also succeeded in that the judge concluded that the directors should have realised from the 1994 accounts that liquidation was inevitable and should therefore have taken steps to minimise loss to creditors. Simply to trade on in the hope that things would pick up was not good enough. Having said that the directors were not to be held liable for all of the subsequent losses suffered by creditors. Unusual weather conditions had played a part and there had been no solemn warnings from professional advisers to cease trading. The relative responsibilities of the directors did differ and the husband was ordered to bear 70% of the award. His wife could not hide behind section 727 of the Companies Act 1985, as the judicial pardon facility was not available in cases of wrongful trading. The wrongful trading award was for the most part not additional to the earlier awards in the case (for misfeasance and preference) because that would involve double counting.

Shadow directors

12-45 We have already seen that any person can in theory be sued for fraudulent trading.[95] On the other hand, wrongful trading only applies to directors (including former directors) and shadow directors (as defined by section 741(2) of the Companies Act 1985). However, the scope of the latter concept is so wide, encompassing any person with whose instructions the directors are accustomed to act (but not professional advisers), as to neutralise any real restriction on the scope of wrongful trading. Thus, in *Re A Company (005009 of 1987)*[96] Knox J. accepted that it was arguable in principle that a bank which was closely supervising a rescue for one of its debtor companies might be regarded as a shadow director. In practice it seems unlikely (particularly in view of this shot across the bows from Knox J.) that any bank would fall into this trap, though the possibility cannot be dismissed entirely. This uncertainty may have discouraged banks from mounting rescue operations. The issue of who might become a shadow director arose more recently in *Re Tasbian Ltd (No. 3)*,[97] a case involving disqualification proceedings. Here the Court of Appeal

[93] The allegation here was that one of the company's businesses had been sold off to the director's son at an undervalue and that bogus redundancy payments had been made to the son and son in law when they left the company. The latter allegation was not fully established. The wife here was able to secure some relief by relying on s.727 of the Companies Act 1985.

[94] The directors had repaid sums of money to themselves on the eve of liquidation. These sums represented funds which they had advanced to the company when it was in difficulty.

[95] See para. 12-28 above.

[96] [1989] B.C.L.C. 13.

[97] [1991] B.C.C. 435. The discussion of the Privy Council in *Kuwait Asia Bank v. National Mutual Life Nominees* [1990] 3 W.L.R. 297 is also instructive on this question, as is the case of *Re Peake and Hall Ltd* 1985 P.C.C. 87.

(confirming a ruling of Vinelott J.) indicated that on the facts of this particular case it was arguable that a management consultant installed by a major investor to oversee the management of the company might have become a *de facto* or shadow director. It should be noted here that the terms *de facto* director and shadow director refer to individuals fulfilling fundamentally different roles. In *Re Hydrodan (Corby) Ltd*[98] Millett J., in dealing with a wrongful trading action, made the point that a *de facto* director is a person purporting to act as director without having been appointed to that position, whereas a shadow director is someone exercising directorial influence whilst "lurking in the shadows". At the end of the day in that case Millett J. found that the liquidator of an insolvent subsidiary had failed to establish that the directors of its parent company were either *de facto* or shadow directors. Furthermore, it did not follow that directors of a parent company, which itself was a corporate director of a subsidiary, were themselves automatically directors of the subsidiary by virtue of their status within the parent.

Judicial guidance

12-46 It has to be said that section 214 of the Insolvency Act 1986 is drafted in somewhat obtuse terms. Statutory interpretation by the courts is therefore invaluable as a guide to practitioners trying to advise clients on the impact of this change in the law. How has this provision been interpreted by the courts in England? The leading case is the ruling of Knox J. in *Re Produce Marketing Consortium Ltd (No. 2)*.[99] Here a company had been slipping into insolvency over a number of years but the directors hoped that things would improve. In the later days of the company's life, accounts were not prepared on time and warnings from auditors were ignored. Knox J. had no difficulty in identifying this as a case of wrongful trading, and he ordered the directors to contribute some £75,000 to the company's assets. With regard to the advent of wrongful trading Knox J. commented:

> "It is evident that Parliament intended to widen the scope of the legislation under which directors who trade on when the company is insolvent may, in appropriate circumstances, be required to make a contribution to the assets of the company which, in practical terms, means its creditors."[1]

Thus, fraud or dishonesty was not a precondition of liability. Knox J. made the point that the directors must be deemed on the facts to have been aware that insolvent liquidation was inevitable. The fact that the accounts which would have indicated this were not available until later, due to delay in preparation, was no excuse for the directors.

12-47 Another significant decision is that of Vinelott J. in *Re Purpoint Ltd*.[2] Here a director of a printing company had presided over the collapse of its finances and had expended corporate funds on assets which it really did not need to continue its business. Once again the accounts were in a mess. In spite of the passing of a resolution in favour of voluntary liquidation, the business continued to trade for several

---

[98] [1994] B.C.C. 161.
[99] [1989] B.C.L.C. 520.
[1] *ibid.*, at 549.
[2] [1991] B.C.C. 121.

months thereafter. Again, the conclusion that this was a case of wrongful trading[3] was predictable. In calculating the quantum of the required contribution from the responsible director, Vinelott J. was unable to say with any real certainty when wrongful trading began—the accounts were in such disarray that he had selected his own "start date", the timing of which worked to the disadvantage of the contributing director.

12-48 The essence of the change in legal attitudes is encapsulated by the case of *Re D.K.G. Contractors Ltd.*[4] Here husband and wife directors of a groundworks company appeared to have operated the business with sublime disregard for the niceties of the Companies Act, and were ordered to make a contribution to its assets when it collapsed with debts approaching £500,000. It was accepted that they were not dishonest, but simply incompetent (or "hopelessly inadequate"). Judge Weeks Q.C. (sitting as a deputy judge of the High Court) indicated that in the new climate, every director should acquaint himself with the minimum standard of performance required by law, *i.e.* the keeping of proper books of account, or face the consequences when the company collapses.

Sanctions

12-49 As section 214(1) makes clear, the normal result of a successful action will be an order that the defendant director make a financial contribution to the insolvent company's assets. The court has complete discretion when making the award, though it should bear in mind that the jurisdiction to grant it is primarily compensatory rather than penal.[5] The question of the available sanctions for wrongful trading is also dealt with by section 215, which identifies examples of ancillary orders the court might wish to make (*e.g.* reducing a debt owned by the company to the contributor to deferred status). Moreover, in the poorly reported county court decision in *Re Fairmount Tours (Yorkshire) Ltd*[6] it was held that the court could reinforce the obligation to make a contribution by imposing a charge on the matrimonial home of the co-directors. The sanction of a contribution order represents an enduring claim against a director. It can be enforced against his estate in the event of the director dying prior to the case coming to trial, a point confirmed by the High Court in *Re Sherborne Associates Ltd.*[7] The question of limitation periods for the initiation of a wrongful trading action was addressed by the Court of Appeal in *Moore v. Gadd (Re Farmizer Products Ltd).*[8] In this case it was confirmed that the limitation period is of six years duration. Moreover, even if the claim is initiated within that period, the court retains discretion to strike it out if it is then prosecuted in a tardy manner.

---

[3] This case also involved a question of misfeasance—see above.
[4] [1990] B.C.C. 903.
[5] See *Re Produce Marketing Consortium Ltd (No. 2)* [1989] B.C.L.C. 520 at 553 *per* Knox J. There are some issues to be resolved on the question of the quantum of the contribution. Can an exemplary award be made, and can particular creditors be given preferential treatment? A perusal of the judgment of Vinelott J. in *Re Purpoint Ltd (supra)* would suggest that the answer to both questions is in the negative. In Ireland it would appear that an individual creditor might benefit directly from a reckless trading award.
[6] (1989) 6 Insolvency Law and Practice 184. For a detailed account of this case see *Doyle* [1996] 18 Insolvency Lawyer 10.
[7] [1995] B.C.C. 40.
[8] [1997] B.C.C. 655.

Fruits of the action

12-50 One issue not addressed directly by the statutory provision, is the question of who gets the benefit of a successful claim for wrongful trading? The common assumption[9] was that it would ensure for the benefit of the general unsecured creditors of the company, but this assumption was thrown into doubt by a statement from Knox J. in *Produce Marketing (No. 2)*[10] to the effect that the proceeds of such litigation could be claimed by a secured creditor having a floating charge over the company's assets. This comment has been greeted with some scepticism[11] and it would certainly seem to fly in the face of the philosophy behind the introduction of the idea of wrongful trading in the first place—*i.e.* to provide a mechanism to improve the prospects of unsecured creditors salvaging something from the wreck of the company. Indeed, in the later case of *Re M.C. Bacon Ltd (No. 2)*[12] Millett J. seemed to take the opposite view to that of Knox J. According to Millett J. (and in the opinion of the authors, this is the correct view) the proceeds of a wrongful trading action should be destined solely for the benefit of unsecured creditors.

12-51 One other issue that is not dealt with by the legislation concerns the funding of a wrongful trading action. It was held by Millett J. in *Re M.C. Bacon Ltd (No. 2)*[13] that the costs of an unsuccessful wrongful trading action cannot be regarded as expenses of the liquidation, and therefore, a liquidator should be cautious before embarking upon such litigation. It may be necessary to secure outside funding and this will only be forthcoming if the prospects of success are good.

12-52 In *Katz v. McNally*[14] (one further stage in the Exchange Travel litigation) the Court of Appeal indicated that it was not in agreement with Millett J. on this issue. Although the case dealt with funding a preference action the Court of Appeal expressed the view that were the liquidator to outlay funds to pursue such claims they might be considered as costs incurred in getting in assets.

12-53 The funding of wrongful trading actions came under the microscope once again in *Re Oasis Merchandising Services Ltd.*[15] Here a liquidator in order to finance a wrongful trading claim had agreed to sell the fruits of the action to a commercial firm specialising in offering litigation support. The liquidator agreed as part of his arrangement to accept instructions as to the pursuit of the claim from the financiers. The Court of Appeal held that such an arrangement could not be tolerated. A wrongful trading claim was vested exclusively by the legislation in the liquidator and could not be sold. Moreover it was contrary to public policy to allow an office holder to pursue litigation whilst acting under the instructions of a third party.

12-54 If the effect of the advent of wrongful trading is to make managers wary of taking "status" directorships and, (all too common in public companies) paper directorships for signing purposes only, that will be no bad thing. It is unlikely that a creditors' meeting (usually sprinkled, at least, with professional insolvency practi-

[9] This assumption is based on the outcome in *Re Yagerphone Ltd* [1935] Ch. 392 (a successful fraudulent preference recovery action).
[10] [1989] B.C.L.C. 520 at 554.
[11] See *Oditah* [1990] L.M.C.L.Q. 205 and *Wheeler* [1993] J.B.L. 256.
[12] [1990] B.C.L.C. 607 at 612–13.
[13] *Supra*. Followed by analogy in *Mand v. Hammond Suddards (No. 2)*, *The Times*, June 18, 1999.
[14] [1997] B.C.C. 784.
[15] [1997] 2 W.L.R. 764.

tioners representing creditors) will receive with much enthusiasm a director's statement that he was really only a director in name and did not attend board meetings.

12-55 Probably the quality of the advice available to directors will determine how quickly things change. It has been very common in the past for honest directors worried about the solvency of their companies to consult their auditors; the auditors normally played safe by advising an immediate cessation of business. In view of the wording of section 214(3), such advice can no longer be regarded as safe, although no doubt a cessation will, in some cases, be a proper step to take with a view to minimising creditors' losses.

12-56 It is commonplace these days for banks who have reason to doubt the stability of a corporate customer to appoint an insolvency practitioner to make a 24 or 48-hour appraisal of the situation before deciding whether to appoint a receiver. Directors anxious about whether they should continue to trade will often need a similar independent appraisal and will be well advised to take the same course.

MISFEASANCE

12-57 A company director may also be exposed to the threat of personal liability on a different front. If it can be shown that he has been in breach of duty to his company[16] which has since gone into liquidation, summary proceedings for misfeasance may be instituted against him under section 212 of the Insolvency Act 1986 by the liquidator, official receiver, or, indeed, any creditor[17] or contributory. The director, or any other officer, may be ordered to restore assets to the company or compensate it for the loss caused by his breach of duty.[18] Section 212 merely offers an effective facility for prosecuting a civil action against a company officer alleged to be in breach of duty; it does not of itself create a new cause of action.[19]

Forms of misfeasance

12-58 Let us consider some possible forms of misfeasance. It seems unclear on the existing authorities whether mere negligence can found the basis of a misfeasance action, though this is not out of the question in an age where the boundaries of professional negligence are being constantly extended.[20] Certainly the making of a

---

[16] It now seems that the word "company" may be sufficiently wide to encompass its creditors at large—see *West Mercia Safetywear v. Dodd* [1988] B.C.L.C. 250 and the discussion above at page 220. Even if this is so, it is doubtful if s.212 can be exploited by an individual creditor or other person having a contractual relationship with the company—see *Nordic Oil Services Ltd v. Berman* 1993 S.L.T. 1164 at 1172 *per* Lord Osborne.

[17] *Re Ayala Holdings Ltd* [1993] B.C.L.C. 256.

[18] It seems that debenture holders secured by a floating charge have first claim on the proceeds of a successful misfeasance action—*Re Anglo-Austrian Printing and Publishing Co.* [1895] Ch. 152, *Wood v. Woodhouse and Rawson United* [1896] W.N. 4, *Re Asiatic Electric Co. Pty. Ltd* (1970) W.N. (N.S.W.) 361.

[19] *Coventry and Dixon's Case* (1880) 14 Ch.D. 660. In *Re Etic Ltd* [1928] Ch. 861, Maugham J. held that proof of a breach of duty was an essential prerequisite to a misfeasance action. A misfeasance action is not subject to limitation periods but the general rules on striking out actions apply—*Re Latchford Construction* [1992] B.C.L.C. 265.

[20] *Re B. Johnson & Co. (Builders) Ltd* [1955] Ch. 634 supports the view that misfeasance proceedings are not available. See also *Re Day Nite Carriers Ltd* [1975] 1 N.Z.L.R. 172. However, in *Dorchester Finance v. Stebbing*, (1977) reported in [1989] B.C.L.C. 498, the fact that directors can be sued in negligence by their own company was confirmed. The rewording of s.212 to cover breaches of any duty may also support the view that negligence is now covered.

private profit in breach of fiduciary duty would be encompassed. Excessive drawing of directors' fees out of capital could fall within the ambit of misfeasance as was confirmed in *Re Halt Garage (1964) Ltd.*[21] Unlawful disposal of company property or wrongful payment of dividends could also constitute misfeasance.[22] Where several directors have been found guilty of misfeasance, the court enjoys complete discretion to apportion liability between them.[23]

Relief

12-59 If a director is sued on the grounds of misfeasance, he may be able to rely[24] on the Companies Act 1985, s.727(1):

> "If in any proceedings for negligence, default, breach of duty or breach of trust against an officer of a company or a person employed by a company as auditor (whether he is or is not an officer of the company) it appears to the court hearing the case that that officer or person is or may be liable in respect of the negligence, default, breach of duty or breach of trust, but that he has acted honestly and reasonably, and that having regard to all the circumstances of the case (including those connected with his appointment) he ought fairly to be excused for the negligence, default, breach of duty or breach of trust, that court may relieve him, either wholly or in part, from his liability on such terms as it thinks fit."

Indeed, it is clear from subsection (2) that such an officer may seek relief under this provision in anticipation of a misfeasance action being instituted against him. This is a useful facility and of some comfort for directors in these troubled times.

12-60 The use of section 727 was considered by Hoffmann J. in *Re Welfab Engineers Ltd.*[25] Here a company in financial difficulties was alleged to have sold off factory premises at an undervalue. Apparently the directors had received a number of offers for these premises and had opted for a bid that, although lower than some of the others, carried the bidder's promise to retain the services of company employees who worked at that particular factory. Hoffmann J. held that had this been proved to be a case of misfeasance he would certainly have excused the directors under section 727. The difference between the valuations of the various bids was small and the directors clearly had a duty to have regard to the interests of their employees (Companies Act 1985 section 309).

12-61 However, section 727 only offers relief where the wrong has been done to the company—it cannot be used as a shield to an action brought by one of the company's creditors. This point was stressed by the Court of Appeal in *Customs and*

---

[21] [1982] 3 All E.R. 1016. See also *Rance's case* (1871) 6 Ch. App. 104.

[22] *Re Park Gate Waggon Co.* (1881) 17 Ch.D. 234. An *ultra vires* transaction causing loss to the company would be similarly regarded—*Viscount of the Royal Court of Jersey v. Shelton* [1986] 1 W.L.R. 985. In this particular case, the directors escaped liability as Jersey company law contains no provision equivalent to s.310 of our Companies Act 1985. *Flitcroft's case* (1882) 21 Ch.D. 519, *Re National Bank of Wales* [1899] 2 Ch. 629.

[23] *Re Morecambe Bowling Ltd* [1969] 1 All E.R. 753.

[24] This does not have to be specifically pleaded—*Re Kirby's Coaches* [1991] B.C.C. 130.

[25] [1990] B.C.L.C. 833. A judicial pardon was also made available to a director in *Re D'Jan of London Ltd* [1993] B.C.C. 646 where a director's errors in checking an insurance proposal form had led to the policy being unenforceable and the company suffering an uninsured loss.

Excise v. Hedon Alpha Ltd,[26] where a director unsuccessfully petitioned the court for relief from liability for the company's unpaid betting duty.

12-62 Formerly only the court could relieve a director from liability for misfeasance. By virtue of section 310 of the Companies Act 1985 any provision contained either in the company's articles of association, or in any service contract, purporting to exempt a director from liabilityfor breach of duty to his company, is invalid. There is a limited exception as regards terms exempting a director from liability incurred (presumably for costs) in defending proceedings in which judgment is given in his favour or he is relieved by the court. The uncertainty that existed previously over whether section 310 outlawed insurance arrangements designed to indemnify directors from the consequences of breach of duty, has been resolved by section 137 of the Companies Act 1989 which introduces an amendment to make it clear that it is lawful for companies to take out such policies for their directors and to pay the premiums thereon. One other important loophole in the prohibition imposed by section 310 is that it does not prevent a third party from offering an indemnity to a director to cover breach of duty to the company.[27]

12-63 The normal limitation period for a misfeasance action would be six years though his would be extended in cases of fraud or breach of trust.

MISCELLANEOUS FORMS OF PERSONAL LIABILITY

12-64 Of the miscellaneous forms of personal liability, mention must be made of section 24 of the Companies Act 1985. This provision rendered a member liable for the company's debts if it had been allowed to carry on business for more than 6 months with fewer than 2 members. Section 24 was successfully invoked against a director who was a sole member in *Nisbet v. Shepherd*[28] but this was a rare example of its being used in practice. This provision has now been largely superseded with the advent of the Companies (Single Member Private Limited Companies) Regulations 1992 (S.I. 1992 No. 1699).

"Phoenix syndrome"

12-65 As a result of the Insolvency Act 1986 and the Company Directors Disqualification Act 1986, personal liability for the company's debts may now be imposed on a director in two new situations. First, personal liability may be imposed on a director who is in breach of sections 216 and 217 of the Insolvency Act 1986. These sections prohibit a director of a company which goes into insolvent liquidation from being involved, for the next five years, in the management of another company which uses either the name of the insolvent company or a name so similar as to suggest association with it. Presumably the many authorities on passing off actions would be relevant when considering whether a particular name suggests an association with another company. The same applies to a former director who left

[26] [1981] 2 W.L.R. 791. It is also not available on a wrongful trading action—*Re Produce Marketing Consortium Ltd (No. 1)* [1989] 1 W.L.R. 745. For a discussion of this statutory provision in New Zealand, see *Re Day Nite Carriers Ltd* [1975] 1 N.Z.L.R. 172.

[27] *Burgoine v. Waltham Forest LBC* [1997] B.C.C. 347—this is a curious case involving a company set up by a local authority.

[28] [1994] B.C.C. 91.

the company within 12 months of liquidation. The new law here seeks to curb the much-criticised "Phoenix syndrome." There are also criminal penalties which may be incurred for breach of this prohibition. The impact of section 216 was considered by Morritt J. in *Re Bonus Breaks Ltd.*[29] Here a director of a company named Bonus Breaks Ltd (which had gone into an insolvent liquidation) wished to be given leave to become a director of a successor company to be called Bonus Breaks Promotions Ltd. Leave was given, because there was no evidence that the director was at fault for the collapse of the first company, but this permission was only granted on condition that the new company did not buy back any of its shares for a two year period following its incorporation, unless the transactions were approved by an independent director.

12-66 A different approach to a section 216 leave application was adopted by the court in *Penrose v. Official Receiver.*[30] Here the directors of the failed company wished to open a new business using a similar name because there was substantial goodwill attached to that name. Leave was granted by Chadwick J. without any pre-conditions. There was no evidence that the directors in question were unfit or in any way responsible for the collapse of the first company. A similar relaxed approach was adopted in *Re Lightning Electrical Contractors Ltd*[31] where the fault for the collapse of the first company appears to have lain at the door of a co-director who was not a party to the leave application. On the basis of these authorities it is safe to assume that the courts will view leave applications in a sympathetic light, provided that the applicant could not be viewed as responsible for the corporate collapse. Having said that, if a director breaches the prohibition on name use without seeking leave the courts will take a very dim view.[32]

12-67 Secondly, section 15 of the Company Directors Disqualification Act 1986 states that a director who contravenes a disqualification order or who becomes involved in the management of a company despite being an undischarged bankrupt, will be jointly and severally liable, with the company, for debts incurred in the period in question. A director who acts, or is prepared to act, on the instructions of an undischarged bankrupt will be similarly liable—this will no doubt eventually eliminate the numerous companies apparently run by members of the families of undischarged bankrupts.

12-68 Personal liability can arise through many other avenues. There are circumstances where a director may be held liable for costs arising in connection with company litigation, even though that director is not formally a party to the said proceedings.[33] Where a company is found to have evaded VAT, a director who is deemed responsible for this default can be held personally accountable by virtue of section 61 of the VAT Act 1994.[34] Companies as employers are required to ensure that their

---

[29] [1991] B.C.C. 546.

[30] [1996] 1 B.C.L.C. 389.

[31] [1996] 2 B.C.L.C. 302.

[32] See *Thorne v. Silverleaf* [1994] B.C.C. 109 where a creditor was able to invoke section 216 to claim money from a director of a debtor company notwithstanding the fact that the creditor was aware of the statutory infringement. An overview of the issues raised in the above section is provided by the author in [1997] J.B.L. 234.

[33] Supreme Court Act 1981, s.51.

[34] See *Stevenson and Telford Building and Design Ltd v. Customs and Excise* [1996] S.T.C. 1096, *Customs and Excise v. Bassimeh* [1997] S.T.C. 33 and *First Indian Cavalry Club v. Customs and Excise* [1998] S.T.C. 293.

employees are properly insured.[35] Failure by the company to do this could result in the directors being made liable.[36]

CRIMINAL SANCTIONS AGAINST DIRECTORS OF INSOLVENT COMPANIES

12-69 A director of a company that goes into liquidation, administration or receivership may attract the attention of the criminal law in a number of ways.

Fraudulent trading

12-70 First, where fraudulent trading has occurred, criminal liability[37] will be imposed by section 458 of the Companies Act 1985. The test here is clearly subjective. It was decided in *R. v. Cox and Hedges*[38] that proof of dishonesty is required. The leading case is *R. v. Grantham*,[39] where the Court of Appeal ruled that the crime of fraudulent trading occurs where a director obtains goods or services on credit knowing the company does not have funds to pay for them. It is not a defence that the director believed that funds might become available at some time in the distant future. The so-called "Blue Skies Test" of Buckley J. in the well-known but unreported case of *Re White and Osmond (Parkstone) Ltd*[40] was rejected. It should be noted that the offence of fraudulent trading can be committed even though the company never goes into liquidation.

Insolvency offences

12-71 There are a number of well-established criminal offences now detailed by sections 206–211 of the Insolvency Act 1986, which may be committed by officers of insolvent companies. Thus, fraud within the 12 months prior to the commencement of the winding up is dealt with by section 206.[41] Transactions designed to defraud creditors are penalised by section 207. It is an offence under section 208 for an officer to conceal company property from the liquidator. Section 209 penalises officers who falsify the company's books, whereas section 210 of imposes criminal penalties upon company officers who make material omissions in any statement relating to the company's affairs. Finally, an officer who makes false representations to the company's creditors in order to secure their agreement with reference to the company's affairs or winding up, commits an offence under section 211. Criminal liability can also result from the breach of a disqualification order, as was indicated

---

[35] Employers' Liability (Compulsory Insurance) Act 1969.

[36] Compare here *Richardson v. Pitt-Stanley*, *The Times*, August 11, 1994 and *Quinn v. McGinty* [1998] Rep. L. Reps 107.

[37] The maximum penalty is seven years imprisonment. If the convicted person is a foreigner deportation may follow—*R. v. Kouyoumdjian* (1990) 12 Cr. App. Rep. (S) 35. A compensation order is also a possibility, but not if the defendant has been deprived of his livelihood as a result of being disqualified—*R. v. Holmes* (1992) 13 Cr. App. Rep. (S) 29. See also *R. v. Smith and Palk* [1997] 2 Cr. App. Rep. (5) 167 and *R. v. Thobani* [1998] 1 Cr. App. Rep. (5) 206.

[38] [1983] Crim. L. Rev. 167. See also *R. v. Miles* [1992] Crim. L. R. 657.

[39] [1984] 2 W.L.R. 815. See also *R. v. Smith* [1996] 2 B.C.L.C. 109—deceiving future creditors.

[40] (1960) unreported.

[41] See *R. v. Robinson* [1990] B.C.C. 656.

above, or from infringement of the prohibition (on the use of similar company names) contained in section 216 of the Insolvency Act 1986.[42]

Theft

12-72 Criminal liability may also arise for theft contrary to section 1 of the Theft Act 1968. In spite of the doubts raised in *R. v. Pearlberg*,[43] a company director who is also the majority shareholder can, in principle, steal from his own company. This was made clear by the Court of Appeal in the *Attorney-General's Reference (No. 2 of 1982)*,[44] which arose out of the *Pearlberg* case. It is, of course, difficult to prove dishonesty in such a case.

12-73 The Theft Acts 1968 and 1978 contain other offences which might apply, such as obtaining property by deception, contrary to section 15 of the Theft Act 1968, and obtaining services by deception in breach of section 1 of the Theft Act 1978.

Prosecution procedure

12-74 Where criminality on the part of company officers has become apparent during the course of the liquidation, sections 218 and 219 outline the mechanisms for pursuing the matter further. In a compulsory liquidation, where the liquidator discovers the possibility of criminal offences on the part of company officers, he must refer the matter to the Official Receiver. No guidance is given on the next stage of the reporting chain, though presumably the Official Receiver will have to notify the matter to the Director of Public Prosecutions. In the case of voluntary liquidation, the liquidator should make his report directly to the prosecuting authority, *i.e.*, the D.P.P. The D.P.P. can then refer the case to the Secretary of State who may appoint D.T.I. inspectors to investigate further.

---

[42] See *R. v. Cole* [1998] B.C.C. 87 where the court concluded that the offence in question was one of strict liability and therefore required no *mens rea*.

[43] [1982] Crim. L. R. 829.

[44] [1984] 2 W.L.R. 447.

CHAPTER 13

Disqualification of Directors

INTRODUCTION

13-01 English law adopts a policy of open access to limited liability. Few qualifications are imposed on company directors and there is no minimum share capital level fixed for private companies. The general rule is that a director whose company becomes insolvent is not automatically disqualified from being given the opportunity of a second chance.[1] The Insolvency Bill 1985 originally contained a provision (clause 7), which created an automatic disqualification for directors where the company went into insolvent compulsory liquidation, but this was dropped due to concerted opposition from persons (including Sir Kenneth Cork) who believed it was too draconian and indiscriminate.

13-02 However, there are exceptions to the general rule and these have been conveniently set out in a separate statute, the Company Directors Disqualification Act 1986.[2]

GROUNDS FOR DISQUALIFICATION

Indictable offence or fraud

13-03 Sections 2 and 4 of the Act provide that if the director has been convicted of any indictable offence connected with the company's formation or management, or appears guilty of fraud (including fraudulent trading) in respect of a company that has been wound up, a disqualification order for up to 15 years may be made. The courts, in recent years, have widely interpreted this ground for disqualification. Fraud committed either against the company itself or a third party will suffice. Such fraud may have occurred at any period during the birth, life or death of a limited

---

[1] If a director has been declared bankrupt, he is automatically disqualified—see Company Directors Disqualification Act 1986 ss.11 and 13. This ban can be lifted with leave of the court, though such leave is unlikely to be forthcoming—*Re McQuillan* (1989) 5 B.C.C. 137. The offence of acting as a director whilst an undischarged bankrupt is one of strict liability—see *R. v. Brockley* [1994] B.C.C. 131. For sentencing aspects, see *R. v. Young* [1990] B.C.C. 549, and *R. v. Theivendran* (1992) 13 Cr. App. Rep. (S) 501. A similar bar applies to a person who has had a county court administration order made against him (C.D.D.A. 1986 s.12). An individual who has entered into a voluntary arrangement under Part VIII of the Insolvency Act 1986 suffers no such disabilities. For a good review of these issues see Griffiths and Parry [1999] Insolvency Lawyer 199. A useful comparison can be drawn with the prohibition imposed by section 216—on this see Milman [1997] J.B.L. 224.

[2] As supplemented by the Insolvent Companies (Disqualification of Unfit Directors) Proceedings Rule 1987 (S.I. 1987 No. 2023) and the Insolvent Companies (Reports on the Conduct of Directors) Rules 1996 (S.I. 1996 No. 1909). For the law in Northern Ireland, see the Companies (Northern Ireland) Order 1989 (S.I. 1989 No. 2404, N.I. 18).

company.[3] Actual conviction of an offence is not essential for the purposes of section 4.

Failure to file returns

13-04 A common ground for disqualification is set out in sections 3 and 5. Where the director has been in persistent breach of the obligation to provide information on a company's affairs to the Companies Registry, he may be disqualified for up to 5 years. Conviction for three defaults within five years is conclusive proof of persistent default. It is clear that, in recent years,[4] both the courts and the DTI have begun to view more strictly company officers who are in default of the filing requirements.

DTI investigation finding

13-05 Under section 8 of the Act, the court may disqualify if it is of the opinion that, in view of the findings of a DTI investigation (formal or informal),[5] into the affairs of the company concerned, it would be in the public interest to do so. The maximum period of disqualification here is 15 years.

Fraudulent or wrongful trading

13-06 Where a director has been made to contribute to a company's assets, as a result of a finding of fraudulent or wrongful trading under sections 213–214 of the Insolvency Act 1996, section 9 of the Act permits the court to disqualify him for up to 15 years.[6]

Unfit directors of insolvent companies

13-07 The most important ground for disqualification is where a case of "unfitness" has been made out in respect of a director of an insolvent company. A company is insolvent[7] for these purposes if it cannot pay its debts (or is asset insolvent) and has gone into liquidation, administration or administrative receivership (but not if it has simply entered into a self standing C.V.A. with its creditors).[8] This "unfitness" ground for disqualification (now found in section 6) has proved to be the most vital in practice, and there have been several thousand disqualification orders granted since the new rules came into operation.[9]

13-08 These new disqualification rules operate not merely against *de jure* direc-

[3] See here the Court of Appeal decision in *R. v. Austen* (1985) 1 B.C.C. 99, 529, where a 10 year disqualification order was imposed. The Court of Appeal followed the earlier decision in *R. v. Corbin* [1984] Crim. L. Rev. 302. In *R. v. Goodman* [1994] 1 B.C.L.C. 349 the Court of Appeal indicated that the phrase "in connection with the management" was to be construed widely, hence a director convicted of insider dealing was disqualified for 10 years. The tariff system of disqualification (discussed below) applies equally to s.2 cases—*R. v. Edwards* [1998] 2 Cr. App. Rep. (S) 213.

[4] Formerly the courts were more liberal—see *Re Civica Investments Ltd* [1983] B.C.L.C. 456.

[5] Under ss.431, 432, and 447 of the Companies Act 1985. For procedural aspects of such proceedings see *Re Astra plc* [1999] B.C.C. 121.

[6] See *Re Purpoint Ltd* [1991] B.C.C. 121 and *Re Purpoint Ltd* [1999] B.C.C. 26.

[7] On the calculation of insolvency for these purposes see *Official Receiver v. Moore* [1995] B.C.C. 293.

[8] Cynics might suggest that this is one attraction in the CVA procedure for directors.

[9] See Insolvency Service Annual Report 1997–98 which records 1267 disqualifications for that particular year! This figure must be viewed, however, against the tens of thousands of directors of failed companies who theoretically come under scrutiny.

tors, but also *de facto*[10] and shadow directors (as defined by section 22(5) of the Company Directors Disqualification Act 1986).[11] Former directors are also within the purview of the disqualification rules. Moreover, in *Re Seagull Manufacturing Co. Ltd (No. 2)*,[12] it has been decided that the rules extend to "true foreigners" (*i.e.* non-British citizens resident abroad) and cover unfitness constituted by acts outside the jurisdiction. This extension of the disqualification regime is necessary in view of the growing number of British companies controlled and managed from abroad. However, there may be procedural difficulties with regard to service of the proceedings out of the jurisdiction. Companies acting as directors of other companies are also susceptible to disqualification.[13]

UNFITNESS: CHANGES IN 1986 ACT

13-09 Disqualification of unfit directors of insolvent companies had been a possibility in English law since the enactment of the Insolvency Act 1976, but the law was amended in 1985 to improve it in a number of respects.

13-10 First, the "two in five years rule" was abolished; a single insolvency would suffice in future.

13-11 The second reform consists of the statutory guidelines which were laid down to assist the court to determine whether a director was unfit (see s.9 and Sched. 1). Section 6 itself does give some help, for example by stressing that the court can consider conduct in relation to *any* company,[14] but the crucial guidance is given by Schedule 1, which lists a wide range of matters from theft to failure to comply with the various reporting requirements of the Companies Acts. Part I of the Schedule refers to misfeasance, misapplication of the company's assets, or failure to keep proper records and make returns. Part II applies where the company is insolvent, and deals with the extent to which the director is responsible for the financial collapse of the company and its failure to honour its obligations. Participation in the grant of preferences[15] and involvement in "*Centrebinding*" (described in Chapter 5) must also be taken into account, as must the failure to co-operate with an office holder[16] or to assist in the preparation of a statement of affairs. This list is purely illustrative: there are a number of other common vices well recognised as indicia of unfitness.[17]

---

[10] *Re Moorgate Metals Ltd* [1995] B.C.C. 143, *Secretary of State v. Tjolle* [1988] 1 B.C.L.C. 333, *Official Receiver v. Kaczer*, *The Independent*, December 7, 1998 (CS). If there is doubt as to the precise role of an individual he should be given the benefit of that doubt—*Re Richborough Furniture Ltd* [1996] B.C.C. 155.

[11] On shadow directors see para. 12-45 above. For the distinction between de facto directors and shadow directors see *Re Laing Demolition Building Contractors Ltd* [1998] B.C.C. 561.

[12] [1993] B.C.C. 833. In a similar vein in an unreported decision of Blackburne J. (sitting in the High Court in Manchester in March 1999) the practice of using Sark-based front men to act as nominees for disqualified persons was blocked by imposing a 12 year ban upon an individual who had been acting as paper director for numerous companies. A serial nominee director was also the subject of a (lesser) disqualification in *Re Kaytech International* [1999] B.C.C. 390.

[13] *Official Receiver v. Brady* [1999] B.C.C. 258.

[14] See *Secretary of State v. Ellis (No. 2)* [1993] B.C.C. 890, *Re Dominion International Group (No. 2)* [1996] 1 B.C.L.C. 572, *Secretary of State v. Ivens* [1997] B.C.C. 396.

[15] *Re Living Images Ltd* [1996] B.C.C. 112, *Secretary of State v. Tighe (No. 2)* [1996] 2 B.C.L.C. 477, *Re Sykes (Butchers) Ltd (Secretary of State v. Richardson)* [1998] B.C.C. 484. See also *Re Verby Print Advertising* [1998] B.C.C. 652.

[16] *Secretary of State v. Tighe (No. 2) (supra)*.

[17] For example, failure to supervise junior managers—*Re Barings plc (No. 1)* [1998] B.C.C. 583.

13-12 To combat the problem of excessively charitable judges, section 6(1) now provides that where unfitness is established, the court is *obliged* to impose a minimum two year disqualification. The significance of this change was borne out by the ruling of the Court of Appeal in *Re Grayan Building Services Ltd.*[18] Here the trial judge had concluded that the respondent director was unfit but declined to disqualify him because he did not appear to pose a threat to the public in the future. The addition of this gloss on the law was criticised by the Court of Appeal; disqualification for the minimum two years was an inescapable result of a finding of unfitness. However, to put things in perspective, it must be remembered that judges do retain considerable discretion in determining unfitness in the first place.

13-13 Finally, and perhaps most important of all, a reporting mechanism was established by section 7(3) to ensure that insolvency practitioners act as "whistle-blowers" on unfit directors.[19] Detailed guidelines on the responsibilities of office holders in this respect are mapped out in delegated legislation and Statement of Insolvency Practice 4 (which is produced by the Society of Practitioners of Insolvency). Although it is clear that not all insolvency practitioners relish their role as unpaid policemen and resent the amount of paperwork involved, the adoption of this new procedure has greatly increased the number of names referred to the authorities, and this, in turn, has led to a corresponding growth in disqualification orders.

13-14 These changes have led to an explosion of litigation in English law. The vast majority of cases are of first instance authority, and some are difficult to reconcile with others. There are, however, some general observations which could usefully be made. Most recently in *Re Landhurst Leasing plc*[20] Hart J. outlined two fundamental aspects of the law. Firstly the aim of the disqualification regime is to promote improved standards of management and those standards are determined in an objective light. Notwithstanding this guidance, in view of the caveat of Dillon L.J. in the Court of Appeal in *Re Sevenoaks Stationers Ltd*,[21] that there is a danger in elevating judicial statements about the effect of the new legislation to the status of a quasi statutory test, it is unwise to treat these points as any more than rough guides.

UNFITNESS: AIM OF DISQUALIFICATION LAW

13-15 Although disqualification proceedings may be characterised as civil in nature they do not involve the settlement of disputes between private parties but rather represent a form of public interest enforcement.[22] There have been repeated assertions to the effect that the aim of the law is to protect the public and not to punish the director. For example, in *Re Rolus Properties Ltd*,[23] Harman J. stressed this rationale when disqualifying a director who had failed to keep proper accounts;

---

[18] [1995] 3 W.L.R. 1.

[19] The details are fleshed out by the Insolvent Companies (Reports on Conduct of Directors) Rules 1996 (S.I. 1996 No. 1909).

[20] [1999] 1 B.C.L.C. 286.

[21] [1990] 3 W.L.R. 1165 at 1171. Although each case turns on its own facts, there are some generally applicable points of legislative interpretation—see, for example, *Secretary of State v. Ellis (No. 2)* [1993] B.C.C. 890.

[22] *Secretary of State v. Jabble* [1998] B.C.C. 39.

[23] (1988) 4 B.C.C. 446. This rationale is questioned by Dine in [1994] J.B.L. 325 who points out that disqualification proceedings are often tinged with an aura of criminal prosecution but without the appropriate safeguards for respondent directors.

the rules in the Companies Acts specifying the requirement of accounts were a *quid pro quo* for the benefit of limited liability, and imposed for the public good. This "protection of the public" imperative also came to the fore in *Re Rex Williams Leisure plc*,[24] where Nicholls V-C refused to postpone disqualification proceedings until related civil litigation had been concluded; the safeguarding of the public could not wait.

UNFITNESS: KEY CONSIDERATIONS

13-16 Central to the whole disqualification concept is the finding of unfitness. Certain factors have attracted special comment from the courts. It must be reiterated that the courts are only concerned to look at conduct in relation to company mismanagement—evidence of general misbehaviour is not relevant.[25] Having said that, the court does have the power to have regard to "spent" convictions.[26]

Failure to maintain accounts

13-17 Apart from default in the statutory obligations with regard to public accounts, the courts will take a dim view of failure to maintain proper financial records as required by Companies Act 1985 s.221, a point stressed in *Re New Generation Engineers Ltd*.[27] In *Re Firedart Ltd (Official Receiver v. Fairall)*[28] Arden J. explained the rationale for this requirement in terms of the need for directors to make properly informed business decisions and also to facilitate the administration of a winding up. In *Secretary of State v. Ettinger*[29] Nicholls V.C. stressed the broader policy considerations; the obligation to maintain proper financial records must be viewed as part of the quid pro quo for limited liability and therefore the courts will view seriously any systematic failure to maintain proper financial records.

Trading errors constituting unfitness

13-08 There is some evidence that the courts are reluctant to disqualify for mere commercial misjudgment. Hoffmann J., in *Re C.U. Fittings Ltd*,[30] indicated that directors who are immersed in a day to day struggle to keep their company afloat cannot be expected to have wholly dispassionate minds. There is also a de minimis rule in operation here, as Mervyn Davies J. was at pains to stress in *Re E.C.M. Europe Electronics*.[31] However, it seems apparent that judicial antipathy towards penalising the incompetent company director is greatly reduced, especially if a pattern of business failures can be established. Thus, although it is no longer a

[24] [1992] B.C.C. 79 confirmed on appeal [1994] Ch. 350. See also *Secretary of State v. Baker (No. 3)* [1999] 1 B.C.L.C. 226 where the Court of Appeal refused to stay disqualification proceedings in circumstances where there were ongoing disciplinary proceedings because the two sets of proceedings covered different issues. The Court of Appeal concluded that to allow the disqualification proceedings to continue would not bring the administration of justice into disrepute.

[25] *Re Dawes and Henderson Agency* [1997] 1 B.C.L.C. 329, *Re Westmid Packaging Services Ltd (Secretary of State v. Griffiths)* [1998] 2 B.C.L.C. 646.

[26] *Secretary of State v. Queen* [1998] B.C.C. 678.

[27] [1993] B.C.L.C. 435. See also *Re Rolus Properties Ltd* (1988) 4 B.C.C. 466.

[28] [1994] 2 B.C.L.C. 340.

[29] [1993] B.C.C. 312.

[30] [1989] B.C.L.C. 556.

[31] [1991] B.C.C. 268.

requirement that the director should have been involved in several failed companies, there is still some significance to be attached to a poor track record.[32]

13-19 Continuing to trade on in the face of insolvency may indicate unfitness,[33] even though this is not specifically listed as a factor in Schedule 1. One significant change that has already been noted in the context of wrongful trading is that there is no longer an automatic "inertia defence". Accordingly, in *Re Majestic Recording Studios Ltd*,[34] an executive director who was viewed as a shirker by Mervyn Davies J. was disqualified for three years; nonfeasance is now quite rightly treated on a par with misfeasance.

13-20 The courts now attach considerable importance to the fact that the director did (or did not) seek professional advice when he realised that his company was in financial difficulties.[35] Failure to respond to professional advice is also a serious matter as far as the court is concerned, as Ferris J. made clear in *Re GSAR Realisations Ltd*.[36] The employment of professionally qualified staff to handle such matters as accounts may also be a saving grace.[37] However, wholesale delegation of one's responsibilities as a director is not viewed as a good defence by the courts.[38]

13-21 On the other hand, professionally qualified directors will be judged more severely. Thus, in *Re Cladrose*,[39] the courts imposed a longer disqualification on a director who was a qualified accountant because they were particularly disappointed with his failure to ensure that the company maintained proper financial records. Again in *Re Continental Assurance Co*[40] a failure by a finance director to display an awareness that financial assistance in the purchase of company shares was illegal (CA 1985 s.151) was viewed with particular concern.

Trading on Crown debts: unfitness?

13-22 The main point on which there has been judicial disagreement is on how to view the common practice of trading on Crown debts, such as PAYE and national insurance contributions deduced from employees' wages.[41] The abolition of the authorities' right of recourse against officers of defaulting companies to make good any shortfall may well have encouraged this malpractice during the years

[32] *Re Ipcon Fashions Ltd* (1989) 5 B.C.C. 773, *Re Keypack Homecare Ltd (No. 2)* [1990] B.C.C. 117 and *Re Travel Mondial (U.K.) Ltd* [1991] B.C.L.C. 120.

[33] *Re Pamstock Ltd* [1996] B.C.C. 341, *Secretary of State v. Lubrani (Re Amaron Ltd)* [1997] 2 B.C.L.C. 115. But compare *Secretary of State v. Tjolle* [1998] 1 B.C.L.C. 333.

[34] [1989] B.C.L.C. 1. Note also *Re A. & C. Group Services Ltd* [1993] B.C.L.C. 1297 and *Re Park House Properties* [1998] B.C.C. 847.

[35] *Re Douglas Construction Services Ltd* [1988] B.C.L.C. 397 and *Re McNulty's Interchange Ltd* (1988) 4 B.C.C. 533.

[36] [1993] B.C.L.C. 409.

[37] *Re Rolus Properties Ltd* (1988) 4 B.C.C. 446.

[38] See *Re Burnham Marketing Services Ltd* [1993] B.C.C. 518 and *Re A. & C. Group Services Ltd* [1993] B.C.L.C. 250. See also *Re Landhurst Leasing plc* [1999] 1 B.C.L.C. 286 on the delegation of responsibilities between board members.

[39] [1990] B.C.C. 11. This is consistent with comments of Foster J. in *Dorchester Finance v. Stebbing* [1989] B.C.L.C. 498.

[40] [1996] B.C.C. 888.

[41] In English law, prior to 1985 (see IA 1985 s.216), directors could be made personally liable to make good any shortfall in Crown debts due from the insolvent company, if they knew or ought to have known that they were not being duly forwarded. By abolishing this form of liability, the legislature may have given the green light to the continued malpractice of trading on Crown debts. The position has now gone full circle with the reintroduction of personal liability by s.64 of the Social Security Act 1998—see para. 12–17 above.

1985–1998. In the early case of *Re Dawson Print Group Ltd*,[42] Hoffmann J. refused to view this practice as more reprehensible than trading at the expense of ordinary creditors. Vinelott J. took the opposite view in *Re Stansford Services Ltd*.[43] In *Re Lo Line Electric Motors Ltd*,[44] Browne-Wilkinson V.-C. favoured the stricter view of Vinelott J., and indicated that he viewed failure to pay Crown debts as being more culpable than failure to pay ordinary commercial debts. However, in an authoritative pronouncement on the subject, the Court of Appeal appeared to ally itself with the view expressed by Hoffmann J. Thus, in *Re Sevenoaks Stationers Ltd*,[45] the Court of Appeal rejected the notion that such behaviour would automatically indicate unfitness, Dillon J. declaring:

> "The official receiver cannot, in my judgment, automatically treat non-payment of any Crown debt as evidence of unfitness of the directors. It is necessary to look more closely in each case to see what the significance, if any, of the non-payment of the Crown debt is."[46]

13-23 This more flexible approach was subsequently adopted by Warner J. in *Re Tansoft Ltd*,[47] where a director had not only failed to pay Crown debts, but had also breached his responsibilities as a director in a number of other respects. A seven year disqualification was imposed. Although it is no longer the case that failure to pay Crown debts will necessarily indicate unfitness, it is a fair assumption that it is the sort of conduct likely to persuade the authorities to institute disqualification proceedings in the first place. Moreover, government policy on non payment of Crown debts has now reverted to its former draconian nature[48] and the courts are also reflecting that change in their disqualification rulings. Thus in *Re Verby Print Advertising*[49] directors who used available funds to settle trade debts but deliberately withheld funds due to the Crown were found to be unfit by Neuberger J.

Remuneration policy: evidence of unfitness

13-24 The courts will pay particular attention to the way directors have treated themselves in the event of the company experiencing financial difficulties. Some evidence of personal belt tightening may make the different between disqualification or not. The courts have repeatedly rejected the argument that a director was paying himself the market rate; once the company becomes insolvent the key factor is what can it afford.[50]

Unfitness: should a director have resigned?

13-25 A director of a company, which is insolvent and heading for liquidation, who remains in office and continues to draw his salary may be unfit. This is a difficult

[42] [1987] B.C.L.C. 601.
[43] [1987] B.C.L.C. 607.
[44] [1988] 3 W.L.R. 26.
[45] [1990] 3 W.L.R. 1165.
[46] *ibid.*, at 1177.
[47] [1991] B.C.L.C. 339.
[48] See Social Security Act 1998.
[49] [1998] 2 B.C.L.C. 23.
[50] *Secretary of State v. Van Hengel* [1995] 1 B.C.L.C. 545, *Re Ward Sherrard Ltd* [1996] B.C.C. 418 and *Secretary of State v. Lubrani* [1997] 2 B.C.L.C. 115.

area and in *Re CS Holidays Ltd*[51] Chadwick J. attempted to offer judicial guidance on the dilemma facing a director in such a situation. Here the respondent had warned his colleagues about the dangers of continued trading but he failed to resign when they disregarded his advice. The court found that he had no part in the continued trading and was not simply clinging to office to draw remuneration.

DISQUALIFICATION OF UNFIT DIRECTORS—PROCEDURAL ASPECTS

13-26 There are a number of procedural aspects of disqualification applications worth noting. The primary legislation[52] gives no guidance on many procedural questions accordingly, the courts have been left to devise their own rules to deal with this matter.

Timing of the proceedings

13-27 Under section 7(2), a limitation period of two years from the commencement of insolvency proceedings is imposed.[53] This time limit can be extended with the leave of the court where the respondent would not be unduly prejudiced, as happened in *Re Probe Data Systems Ltd (No. 3)*.[54] However where prejudice is shown to exist the court will refuse its leave.[55] The leading case on this decision is the Court of Appeal authority of *Secretary of State v. Davies*.[56] Here the court indicated that it may grant leave for out of time proceedings even if it has doubts about the validity of the excuses of the authorities for the delay. The crucial factor must be the proper exercise of judicial discretion in the particular case.

13-28 Conversely, the courts might quash proceedings commenced within the two year limitation period, if the delay in bringing the matter to court has caused prejudice to the defendant. In *Re Noble Trees Ltd*,[57] Vinelott J. quashed proceedings that had been instituted just a few days before the limitation period had run out (the prosecution of these proceedings had been further delayed by the authorities). In *Re Manlon Trading Ltd*[58] the Court of Appeal indicated that the general rules on want of prosecution in civil litigation applied to disqualification cases.

---

[51] [1997] B.C.C. 172 reported *sub nom. Secretary of State v. Gash* [1997] 1 B.C.L.C. 341.

[52] But note the Insolvent Companies (Disqualification of Unfit Directors) Proceedings Rules 1987 (S.I. 987 No. 2023) as supplemented by the Insolvent Companies (Disqualification of Unfit Directors) Proceedings (Amendment) Rules 1999 (S.I. 1999 No. 1023) which seek to ensure as much terminological and procedural consistency with the regime introduced generally by the Civil Procedure Rules 1998 (S.I. 1998 No. 3132) in April 1999.

[53] Leave may be granted by the court to waive this time limit. For the relevant principles to be applied, see *Re Probe Data Systems Ltd (No. 3)* [1992] B.C.C. 110 (*Secretary of State v. Desai*), *Re Tasbian Ltd (No. 3)* [1992] B.C.C. 358 (*Official Receiver v. Nixon*), *Secretary of State v. McTighe (Re Copecrest Ltd)* [1994] 2 B.C.L.C. 284 and *Secretary of State v. Ellis (No. 2)* [1993] B.C.C. 890. As to when the time begins to run out, see *Official Receiver v. Jacob* [1993] B.C.C. 512, and *Secretary of State v. Houston* [1993] G.W.D. 30–1861, *Re Phillipp and Lion Ltd* [1994] 1 B.C.L.C. 739, *Secretary of State v. Normand* [1995] 2 B.C.L.C. 297.

[54] [1992] B.C.C. 110. See also *Secretary of State v. Carmichael* [1995] B.C.C. 679.

[55] *Re Packaging Direct Ltd* [1994] B.C.C. 213, *Re Cedar Developments Ltd* [1995] B.C.C. 220, *Re NP Engineering and Security Products* [1995] 2 B.C.L.C. 585, *Secretary of State v. Morrall* [1996] B.C.C. 229 and *Re Westmid Packaging Ltd (No. 2)* [1996] B.C.C. 229, *Secretary of State v. Martin* [1998] B.C.C. 184.

[56] [1997] B.C.C. 235.

[57] [1993] B.C.C. 318.

[58] [1995] 1 B.C.L.C. 578. See also *Official Receiver v. B. Ltd* [1994] 2 B.C.L.C. 1 and *Re Dexmaster Ltd* [1995] 2 B.C.L.C. 430.

Notice of proceedings

13-29 Section 16(1) states that there should be 10 days minimum notice given to the defendant that disqualification proceedings are to be instituted against him, but this direction has been watered down as a result of the Court of Appeal's majority ruling in *Secretary of State v. Langridge*,[59] where it was held (Nourse L.J. dissenting) that failure to give proper notice did not invalidate the subsequent disqualification proceedings. In reaching this somewhat surprising conclusion, the majority of the Court of Appeal (which was constituted differently from the bench in *Re Sevenoaks Stationers Ltd*)[60] laid great weight on the aim of the law, which was to protect the public by restricting the privilege to trade under limited liability, and afforded this policy aim priority over the rights of individual directors. Leggatt L.J. declared:

> "Standing back and looking at this problem in perspective, it makes no sense to me that Parliament should have intended to shut out an applicant from applying for a disqualification order (in default of an extension of time) merely because he failed to serve timeously on the director concerned what has accurately been called 'an unparticularised letter before action'".[61]

13-30 A similar attitude surfaced more recently in *Official Receiver v. Keam (Re Surrey Leisure Ltd)*[62] where the courts indicated that it was not necessary for the notice to itemise the names of all the companies involved in the forthcoming disqualification proceedings.

Appropriate court

13-31 Occasionally disputes arise as to whether disqualification proceedings have been commenced in the appropriate court. Such cases may in English law be heard in either the county court[63] or the High Court. In *Re Lichfield Freight Terminal*[64] Neuberger J. indicated that the crucial determining factor was to identify the court with jurisdiction when the disqualification proceedings began and not the court enjoying jurisdiction at the onset of insolvency. In Scotland in *Secretary of State, Petitioner*[65] the same point was made by the Court of Session (Inner House).

Evidential aspects

13-32 Disqualification proceedings represent a curious genre, procedurally speaking. The courts have been left to devise their own rules by adapting general rules of civil procedure. What is clear is that as we are dealing with a civil case the authorities need only establish their case on the balance of probabilities, and not beyond reasonable doubt.[66] The Court of Appeal in *Re Rex Williams Leisure*

---

[59] [1991] 2 W.L.R. 1343. Leave to appeal to the House of Lords was refused—see [1991] 1 W.L.R. 606.
[60] [1990] 3 W.L.R. 1165.
[61] [1991] 2 W.L.R. 1343 at 1357.
[62] *The Times*, January 25, 1999.
[63] The county court is not appropriate if the company has already been dissolved—*Re NP Engineering and Security Products Ltd* [1995] 2 B.C.L.C. 585.
[64] [1997] B.C.C. 11, following *Re The Working Project* [1995] 1 B.C.L.C. 226.
[65] [1998] B.C.C. 437.
[66] *Re Verby Print Advertising* [1998] B.C.C. 652.

plc[67] dealt with the use of hearsay evidence and indicated that it could be admitted in disqualification proceedings. Central to the proceedings are the affidavits used by the "prosecuting" authorities.[68] Rules have also been developed by the courts to regulate the collection and presentation of evidence by the respondent.[69]

Costs

13-33 Once again the rules here have been developed ad hoc by the courts, the matter not being dealt with by primary or secondary legislation.[70] The principles that have been developed are complex what is recorded below is but a summary of the key points.

13-34 Where proceedings are initiated but then withdrawn it would be the normal result that the authorities would have to pay the respondent's costs, as the Court of Appeal concluded in *Re Southbourne Sheet Metal Ltd*.[71] If the authorities win the disqualification they will be allowed costs against the respondent director, but normally only on the standard, as opposed to indemnity, basis.[72] The indemnity basis can however be used if either party has behaved in an unacceptable manner, as was the case in *Secretary of State v. Blake*[73] where the court declared that the proceedings were entirely misguided. It sometimes happens that a disqualification is secured whilst many of the allegations are rejected. The position here was reviewed in *Re Pamstock Ltd*[74] where the Court of Appeal upheld the decision of the trial judge to deprive the successful applicant of half of his costs because of the broad brush approach adopted in putting complaints before the court.

13-35 In *Re Minotaur Data Systems Ltd*[75] it was held that if the Official Receiver does not use legal representation he can be regarded as a litigant in person for the purpose of claiming an allowance.

Period of ban

13-36 Once the court finds a director to be unfit, it must by virtue of section 6(1) and (4) impose a two year minimum disqualification.[76] Having said that, a disqualification order imposed on an unfit director can be extended for up to a fifteen year period (see section 6(4)). The court may be prepared to impose a discount to compensate for the period of uncertainty awaiting trial when a director will often be unable to obtain work in his chosen career.[77]

---

[67] [1994] Ch. 350—this was a section 8 case but it was applied to s.6 proceedings in *Secretary of State v. Ashcroft* [1997] B.C.C. 634. See also *Secretary of State v. Moffatt* [1996] 2 B.C.L.C. 16, *Re Sutton Glassworks Ltd* [1997] 1 B.C.L.C. 26 and *Secretary of State v. Baker (No. 3)* [1999] B.C.C. 146. Note that generally the law has adopted a more liberal approach to the use of hearsay evidence in civil cases since the enactment of the Civil Evidence Act 1995.

[68] See here the comments of Neuberger J. in *Re Park House Properties* [1998] B.C.C. 847. Note also *Re Dominion International Group* [1995] 1 B.C.L.C. 570.

[69] On the use of subpoenas by respondent directors wishing to acquire evidence to build the defence case see *Re Global Info Ltd* [1999] 1 B.C.L.C. 74. Note also *Secretary of State v. Baker (No. 2)* [1998] B.C.C. 888.

[70] On the costs position for a s.17 application see *Secretary of State v. Worth* [1994] 2 B.C.L.C. 113.

[71] [1993] 1 W.L.R. 244.

[72] *Re Dicetrade Ltd* [1994] B.C.C. 371.

[73] [1997] 1 B.C.L.C. 728.

[74] [1996] B.C.C. 341.

[75] *The Times*, March 18, 1999.

[76] *Re Grayan Building Services Ltd* [1995] 3 W.L.R. 1.

[77] *Re Westmid Packaging Services Ltd (Secretary of State v. Griffiths)* [1998] 2 B.C.L.C. 646 rejecting the view taken in *Secretary of State v. Arif* [1996] B.C.C. 586. A discount will also operate where the case is protracted through no fault of the respondent—*e.g.* where the authorities appeal successfully as in *Re City Pram and Toy Co. Ltd* [1998] B.C.C. 537.

13-37 It must be remembered that often there are several directors before the court. Their culpability may vary and accordingly differential disqualification periods may be imposed. Thus in *Re Peppermint Park Ltd*[78] the three respondents consisted of a dominant controlling shareholder who actively ran the business, a passive wife who had only been a director for a short period and a managing director who was largely dominated by the first respondent. The High Court after reviewing the responsibility of each individual imposed disqualifications of nine, two and two and a half years respectively.

13-38 Rough guidelines on appropriate disqualification periods were laid down by the Court of Appeal in *Re Sevenoaks Stationers Ltd*,[79] where it was indicated that there were three bands, depending upon the seriousness of the case; namely 2–5 years for minor cases, 6–10 for the middle bracket, and 11–15 years for bad cases. The court has complete discretion in determining the disqualification period, and the authorities also enjoy discretion on the question of whether to institute proceedings; it is no defence for a director facing disqualification to complain that his co-directors have not been proceeded against.[80] A recent instructive authority here is provided by *Re Melcast (Wolverhampton) Ltd*,[81] where Harman J. refused to accept as relevant, the argument that the defendants had not benefited personally from their incompetence. However, the judge did take into account the fact that one defendant was aged 68, and therefore it was not necessary to impose more than a seven year disqualification, because he was unlikely to be involved in company management after the age of 75. The issue of appropriate periods of disqualification was revisited by the Court of Appeal in *Re Westmid Packaging Ltd (Secretary of State v. Griffiths)*[82] where the focus was placed upon the need to deter, the age and health of the respondent, whether he had cooperated with the court, and the period during which he had been awaiting trial of his case.

13-39 A disqualification order, once granted, prohibits any managerial involvement in the affairs of a limited liability company, whether direct or indirect. Indeed, it has been held in one case that a disqualified director could not, in future, seek to ply his trade as a "company doctor".[83]

13-40 The disqualification order must be in an authorised form[84] and must be registered at the Companies Registry.[85]

---

[78] [1998] B.C.C. 23. Where the authorities proceed against several co-directors, different disqualification periods can be imposed where the degree of culpability varies—*Re City Investment Centres Ltd* [1992] B.C.L.C. 956, *Re Austinsuite Furniture Ltd* [1992] B.C.L.C. 1047.

[79] [1990] 3 W.L.R. 1165.

[80] *Re Tansoft Ltd* [1991] B.C.L.C. 339.

[81] [1991] B.C.L.C. 288.

[82] [1998] 2 B.C.L.C. 646.

[83] See *R. v. Campbell* (1984) 78 Cr. App. Rep. 95.

[84] See Companies (Disqualification Orders) (Amendment) Regulations 1995 (S.I. 1995 No. 1509). On the form of the order see *Re Gower Enterprises (No. 2)* [1995] B.C.C. 1081, *Re Seagull Manufaturing Ltd (No. 3)* [1995] B.C.C. 1088 and *R. v. Cole* [1998] 2 B.C.L.C. 234. An order can be amended by using the slip rule—*Re Brian Sheridan Cars* [1996] 1 B.C.L.C. 327 and *Official Receiver v. Hannan (Re Cannonquest Ltd)* [1997] B.C.C. 644.

[85] The Secretary of State is required to keep this register by virtue of section 18(2) of the Company Directors disqualification Act 1986. The onus is on the disqualifying court to see that the order is filed but this is not always done, as the National Audit Office noted in its 1993 report (q.v.) (para. 4.14). On when the order takes effect see *Secretary of State v. Edwards* [1997] B.C.C. 222.

Summary procedure

13-41 It is well known that some senior judges have been concerned about the amount of judicial time being consumed by hearing disqualification cases, many of which involved little in the way of technical law. The government is also concerned about the public expenditure implications of the tide of disqualification cases coming before the courts. Ferris J. offered a solution to these concerns in *Re Carecraft Construction Ltd*[86] by developing a procedure under which the parties could present the court with an agreed statement of facts and allegations which had been accepted whereupon the court could impose a disqualification based upon these facts. This practice looks suspiciously like plea bargaining but the courts have always resisted that inference.

13-42 Central to this summary procedure is the agreed statement of facts. In *Re Banarse & Co. Ltd*[87] the importance of having an unambiguous agreed statement was stressed; there must be no need for the court to have to make secondary inferences of fact. Once the statement is agreed a judge who hears a case on the basis of this summary procedure is not allowed to fix a disqualification period by reference to allegations outside the agreed schedule.[88]

13-43 The sensitivity of this procedure came to the surface in *Secretary of State v. Rogers*.[89] Although it is common for the authorities to indicate to the court what they think would be an appropriate period of disqualification the court is not bound by that suggestion. It is the final arbiter in such matters. This essential fact was reiterated by Rimer J in *Re BPR Ltd*,[90] though with the rider that if the judge is minded to impose a period of disqualification much longer than the parties had anticipated he should alert the parties to allow them to consider their position.

13-44 The *Carecraft* procedure is now well established and is indeed underpinned by a *Practice Direction (No. 2 of 1995)*.[91] Further judicial encouragement was offered in *Official Receiver v. Cooper*[92] where it was held by Jonathan Parker J. that any admissions made by the respondent director in the agreed statement of facts can be kept confidential so that they are not used to haunt him in other civil proceedings. The purpose of disqualification proceedings was to protect the public and not to assist office holders in litigation. This is a subtle distinction and many commentators might view successful proceedings against miscreant directors as a good way of protecting the public.

Undertakings as an alternative to a disqualification

13-45 Another opportunity to reduce the number of disqualification cases coming before the court arose fortuitously in *Re Homes Assured Corporation*.[93] Here a director facing disqualification proceedings preempted the decision of the court by pointing out that he was of advanced age, in ill health and would not be undertaking any directorships in the future. In these circumstances the court felt able to stay

---

86 [1994] 1 W.L.R. 172.
87 [1997] B.C.C. 425.
88 *Re SIG Security Services* [1998] B.C.C. 978.
89 [1996] 1 W.L.R. 1569.
90 [1998] B.C.C. 259.
91 [1996] B.C.C. 11.
92 [1999] B.C.C. 115.
93 [1996] B.C.C. 297.

the proceedings in lieu of this legally binding undertaking. A similar result occurred in *Secretary of State v. Cleland*[94] where the director in question was also in poor health. However, neither the court nor the authorities are obliged to accept such an offer in return for dropping the proceedings, a fact confirmed by the Court of Appeal in *Secretary of State v. Davies (No. 2)*.[95]

13-46 The availability of this cost effective solution has attracted the attention of the government which intends to confer statutory approval on the practice in appropriate cases.[96]

Appeals

13-47 It is possible for a director against whom a disqualification order has been made to appeal against it.[97] Where such an appeal is mounted the court does have the power to stay the disqualification until the appeal is resolved but it is most reluctant to do so, as was explained by the court in *Secretary of State v. Bannister*.[98]

13-48 The authorities can also appeal against a ruling of a trial judge that is considered to be excessively lenient. A good illustration of this happening is afforded by *Re City Pram and Toy Co. Ltd*[99] where the trial judge concluded that the behaviour of the respondents did not constitute unfitness. On appeal this conclusion was rejected—the directors should not have continued trading for so long and they should not have continued to accept advanced deposits—with the result that a two year period of disqualification was imposed. Having said that, the appellate court is naturally reluctant to interfere with the exercise of discretion of a trial judge in such matters.[1]

Applications for leave to act

13-49 A disqualified director can apply to the court for leave to modify its effect. In practice, this is often done as part of the disqualification proceedings themselves,[2] and a form of "plea bargaining" has thus developed. A director may be willing to accept a disqualification order at large, provided he can be given leave to remain on as a director or manager[3] of a particular named company. The courts have shown themselves willing to accept such a situation, particularly where the conduct of the director with regard to that named company has been unimpeachable, and where the jobs of employees may be threatened by disqualification and subsequent closure of business.[4] An undertaking to introduce some form of independent supervision will

---

94 [1997] B.C.C. 473.

95 [1998] B.C.C. 11 reported *sub nom. Re Blackspur Group*.

96 See below at 13-62.

97 For appeal routes, see *Re Langley Marketing Services Ltd* [1992] B.C.C. 585, *Re Probe Data Systems Ltd (No. 3)* [1992] B.C.C. 110 (*Secretary of State v. Desai*).

98 [1996] 1 W.L.R. 118. See also *Secretary of State v. McTighe* [1997] B.C.C. 224.

99 [1998] B.C.C. 537. See also *Secretary of State v. Tighe (No. 2)* [1996] 2 B.C.L.C. 477 and *Re Saver Ltd* [1999] B.C.C. 221.

1 *Re Westmid Packaging Services (Secretary of State v. Griffiths)* [1998] 2 B.C.L.C. 646. See also *Re Hitco 2000 Ltd* [1995] 2 B.C.L.C. 63.

2 Indeed this practice is to be encouraged to save on costs—*Secretary of State v. Worth* [1994] 2 B.C.L.C. 113.

3 In *Re Cargo Agency Ltd* [1992] B.C.C. 388, a disqualified director was given leave to act as a manager of a company, but was refused leave to become a director.

4 For illustrations, see *Re Lo Line Electric Motors Ltd* [1988] 3 W.L.R. 26, and *Re Majestic Recording Studios Ltd* [1989] B.C.L.C. 1.

also impress the court. A good example of this practice at work is provided by *Re Chartmore Ltd*,[5] where Harman J. accepted undertakings from a disqualified director who wished to remain in a managerial position with respect to a particular named company. In return for this concession (which was being sought for a one year trial period only), the director agreed to hold monthly board meetings at which a representative of the firm's auditors would be present. Chadwick J. adopted a similar approach in *Re Godwin Warren Control Systems*.[6]

13-50 The question of leave applications has been reviewed in several recent decisions. In *Secretary of State v. Griffiths*[7] the Court of Appeal offered some general guidance and made the point that the existence of the leave facility should not be relevant to the primary question of determining an appropriate period of disqualification. Arden J. added to the jurisprudence on the subject in *Re Tech Textiles Ltd*.[8] A further pronouncement on leave applications was offered by Scott V.C. in *Re Barings plc (No. 4)*[9] where a generous view was taken of a disqualified individual who sought permission to remain as a non executive director of three named companies, with leave being granted (subject to conditions) largely on the basis that this would pose no threat to the public. Notwithstanding these indications of general attitudes it was stressed by the court in *Shuttleworth v. Secretary of State*[10] that the court is endowed with complete discretion which should not be fettered by developing a gloss on the legislation.

13-51 This is a strategy that is to be commended to a director facing disqualification, where his conduct with regard to some of the companies he has managed has been unobjectionable. However it is important that a director given leave respects the terms under which it was granted; failure to do this will guarantee a severe response from the courts.[11]

Ignoring disqualification

13-52 One fault in the regime is that it is believed that many directors flout the terms of their disqualification. The prospects of them doing this are reduced by the establishment of a public hotline which can be used to inform on directors breaching the disqualification.[12]

13-53 Breach of the disqualification order is a criminal offence under section 13. This carries a maximum penalty of two years imprisonment and a fine.[13] It has been held in Australia that the offence of infringing a disqualification order is one of strict liability, requiring no proof of mens rea.[14]

13-54 Failure to comply with a disqualification order can also lead to personal

---

[5] [1990] B.C.L.C. 673. See also *Re Gibson Ltd* [1995] B.C.C. 11, *Secretary of State v. Palfreman* 1995 S.L.T. 156, *Re Verby Print Advertising* [1998] B.C.C. 652.

[6] [1992] B.C.C. 557. However the court will not ask the Official Receiver to police any undertakings; that is a matter for the court—*Re Brian Sheridan Cars Ltd* [1996] 1 B.C.L.C. 327.

[7] [1998] B.C.C. 836. See also *Secretary of State v. Barnett* [1998] B.C.L.C. 64.

[8] [1998] 1 B.C.L.C. 259.

[9] [1999] 1 B.C.L.C. 262.

[10] *The Times*, February 9, 1999.

[11] See the county court case of *R. v. Davies* (unreported but noted in Butterworths Disqualification Newsletter No. 1).

[12] See the news report in *The Times*, January 5, 1999 on usage.

[13] Where a disqualified person is imprisoned, it would appear that the disqualification order takes immediate effect and will not be postponed until his release from prison—*R. v. Bradley* [1961] 1 All E.R. 669.

[14] *Poyser v. Commission of Corporate Affairs* [1985] V.R. 553.

liability for company debts (section 15). The practice of using a nominee to act as director is dealt with by section 15(1)(b), which, in combination with the remainder of section 15, imposes full personal liability both on the disqualified director and the nominee. It is a defence for the nominee to show that he was unaware that he was following the instructions of a disqualified person or did not willingly so act.

THE DISQUALIFICTION REGIME AND FUNDAMENTAL HUMAN RIGHTS

13-55 When the current system of director disqualification was introduced some 15 years ago few questions were raised as to the fundamental compatibility of the system with the European Convention on Human Rights. The business community were somehow seen as being outside the protection afforded by the Convention. The controversial *Saunders*[15] decision, although dealing not with disqualification but rather with the conduct of DTI investigations and the use of compelled evidence acquired through the investigation process, changed that complacency and questions have been asked as to whether various aspects of the disqualification regime comply with the Convention.

13-56 In *R. v. Secretary of State ex parte McCormick*[16] the Court of Appeal held that the prohibition on the use of compelled evidence against a company director did not apply in disqualification proceedings as these were civil in nature and therefore the *Saunders* principle was inapplicable. This seems an odd interpretation and were the point to be pursued in Strasbourg a different conclusion might well be reached.

13-57 In *EDC v. U.K.*[17] the Commission indicated that the substantial delay often associated with the prosecution of disqualification cases may itself infringe the right to a prompt trial within a reasonable time as guaranteed by Article 6. In fairness this point has already been recognised by the English courts who often factor delay into the calculation period of disqualification if a director is found to be unfit.

13-58 At present it is still necessary for a disgruntled director to pursue his case in Strasbourg. The English courts will not defer their consideration pending a ruling on the Convention. The issues identified above are likely to become more heated once the Human Rights Act 1998 becomes fully operational.[18]

THE DISQUALIFICATION REGIME: AN EVALUATION AND REFORM PROPOSALS

13-59 It must be conceded that the development of the jurisdiction to disqualify unfit directors of insolvent companies was by far the most significant of the changes introduced in 1985–86. However the question remains as to whether the present regime is the most efficient method of dealing with such individuals.

13-60 The National Audit Office reviewed[19] the system in 1993. Its main concern was that of the thousands of cases referred to the authorities by office holders

---

[15] [1997] B.C.C. 872.
[16] [1998] B.C.C. 379.
[17] [1998] B.C.C. 370.
[18] In *Hinchcliffe v. Secretary of State* [1999] B.C.C. 226 the court refused to adjourn proceedings pending the passage of the Human Rights Act.
[19] HC No. 907.

only a small percentage (less than 10 per cent) were pursued to the point of disqualification. The Public Accounts Committee reinforced these criticisms.[20] As a result of this criticism the Insolvency Service adopted a more aggressive policy with the result that the number of cases coming before the court has trebled in the space of a few years. This in turn produced difficulties with regard to delay in proceedings[21] and marginal cases being pursued unsuccessfully. More importantly the cost of the disqualification regime rose sharply to the point that its net cost is now believed to be in the region of £20 million.[22]

13-61 The courts became aware of this problem and some judges sought to streamline procedures by adopting the *Carecraft*[23] summary procedure and by expressing a willingness to accept undertakings in lieu of disqualification proceedings.

13-62 The current position is in a state of flux. The National Audit Office[24] has now reviewed developments since 1993 and has noted an improvement of performance by the bureaucratic authorities entrusted with managing this regime. Certainly the figures show some 399 directors being disqualified for unfitness in 1993–94 with the comparable figure for 1997–98 being 1267. To some extent this is the result of increased resources being devoted to this area of enforcement. Variations of practice between local offices of the Insolvency Service have also been reduced. The problem of delay in completing the disqualification process through the court system is still unresolved. The government has hinted at an intention to legislate to facilitate the use of binding undertakings but no firm proposals have been tabled. Nevertheless some commentators[25] have raised fundamental doubts about the present regime. Should the courts be employed in dealing with these cases, many of which involve little legal principle, or would the use of a tribunal system involving participation by the business community be more sensible? Would a more proactive approach be more effective—*e.g.* by introducing some form of qualification for a company director wishing to access limited liability or by imposing a minimum capital requirement for private companies, as is the norm in the rest of Europe.

---

[20] (18th Report, 1993–94) (HCP 167). The Insolvency Service undertook to respond positively to these criticisms (see Cm 2062) and the 1999 Report of the National Audit Office does testify to an improved performance.

[21] For criticism of this growing problem and suggestions to alleviate matters by better case management see *Re Westmid Packaging Services Ltd (Secretary of State v. Griffiths)* [1998] 2 B.C.L.C. 646 and *Secretary of State v. Tjolle* [1998] B.C.C. 282.

[22] For details see C.C.H. Company Law Newsletter (Issue 26, 1999) at 4. Note also National Audit Office Follow-up Report (HC 1998–99, No. 424) where the cost of Insolvency Service resources invested in the director disqualification regime for the year 1997–98 was estimated at £22 million.

[23] See the discussion above at para. 13-41.

[24] Company Disqualification: a Follow-up Report HC 1998–99 No. 424.

[25] See for example Milman, Palmer's In Company (May 1997) and Hicks, "Disqualification of Directors: No Hiding Place for the Unfit?" (ACCA Research Report No. 59, 1998).

Index